# Birds

2nd Edition

## by Brian L. Speer, DVM; Kim Campbell Thornton; and Gina Spadafori

for dummies®

A Wiley Brand

## Birds For Dummies®, 2nd Edition

Published by: **John Wiley & Sons, Inc.,** 111 River Street, Hoboken, NJ 07030-5774, www.wiley.com

Copyright © 2021 by John Wiley & Sons, Inc., Hoboken, New Jersey

Published simultaneously in Canada

For general information on our other products and services, please contact our Customer Care Department within the U.S. at 877-762-2974, outside the U.S. at 317-572-3993, or fax 317-572-4002. For technical support, please visit https://hub.wiley.com/community/support/dummies.

Wiley publishes in a variety of print and electronic formats and by print-on-demand. Some material included with standard print versions of this book may not be included in e-books or in print-on-demand. If this book refers to media such as a CD or DVD that is not included in the version you purchased, you may download this material at http://booksupport.wiley.com. For more information about Wiley products, visit www.wiley.com.

Library of Congress Control Number: 2020949856

ISBN 978-1-119-64322-7 (pbk); ISBN 978-1-119-64315-9 (ebk); ISBN 978-1-119-64325-8 (ebk)

Manufactured in the United States of America

SKY10022857_112520

# Contents at a Glance

# Table of Contents

# Introduction

Welcome to *Birds For Dummies*, the only book you need to turn your admiration and appreciation of birds into a lasting, loving relationship with an avian companion!

Many people purchase birds for their status, for their beauty, for their song, or even for how well they match the furniture! But no one wins when someone picks a pet for the wrong reasons or has odd ideas about what it takes to properly care for a new family member.

This book has everything you need in order *not* to end up in that group of uneducated bird owners. Whether you already have a bird or you're thinking about getting one, this book is your guide to caring for your bird for years to come!

## About This Book

Birds are *not* simple creatures. They have needs and desires (some people call them demands!), and many are highly affectionate and social. Some birds can test your tolerance when it comes to noise and mess. You need to know all this going in, along with which bird to buy, where to buy one, and how to deal with the inevitable behavior problems that challenge nearly every bird owner from time to time.

Successful bird lovers are knowledgeable, realistic, and flexible, and most of all, they have a good sense of humor. If that description fits you, you'll be rewarded by sharing your life with a marvelous feathered friend. We want you to be among the successful bird owners, and every line in this book is part of our heartfelt effort to help you be exactly that.

This book is a reference, which means you don't have to read it from beginning to end. Instead, you can dip into the book to find the information you need, whenever you need it. Also, you don't have to remember what you're reading — there isn't a test at the end.

If you're short on time, you can skip anything marked with the Technical Stuff icon, as well as text in gray boxes (called *sidebars*). This information is interesting, but it's not essential to your understanding of the subject at hand.

Within this book, you may note that some web addresses break across two lines of text. If you're reading this book in print and you want to visit one of these web pages, simply key in the web address exactly as it's noted in the text, pretending as though the line break doesn't exist. If you're reading this as an e-book, you've got it easy — just click the web address to be taken directly to the web page.

Finally, a word on gender: We use male and female pronouns to refer to pets. Although many bird owners don't even know the gender of their birds (see Chapter 3 for more on that subject), we think using the word *it* for any living being sets up an association that's just not right. Animals aren't *things* like a piece of furniture or this book. They're living, thinking, loving beings — hes and shes. We alternate the use of the male and female pronouns throughout the book, but in any given reference, you can rest assured that the information applies to both genders, unless specifically noted otherwise.

# Foolish Assumptions

As we wrote this book, we made some assumptions about you, the reader:

>> You already own a bird or you're considering adding one to your home.

>> You may have no experience with birds, or you may have lived with them for years. Either way, you're sure to find valuable information to make life with your avian companion even better!

>> You're interested in being the best bird owner you can possibly be.

# Icons Used in This Book

Every *For Dummies* book has little pictures in the margins called *icons* that help you navigate through the book. Here's a rundown of what each icon means.

TIP

The Tip icon flags especially useful clues to make life with your bird easier or help your pet be happier and healthier. It highlights time-savers and money-savers, too!

**REMEMBER**

If we think something is so important that it deserves restating or remembering, we flag it with the Remember icon to make sure you don't jump over that vital information.

**WARNING**

The Warning icon denotes some common mistakes bird owners make, along with advice for avoiding them. Pay heed! Some of these errors can be deadly to your pet.

**TECHNICAL STUFF**

We're bird experts, and sometimes we like to get a little technical. When we do, we use the Technical Stuff icon. You can safely skip anything marked with this icon without missing the point of the subject at hand.

## Beyond the Book

In addition to the material in the print or e-book you're reading right now, this product also comes with some free access-anywhere goodies on the web. Check out the free Cheat Sheet for information on what to buy for your new bird, signs of a healthy pet bird, and a schedule of routine care. To access the Cheat Sheet, go to www.dummies.com and type **Birds For Dummies Cheat Sheet** in the Search box.

## Where to Go from Here

If you've never had a bird in your life and you're just starting to entertain the idea of adding one, you may want to start at the beginning of this book. If you already have a bird, you can skip around, checking out the chapters that address your needs at the moment. Either way, let the Table of Contents and Index be your guides.

# 1

# Getting Started with Birds

# Chapter **1**

# Birds and Humans: It's Only Natural!

Who among us hasn't looked up with awe and even envy at the sight of a soaring hawk or the V formation of migratory waterfowl? Who hasn't smiled at the clever capering of chickadees or the luminescent colors of a hovering hummingbird? And what about the sweet song of the canary or the clever mimicry of the parrot? For as long as our collective consciousness can remember, we've shared our environment with birds, creatures of myth and magic, soaring spirits who remind us of a dimension beyond our own. Look up, they remind us, and in so doing we gain both perspective and inspiration.

Perhaps humans have always wondered what it would be like to bring birds closer to us, out of the heavens and into our lives. And in response to the immense and primeval appeal of these flighted creatures, we've done exactly that, enjoying their song and their beauty in our homes. Ancient civilizations in China, Egypt, and Rome, among others, found pleasure in bird keeping, a joy that follows us to modern times as more people than ever discover the benefits of sharing their lives with avian companions. According to the latest statistics from the American Pet Products Association, approximately 5.7 million U.S. households live with a pet bird.

But have we done birds any favors by taking them under our wings? Clipped and caged, often admired more for their ornamental presence than for their companion qualities, these marvelous creatures are too often sold short. When we treat them with less respect than they deserve, we can make our birds miserable and sick, and we deny ourselves the full pleasure of their company. Even worse, through greed and ignorance, we decimate their numbers in the wild, driving some incredible species to extinction in our quest for their uniqueness and their habitat.

Fortunately, knowledge of how to properly care for pet birds — physically *and* emotionally — has grown in the last several decades, thanks to pioneering avian veterinarians, researchers, breeders, and bird lovers themselves who are no longer satisfied to allow birds to be second-class compared to pet dogs or cats. We're part of an evolving society that increasingly appreciates the creatures with which we share our world.

The changing times are exciting, and by buying this book you're claiming your interest in becoming part of the new and improved perspective on pet birds. Finding out how to care for them properly is a wonderful first step on the road to bird keeping. First steps lead to lots of new territory, and in this chapter we help you explore a promising trail of information.

**REMEMBER**

As with all companion animals, doing your homework is essential to success as a bird parent. You need to know what you're getting into and where to find the bird of your dreams. And you need to know how to care for your bird and what to do when things go wrong (and they will, sometimes!). So, don't rush! Enjoy discovering details about birds, and you can expect to be better prepared for the time you bring home a bird of your own.

# Getting to Know the History of Birds

*Birds For Dummies* isn't a history book, and we aren't historians — and we certainly don't want to bore you! But we think some historical perspective is both important and interesting. And besides, sometimes looking back helps clear the vision of what's ahead. So, read on! We promise: You won't face a test at the end of this section.

**BIRD TALK**

Because birds have been a big part of our lives and cultures for so long, many of the words we use when we talk about our feathered fellows are ancient in origin, derived from *avis*, the Latin word meaning "bird." Count in this group the words *avian* (having to do with birds), *aviculture* (the keeping of birds, especially for breeding purposes), and *aviary* (a place to house birds). And what about *aviation, aviator,* and *avionics?* You got it: When you see the letters *avi-* at the beginning of a word, you can figure a connection to birds or to one of their most notable qualities — flight!

## Food, feathers, and (finally!) friendship

Our earliest ancestors didn't have the luxury of enjoying birds as pets — they needed them for food, and they hunted birds and collected eggs to meet their most basic sustenance needs. Before long, though, humankind started to realize the benefits of *domestication* (changing wild creatures so that they not only provide us with food, but also serve as helpers and companions). These changes began 10,000 to 12,000 years ago and haven't stopped since. The worldwide growth of fried-chicken fast-food chains is just a modern milestone on the road that began in the jungles of Asia, where people first discovered the tasty ancestor of domestic chickens, the red jungle fowl.

Domestic fowl were admired and worshipped for their fertility, their courage, and even their role as the earliest alarm clocks. With so much going for them, birds quickly graduated to a place of honor for their nonmeat attributes — their beauty became reason enough to keep them around.

Although many of the world's cultures are horrified at the very idea of eating dogs and cats, the use of birds for food is nearly universally accepted (with the exception of individuals who abstain for philosophical or religious reasons). Why is it that some birds are prized as family members and others are best appreciated when served with orange sauce? We don't know, but in Chapter 2 we show you how some of the birds we routinely consider "food" really have decent pet potential!

## Humans' enduring involvement

People keep birds today for many of the same reasons Egyptian pharaohs or ancient Romans captured them — for beauty — as well as for some reasons bird fanciers of times past probably never gave much thought to. Figuring out what attracts you to birds can give you an understanding of the trade-offs you can live with (and those you can't). And those realizations are bound to set you up for success in choosing your avian companion.

## The beauty of birds

Let's face it: Humans are plain. Oh sure, we have some different skin tones and different hair and eye colors, but put us next to birds, and we have to admit to being pretty dull. And that's probably one reason why humans appreciate the beauty of birds and why our history with them in close company spans hundreds of years — we just want to be able to gaze upon (or wear) their glorious feathers.

Is it any surprise that some of the more popular pet birds are also the flashiest? The beautiful macaws — the scarlet, the blue-and-gold, and the giant blue hyacinth — are breathtaking to behold, as are their glorious smaller relatives, such as the dazzling sun conure, with a beautiful complement of sun-yellow feathers. And non-parrot species are not to be left out! Just consider the beauty of some of our fancy chicken and waterfowl breeds, as well as prize pigeons. Even smaller birds are prized for their plumage. From a simple singer discovered on a far island, the canary has been bred into all kinds of fancy feathered forms.

The lust for beauty spelled extinction for more than a few species of birds, ruthlessly slaughtered for feathers to adorn ladies' hats in the last century — as many as five million a year died for their plumage. Among the victims: one of the only two parrot species native to the United States, the Carolina parakeet. By the turn of the century, groups such as the Audubon Society were working to stop the killings. Too late for the Carolina parakeet, though: The last one died in the Cincinnati Zoo in 1918.

TIP

How beautiful do humans consider birds? So much that if you're trying to attract attention to a product or service, a picture of a bird typically works wonders. The eye-catching potential of birds makes them popular with the folks in the advertising and marketing businesses. Fans of the sketch comedy TV series *Portlandia* may recall the catchphrase "Put a bird on it," satirizing the trend toward avian motifs. Brian, who always has his eye out for birds, has noticed that about a quarter of the booths at veterinary conferences use birds in their displays, even if birds can't use the products!

TECHNICAL
STUFF

The Latin term *rara avis*, meaning "rare bird," is often used to reference an unusual or unique person or object. Roman poet Juvenal is credited with it in a sentence describing "a bird as rare upon the earth as a black swan."

## Of song and speech

Birds use song and mimicry to protect their territory, warn of danger, and attract mates, and throughout history, their fascinating music has also engaged a human audience. Such birds as the canary and the singing greenfinch have long been prized for their song, and the members of the *Psittaciformes* order — otherwise known as parrots — are so well known for their vocal talents that they've inspired a figure of speech. (To *parrot* something means to repeat it, whether you're a bird or a human being.) Even finches such as the ones shown in Figure 1-1 keep up a companionable twittering.

Photograph courtesy of Claudia Hunka, Your Basic Bird (Berkeley, California)

The breeding of canaries dates to the 16th century, and humans' relationship with wild-caught parrots is traceable to even earlier times. Ancient Greeks and Romans fell in love with parrots, so much so that a trained one was considered more valuable than the slave who trained him. A favorite phrase to teach a Roman parrot? Why, "Hail the Emperor!," of course.

Some 1,800 years later, companion birds were still found in the highest halls of government. Yes, the White House. James and Dolley Madison brought their "green parrot" with them to the Executive Mansion, Thomas Jefferson kept mockingbirds there, and Andrew Jackson had a parrot named Polly known for her (pardon the pun) "fowl" language. John Tyler had a pet canary he called Johnny Ty — nothing like naming a bird after yourself — and, of course, Abraham Lincoln is known for the earliest of the presidential turkey pardons. An admirer sent James Buchanan two bald eagles, whom he sent to live at his home in Pennsylvania. William McKinley had a parrot named Washington Post, known for whistling "Yankee Doodle." Calvin Coolidge may well have had the greatest number of presidential pets, including four canaries, a thrush, a goose, a troupial (the national bird of Venezuela), a mockingbird, and a "yellow bird" named Goldy. Dwight Eisenhower's parakeet, Gabby, died while he was in office and is buried on White House grounds, as is Caroline Kennedy's pet canary.

Recent research strongly suggests that birds don't, in fact, merely parrot, or repeat, what they hear — some understand the words they're saying. The work of Dr. Irene Pepperberg and her African grey, Alex, changed everyone's understanding of the intelligence of birds. Sadly, Alex passed away in his sleep at the young age of 31, as a result of *atherosclerosis* (hardening of the arteries), but his legacy continues to be a guiding light for us all. Alex didn't just talk — he had the ability to identify objects and colors and understand concepts such as "bigger" and "smaller." You can learn more about him at the Alex Foundation (`www.alexfoundation.org`).

## A charming companion

Although birds have lived as part of the human family for tens of thousands of years, the here and now may be the best time to enjoy an avian companion. Laws enacted to conserve birds in the wild and to stymie the worst sins of the importation trade (in which thousands upon thousands of birds died, either in transit or after entering the public realm as pet birds) have put the focus on breeding. The birds who come out of the best breeding programs make the very best quality pets, better than any Caesar could have known.

## CLOUD: A THERAPY BIRD

Our flying friends can be much more than companions in our homes. Birds have made a place for themselves as our helpers as well. Pet birds help children with autism improve their social skills, gain self-confidence, and develop trust. Parrots have helped people with disabilities manage stress and anxiety. Some emotional support parrots have learned to recognize stress in their humans and to say calming phrases that help them to relax or overcome anger. And although they aren't as common as therapy dogs or cats, therapy birds bring joy to patients in hospitals, residents of nursing homes, and children in schools.

Cloud, a ringneck dove (shown in the nearby photograph), was handled by humans — including kids — from the time he cracked out of his shell. He grew up to be a docile, friendly bird who was especially used to interacting with children. His owner, Daleen

Comer, was involved in pet therapy visits, and she thought Cloud would be a natural for the children's reading program. She trained him to wear a flight suit (think of it as a bird diaper) and created a special basket in which he could ride and be secure. To help prepare him for making visits, she began taking him places: the bank, the dry cleaner, the pet store, hobby shops. He wasn't afraid of anything. When Cloud was 2 years old, she had him evaluated by Pet Partners to see if he was suited to the work, and he received a perfect score.

They started making visits to the library and then weekly visits to classrooms. Cloud, now 12 years old, sits on his blanket on a table at school. Kids take turns coming up to see him, give him a treat, and read to him to practice their skills with a noncritical listener. He attends programs where students learn about the differences between therapy animals and service animals and demonstrates how therapy animals can help people. College students at exam time also benefit from his stress-relieving presence. Comer says Cloud is an ideal partner for the communities in which they visit and hopes he has several more years of bringing happiness to people.

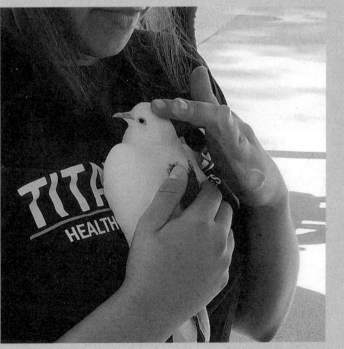

*Photograph courtesy of Daleen Comer*

Socialized since infancy to see humans as part of their "flock," many of today's pet birds have companionship potential that can amaze anyone who believes the old stereotypes about wild-caught birds. Every bit as beautiful as their wild relatives, breeder-raised babies are loving and intelligent, and improvements in what we know about their care keep them healthier than ever before. Our newfound knowledge, combined with centuries of experience and perspective, means that if you educate yourself to care for your pet, you can expect a phenomenal relationship — better than you may have imagined when you decided to become a bird owner. The depth of a healthy and interactive relationship with another living being is immense. Birds can certainly be a part of our lives and we a part of theirs.

# Deciding If You're Ready for a Bird

Pet birds bring so much to their owners' lives — color, song, speech, and a relationship that, at its best, approaches what you would find with a mate or a child (and, at its worst, approaches what you would find with a mate or a child). And that, for some people, is the problem. Birds give as good as they get. Sometimes birds are a joy to live with, and other times, they're a big pain in the tail feathers.

Having a bird in your home is different from having a dog or a cat (we have both). Birds are birds, unique and magical in their own right. To be ready for them, you have to be open to their own feathered flavor of magic.

Having a bird is more rewarding than you could ever imagine. We believe that learning to share life with a bird can make most of us better people. When you understand your bird's wide range of nonverbal communication, your own communication skills are enhanced, making you more sensitive and better able to interact with others (of all species).

But living with a bird isn't easy. For your own sanity, and for the health and happiness of the bird you hope to introduce to your world, you need to ask yourself whether you're really up to the challenge. Forewarned is forearmed, after all.

## Putting in the time

Forget any notion you ever had about birds being low-maintenance pets. Canaries and finches can fall loosely into that category, although even those species require more attention than you may expect, but the same can't be said of all the other birds we love as pets. From budgies to cockatiels to the flashiest of macaws, birds can be — how shall we say this politely? — *demanding.* You can't just put them in a cage, change the papers, add food and water, and ignore them. They won't let you.

Most of the birds people keep as pets are highly intelligent and very social. People often have denied them the company of their own kind and the stimulation of an appropriate environment. We ask them to be happy with us — and they *can* be, but not without effort on our part. And effort takes time. When you take one of these sentient beings into your life, you must take responsibility for her health, happiness, and welfare. If you're not prepared to spend that time working with your bird, training your bird, providing healthy social interaction for your bird, and allowing your bird plenty of supervised out-of-cage time to enjoy, you're going to have an unhappy bird. An unhealthy bird. A biter. A screamer. A feather-picker. And it doesn't need to be that way.

Cared for properly, birds can be as time-consuming as dogs. Really. They need to be loved, handled, trained, fed, and cleaned up after — a lot! If you don't have that kind of time and energy, reconsider choosing a bird as a companion unless you're sure you'll enjoy the pleasant sounds of a *charm* of finches (*charm* is the delightful term for a group of finches), who prefer the society of their own kind rather than interactions with humans.

**REMEMBER**

With any relationship, the more you put into it, the more you get out of it. The same is true when it comes to birds. The more time you spend with your bird, the more loving and socialized she'll be — and the more time you'll want to spend with her as a result! But don't forget to grant these individuals the opportunity to be just that: individuals. Their personalities and their likes and dislikes vary just as much as ours do. Not all birds are suited to all people and living circumstances. In this regard, think of them as feathered humans.

Another aspect of time that you need to consider when it comes to birds: longevity, yours and theirs. Healthy pet parrots can live for *decades,* which requires a major commitment to such companionship. In general, the larger the parrot species, the longer the life expectancy. For example, the large macaws can live 70 to 100 years or more, while the little budgerigars rarely will live to be 20 years old.

Can you imagine spending most of your life with a pet? Are you able to plan for the pet who outlives you? These issues are very real for bird owners, and you need to factor them into your decision-making. Some pet trusts, which ensure that pets are cared for after an owner's death, can be in effect for up to 150 years — a must if you have a long-lived pet such as a macaw, Amazon parrot, or tortoise.

**TIP**

For help in understanding an older bird and in keeping her healthy, check out Chapter 11.

# PARAKEETIS TYRANNOSAURUS?

One of the more unusual aspects to consider when taking a bird into your life: This association is likely to be the closest you'll ever get to sharing space with a dinosaur. Although scientists once figured that reptiles were next of kin to dinosaurs, they now believe birds are even closer. Birds are descended from a small meat-eating dinosaur that walked on two legs. The link between the two was made with the discovery of *Archaeopteryx* (meaning "ancient wing"), a Jurassic-period fossil of a creature that was part bird and part dinosaur.

If you have a hard time making the leap between birds and dinosaurs (the word *dinosaur* means "terrible lizard," after all, not "terrible bird"), check out the foot of an ostrich sometime — but not closely. The claws alone may give you *Jurassic Park* jitters. Scientists have learned that many of the dinosaurs once considered to be reptiles actually had feathers. Based on fragmented DNA recovered from a T. rex fossil found in the United States, one published study found that the closest living relative to a T. rex is, yes, the chicken! We love that.

*Photograph courtesy of D. Davidson Harpur*

## Shelling out the bucks

Birds are expensive to care for properly, much more so than most people anticipate. The price of acquiring a bird itself can run from the inexpensive for finches, canaries, and budgies to the monthly-salary figures some people are willing to shell out for large, flashy parrots. And that's just the beginning.

Safe, roomy caging isn't cheap, nor is a proper diet of pellets and fresh foods. Preventive veterinary care to keep your bird healthy is a pricey must, and if your bird gets *really* sick, be prepared to dig deep. All these aspects of care must be factored in, along with such necessities as toys, which a large parrot can go through with awesome efficiency. It all adds up.

TIP

Throughout this book, we note places where you can save money without cheating your bird. A good place to start is with your choice of bird. Although many people are drawn to the largest and most colorful of parrots, some of the other species are less expensive to acquire and maintain. We highlight these alternatives in Chapters 2 and 19.

## Dealing with the noise and mess

To hear some people tell it, the best tools for anyone who wants to keep a bird are earplugs and a handheld cordless vacuum. And it's true: Some birds can give a rowdy rock band a run for their money when it comes to decibel levels and the ability to trash a room.

Some of the problems are natural and normal, and some are caused by humans, but either way, the potential for noise and mess is an important consideration when you're thinking about a bird.

But then again . . . these problems shouldn't stop you, unless peace, quiet, and a clean house are the things that matter most to you in life.

TIP

For a better handle on which birds are noisiest, see Chapter 2. For ways to minimize mess, see our cage and cage setup information in Chapter 4.

REMEMBER

We're not trying to put you off bird keeping. But we believe in the importance of understanding potential problems *before* you take the plunge. The best attributes a bird lover can have are the same as a good parent — love, patience, structure, and a good sense of humor. You'll need them all! But the payoff . . . oh, it's grand. (And unlike being a parent to a human child, you don't have to save for a college fund.)

## A BIRB IS A BIRD IS A BIRB

Who doesn't love birbs? No, we're not misspelling that. *Birbs* is an affectionate term used on the Internet to refer to our feathered friends. What qualifies as a birb? According to Audubon (www.audubon.org/news/when-bird-birb-extremely-important-guide):

> The subreddit r/birbs [www.reddit.com/r/Birbs] defines a birb as any bird that's "being funny, cute, or silly in some way." Urban Dictionary [www.urban dictionary.com/define.php?term=birb] has a more varied set of definitions, many of which allude to a generalized smallness. A video on the YouTube channel Lucidchart [https://youtu.be/FpCX1BWA6do] offers its own expansive suggestions: "All birds are birbs, a chunky bird is a borb, and a fluffed-up bird is a floof."

Birb, borb, or floof, we love them all. #BirbsForever

# Chapter **2**

# Narrowing the Choices

You may find bringing a bird into your life an easy decision. But what kind of bird? That call can be the most difficult of all. So many choices, so much stunning beauty, cleverness, and personality. How can you choose? We say: Choose carefully!

We know people who've chosen birds based on some really awful criteria, like which bird best matches their new carpeting — a parrot in just the right shade of blue. Other people choose birds for status — some rare birds can set a buyer back thousands or even tens of thousands of dollars. A decision based on these criteria can be a disaster. You may miss out on one of the big benefits of bird ownership — the company and closeness of a new family member — and the mess and noise delivered by that decorative avian status object aren't likely to win any adoring coos. Vanity can be a pretty expensive lesson, especially when a bird who isn't getting the care and attention she needs becomes sick or dies.

How can you avoid such a scenario? Start by understanding what birds really are about and what they need, and determine what you can and can't live with. Even a *little* knowledge can be good — and the more you know, the better!

**REMEMBER**

We're not saying you shouldn't choose a bird strictly for aesthetics. Some pet birds, such as finches and canaries, are content to live with as little human contact as possible, spending their days delighting our lives with song, color, and playful antics in their cages. But expecting a larger and more social parrot to adapt to such a situation isn't a good idea. We want you to recognize not only the remarkable variety of birds available but also that the bird you're naturally drawn to may or may not be the right one for you in the long run. Consider your lifestyle, your personal tolerances for noise and mess, and the amount of time you have to care for and interact with a bird. With this information at hand, you have the best chance of pairing up with the particular species that suits you.

Although we feature many varieties of companion birds in this chapter — including a few that the vast majority of bird lovers are best off avoiding — we offer a list of the ten best birds for beginners in Chapter 19.

TIP

Here's a different way of looking at the question: What is a bird looking for in you? When you visit a retailer with birds, look for that individual who comes to you, wants to interact with you, and tells you, "I think you're kind of special." This bird may be an entirely different species from the one you were thinking of, but keep in mind, you're looking for the *right* relationship with the *right* bird.

# Deciding What You're Looking for in a Bird

If you can't just fall in love with the look of a bird, what characteristics are worth considering? In the following sections, we describe the traits most people love or hate, so you can develop your own standards and compare them to the various species.

## Judging interactivity

Bird species range in friendliness from the "don't touch me" attitude of most finches to the Velcro-like manner of some cockatoos. That said, some finches can learn to interact with you and come to your hand, and cockatoos often probably shouldn't be encouraged to live their lives attached to you — a little independence is a good thing.

Do you want a bird in the hand or one in the cage? Even within the highly intelligent and social parrot species, you can find differences in the amount of attention a bird wants — or demands, in some cases.

Are you comfortable being the center of another being's life, or are you likely to find the demands for attention from such a bird to be tedious or entrapping after a while? The answer to this question can take you a step closer to one group of birds or another, and responding too casually to the question can lead both to your own unhappiness and your bird's. So, give it some serious consideration.

## Considering size

No matter how friendly they are, large birds scare some people. Their flapping wings and impressive beaks have only a distant appeal to the person whose idea of the perfect pet bird is a budgie who can balance easily on a single finger. Other folks love the dramatic presence the larger birds command.

You can find charming personality types in all sizes. If you like a social bird in a small package, parrotlets, lovebirds, and budgies can fill the bill. You don't have to buy a big parrot to get a big personality!

Size counts for more than presence, however. Large birds require larger, more expensive cages. Plus, they go through food, toys, and perches more rapidly than their smaller counterparts and generally make a much larger mess. The initial price of a large bird is often greater, too.

## Making a mess

Logically, larger birds make larger messes, but some birds really are over the top when it comes to covering every available surface with feces, feathers, and food. Top of the list: lories and lorikeets, lively and colorful nectar eaters with the ability to shoot their runny droppings some remarkable distances. This trait limits their pet appeal for many people, but some folks take these talents in stride, figuring the extra work is worth the companionship of these charmers.

### A BRAVE-HEARTED PIGEON

Pigeon-hearted? It doesn't mean what you think. G.I. Joe was a homing pigeon noted for his service in the United States Army Pigeon Service, used for communication and reconnaissance during World Wars I and II. Hatched in March 1943, he was presented with the Dickin Medal — the equivalent for animals of the Victoria Cross or Medal of Honor — for gallantry, awarded for "the most outstanding flight made by a United States Army homing pigeon in World War II." His 20-mile flight, achieved in an impressive 20 minutes, saved the lives of more than 100 troops by delivering a message that prevented a friendly-fire event. After World War II, he was housed at the U.S. Army's Churchill Loft at Fort Monmouth, New Jersey, and died at the age of 18 at the Detroit Zoological Gardens. In 2019, he was posthumously awarded the Animals in War & Peace Medal of Bravery.

Although lories and lorikeets may be the messiest, no bird can be considered truly neat. Well-designed cages, plenty of newspaper, a hand-vacuum, and a large assortment of cloth and paper towels can keep things under control, for the most part. Again, it's all a matter of preference, tolerance, and mutual compatibility.

You can train many different kinds of birds to eliminate on cue. This allows you to hold them over a wastebasket or other container to capture the mess. For help in accomplishing this nifty feat, see Chapter 7.

## Bring in da noise

No bird is perfectly quiet. Finches keep up a constant chatter, and canaries have been encouraged through centuries of breeding to sing. Some birds, however, can make you yearn for the relative quiet of a house next to a major airport. Birds use their voices to communicate their feelings — of loneliness, of boredom, of isolation, or of just being alive. Some pet birds are noisy only at certain times, such as in the early morning or at dusk, while others can start up at any time.

You need to figure out your tolerance levels and balance them with the bird you're considering. If peace and quiet is of paramount importance to you, no bird may fit into your life. Even the most patient souls may discover that the real screamers push their limits at one time or another.

Consider, too, your living situation — apartment, attached house, suburban dwelling, or acreage. The walls of an apartment building or attached house do little to muffle the sounds of the loudest birds, and that could lead to trouble with the neighbors — or even get you evicted. If you're considering chickens or other backyard poultry as companions, keep in mind that zoning and homeowner's association regulations may prevent the keeping of those birds. As an example, many cities have ordinances prohibiting the keeping of roosters or limiting the numbers of birds that a household can keep.

Sometimes bird lovers make matters worse by their reactions to screaming birds. For tips on what to do — and what not to do — with a screaming, noisy, disruptive feathered child, see Chapter 12.

## Talking ability

The ability to mimic sounds is one of the things that makes parrots so popular, but the skill and ability of mimicry isn't found equally in all parrots. With patience and work, many parrot species can utter a few words or phrases, but if you're really looking for the gift of gab, be sure to choose a yellow-naped or double-yellow-headed Amazon parrot or an African grey parrot, species especially known for their speaking ability. Even then, you can't be sure you're getting a bird who will talk unless he was talking when you bought him. (The same thing, incidentally, goes for the singing skill of canaries. Make sure you hear singing before you buy, if that's what's important to you.)

For tips on teaching a bird to talk, see Chapter 7. Chapter 12 is the place to go for hints about how to coax your bird to be quiet for a while!

What do you call a group of parrots? A *pandemonium*, of course! They're sometimes also referred to as a *company* of parrots.

## Paying attention to price

The price of a pet bird can be considerable, starting from less than $20 for some small budgies or finches and climbing rapidly into the hundreds of dollars for some of the large common parrots and into the thousands and tens of thousands for species that are especially rare, large, or difficult to breed in captivity.

Bargain hunting is usually a bad idea when it comes to birds. Raising healthy, well-socialized birds is time-consuming and expensive, and the prices for these birds reflect the labor that goes into their raising. You have to wonder what kind of corners were cut when you find a price that's out of line with what's normal for a particular species in a particular area. Is the bird a medical time bomb just waiting to explode with the stress of a new home? A simmering behavior problem waiting to develop? Too often the answer is "Yes" to one or both questions.

Figure out the price you can afford to pay, and then shop for the best bird possible for that money. Don't fret over the bird you can't afford, because you can find many wonderful and underappreciated species in every price range, and they make wonderful pets. We'd rather see you spend what may seem to be an "outrageous" $50 on a healthy, well-socialized budgie with great pet potential than $20 on a mass-produced budgie of unknown genetics or health, or $300 on a sick or emotionally crippled parrot of a species that usually retails for considerably more. You're better off with the well-raised and socialized budgie, trust us. Budgies are cool.

Also, consider reaching out to rescue groups for birds in need of a second chance at life with the right forever home. Just as in animal shelters with dogs and cats, numerous shelter birds may be just the right fit for you!

The cost of a bird is only part of the hit you take when you bring home a feathered companion. Cages, perches, toys, and more are expensive, and so is that post-purchase veterinary examination, but they all need to be factored in to keep your pet bird healthy and happy. For more on bird gear — what you need, what you don't, and more — see Chapter 4.

## PET PREFERENCE: CUDDLE-BUG, "WILD" THING, OR BREEDER?

Most of the birds commonly available as pets today are valued as much for their companionship as anything else. Socialized, hand-raised babies grow up thinking humans are pretty cool, and they want us to be a member of their flock. We become their family!

The new emphasis on companionship of the pet bird reflects a change in the way many people interact with their birds. In this regard, people often want birds to be family members. Some folks, though, still want birds more to look at than to cuddle, and those people are likely to be happier with birds content to live in an aviary with little or no human contact. Although these are domestically raised birds, to be sure, they're typically as little interested in us as their wild-born relatives may be.

A third group, the hobby or professional breeder, may have a different goal altogether. Just like a farmer who cares for the animals she stewards, aviculturists do, too. Often, the intended goal is to allow successful breeding and rearing of young birds. An aviculturist's sole objective may be to allow their birds to procreate and raise their young. Some breeders want to successfully raise a particular species or subspecies. Others may work to develop new colors or varieties, win prizes at shows, make money (or at least pay the costs of production), and enjoy the intense joy and satisfaction that comes from successfully breeding and keeping healthy birds — or all of the above.

What are you looking for in a bird? We talk about the joys as well as the challenges of breeding and raising birds in Chapter 13, and you can find plenty on both the hands-off and hands-on species later in this chapter. But you're the one who must consider what relationship you're looking for with your bird, because your decision affects the kind of bird you choose — not just the species, but in many cases the individual bird.

Keep in mind that we're talking about unique species from a variety of different environments, not simply "breeds of birds." Our avian friends originate from all around the globe and have evolved to live comfortably and successfully in a particular habitat. When we bring them into our homes to share their lives with us, we have an obligation to think in a species-specific way about what we do with them and for them.

# Considering the Species

After you figure out what you want in your feathered companion, you can realistically look at what's out there and start matching the species that connect with your personality and lifestyle. Don't feel restricted! The variety of species and types of pet birds available today is so broad that all except the most dedicated quiet-and-neatness types can find more than one species to fill the bill — and probably several!

We put our observations on the record here to let you know what each species is really like, both the good and the not-so-good qualities. Nobody's perfect — not you, not us, and not any single bird. But getting the match as close as possible is your best bet for a long, happy, and healthy relationship.

**WARNING**

Make no mistake: The qualities we're talking about in this chapter refer to truly healthy pet birds acquired from reputable sources — and in the case of the parrot species, well-socialized birds to boot. Brian's experience confirms that a healthy, well-cared-for bird can live roughly twice as long as some of the generic life expectancies published in most of the older reference books. You'll never find a better testimonial to good preventive care. Poor living conditions combined with an unhealthy diet and risky behavior also limit our own life expectancies — similar to what we see in the birds we keep.

**TIP**

For information on choosing a reputable bird source, see Chapter 3. And don't forget that a good start is *only a start:* Explore the latest on avian nutrition in Chapter 6 and on preventive care in Chapter 9.

# The hands-off color and songbirds

Finches — and canaries are finches, too — have been popular for centuries, with good reason. They're attractive, active, and fill our world with sound, including the sweet songs canaries are known for. Well-suited to life in a cage or aviary, these canaries and other finches (see Figure 2-1) are perfect for people who don't want a lot of physical interaction with their pet birds. If you keep the cage or aviary clean and make sure your pets are healthy and well fed, they're quite content to keep you on the periphery, sharing their lives with you from afar. These small charmers can also be interesting to breed, without the time-consuming hand-feeding that parrots may require.

## Finches

Relatively inexpensive with a couple of very hardy species in the group, finches make a good first bird, a child's pet, or charming aviary residents for both experienced or beginner bird keepers. Best bets: society or zebra finches, which are very common and relatively inexpensive (usually starting at around $20). Although small in stature, these little birds do need comfortable housing and a stress-free existence in your home. If you provide a finch with enough enrichment in her enclosure to allow her to choose if she can be seen or not, she'll feel great comfort and security. Sadly, stress is one of the leading contributors to some of the health problems Brian sees in finches.

Photograph by Kim Campbell Thornton

Beyond society and zebra finches is a world of exotic and lovely finches, such as the multicolored Gouldians or the Fischer's, with their long tail plumes. The more unusual finches are much more expensive than the society or zebra finches — they cost up to $250 — and they're also more difficult to keep. Easily chilled and quickly stressed, many of the more unusual finches are best left in the hands of experienced bird lovers.

TIP

Society and zebra finches are the best bet for anyone looking to bring the zest of these little guys into their lives. They're both easy to keep. A pair or handful of zebras or societies can comfortably keep themselves amused while you're at work.

The finch's life span is around 3 to 6 years for a "typical" pet, but a healthy bird from a reputable source, cared for properly, can hit the 20-year mark. Finches can thrive in almost any living situation, from studio apartment to outdoor aviary.

## Canaries

The Sinatras of the pet bird world, canaries have enjoyed a long run of popularity — and a fair amount of fame, too. Consider the classic Warner Brothers cartoon character, Tweety Bird, who has done plenty to promote his real-life counterparts. (We won't quibble with the fact that Tweety doesn't seem to sing much at all, since his uncharacteristic gift of conversational skills makes up for the deficit.)

Canaries have been bred for centuries and, as a result, come in a wide variety of colors, shapes, and feather patterns. The yellow border fancy is perhaps the one who looks the most like Tweety, a clear, vibrant burst of sunshine in any room. Borders are available in other colors, too, including white, blue, and green. Canaries also come in a dramatic red-orange and a cinnamon color. Fancy feathers were the aim of other breeders, who've produced frilled versions with elegant feather puffs or fringes over the eyes.

**TIP**

Red canaries need a little human help to maintain their breathtakingly vibrant color. People who exhibit their birds add special ingredients — color foods — to their red canaries' diets to help them become just the right hue. A more natural way to bring out the red is to feed foods high in beta-carotene, such as freshly grated carrots, chopped broccoli, or pieces of cooked sweet potato, when the bird is *molting* — the time when new feathers are coming in.

When it comes to what canaries are best known for — song — the green roller takes the prize. The roller is humble in appearance, perhaps, but eagerly sought out for the complexity and length of his song. (And we do mean "his," because in canaries, the girls leave the singing to the boys.)

Canaries can start at prices not much higher than the common finches ($60 to $75 for females and $80 to $100 for males, because of their singing ability), but if you're really looking for great singing or distinctive colors or feather patterns, you can easily shell out $300 to $400 or more in some cases. Ordinary life span for most canaries is roughly 8 to 16 years, but 20- and 30-year-olds who enjoy good care turn up fairly regularly. The canary is another fine bird for any living situation, from small apartment to outdoor aviary.

## Small parrots

Quieter, neater, and, of course, smaller than their larger relations, the parrots we group together in this section include what may be the world's most popular pet bird, the budgerigar, and others with loads of fans, too, such as the cockatiel. And don't forget the parrotlets and the lineolated parakeets, both popular and rising in popularity. These little guys are known for being among the smallest members of the parrot family. Don't let their size fool you: Some of these small parrots have plenty of personality, and some can be more than enough to intimidate people. That said, parrotlets and linnies often make affectionate companions, and offer surprising talking ability. Most are reasonably priced, as well.

### Parakeets

When Americans think "parakeet," they're usually picturing what the rest of the world calls a *budgerigar*, or *budgie* (see the next section). A budgie is a parakeet, but to believe that it's the only parakeet sadly ignores some of the more magnificent pet birds available. Most popular among these birds are the Asiatic parakeets — ringnecks, Alexandrians, derbians (also known as the Lord Derby parakeet), plum-heads, and mustached parakeets. As a group, they're known for flashy, vibrant color and long, elegant tails.

Once considered hands-off aviary birds, Asiatic parakeets are gaining ground as more up-close-and-personal pets. When captive raised and well socialized, some of these birds have great potential as affectionate companions and even great talkers — one of the better talkers Brian has ever met is a blue Indian ringneck parakeet named Sid. These species are gorgeous in an aviary, however, and seem to be happy there, too. Some Asiatic parakeets — either in the home or the aviary — have a pleasant and soothing call, while others have a reputation for being moderately noisy.

Parakeets have a wide price range. Smaller, more common varieties may cost as little as $20 to $50. Prices climb according to color or species rarity, to as much as $800 or $1,000. Life spans for well-cared-for birds run from 20 to 40 years. Kim's African ringneck parakeet, Larry, lived to be 29 years old.

The Asiatics aren't the only parakeets around. One popular parakeet native to South America is the Quaker, also called the Monk. Quakers are so adept at establishing themselves in the wild in places where they don't belong, however, that some states and countries don't allow them to be kept as pets. If your part of the world doesn't have a regulation against ownership, though, these parakeets can be good companions. (Check with your local agriculture department for restrictions.) States that prohibit or restrict keeping Quaker parakeets include California, Georgia, Hawaii, Kansas, Kentucky, New Jersey, Pennsylvania, Rhode Island, Tennessee, and Wyoming.

Quakers are handsome green-and-silver birds with decent talking potential and affectionate natures, when raised and handled properly. Prices are reasonable for these charmers, from $300 to $700, with an average of $475.

**TECHNICAL STUFF**

Quaker parakeets earned their name because of the way babies "quake" when being fed in the nest.

The *Brotogeris* gang are also parakeets of South American origin. These little guys love riding in pockets, are pretty quiet, and aren't very messy. Primarily green in color with small, contrasting markings, *Brotogeris* are big guys in little bodies — some even like to pick fights with much bigger birds! The canary-winged parakeet — green with bright yellow under the wings — and gray-cheeked are two of the more commonly available *Brotogeris* parakeets in the United States. A little more expensive than some other parakeets, well-socialized individuals can start at $400 and go up from there. The *Brotogeris* species are difficult to breed and rear successfully, making them less common than in years past.

## Budgerigar

When budgies were discovered by Europeans in Australia in the mid-1800s, they created quite a stir back home in Europe. They had everything going for them — bright color, an affectionate nature, and a real facility for talking. These same traits make this awesome little bird the world's most popular today. You just can't top a nice budgie — they have it all!

In some ways, the popularity and availability of budgies has led many people to dismiss them, more so in recent years. Too common, too cheap, too ordinary, these lovely pets are too often considered just a "starter" bird, especially for children. And that idea opens the doors to mass breeding to fill public demand for low-cost sources of budgerigars, which further reinforces any perception of the budgie as a "throwaway pet." What a waste!

TIP

Budgies (shown in Figure 2-2) are remarkable pets, for children, adults, beginners, and experienced bird lovers alike.

**FIGURE 2-2:** Budgies are often dismissed as common, but they're fun-loving, beautiful, and smart.

*Photograph courtesy of Claudia Hunka, Your Basic Bird (Berkeley, California)*

Budgies come in many colors and patterns and two basic body types. The American style of budgie is slender and long, whereas the English budgie is husky, with an almost bulldog look. Their personalities are the same, though, so color or body type is strictly a matter of personal preference.

These versatile birds are suitable for any living situation. Prices range from under $20 for what are typically mass-produced birds to around $100 for more unusual colors in hand-raised birds. You can probably find a hand-raised American type for around $40, and we say that's a good deal. Although eight years is the common forecast on life span, a well-cared-for budgie can make it well into the teens and beyond.

**TIP**

To make sure you have the best experience with a budgie as a pet, skip the under-$20 mass-produced specimens (which are often a bit of a gamble because of uncertain health, background, and pet potential) and search out a hand-raised baby. A hand-raised little budgie who is really well socialized, already eating a good diet, and shows interest in interacting with you can carry you a long way! Parent-raised birds can be fine as hands-off cage or aviary pets, but we think you can enjoy the greatest rewards from your relationship if you choose a bird you can become friends with.

A talking budgie has the charm to make a statue break out in a smile. If you listen carefully, you may figure out why we think these little guys are equipped to give the better-known big-parrot talkers a run for their money! Their lispy little high-pitched voices are adorable! Some are incredibly good talkers, learning 300 or more words or phrases. A budgie named Puck, from Petaluma, California, holds the record for largest avian vocabulary, according to Guinness World Records, which documented his knowledge of 1,728 words. We think that tiny hand-raised budgie you can carry around in your shirt pocket is worth his weight in gold!

## Lovebirds

Peach-faced, black-masked, and Fischer's lovebirds are small, sweet companions who come in a rainbow array of colors, thanks to human genetic meddling. Natural-born snugglers, lovebirds adore holing up in a pocket or other warm, hidden place. They aren't great talkers, but some can learn a few words and phrases if you have the time and patience to work with them.

**TIP**

For a pet, a single lovebird is best; otherwise, your pair will only have eyes for each other, not for you. Forget that old myth about them dying of loneliness — it just isn't true. One healthy, well-socialized lovebird will be your contented pal.

Lovebirds are also popular as aviary birds and for breeding purposes, and many hobbyists are working hard to increase the available varieties of these lovely birds.

Fine for almost any living situation, lovebirds have life spans of 8 to 14 years, and well-cared-for birds over 20 years old are out there. Costs run from $50 for the normal peach-faced variety to $200 for newer color variations or less-common lovebird species.

## Parrotlets and lineolated parakeets

The tiny parrotlet (see Figure 2-3) can fit in your hand, but anyone who owns one can tell you they have as much attitude as any macaw, more proof that good — no, make that *great* — things can certainly come in small packages.

**FIGURE 2-3:** Parrotlets (like this blue mutation of a Pacific parrotlet) are packed with personality and love to be part of your life.

*Photograph courtesy of Amy Baggs*

A newer arrival to this group is the lineolated parakeet. These vibrant green, yellow, or blue wonders have great potential for companionship and make wonderful friends to hang out with.

Parrotlets and linnies generally have minimal talking ability, but they're great fun to handle and to watch. Both can be fabulous to train and can do impressive things! In so many ways, they demonstrate how they're just big parrots inhabiting a little parrot body!

Reasonably priced, starting at $150 and going up to $500 or so, parrotlets can and should enjoy a life span of up to 20 years. Linnies are priced at about $300 for a pair and typically have a ten-year lifespan.

## Cockatiels

The cockatiel is likely the most popular single pet bird species, at least among the parrot family. With crests reminiscent of the larger cockatoo, these birds were, for a while, known as "cockatoo parrots" until the modern coinage of *cockatiel,* from the Portuguese word *cacatilho* (meaning "little cockatoo").

Cockatiels (shown in Figure 2-4) justly deserve their legions of fans. Handsome and affectionate, the cockatiel is a perfect fit for any living situation, and a relatively easy breeder for anyone who wants to give that hobby a try. Many people have enjoyed the adventure of breeding cockatiels over the years, producing lovely varieties of colors and patterns, from the naturally occurring gray to the pale yellow lutino, the *pied* (blotches of two or more colors), cinnamon, pearl, and albino.

**FIGURE 2-4:** Cockatiels are pleasant to live with and come in a range of color mutations.

*Photograph by Kim Campbell Thornton*

Prices can start at $50 for some of the mass-produced birds, and rise as high as $275, with the cost of most pet cockatiels somewhere in the middle. Hand-raised babies and the rarer colors and patterns are at the higher end of the scale. Life spans for most cockatiels are often quoted to run 10 to 14 years, but again, a bird who starts healthy and is well cared for can live well into the twenties and beyond. In Brian's practice, birds in their late twenties and early thirties are not uncommon.

## PET BIRDS AND CHILDREN

Birds can be wonderful companions for children, but sometimes the reverse isn't so true. Children who are too young or unable to understand the importance of gentle, respectful handling can end up with a dead bird pretty quickly — truly a tragedy for all involved.

The look-don't-touch birds such as canaries and other finches are best for very young children. From the age of 8 or so, a child can begin to understand instructions for correctly handling smaller parrots, making budgies and cockatiels a good match for these older children. When kids enter their teens, almost any bird who fits the family's lifestyle can be a good match.

In Brian's experience, children who learn to communicate nonverbally with a bird in a constructive, mutual way often have a great learning experience that stands them in good stead later in life, both with humans and with other animals. Birds can really help to teach us how to be better people, as well as better communicators with other humans and with birds.

Remember, though, that taking proper care of any pet is the parent's responsibility. Lead by example. Don't make the pet the focus of a tug-of-war between you and your child. The lesson of responsibility is a good one to draw from a relationship with a pet, but so, too, are the lessons of compassion, caring, and respect for another living being.

**TIP**

As with budgies, you can find plenty of mass-produced cockatiels with price tags that may seem irresistible. If you're looking for a healthy, long-term companion, however, the hand-raised bird is a much better bet, even if the price is higher.

**WARNING**

As interesting as the many variations of cockatiels can be, some health problems have slipped into the mix. Some varieties, such as the white-faced and cinnamon, may develop problems on certain formulated diets. Talk to a veterinarian who is qualified and experienced in avian medicine to determine how to best keep these birds in optimal health and how to detect or avoid early problems.

Males are usually better at vocalizing, with whistling a specialty. Cockatiels are generally not the best talkers, but males can pick up a few words or phrases. Don't let the lack of verbosity dissuade you, though: The gentle cockatiel is about as fine an avian companion as you can imagine.

## Medium-size parrots

Pricier and less commonly available than budgies and cockatiels — and generally less flashy and colorful than their larger relatives — the medium-size parrots are often overlooked and underappreciated. And that's a shame, because in this group you can find some wonderful companions — handsome birds who are relatively neat and quiet (with a couple of notable exceptions) and reasonably priced to acquire and care for. A great bunch!

## Poicephalus

The Senegal (shown in Figure 2-5) is probably the most popular of the class of smaller African parrot species known collectively under the genus *Poicephalus*. The Senegal parrot is reasonably priced, at around $600 to $800 for a hand-fed baby. Senegals are neat and quiet as parrots go, and handsome in a somewhat unspectacular way — green feathers on the back, a mango-colored breast, and a gray head.

**FIGURE 2-5:**
Quieter and more easygoing than many other parrots, the Senegal is a good choice for first-time bird owners.

*Photograph courtesy of Amy Baggs*

Personable and affectionate, Senegals are capable of picking up a few words and phrases, but they're not generally known for their talking ability. Good for many living situations, small apartments included, Senegal parrots have much to offer as companion birds for many people.

**WARNING**

You need a critical eye when it comes to interpreting the behavior of a Senegal. It's easy to underestimate them and cause more behavior problems if you don't look, listen, and train well.

The others in this group — including the red-bellied, Meyer's, and Jardine's parrots — are comparatively more difficult to find and notably more expensive (up to $1,200 or so) than the Senegal parrot but are well worth seeking out. The life span of a healthy, well-cared-for *Poicephalus* can range from 20 to 40 years.

## Lories and lorikeets

You see a lot of lories and lorikeets in zoos and commercial aviaries — their fantastic good looks and clownish personalities are undeniable attractions. They're a delight to watch, a rainbow of intense, vibrant color. The lory feeding exhibits in many zoos and wildlife parks are popular draws for thousands of people worldwide.

**WARNING**

As household pets, though, these guys have one decided drawback — they're incredibly messy. Unlike most of the birds available as pets, most lories and lorikeets don't eat hard food, for the most part, but instead consume more liquid rations — in the wild they're nectar eaters. This sticky diet is harder to keep up with than that of other commonly kept birds, and that's not the only problem. Their diet results in oodles of watery droppings, which the birds seem to delight in shooting as far from their cages as possible.

If you can overlook the mess — and many people cope just fine — lories are lovely pets. The spectacular rainbow lory, in particular, is a good choice in this group, goofy and fun to be around. Lories aren't suited for close-quartered living, however, because of some decidedly high-decibel noise. Prices of lories are moderate: $400 and up, depending on the species.

The difference between lories and lorikeets is generally the length of their tails. Lorikeets, like parakeets, have longer tail feathers. If you get a chance to meet some of these birds in person, you're in for an olfactory experience you won't believe! The feathers of lories and lorikeets smell absolutely fabulous, perhaps because of their fruit-centric diet. Other bird species have their own unique odors, but these guys take the deliciously scented cake!

## Conures

The rap on conures is that they should be sold along with earplugs for everyone around them — neighbors very much included. Some conures well deserve this reputation for noisiness — those vociferous sorts may be more closely related to macaws — but not all conures can be credited with a noisy nature.

We include conures with the medium-size parrots because some of the most common ones, such as the sun conure, aren't all that large. As a group, though, conures display a wide range of size, with species such as the mitred really qualifying as a large parrot.

The conures of the *Aratinga* genus are usually the real noisemakers — the sun, jenday, golden-capped, mitred, red-fronted, dusky, and white-eyed, to name a few. Although not of the *Aratinga* genus, the nanday and the Patagonian conures are other conures with a well-earned reputation for noise.

*Aratinga* conures have formidable vocal abilities when it comes to shrieking and frequently have little hesitation to share their talents. Of these, the sun conure is probably the most attractive, enticing people to figure they can live with the noise just to enjoy the beauty and antics of these clever parrots.

REMEMBER

The bottom line with these birds is the same hard truth you have to face with any winged pet: knowing what you can live with. You can't change the nature of a bird; the best you can do is live with the traits that are challenging, to say the least. If the appearance and liveliness of a sun conure overwhelms any doubts you have about the noise, maybe you're meant to have one (as long as you're not living with close-by neighbors, that is).

The conures of the genus *Pyrrhura* are smaller and not nearly as loud. The green-cheeked, maroon-belly, and black-capped conures are the most popular in this group. Like the parrotlets and lineolated parakeets, green-cheeked conures can be quite the rock stars, easily learning many tricks and behaviors.

Conures range in price from $200 or so for some of the *Pyrrhura* to considerably more for flashier or rarer species or color variants, up to as much as $3,000. Life expectancies for healthy, well-cared-for birds can run from the twenties to the forties.

### Caiques

There are two species of caiques: white-bellied and black-capped. The names are a tad deceiving, because both kinds have white fronts. The black caps have — you guessed it — black heads. Caiques are lively, busy birds, highly entertaining as companions, and real clowns. Everybody's business is a caique's business. They often want to be a part of whatever is going on or whatever they can get started! Their popularity is solid, and for good reason.

Like most of the medium-size parrots, life spans range from the twenties on up for healthy, well-cared-for birds. You can find caiques at a price range of $900 to $2,000, with most falling into the $1,200 to $1,500 range.

## Large parrots

Flashy, colorful, noisy, intelligent, and talkative, large parrots are the ones folks usually visualize when they hear the word *parrot*, partially because some of these guys can *really* talk! You can find some excellent companions among these birds — and some challenging ones, too. But don't expect to ever run across one that isn't a parade-stopper — these birds have star status, without a doubt!

## Amazons

Clever, colorful, talkative, and often bratty, Amazon parrots are sometimes considered a handful — but within the group you can find some species that defy commonly held beliefs.

First, the characters: There are about 30 species of Amazon parrots. Amazons undoubtedly have command presence. The yellow-naped and double yellow-heads are generally good talkers, but they can also be loud and demanding. They have the potential to become possessive of the person they may perceive as a mate, leading to the misleading description of being a "one-person bird." You need to know about these possibilities before you start out with an Amazon. Some people like their in-your-face attitude; some don't.

Other Amazons may be easier to live with, among them the lilac crowns, red-lored, blue-fronted, and white-fronted. These smaller species are less likely to push, are generally quieter, and are typically easier to handle. The trade-off: Their talking ability is usually not as good as that of the yellow-naped or double yellow-head.

Life expectancies for Amazon parrots are among the longest of pet birds; up to a hundred years is possible, particularly because we now better understand what it takes to keep these birds healthy. Unfortunately, poor diets and lousy care limit the life expectancy potential of many of these impressive birds; most of the pet population is gone long before the age of 50, with geriatric problems showing up in birds as young as 20 years old. Prices typically range from $500 to $2,500.

**WARNING**

A common health problem seen in Amazons is obesity. If you have an Amazon, make sure you offer her a healthy diet and plenty of exercise, or else these natural perch potatoes will go to, er, seed, rather easily.

## African greys

Introducing the undisputed Einsteins of the parrot world! African greys — both the more common Congo and the smaller Timneh — are marvelous talkers who have demonstrated that they actually understand what they're saying.

**WARNING**

Grey parrots need attentive owners. They need to be kept engaged and challenged. Without a good relationship with a human caretaker, the birds can become fearful, sullen, or even aggressive. Boredom and a lack of variety and intellectual stimulation make for a miserable life for these clever pets. Compared to Amazon parrots, grey parrots generally have less volume, typically vocalizing more beeps, whistles, and other sounds much more than many other species. Regardless, even those sounds may not necessarily be suited for close-quartered living or easily annoyed neighbors.

TIP

Most African greys kept as companions are of the larger species *(Psittacus erithacus)*, with a tail that is more vividly colored than that of the Timneh *(Psittacus timneh)*. In terms of personality, though, there's little overall difference. The secret's out: Timneh greys are pretty cool, too! Expect to pay $800 to $3,600 for either species of these clever birds.

## Cockatoos

Cockatoos have a reputation as "love sponges" — birds who, in some folks' minds, would choose to be "surgically grafted" onto their human companion. That's only half the story, though. Cockatoos are often said to come in two basic behavioral types: the "love sponge" and the "hyperactive child."

WARNING

Umbrellas, Galahs (see Figure 2-6), and Moluccans are in the first group. These flashy birds can easily be taught or led to expect close human contact, all the time. Needless to say, a bird who demands attention 28 hours a day can be a royal pain in the tail feathers. Ultimately, the relationship doesn't end well if the birds are denied what they've come to expect as normal. They can develop significant behavioral problems (aggression, screaming, feather picking), as well as a number of medical problems.

The "hyperactive child" is best represented by Goffin's and bare-eyed cockatoos. Not always so keen on snuggling, these clowns never met a toy (or cage door) they couldn't figure out and take apart. Some of these birds require padlocks on their cages to keep them from escaping — and not combination locks, either! Goffin's and bare-eyeds learn trick behaviors quickly and perform them with great enthusiasm. These guys really need to have lots of jobs to do. Keeping their minds and bodies engaged is an essential part of helping them maintain a balanced life with you.

Living with a cockatoo means never a dull moment in your household, that's for sure. Prices range from $700 for some of the smaller species, such as Goffin's cockatoos, or $1,000 to $5,000 for species such as umbrella cockatoos, Moluccans, or Major Mitchell's. Rare species such as some of the black cockatoos can run $20,000 and up. Life expectancies can theoretically hit 100 years for the larger species, although in most countries, birds over 60 to 70 years are relatively uncommon. Most can and should live longer through better care and nutrition.

WARNING

We recommend that people with allergies (particularly to feathers or feather dust) steer clear of cockatoos. They're among the dustiest of birds, distributing lots of feather dust and dander.

**FIGURE 2-6:**
Galahs, sometimes referred to as rose-breasted cockatoos, aren't necessarily cuddlers but they are friendly and affectionate.

## Eclectus

WARNING

One of the more interesting pet birds and certainly among the most beautiful, Eclectus have a few characteristics that make them less than suitable for beginners. They can be more sensitive to their environment than many other parrots, and you may need to feed them a higher percentage of fresh fruits and vegetables to keep them healthy. Seed-only diets are particularly hard for the Eclectus parrot to survive on for long, one of the reasons why the Eclectus rarely did well in captivity until humans developed a better understanding of optimal nutrition for these wonderful birds.

Unlike many companion birds, with the Eclectus, the female is more often the "boss" — and certainly more beautiful (at least if you like red). Four common subspecies of Eclectus parrots are available for the pet trade — the red-sided, vosmaeri, grand, and Solomon Island. Prices start at around $1,000 and can go up to $2,500 for these showstoppers.

## Pionus parrots

The Pionus (pronounced "pie-*oh*-nus") could be the poster child for the under-appreciated parrots. Relatively quiet and easygoing, these birds can be excellent choices as companion parrots. They're not necessarily the best talkers, but they're quite capable of picking up a few words and phrases. Because of their gentle nature, the Pionus parrots, including the blue-head, white-cap, dusky, Maximillian's, and bronze-wing, are ideal for any living situation.

Why are these fabulous pets passed by? Probably because their coloration isn't as striking as other parrots' — you could even call them plain. Don't overlook them, though: Pionus parrots have fantastic potential to become wonderful companions. Depending on rarity or popularity, you can purchase these birds starting at $500, with some going for $2,500 or more. With good nutrition, husbandry, and love, their life expectancy can reach 30 to 40 years.

An interesting characteristic of the Pionus is the *Pionus snarfle,* which sometimes frightens new owners, and even some veterinarians who've never heard the sound, into believing that some sort of serious respiratory problem is present. When under stress or excited, the birds occasionally breathe rapidly in and out through their nares, making an impressive ear-catching sound until they calm down. We don't really know why they do this, but the Pionus snarfle is nothing to worry about other than the need to try to figure out what's causing the agitation or excitement, and it's actually often the subject of a good laugh!

## Macaws

Macaws can be sought-after pet birds, treasured for their stunning looks and, increasingly, for their companionship potential. You can find a range of personality types and prices within the collection of birds known as macaws. The large macaws can live up to 80 or even 100 years, while smaller macaw species can hit 40 years — a long time to have a pet. No macaw is particularly suited for apartment living — their caging requirements take up a lot of space, and they're not quiet.

Here's the breakdown on these popular parrots:

>> **Blue-and-gold:** The most popular pet among the macaws, the blue-and-gold shares with his relatives the desire to physically and socially express his opinion about a lot of things, sometimes to the dismay of those he lives with. Blue-and-golds are fine for educated beginners, as long as the owner understands the occasional social-climbing drives these birds attempt and knows how to deal properly with the situation. In the right hands, blue-and-golds make beautiful and enjoyable companions. The price range for blue-and-golds runs from $800 to $2,500.

>> **Scarlet:** Popular in show-biz as well as pet homes for their stunning looks, scarlet macaws sport a long tail and red, yellow, and blue feathers (primarily

red — hence, the name). Like the blue-and-gold, the scarlet can be opinionated. In reality, these labels of being "opinionated" likely are merely some normal manners of expression that can also be seen in their wild counterparts. Although the scarlet macaw may have a reputation for becoming "bitey," this behavior has a purpose and can be properly directed with appropriate intervention. Scarlet macaws are probably not the best birds for beginners, but they're fine companions for experienced bird lovers. Prices range from $2,500 to $3,500.

>> **Military:** Overshadowed by the blue-and-gold and scarlet macaws, military macaws are, in our opinion, underrated and underappreciated as companions. Slightly smaller than their blue-and-gold counterparts, these birds seem to be much more active, busier little guys, and they can make wonderful pet birds. Good training and guidance can help avoid some of the common problem behaviors they may demonstrate. Prices typically range from $1,200 to $1,800.

>> **Green-wing:** These birds are the second largest of the *Ara* genus macaws. (All the common large macaws, except the hyacinth, belong to the genus *Ara*.) The green-wing macaw is an impressive individual, indeed. Although these birds are large and very strong, they can learn to be quite fearful, especially in the face of forceful or frightening experiences. The best advice for anyone with a green-wing macaw: Take your time and don't force your attention. If the bird says "no," stop and reassess your behavior. (This is good advice for any companion bird or animal with whom we share our lives.) For the experienced bird lover, though, green-wing macaws, like most other macaw species, can be wonderfully rewarding friends. Prices range from $1,200 to $1,800.

>> **Hyacinth (see Figure 2-7):** So special, this guy's in a class of his own — in scientific classification *(Anodorhynchus),* as well as price. The domestically raised hyacinth macaw is often known as the "gentle blue giant" and is the largest of all commonly available parrots. In spite of their immense size, these birds are dramatically gentle and easily handled by most people. The birds can be quite noisy, however, and their huge beaks give them major destructive potential. As with the green-wing macaw, you need to be willing to negotiate behavior and even change your own behavior instead of defaulting to force. The price? Are you sitting down? $10,000 and up.

>> **Small macaws:** The "mini macaws" include the yellow-collared, Hahn's, noble, red-bellied, severe, and Illiger's. Small macaws are taxonomically quite different from their larger counterparts, but they're similar in that they can be enjoyable companions. Prices range from about $700 to about $2,000, depending on the species.

Photograph by Brian L. Speer, DVM

## Toucans, mynahs, and some others

Toucans and mynahs are two species that took a big hit when laws were passed banning importations. They aren't commonly bred and raised in captivity, and their available numbers in the pet world have fallen steadily. They're fascinating birds to live with, however, and stunningly beautiful. Although not easy to keep, we know much more today about how to successfully keep toucans and related family birds.

The mynah's main claim to fame is mimicry, and they're good at it. (One horrible myth that seems to follow them is that you have to split their tongues for them to talk — not true!)

Toucans can't talk and largely are kept as attractive aviary species because of their striking looks. And if you haven't yet "played catch" with a toucan, try tossing a blueberry for one when you have the chance! Their skill at fielding a toss is legendary. Expect to pay anywhere from $4,000 to $15,000 for one of these colorful birds.

## Chickens, ducks, geese, pigeons, peafowl, and turkeys

Chickens' popularity as backyard birds has risen astronomically in the past two decades. Although many people may raise their eyebrows at the idea of a pet chicken (like the one in Figure 2-8), common (and not-so-common) barnyard fowl can be absolutely charming, ideal for the person with a bit of land. They're cuddly and trainable — we're not kidding! — and come in a variety of colors and sizes. They're often flamboyantly feathered, right down to their feet. Many chicken breeds are docile, confident, and friendly. Bonus: Eggs for breakfast!

**FIGURE 2-8:** Spicoli, who resembles the avian version of a Dalmatian, is a silver-spangled Hamburg.

*Photograph courtesy of D. Davidson Harpur*

Chickens have been domesticated for more than 7,000 years, but only recently have they become widely popular as pets. Some people keep exotic and heritage breeds of chickens for their beautiful or unusual appearance (the Appenzeller Spitzhauben is described as resembling a Dalmatian with a mohawk), while others consider such factors as temperament, adaptability to cold or hot weather, small size (the better to keep one in a condo), and laying ability.

**WARNING**

Many municipalities do not permit the keeping of *roosters* (adult male chickens) because they can be extremely noisy, especially early in the morning or any time they feel the need to declare their territory. They may also be aggressive toward people or other animals. To keep peace in your neighborhood, if you buy an assortment of unsexed chicks, be prepared to find a new home for any that turn out to be roosters. If you don't want to run this risk, consider purchasing chicks from a sex-linked breed, meaning males and females are easily distinguished at hatch.

Prices can range from $5 for a day-old *unsexed* (meaning you may get a rooster) buff Orpington chick to $99 for a day-old unsexed Deathlayer chick, known for a luxuriant tail and black feathers glistening with iridescent green and purple. Chickens are social, so you'll want to have two or more. Don't forget to factor in the cost of a coop, nest boxes, and other equipment.

Like chickens, ducks come in some striking varieties and can provide you with delicious fresh eggs! Geese can be outstanding watch-birds, and even turkeys can be beautiful and affectionate. Peafowl, the males at least, are gorgeous, but the loud screams of the males are not for everyone and may not contribute to good relationships with your neighbors.

Although none of these birds is known for their intelligence, many are kept and enjoyed as companion animals. Brian works with many clients and rescue groups with pet chickens, ducks, and geese who come when they're called and seek out their owners for affection. On his own happy "birdstead," Brian has several geese, ducks, and pigeons, as well as macaws.

**WARNING**

Chickens, ducks, and geese can live comfortably on a large suburban lot (if your community's zoning allows it, of course), but the same can't be said of the glorious peacock. Prized for their fantastic plumage, peacocks (the female is a *peahen*, and both are *peafowl*) can get you in trouble with the neighbors in short order for their amazingly high-decibel calls at night. These lovely creatures are best suited to houses on large acreages — or to places with deaf neighbors.

## THE DINOSAUR BIRDS: OSTRICHES AND EMUS

To look at the feet of an ostrich or emu is to recognize the link between birds and dinosaurs. These massive, flightless birds have a small but devoted core of fanciers. Should you be among them? That depends.

The larger of the species, the ostriches, are popular as breeders and suppliers of meat, hide, and feathers, but now and then you can find people who keep them as pets. Female ostriches are often manageable, but males can be extremely difficult to control and flat-out intimidating. They're really not for most people.

Ostriches are larger than any other modern bird, and they're the only bird with two toes on each foot. They can run up to 40 miles per hour for sustained periods, so don't be gulled into taking one on in a race. Ostriches can live 50 to 75 years, so have a long-term plan in place for care and maintenance should you decide to acquire one. They're neat to have around if you have the land and space, for sure, but they're not really "pets." Still, ostriches certainly offer you the ability to hang with a "dinosaur."

*Photograph courtesy of Jerry M. Thornton*

Emus, on the other hand, are potentially interesting pets. Baby emus are really cute (not that baby ostriches aren't), marked with their own little "racing stripes" that fade as the bird matures. If you're able to locate an emu raised to see humans as "family," you're likely to have one who thinks she's a person. These friendly birds love to be hugged and are wonderful at pest-control in your yard. Still, they're not for the timid — full-grown birds are 5 feet tall and 80 to 100 pounds.

If you ever run into an ostrich or emu (or, even rarer, a cassowary), don't be as concerned about their heads as their feet. These forward-kicking birds can really pack a wallop, enough to knock the breath from you — or worse. Their beaks can hurt, too.

Brian has raised ostriches and emus, and there will always be a special place in his heart for these big, not-so-bright birds. Brian's two emus, Big Bird and Ernie, are both 45 years old and still going strong. He's experienced in handling them, and he's always careful to keep an eye on their movements. Kim and Gina, however, are content to watch these interesting birds from the inside of a safari vehicle or the other side of a very solid fence.

# Chapter **3**

# Deciding on a Bird of Your Own

From all the plumed possibilities, you now have in mind your pick of potential pet birds — hands-on or hands-off, small or large, noisy or relatively quiet. Your homework complete, you're moving marvelously closer to sharing your home with the bird of your choice.

But where do you find that special bird?

Perhaps you believe the selection process is simple, a matter of going to the nearest pet store or checking craigslist. If only choosing wisely were that easy! Unfortunately, Brian sees evidence to the contrary in his practice every day — birds too sick, too young, or too wild to be good pets. Some of them pay with their lives for the poor choices their owners make, suffer from illness, or become unwanted because they weren't the pets their owners expected.

What can you take away from other people's sad mistakes? Two words to remember: *Buyer beware!*

All sellers are *not* the same, which is why you need to arm yourself with knowledge and take your time before plunking down your cash, whether the outlay is a few dollars for a budgie or several thousand for a more exotic bird. The shopping experience offers all the security of a minefield. Take our hands, and we can walk you through it, safe and sound.

## DID WE HEAR A "YES, BUT"?

For all we say about the best way to choose and buy a bird, we know people who did the opposite and everything worked out fine. These exceptions usually take the form of "Yes, buts," if you will, as in "Yes, but we didn't do that, and our bird is great." And it's true, some folks have bought birds from less-than-ideal sources, or bought them too young, or bought birds other people couldn't handle, and the situation worked.

For all those folks, we have a "Yes, but" of our own: "Yes, but you were *lucky*." From a more critical point of view, what does a situation that "worked" look like? A bird who is not a problem for the family? How does that living situation look from the bird's point of view? One key thing to keep in mind, given the sentient nature of these amazing animals, is that the relationship is not only about you and your perception of what works or doesn't. It's also about how well the relationship works for your avian buddy.

Everything you read in this chapter is about minimizing risk, avoiding the most common ways people end up with birds who break their hearts and their budgets, and preventing birds from suffering the consequences of being in the wrong place with the wrong company at the wrong time Don't rely on luck: Approach bird buying sensibly and get the healthiest and best companion-quality bird you can. There's plenty of time afterward for falling deeply and irretrievably in love.

## WILD-CAUGHT VERSUS CAPTIVE-RAISED BIRDS

The Wild Bird Conservation Act of 1992 changed the pet bird landscape dramatically in the United States, virtually eliminating the flow of wild-caught birds into the country for the pet trade. Similar acts have been implemented in many countries as well, helping to keep wild birds where they belong — in their wild habitats — and domestically reared birds with humans. The bill was a huge victory for animal activists who documented problems in the import trade, where birds, at times, died before ever coming close to a caring home and their habitats, nesting sites, and family structures were damaged or destroyed during their capture.

This shift toward captive breeding of pet birds has provided an unintended benefit: improved availability of better pet birds, from both a health and a temperament perspective. Caring, informed *aviculturists* (people who raise and care for birds) stepped up to the challenge to produce companion birds who are well raised, see humans as friends, and aren't damaged by the stresses of being captured and removed from their natural environments.

The reduction in the demand for wild-caught birds for the pet bird trade hasn't ended threats to the survival of parrot species in the wild. Habitat destruction is proving to be just as damaging, if not more so, to many bird species. Organizations such as the World Parrot Trust (www.parrots.org) are fighting to preserve birds in the wild. We encourage you to support them.

**REMEMBER**

Review Chapter 2 for our evaluation of each of the popular pet bird species — and some of the more unusual ones, too. If you're just starting out, you may want to explore Chapter 19, which features our picks of the ten best birds for beginners. And no matter whether this is your first bird or you're an experienced bird keeper, check out Chapter 17 for a quick rundown of the right questions to ask when you buy a bird.

# Telling the Girls from the Guys

Which do you prefer — a male bird or a female? Does gender really matter? How can you tell the males from the females, anyway?

Selection of one sex or the other depends on the qualities you're seeking in your new family member. If you're buying a canary and you want a singer, a male is your choice. (And still, you should hear the bird sing before you buy him.) Male cockatiels are usually better whistlers than females, and the red and blue female Eclectus parrot is considered the real looker of her kind — much flashier than her green and red mate, although he's not bad looking, either. In terms of health, females sometimes have obstetric problems, such as *egg binding*, where eggs get trapped inside, especially in smaller parrot species such as budgies, cockatiels, or lovebirds. And of course, the folks who breed birds have preferences: They don't want to end up with all males or all females!

In many cases, though, gender makes no difference in terms of pet potential. The basics of caring for, training, and feeding a bird, as well as the bird's intelligence, will be the same, male or female.

The sex of a pet bird is most commonly determined by DNA evaluation (see the nearby sidebar), although birds can also be *surgically sexed,* a procedure in which a veterinarian examines the animal under anesthesia in order to determine gender.

The term for males and females who don't look alike is *sexual dimorphism.* Many species of birds don't exhibit any differences, at least not as far as we mere humans can tell. Birds themselves can tell the difference, of course, although we don't always understand how. We do know, however, that many birds can see a larger color spectrum than humans do, and likely, they can much more easily see the differences between genders.

Some species have gender identities that are obvious to human eyes. The Eclectus is certainly one of the more extreme examples — the male and female are so different that folks once believed the two genders were separate species — but other, more subtle differences exist in many species. An experienced seller can usually tell the girls from the boys in adult budgies, cockatiels, and some of the other parrot species where the colors are the same but the marking pattern is just a wee bit different, such as in the Senegal parrot.

In their quest for birds with that something special, some aviculturists have created a number of color varieties, in the process adding another level of confusion to the identification of some species. The classic example is the cockatiel. The common normal gray cockatiel is easy to sex: Males are gray, with bright orange cheeks and no white on the underside of their wing feathers. Females have gray heads with duller-colored orange cheeks and cross bars underneath their outer tail feathers and wing feathers.

## DNA TESTING: WHEN YOU JUST HAVE TO KNOW

Do you really need to know whether any bird is a boy or a girl? In general, both males and females make equally fine pets, so determining gender is not a necessity — unless, of course, you plan to breed your bird. Give your pet a nice non-gender-specific name, like Avery or Flynn, and go on with your life. Some folks, though, can't leave it at that. They *have* to know.

Enter DNA testing, where a blood sample is sent off to a special lab for gender determination. The cost: Depending on the number of birds you're testing and whether you're sending in blood or feather samples, prices start at $17 and go up from there. Most services offer discounts for multiple birds. DNA testing may be a pricey investment for a $60 cockatiel, or a relative drop in the bucket when the bird is a $10,000 hyacinth macaw.

Simple? Sure, but thanks to new color mutations among cockatiels, it can be much more difficult to differentiate the sexes. In varieties such as the cinnamon, the white-faced, and the albino, telling male from female can be difficult, if not impossible.

TIP

The outcome of a sex determination test is usually documented in writing. If you're considering buying a bird represented as either male or female (in species where the difference isn't visible to the eye), ask to see the documentation. Don't just take the seller's word for it. Birds who have been surgically sexed typically have a tattoo under their wing webs; males on the right, females on the left. Chromosomal or DNA sexing results also are recorded on a certificate that correlates to the identification number of the bird's leg band, if she has one, or microchip number. (You can find more information on identification in Chapter 5.)

Again, buyer beware: If there's no ID to match with the sexing result, you can't be sure you have the same bird, can you?

WARNING

Labs offering DNA tests are not necessarily overseen by any regulatory authorities and quality-control measures may or may not be in place. Brian occasionally sees DNA-sexed "male" birds who are egg-bound or have ovarian or uterine disease.

# Checking Up on a Bird's Good Health

In the wild, a big part of a bird's survival depends on not presenting a tempting target to predators, who actively seek out the sick, old, and weak. Even in birds who are in little danger from predators — generally safe souls such as our own pet birds — the genetic imperative to hide illness still holds. Some signs of sickness often are visible, however, and you need to look for these tip-offs as you form an overall impression of good health.

REMEMBER

A bird can be a big investment, and one of the better ways to protect that investment is to have your new pet thoroughly examined by a veterinarian who is experienced and qualified in the field of avian medicine before your warranty period expires. (You can find more on warranties in the "Protecting Your Rights" section, later in this chapter.)

TIP

Any pet bird you consider buying should display the following characteristics:

>> **He behaves normally — perching without problems, moving with coordination, and using his full body without favoring one side or the other.** The bird should bear weight evenly, all four toes present on each foot

and in proper position — two toes forward, two backward, in the case of parrots.

>> **He's alert and responsive.**

>> **He breathes easily.** He should display no sign of laboring to move air and no tail bobbing, which is another indicator of breathing problems.

>> **His eyes, ears, and nostrils (nares) are clean and free of debris and discharge.**

>> **His plumage appears healthy.** The bird's feathers should have normal color and structure, showing no signs of *stress bars* (horizontal lines indicating problems with feather development) or excessive wear. Look for evidence of damage from feather picking, improper housing, or other trauma.

>> **He consistently produces droppings that are normal in appearance.** All three components — urine (liquid), feces (solids), and urates (white semi-solids) — should be normal in appearance and quantity. Check for pasting of waste around the fanny. (For the complete scoop on poop, see Chapter 8.)

>> **He has a well-muscled body of appropriate weight, with no signs of obesity.** His skin should be smooth and translucent, without excessive amounts of fat showing underneath. You should see no excessive flakiness, scabs, areas of damaged skin, or crustiness.

**WARNING**

A bird who's showing even *some* of these general signs of illness may be gravely ill and may die even with veterinary intervention. Spare yourself the expense and heartache that bringing home such a bird will entail. Suggest to the seller that the bird needs help, but think twice before taking on the project of nursing the bird yourself.

# Making Mature Decisions about Age

Many species of pet birds live for decades with proper care, even to the point of outliving their original owners, which means that birds for sale or adoption are available in a wide spectrum of ages. Most people are probably best off with a fully weaned baby bird, and you may be among them. But we recommend that you consider all the possibilities.

## Weighing the pros and cons of baby birds

The appeal of babies is obvious: They're adorable, they should have no bad habits that you'll have to deal with, and they're ready to bond with you and grow into a perfect lifelong companion. Still, problems can surface even with baby birds.

## The problem with unweaned birds

Baby birds come in two varieties: weaned and unweaned. *Weaned* is a term for a bird who can eat on her own, instead of relying on parent birds or human surrogates to feed her. (When humans assume the duties of parent birds, they're *hand-feeding.*) Fully weaned baby parrots are able to maintain their weight on their own for at least two weeks after the last hand-feeding. Regardless, these functionally weaned kids still have a lot of life lessons to get under their feathered belts, and they're far from a "finished product."

**WARNING**

We do *not* recommend buying an unweaned bird. Some folks believe that bringing an unweaned bird into their hearts and homes is the best way to end up with a strongly bonded pet. Others push the economic aspect of such a purchase: Because the buyer takes over the round-the-clock work of hand-feeding, the cost of an unweaned bird is usually less. To put it bluntly: A dead or dying baby bird can't bond with you, making her something less than a bargain. Too many things can go wrong when novices attempt to hand-raise a bird.

Take the typical blue-and-gold macaw baby, who crawls out of the egg weighing less than an ounce. That baby gains more than 30 times her body weight in the first eight weeks if properly fed and cared for. And "properly fed and cared for" usually means feeding *every two hours,* especially during the first couple of weeks of life. Experienced hand raisers can feed on autopilot. They fall out of bed, warm the formula, feed the babies, and go back to bed without ever really waking up.

When a novice tries hand-feeding while half-asleep, however, the lack of experience can really hurt. Formula can be overheated, burning the baby bird's food-storage organ, called the *crop.* Formula can be fed too fast, flooding down the windpipe and into the bird's lungs. The brooder where she's kept can be too cold or too hot for the true needs of the baby — weakening her and setting the stage for other problems to develop.

**WARNING**

A baby can die, very easily, from your mistakes, leaving you at 2 a.m. feeling like a bird murderer, all alone with no one to call for help. Don't put yourself through the pain, and please try not to put any baby bird through the torture. Brian all too often performs postmortem examinations on baby birds from these settings to pinpoint the reason they died. We strongly suggest leaving the baby raising to folks who know what they're doing.

If, after having birds for a while, you decide you want to go the breeder route, you certainly need to learn how to hand-feed babies. Turn to Chapter 13 to discover more about the joys and challenges of being a bird breeder and the thrills and chills of hand-raising bird babies of your own. Although Brian admits that the excitement, satisfaction, and fulfillment of successfully raising baby birds is immense, he also warns that the endeavor of bird breeding is not an easy one and is certainly not for everyone.

## Socialization — not just hand-feeding — is everything

A hand-raised bird has the best pet potential in those species that humans enjoy interacting with — the parrots, from budgies and cockatiels all the way through to the giant hyacinth macaw. As aviculturists learn more about raising birds in captivity, though, they repeatedly find that it's not the hand-feeding so much as the social contact with humans (really just a by-product of handfeeding) that increases the pet potential of birds.

In one study, orange-winged Amazons were allowed to raise their own babies, while they were also handled regularly by humans during the preweaning period. The results? The human-socialized, parent-raised babies made fine pets.

The study's results make good sense, considering what we know about other companion animals. For example, experts recognize the importance of a puppy being fed by his mother and of the lessons he can learn from his mother and siblings. We don't hand-raise puppies or kittens (unless they're orphaned, of course), but we do understand the significance of socializing them. The best breeders of dogs and cats make sure their babies are gently handled from the time they're born and are exposed to the sights, sounds, touches, and smells of human existence. Logically, the same rules apply to birds: Breeders should ensure they're positively exposed to a variety of foods, objects, sounds, and situations. Without such socialization, baby birds will grow up to be suspicious or fearful of unfamiliar foods or objects. And yet, until recently, hand-feeding was the gold standard for raising and socializing baby birds. We think it's time to change that belief: Successful raising of baby birds may rely on hand-feeding, but proper socialization is the key to developing companionship qualities in many ways. The two do not necessarily have to go together (and often don't).

**REMEMBER**

Although the situation may change in years to come, the practical reality for now is that if you want a baby bird who has been lovingly handled, you're likely to buy one who has been hand-fed. And that's fine — they make outstanding pets. But ask the seller about socialization — have the babies been handled regularly and gently? If you run into a breeder who lets parent birds do the feeding but still makes sure the babies are socialized, you're probably in good hands — and you may have found the best of both worlds.

## Considering the prospect of an older bird

When you start looking for birds, you can expect to find a fair number for sale who are past — and in some cases, long past — their adorable baby stage. They become available for all the reasons other pets do — their owners died, moved, divorced, became bored with their birds, or couldn't deal with their behavior problems. Are older birds eligible for your consideration? Yes! But you need to look at each candidate individually, because the details of every situation — such as behavior patterns reinforced over the years, good and bad — will vary.

## Before the age of sexual maturity

**TIP**

Young birds who are between the baby stage and the age of sexual maturity are often better candidates for settling in with a new owner. You're more likely to be able to alter or outright prevent many behavioral problems, and your chances are greater for successfully converting a young bird to a healthier diet (if she isn't on one already).

**TECHNICAL STUFF**

The onset of sexual maturity varies from species to species. Budgerigars and lovebirds become sexually mature rather quickly, at the age of 6 to 12 months or so. Other birds can take years before becoming sexually mature; for example, the hyacinth macaw often turns 7 years old before becoming interested in a mate.

## After the age of sexual maturity

**WARNING**

Birds beyond the age of sexual maturity may be among the riskiest purchases you can make. Like people, grown-up birds are often set in their ways, and if their ways include some undesirable behaviors, you can expect to have a difficult time making any changes.

Adolescent birds often go through a bitey period. Other behaviors that emerge during this "teenage stage" include sexual behaviors, whistling, singing, talking, and territorial behavior — metaphorically placing a "Keep Out!" sign on the front door of the cage. Now is a good time to stock up on toys and other items that it's okay for your bird to destroy. When their African ringneck, Larry, went through this phase, Kim and her husband went through dozens of pairs of wooden chopsticks acquired from Chinese restaurants and sushi bars. Larry loved reducing them to wood chips.

Some birds also become available *because* they're sexually mature. Like human teenagers, birds can drive you crazy because hormones are driving *them* crazy. Some birds change from Jekyll to Hyde seemingly overnight, and people who don't understand or know how to cope often give up their pets in frustration. Sometimes such birds pass from home to home to home, sold and sold again, becoming bigger problems at each stop. These birds are not necessarily good pet candidates; realistically, they're rehabilitation projects at best and may be suited only for experienced bird keepers. These birds deserve a good home, but it needs to be the right home, with a loving and experienced owner.

**REMEMBER**

With that word to the wise in mind, know that even among older birds, some real gems become available — birds with good manners and good health; loving, well-socialized birds who are fully capable of bonding with a new owner. Move with all due caution, but if you find such a bird, buy her. She's a good deal and a good deed, all rolled into one.

As the popularity of pet birds continues to hold, so, too, does the number of birds given up by their owners. The typical dog- and cat-oriented animal shelter isn't really equipped to accept and rehome birds (although some do, of course). A variety of groups now operate to fill the gap, serving solely to rescue, rehabilitate, and rehome pet birds. Some of these groups provide careful screening and extensive education of prospective owners to increase a bird's chances of sticking in a new home. These organizations can be an excellent source of pet birds. To find one, talk to veterinarians, pet stores (especially those specializing in birds), and shelters in your area. We list a few in the appendix at the back of this book.

# Finding a Reputable Source

Two factors are arguably more important than any others when it comes to buying the right bird with pet potential:

>> **Species selection:** Have you chosen the right kind of bird for what you want in a pet? Have you looked beyond the flash and feathers and selected the bird with the level of care, interactivity, and noise that you can live with? (If you're not sure, turn to Chapter 2 for a look at pet bird species, or visit Chapter 19 for our list of best birds for beginners.)

>> **Finding a reputable source for a healthy, well-socialized pet:** If you choose a species that's right for you and then go to the wrong source to purchase your bird, you may be in store for a disaster as big as, if not bigger than, picking the wrong kind of bird in the first place.

Retail outlets are not only the most popular places to get pet birds but also among the better sources. This advice is the opposite of what experts advise when people are looking for puppies and kittens. Reputable dog and cat breeders do *not* sell to pet stores. Pet-store puppies and kittens too often come from breeding operations where animals are mass-produced with no consideration for health or temperament, often under unspeakably cruel conditions. Others may come from casual local breeders with accidental litters to place.

The bird world is different. Although sickly, mass-produced birds are an occasional problem in the pet-bird trade, many pet stores either breed their own birds or contract exclusively with reputable local breeders. (Some retailers take care of the hand-feeding, while others buy only fully weaned babies.)

For the bird buyer, putting pet stores into the mix means you don't have to deal directly with a breeder to get a great pet bird. Sometimes you *can't* go straight to the breeder — they work through pet stores because they don't want contact with the public.

When you visit a reputable store or retailer, don't be surprised if it seems as if you're being interviewed as if you were adopting a human child. It's a good sign if a retailer or breeder's questions send the message, "Are you a good enough candidate to take home one of our babies?" It suggests they've put a lot of time and effort into raising special birds, and they want to make sure their birds go to the best homes possible.

Why do many aviculturists steer clear of selling directly to the public? The reasons are as varied as the breeders themselves, but commonly they're concerned about privacy and security. As any police officer can tell you, inviting strangers into your home is risky. The risk increases when you have an aviary full of breeding birds whose potential worth runs into thousands of dollars each. Easily stolen, these birds can be sold through ads or at flea markets, netting the thief a few hundred quick dollars for not much effort. (Another reason for thinking twice before buying a "bargain" bird: He could be stolen!)

## THE AVIAN VETERINARIAN AS A BIRD-BUYING RESOURCE

If you're fortunate enough to have an experienced and qualified avian veterinarian in your area, consider tapping into her knowledge of bird sellers in your vicinity. Veterinarians see and hear it all — the healthy birds and the sick ones, the good advice people get from reliable sources and the counsel so poor that the vet must struggle to keep her jaw off the floor. Over time, any good veterinarian makes sense of trends — good birds and good advice from some sources, and the opposite from others.

Don't expect a veterinarian to trash-talk any particular source, though. Aside from demonstrating a lack of professionalism, a veterinarian who issues negative comments leaves herself vulnerable to accusations of violating the doctor–client relationship and to possible litigation. But any good veterinarian will be happy to steer you toward pet stores and breeders who consistently sell healthy, well-socialized pet birds and dispense up-to-date advice. Just ask!

Reputable sources show themselves by their actions and their words. So, leave your credit card at home — you're going shopping. The buying comes later.

# Pet stores

A retail bird or pet store has to have a lot on the ball to make it in a competitive marketplace. Before you even consider making a purchase, check to make sure all aspects of the business are up to snuff. The following sections cover some key areas to check out.

## The staff

People working in a pet or specialty bird store should know what kinds of birds they have and be able to discuss the characteristics of each species. If you're dealing with salespeople who can't tell you the difference between a yellow-naped Amazon and an African grey (beyond appearance), you have to wonder what else they don't know about birds, like proper care, nutrition, and preventive healthcare of the animals in their charge.

Speaking of proper nutrition, a qualified employee can talk to you in an educated manner about proper feeding, such as formulated diets and the choices that are available. Look and listen for a staffer who is knowledgeable about proper cages, toys, and other bird gear.

WARNING

A staffer who staunchly defends an all-seed diet and wants to sell you birds trained into this dietary approach is, at the very least, not current on the latest nutritional knowledge. Retailers are not in the business of seeing or recognizing how birds ultimately develop illness and even die because of those diets. (Turn to Chapter 6 for the latest on feeding.)

Pet-store staff need to know their limits. Medical advice is best left to a qualified veterinarian. Avoid any retail outlet where the staff is eager to recommend and sell useless over-the-counter products.

Expect the staff of a reputable store to truly care about any available birds. After all, birds aren't "merchandise" for sale; they're living, breathing, sentient beings, in need of proper placement in appropriate homes. A conscientious operation wants to make sure you're the right person for the role of bird companion and that you're going to take good care of your pet. Listen for it — a caring and sometimes detailed inquisition is a very good sign.

A first-rate pet store employs people who are clearly interested in and knowledgeable about birds and who understand the importance of a good working relationship with veterinarians and bird trainers. The emphasis, always, should be on prevention of problems through education of the customer — that's you.

## The store

A good pet store should be clean and bright (see Figure 3-1) and odor-free. But before you find any operation guilty of unsanitary surroundings, consider the difficulty of maintaining a single bird, much less a shop full of them. So, cut the staff some slack if a bird has made poop soup in her water dish or if her food-scattering antics have made the floor a little cluttered. Temporary untidiness is to be expected, especially if you come in several hours after the store opens. What's not acceptable, however, is evidence of long-term sanitation problems — a 3-inch pile of feces underneath perches, for example.

**FIGURE 3-1:**
A clean and well-lit bird store is a wonderful place to familiarize yourself with birds before you buy.

*Photograph by Kim Campbell Thornton*

Pay attention to how well the store attends to its animals. Make sure that birds are kept in a controlled situation, where staff can oversee any interaction between them and the customers. Note whether the birds are placed near other stress-provoking pets.

Look, too, for a variety of appropriate cages, toys, and perches. A selection of good reference books and magazines is another plus. You should see pelleted (formulated) diets on the shelves and in the food dishes. Seeds, nuts, and other foodstuffs are fine, as long as the store clearly recommends a balanced basic diet. A good pet store avoids unproven or dangerous products such as over-the-counter antibiotics or mite treatment products. (And make sure the staff doesn't use these questionable remedies on the birds in the store!)

TIP

A store that operates safely and sensibly keeps grooming and boarding services in a completely separate part of the establishment, to protect its birds from exposure to disease.

As you develop an overall impression of a pet store, look carefully at the birds themselves. Consider how healthy and well cared for they appear to be. Pay attention to telltale details such as appropriate cages, as well as toys and perches to keep them happy. Available birds should be interested in people and want to be held (some species more than others, of course — not all birds are born to be love sponges). If the store is hand-feeding babies, you may be able to see them through a window, but beware of any store that invites you in to handle these young birds, at least not without requesting that you wash your hands and put on some protective clothing.

TIP

You can glean the most from visiting a pet store by being friendly and open. Being opinionated is one thing, but you won't get very far being judgmental. Watch, listen, and learn.

REMEMBER

More than anything else, you're looking for evidence of current knowledge, progressive thinking, and a willingness to share information. A cage label that clearly identifies a bird's age and indicates that the bird has been started off right with a high-quality food is one example of that kind of evidence. Proper care, including proper diets, is the sign of a store owned, managed, and staffed by people who are in the business because they love birds.

## Breeders

Some breeders sell directly to the public. To evaluate them, you need to use many of the same criteria you would apply to pet stores. Evidence of current, accurate information is probably the most important sign that you're dealing with someone of merit. The odds are greater that their birds will be of merit, too.

TIP

Good breeders, like good pet stores, don't want to place their babies, to whom they've devoted so much time and attention, into a home where they won't be cherished. Don't be offended if you're asked lots of questions — it's the sign of a caring seller. Expect to be asked about your living circumstances, how long you're away from home every day, if you've ever had birds before, how many birds you have now, and so on.

**REMEMBER**

A good seller will refuse to place a bird with a person who's looking for a bird to match the color of the carpet. Folks with character and integrity want their babies to match your heart.

## Private parties

A person selling a single bird can be the hardest of all to get a read on. Of course, the first question you need to ask is, "Why is this bird for sale?" A good answer may be "The owner died." A response such as "It bit the heck out of my husband" warrants a little eyebrow raising.

In the same way you should check out a bird in a pet store, look for signs of quality care and good health in a pet being offered by an individual. We think everyone deserves a second chance (or third, or fourth), and birds are no exception. If only we could put every one of the unwanted birds back into their natural habitats! But because that dream is unrealistic, we promote the importance of connecting with the kind of human care these animals so richly deserve.

**REMEMBER**

Don't let your altruism override your common sense. Go into any purchase with your eyes wide open — especially when you're dealing with a bird someone else is dying to get rid of.

### STICKER SHOCK

Don't bargain-hunt when it comes to birds. Raising healthy birds to be good pets is expensive, time-consuming work. If you find a "bargain," stop and ask yourself what corners may have been cut in the nurturing process. The bird may come from a mass-production facility that made little or no socialization effort or may be ill or in unknown health. In either case, the bird's potential for becoming a good pet is greatly reduced. He's no bargain, at any price!

If a bird's cost exceeds your budget, you're better off choosing a less expensive species than trying to get a "bargain" on a more expensive bird. You can purchase some of the smaller parrots, for example, for a fraction of the price of their larger cousins. Better to spend $100 on a healthy, well-socialized cockatiel than $100 on a sick Amazon with behavior problems — even if the Amazon's price is touted as the "sale of the century." A sick or unmanageable bird is no bargain. Price is one factor to consider, but it's not the primary one.

# Protecting Your Rights

No matter where or from whom you buy a bird, don't proceed without a written sales contract and warranty. That's for your protection, and for the seller's protection as well. As with any legal document, read it carefully and make sure you're comfortable with the terms before closing the deal.

A good sales contract strongly recommends or requires that the bird be examined by a veterinarian, usually within 48 to 72 hours of purchase but sometimes within a 14-day period. The warranty should spell out what will happen if your bird is found to be ill or have a preexisting medical problem. Some agreements may require a second opinion to confirm the problem. Compensation for medical expenses to treat a sick bird may be limited or nonexistent.

As a buyer, you may have some responsibilities set forth in the contract, too. For example, the sales contract may require you to keep your new bird separate from other birds in your home for a set period of time so that, if you return her, she won't pose a hazard to others in the breeder's aviary or nursery or to avian residents of the pet store.

Under the terms of most contracts, the seller may offer a refund after you return the bird or, more likely, the seller will replace the sick bird with another one. This is especially true when you're dealing with the more costly species. An aviculturist or pet store is unlikely to give you a refund or replace a sick bird unless you return the original bird. That is one very good reason to take a new bird for a veterinary check immediately, before you become attached, although even then it may be too late — when you take possession of a bird, you may fall in love quickly. This is also why it's so important to investigate the seller and make sure you're satisfied with the care she provides to the birds being bred or sold. That's the best way to save money on a bird purchase.

# 2

# Caring for Your Bird

**IN THIS PART . . .**

Find out what you need for your bird.

Know what to do when you bring your bird home.

Feed your bird what she needs.

Handle your bird the right way.

Chapter **4**

# Preparing for Your Bird's Arrival

Love to shop? Need a reason to? You're in the right place at the right time. Your bird needs some gear, and you want to shop — you're a perfect match!

If you like to spend money on your pets, you're certainly not alone. The pet-supplies industry is huge, a multibillion-dollar dynamo that thrives through boom times and recessions alike. From mom-and-pop pet stores to big chain stores to online pet shops, a whole lot of spending's going on — and, for the most part, our birds end up much better off for the investment we make in their comfort, amusement, and safekeeping.

But not always. You can find unsafe or unnecessary products anywhere pet supplies are sold. Some are just a waste of your money, but others can be a risk to your bird's health. And you can't always rely on the advice of a pet-store owner or employee to help you sort out the good from the bad. Although most sales personnel mean well, many may not have up-to-date information on the best products for your pet. Some inadvertently pass on very outdated and even dangerous information.

The good news is you can find correct and current information right here. This chapter equips you with the knowledge you need to buy safe and reasonably priced cages, perches, toys, and all the other necessary paraphernalia that goes with bringing a bird into your life.

**REMEMBER**

Although the situation is improving, plenty of outdated advice about avian nutrition still exists — and much of it is shared in pet stores and by other bird retailers or even veterinarians. These folks are often the same people who may give you bum advice on bird gear. Make sure you're offering the best food to your pet by checking out Chapter 6 for current advice on the appropriate diet for your bird.

# Shopping for Cages

No purchase is more important than your bird's cage. The cage is the safe haven where your pet will spend time when you're not home, when the family is sleeping, or when you're doing other things and can't pay attention to your pet. Some birds — we call them the "hands-off" varieties — almost never leave their cages. A cage is security and protection, a place to play, and a place to rest. For all these reasons and more, it pays to shop carefully. The cage is a big-ticket item — in some cases costing more than the bird himself.

**TIP**

If you stay alert to the possibilities offered on craigslist or eBay, you can save some serious change by buying a cage secondhand. Be sure the cage is high-quality, and then make your best deal. Plan to scrub the used cage before introducing your bird to it, though. Here's an easy way to clean a cage: Take it to a do-it-yourself car wash and use the high-pressure hose on it. Just be sure to rinse all the soap off well when you're done. After cleaning a secondhand cage thoroughly, play it safe by disinfecting it, too. Use diluted bleach, at about ½ cup per gallon of water, and then let the cage air-dry.

Turn to Chapter 5 for tips on how to set up your cage.

## Considering size: Bigger is better

The first rule of caging: Buy the biggest cage you can afford. Forget the generic categorization you'll find in pet stores of "finch cage," "budgie cage," "small parrot cage," and so on. Those descriptions represent the *minimum* size to consider — a better bet is at least one size bigger. No cage is too large, but plenty are too small for a bird's needs.

No matter how much attention you're able to devote to your bird, she'll still spend a lot of time cooped up — almost all her life, in the case of canaries and other finches. Give your bird a break, right from the start, and buy a cage that will allow her as much freedom of movement as possible.

TIP

Cages may lack in an important dimension: width. Those tall and narrow circular cages may look nice, but they force birds to fly more like a helicopter than in the style that comes naturally for them. Remember to consider the way the birds move. Finches and canaries usually prefer to fly horizontally, not vertically. Parrot species like to fly horizontally, as well as climb up and down in their cages.

WARNING

The only problem with buying a cage larger than commonly recommended is that the bar spacing may be the wrong size for your bird. Before you buy any cage, make sure your bird can't put his head through the bars. Some pets accidentally catch themselves this way, resulting in injuries or even death. Fortunately, many manufacturers of high-quality cages offer different bar-spacing options on their models, so you can get a large cage of the dimensions that are best for your individual bird's needs. The basic bar spacing for cockatiels is about ¾ inch; finches require smaller bar spacing, and Amazons and macaws need larger.

## Focusing on material: Wood or metal?

Metal is the best material for cage construction. Wood is too hard to clean and usually won't stand up to the abuse birds can give out. Some manufacturers are experimenting with acrylics; these components can make attractive housing for your pet, but they may not offer enough social interaction and ventilation to keep a bird happy. (Acrylics do make some of the best toys, though.)

Metal cages are made of stainless steel, brass, aluminum, galvanized wire, or iron and come in all kinds of designs, with or without paint. Choose a model without fussiness — an embellished lodging may look good in the store, but you're apt to regret the purchase every time you try to clean poop out of the decorative elements. Pay attention to safety and practicality when you're shopping for your bird.

Galvanized metal is fine — at least it won't rust — but look for galvanizing material that's electroplated on, not dipped. The latter process too often leaves beads of material that parrots can chip off and swallow, putting them at risk of zinc or lead poisoning or both. Powder coating is popular in many decorator colors and is fine for most birds. (Some dedicated chewers can remove the paint, though, and some paints can contain risky levels of zinc, lead, or other heavy metals.) If you think about it, nothing about paint should be acceptable for consumption.

# Knowing what to look for in a cage

With so many cages on the market (or available secondhand), how can you be sure you're buying one of high quality? Here are a few points to consider:

» **Design:** You want a cage to be attractive, but even more important, it should be workable for your bird. Fortunately, if you shop well, you can find a cage that's both well designed and good-looking.

Look for features such as a bird-proof latch (especially if you have an escape artist like the Goffin's cockatoo); dishes that are easy to move, remove, and clean; and a droppings tray that takes standard-size newspapers. Make sure that you can easily reach in and make contact with your bird, wherever she may be within the cage. In some emergencies, easy access is a critical concern. Make sure the food and water sources provide no "traps" to catch and injure toes, heads, wings, and so on. A mess catcher can be helpful, too — it looks like an inverted metal skirt around the base of the cage.

The best position for the slide-out droppings tray at the bottom of the cage is under a grid so your bird can't access it. High-impact, durable plastic or metal is a good choice for a droppings tray — no matter what the material, the tray should slide out smoothly and be easy to clean.

**WARNING**

Check your bird's ability to move freely and comfortably in his cage without bumping into some obstruction. Too many perches, bowls, toys, or corners within the cage can lead to a loss of freedom of movement and a reduction of quality of life.

Most people prefer vertical bars with the idea that they're easier on long tail feathers. Horizontal bars are easier to climb for some birds, though. Either kind is fine, and some cages even mix them up, with vertical bars on some sides and horizontal on others.

» **Sturdiness:** You're going to have your bird and the cage for a long time, so you need to make sure the construction is solid. Check seams, welds, and places where wires and corners meet. Is everything all smooth and sturdy, with nothing for a bird to chip off and chew? Beware of chipping or flaking paint.

» **Convenience:** A stand is great, especially with cages designed for smaller birds. You and your bird are likely to appreciate having the cage off the ground. You'll appreciate the ease of access, and she'll appreciate the visual perspective. Some stands come with shelves, handy for storing newspapers, food, and other supplies. Casters are a blessing, too, because you can easily move the cage and stand out from the wall to clean behind it.

**WARNING**

Placing a cage directly on the ground puts your bird in a vulnerable "low-altitude position" — one that can be stressful and psychologically undesirable for many birds. Even backyard chickens prefer to roost and rest on perches, up and off the ground. Ideally, a cage, perch, and stand combination that enables the bird to perch comfortably at about mid-chest height (yours, not his) is a great goal. Watch out, though: If you have medium to large parrots, and you allow them to get outside their cages and onto the tops —you may set the stage for a bit of a challenge to get your bird back in, particularly if he doesn't want to, or sees no reason to do so. All the more reason for good training to be put in place! Too high can be as problematic in a different way as being too low. For more on behavior problems, as well as how to build and shape desirable behaviors, see Chapter 12.

**TECHNICAL STUFF**

Most cages come in one or two solid pieces — typically the cage part and the base, in the two-part variety — but you can buy some models that ship flat and require reassembly. These cages, called *knockdowns*, are held together with nuts and bolts, and a well-designed one has these fasteners in places where a busy bird is less likely to find them. Knockdowns are fine, but you have to remember to check the nuts and bolts from time to time to be sure they're still tight. Parrots are really good at undoing your best efforts to keep nuts and bolts fastened.

## Shopping for a travel carrier

Small birds such as finches are able to travel in the cage they live in every day (and usually more comfortably, too), but that's not an option for bigger birds whose large cages aren't made to move much. For these birds, a separate cage is well worth the investment for trips to the veterinarian or a move to the family's new home.

### ANTIQUES ROADSHOW

Although largely inadequate for the needs of modern pet birds, some antique birdcages are beautiful, ornate works of art, meant to mimic temples, mansions, and other examples of architectural splendor, created from the finest woods and jewels. According to information from London's Victoria and Albert Museum, birdcages were probably a common sight in many 17th-century Dutch homes, where pet birds were valued — as they are today — for their song, liveliness, and bright plumage. Birds such as canaries or singing finches were first brought over to Europe by Portuguese trading ships. They were splendidly kept in cages often made of fine materials such as ebony and ivory (or their imitations, ebonized wood and bone). Sometimes the cages contained feeding dishes made of blown glass or beautiful ceramic feeding pots or were embellished with tassels hanging from their bases. Although antique cages make poor living accommodations for today's pet birds, houseplants look great in these delightful relics!

## PUTTING YOUR BIRD IN A TIME-OUT

Some bird owners may benefit from the purchase of a smaller *time-out* cage for use when your bird is driving you crazy. (It happens in the best of families, believe us!) The cage doesn't have to be elaborate — sturdy and just large enough to fit your bird comfortably, and portable enough to allow him to chill for a while — out of the traffic flow in the home. The time-out cage can also double as your bird's travel cage, a sleeping cage, or an outside "shower cage," when set beneath a fine mister outdoors.

If you've ever seen how happy birds are at a bird bath, it'll come as no surprise to you that your pet bird will enjoy getting wet from time to time. And it's good for her, too! For more on showers, see Chapter 7.

Although you never need a cage cover to keep your bird warm in a heated home, sometimes this tool is useful in handling an out-of-control bird. For more on the use of cage covers, see Chapter 12.

A small travel cage is fine, but so, too, are carriers designed for cats or small dogs (see the Figure 4-1), the kind made of high-impact plastic with vents on the side and a grid door on the front or top. For short trips, no perch is necessary — just put down a clean towel to give your bird solid footing. For longer trips or for your bird's increased comfort even on short trips, however, fasten a perch dowel near the base of the carrier with two screws placed through the walls and into the ends of the perch.

Travel cages and carriers are important for reasons beyond the occasional trip to the veterinarian. In times of disaster, these transportable homes make it far easier to evacuate your pet and keep him safe until conditions improve.

Although you can carry a small bird in a paper bag, the benefits of owning and using a safe carrier far outweigh the modest price of acquiring one. Just as is commonly done with dogs and to some degree cats, birds can learn to enter their travel carriers on cue. (See Chapter 21 for more on carrier training.) This is an important skill to teach your bird. With the right training, he'll enjoy going into his carrier and being rewarded for it, making it easier to take him to the vet or anywhere else he needs to go.

Carriers should have a large enough door for your bird to enter and exit comfortably. Cat carriers work well for small and medium-size birds and even some larger birds with short tails.

Add a perch for additional comfort. Even something as simple as a rope perch placed on the bottom of the carrier can increase your bird's comfort inside the carrier.

**FIGURE 4-1:**
Many different
types of carriers
can be suitable
for birds.

*Photograph courtesy of Melody Hennigh, Busy Beaks Academy (Oakley, California)*

If your bird is likely to chew through a plastic carrier, look for an acrylic carrier with a perch already installed. Some models are long, which is useful for parrots with long tails, such as macaws. Wire dog crates, which come in many sizes and can easily support a perch, are another option. Wire crates may require additional locks or carabiners to prevent parrots from opening the doors and high-tailing it out of there.

Most birds appreciate having toys inside their travel carriers. Something they can shred and something they can hide inside or behind will make the carrier much more attractive to them.

# Perch Perfect: Finding the Right Perch for Your Bird

Gravity being what it is, even a creature made for flying spends a lot of time on his feet. And pet birds spend even more time on their feet than their wild relatives do. That makes what's under those feet — *perches* — very important. Perches give birds something to stand on, something to chew on, something to rub and groom their beaks on, a vantage point from which to survey their domain, and a secure home base to rest on.

Three factors apply to perch selection: safety, variety, and destructibility. Safety because, well, that's kind of obvious. Variety because a wide array of shapes, sizes, and materials can go far in keeping your bird's feet healthy, as well as helping him stay busy, fit, and free of boredom. Destructibility? Perches, in particular, are common and appropriate targets for demolition for birds. For a bird, the need to rip the snot out of something is of paramount importance. It's only natural!

REMEMBER

And now for an illustration of the importance of destructibility: When Brian was in Australia a few years ago, he watched in awe as a flock of about 20 red-tailed black cockatoos (birds that retail for up to $40,000 each in the United States, if you can even find one!) landed in a small stand of pine trees and proceeded to rip the trees apart. Limbs, bark, and pulp rained down, as nature's pruning service did their work. How does this story relate to your pet bird? By making you remember: Buy cages and dishes that are bird-proof (or as near to indestructible as possible), but make sure everything else is chewable, shredable, and completely destroyable. It's good for your bird — it's part of what they're built to do!

TIP

An ideal perch is not too smooth, not too hard, and not too soft. Excessively smooth perches may be hard to maintain balance on — and in a wing-clipped bird, that lack of traction may result in a bad fall. Perches that are too hard are difficult to chew up and have fun with, and perches that are too soft get destroyed too quickly. What we're saying, in other words, is plan on buying multiple perches throughout your bird's life.

Here's what's out there in the perch world:

>> **Wood:** Plain pine perches come standard with nearly every cage, and there's nothing wrong with them, except you can do better for your bird. One way is to harvest your own wood for perches (see the sidebar "Perches *au naturel*"); another is to vary the sizes and shapes of the perches you buy. Some ready-made dowels are available in different diameters along the length of the perch, and these at least add some variation on the boring old theme. If you don't want to or can't find tree branches like the one shown in Figure 4-2, a good bird store probably offers a supply of these perch prospects, too.

>> **Rope:** Great foot feel! Rope perches give your bird something decent to hold on to and double as good playthings. The neat thing about rope perches is that you can just throw them in the washing machine or dishwasher when they get dirty. The downside to rope is the possibility of your bird catching a toe in a worn and frayed part of the perch. Also, your bird may chew and swallow strands of the rope, which can cause problems as well. Watch closely and discard the perch when the rope gets stringy.

**FIGURE 4-2:**
This finch is enjoying his natural perch.

*Photograph courtesy of Claudia Hunka, Your Basic Bird (Berkeley, California)*

**TIP**

Rope perches can be expensive if you buy them ready-made for use with birds. You don't have to, though. Check out untreated cotton rope at a boating-supply outlet and make your own perches. By exercising your creativity, you can save money, have fun, and do right by your bird!

**TIP**

One kind of rope perch rates our complete endorsement: the stiff rope coil. These perches combine the best elements of rope, a swing, and a bungee cord, all of which provide exercise for your bird. Plus, they're absolutely fantastic for overweight birds!

>> **Mineral:** Most pet parrots should have one mineral perch, also called a *concrete, cement,* or *grooming perch.* The rough texture feels good underfoot, and the surface is great for helping to keep nails blunt and beaks clean and well groomed (birds like to wipe their beaks against the rough surface). Make sure the size of perch you select is large enough to allow normal weight-bearing and provide some abrasion of the nail tips at the same time. A concrete perch that's too small won't necessarily help blunt nails, unless it meets the tips of those nails. Some birds with particularly strong wills and jaws may decide to chew up, destroy, and eat the concrete, though, and those characters shouldn't have this particular perch. Keep your eyes open for birds who chew up, fragment, and swallow this material, though. If you see such behavior, get rid of that type of perch!

>> **Plastics:** Two kinds of plastic perches are available — acrylic and PVC. Both are popular because of their sturdiness and relative ease of cleaning. We're not real keen on either kind, although, of the two, acrylic is a better choice because it's virtually indestructible.

**REMEMBER**

**WARNING**

Having a perch to chew up is important to most parrots. If you use plastics, add other chewable perch options to your bird's environment.

PVC too often and too easily ends up in pieces in a bird's stomach and can cause some medical problems, as well as slippery footing and boredom. Plastic perches may be too slippery to be comfortable (particularly for heavy-bodied, wing-clipped birds), although some manufacturers compensate for this problem by abrading the surface of the perch. You can do the same with a little sandpaper or an abrasion tool if you want to offer a plastic perch.

For tips on how to place perches in the cage, see Chapter 5.

## PERCHES AU NATUREL

If you're looking for a real bargain in bird equipment, search no further than the perch. No, not that plain pine dowel that came with the cage or that you can find by the scores at any pet-supply store. Some of the best perches around are free and easy to find. They grow on trees, you could say.

Tree branches make great perches. They add variety to your bird's environment, help him maintain healthy feet and legs, and give him something else to rip up for entertainment. Most fruit and nut trees (almond, apple, prune, and all citrus) are fine to use, as are ash, elm, dogwood, and magnolia. If you can get your pruners on some manzanita, go for it — it's a hard wood that can stand up to a lot of abuse. Try grapevines, too. And leave the bark on for your bird to peel off.

Cut branches to a length to fit in your cage, scrub and clean them well with detergent, rinse them, and let them dry in the sun. Check for insect egg pods, and if you find them, just break them off and throw them out before putting the branch in your pet's cage. (If you don't, you may find a zillion little bugs thinking it's springtime in your home.)

You can entertain bigger parrots with scrap lumber. Just be sure you know the source of the wood. You don't want to offer your bird pressure-treated lumber or wood that may be coated with preservatives or other potential toxins.

Think of perches as replaceable cage furnishings: When your bird rips them up, that's great — it means he likes them! Replace them with more of the same when he destroys them. The extra labor and cost involved in replacing those perches is well worth the knowledge that, in your bird's eyes, you're doing a great job.

# Diving into Dishes and Waterers

Your cage probably came with bowls for food and water, and these containers are likely to be perfectly fine for your bird's dining pleasure. Look for bowls constructed of stainless steel, crockery, or high-impact plastic. They should be dishwasher-safe, because you're going to be running them through the hot cycle — a lot.

**WARNING**

We don't recommend galvanized crocks or bowls — they can oxidize, are harder to clean, and pose some potential toxic risks to your birds.

Dishes seem to inspire a lot of creativity on the part of manufacturers, who do their best to come up with designs to minimize mess, stand up to the abuse some parrots can dish out, and retain an attractive appearance and washability. Experiment with dishes all you like until you find the combination that works best for you and your bird.

The workhorse of the cage is always going to be the plain dish, and we encourage you to keep a few of these on hand so your bird isn't without food and water when you're cleaning dirty ones. With larger parrots, make sure the dishes are not easily upended, picked up, thrown, or broken. Although bowl tossing may be a lot of fun from a bird's point of view, damaged crocks can be frustrating and costly.

Birds can drink water from a dish or from a water bottle the way guinea pigs and rabbits do. If you choose to use a water bottle, make sure your bird knows how to use it, and check the spout frequently with a touch of your finger to ensure that water is still flowing. Dehydration from water deprivation can rapidly deal a lethal blow to birds.

**WARNING**

Some bird keepers prefer bottles because it's harder for their pets to dirty the water supply — some birds actually poop in their water dishes, or they love to make "soup" by carefully carrying their food over and dumping it into their water bowls. Don't let the relative convenience of the water bottle give you an excuse to change it less frequently than you would a water dish. Water bottles need to be emptied, cleaned, and refilled daily with fresh water. (Keep a bottle brush handy for cleaning.)

**REMEMBER**

Many birds enjoy using water bowls as bathtubs. For them, the water bowl is not only a location where they can get a drink; it's also a place to get gloriously wet and freshen up.

# Keeping Your Bird Entertained

Toys, like the ones shown in Figure 4-3, are not optional when it comes to pet birds. A constant variety of interesting and destructible toys is essential to your bird's mental and physical well-being. They give your bird something to do with both his mind and his body, keeping him fit and staving off boredom. A bored bird is at high risk for behavioral and health problems, such as feather picking.

**FIGURE 4-3:** Good bird stores, pet stores, and online retailers carry every kind of toy your bird could possibly want or need.

Photograph by Kim Campbell Thornton

Providing play and opportunities to perform natural behaviors such as foraging for food are an essential part of living with a bird. You may have heard it called *enrichment,* a term that encompasses puzzle toys; destructible toys; multiple perching sites; stainless-steel baffle cages filled with treats, fruit, veggies, toys, or shredding material; and play areas with climbing and swinging objects, to name just a few of the ways we can benefit birds by addressing their mental health needs.

Different types of toys serve different functions. Some toys entertain, some are brain games, some let birds practice their amazing manipulation skills, and some are just for tearing apart. Anyone with a young child — or who remembers being one — knows how much fun that is.

**TIP**

*Foraging* (the act of searching for and finding food) is a natural behavior of birds and other animals. Many avian species spend more than half their day foraging and eating. Birds who don't have the opportunity to forage are missing out on an important normal part of bird life. Ways to encourage foraging include toys that require birds to "work" for their meals by chewing, manipulating, or opening objects to get at food. You can scatter foraging items on cage bottoms; use branches, leaves, or clean shavings to hide food for your bird to seek out; and offer whole nuts for your bird to crack.

## Play stands and gyms

Most pet birds — from budgies on up in size — need time out of their cages to explore, exercise, and socialize (the exceptions are canaries and other finches, who are happy to be left alone in roomy cages). You could allow your birds to explore, taste, chew, and destroy your furniture, or you could offer them an alternative — a play stand, gym, or other safe location (see Figure 4-4).

**FIGURE 4-4:** A rose-breasted cockatoo has an assortment of toys on the play stand that tops her cage.

*Photograph courtesy of Rachel Baden, DVM*

Play stands come in two varieties, for the most part: large, freestanding models or those designed to rest on a table. The freestanding models are fit for the largest parrots.

Any size stand or gym offers a variety of perches, swings, and ladders; places to attach toys; and usually a container for food and water. They can be made of natural material (such as grapevine or wood branches) or of turned-pine dowels or hard plastics. A skirt or tray incorporated into the design helps capture mess and thrown food.

**TIP**

When choosing a play stand or gym, look for a model that combines entertainment for your bird with easy cleanup for you. Turned pine or abraded hard plastic is fine, but more natural pieces of wood are likely easier on your bird's feet.

**WARNING**

Some cage designs feature a play gym on top, or they're flat-topped to accommodate the addition of a separately purchased setup. Although a gym on top of your bird's cage may be okay, it may also make it challenging to persuade your bird that it's time to come down, particularly if your bird isn't well trained.

**REMEMBER**

Height generally equals comfort and security in the bird world. When you ask your bird to come down from a high position, there has to be something of greater value to make it worth his while. From a training perspective, examples of this "added value" may include the ability to spend time with you, to be moved to other locations by you, or treats. (For more on avian behavior problems, see Chapter 12.)

## Food as entertainment

Don't underestimate food as a way to keep your bird busy and amused. Check out puzzle toys designed to make eating a challenge. These challenging toys have skewers or nooks to hold foods such as fruits or nuts and are meant to make a game out of getting to these treats. One of our particular favorites is an acrylic tube you load up with favorite items, with holes to insert plain wooden pegs. To get the treats or toys out, the bird has to figure out how to pull the plugs. Ingenious!

Puzzle toys vary in complexity and may require birds to unscrew the toy, find food hidden in pockets or other compartments, lift flaps, or shake food out. Depending on the level of difficulty, you may have to help him learn how to successfully acquire the hidden delights. Break up training into small steps and be patient. You'll be rewarded by your bird's enjoyment when he figures out how to work the puzzle. Rotate different puzzles so he doesn't get bored.

Look for these kinds of accessories in a good bird shop, at a bird show, or online.

Fortunately, toys are fun — to buy, to give to your bird, and to watch her enjoy. Knock yourself out, and know that your bird appreciates the effort. Try toys your bird can hold, toys that hang from the top and sides of the cage, and toys that also serve as perches, such as swings. Twirlies, holdies, chewies, puzzles, bright colors, and noisemakers all can keep your bird occupied.

**WARNING**

Do you know the saying, "He who dies with the most toys wins"? Although a large number and variety of toys is important, you can go overboard — sort of. If your bird's entire treasury of perches, dishes, and toys is stuffed in his cage, you may be limiting his movement and reducing his quality of life. Instead of giving your bird everything, get in the habit of rotating toys on a regular basis. Rotation every month or even every week not only reignites your bird's interest but also helps you spot toys that need to be cleaned or replaced.

**TIP**

Toys come in an almost unimaginable array, and many are lovingly handmade. Some basic rules apply when shopping for toys to ensure they're suitable for your bird and, of course, safe. Look for the following things when you're in the market for toys:

>> **Materials:** Like perches, toys are subject to your bird's destructive nature — and safety during demolition is a must. Wood, rawhide, plastic or steel chain, rope, cloth, and hard plastic are among the more popular construction materials. Be sure to choose toys that can break down without splintering or breaking into pieces small enough to be swallowed. (Clappers on bells, for example, often require removal. If you don't remove them before giving a toy to your bird, your veterinarian may be removing them from his gullet.)

>> **Construction:** Challenging toys, the best choice for busy birds, feature pieces combined in ways that make it hard for birds to pull the whole product apart — but not too hard. Indestructible toys are not appropriate for most birds, because the fun of ripping the gadget apart is missing.

>> **Size:** Little toys for little birds, big toys for big birds. A big bird can catch and lose a toe in a toy made for a smaller bird, and small birds can get their heads trapped in toys made for larger relatives.

>> **Connectors:** If the toy isn't already equipped with a connector, a simple key ring, available from any hardware store, is one way to attach the toy to the cage. Not all birds can safely have access to key rings, though. The larger the parrot, the greater the potential for them to pry it open and then injure themselves if their tongue or beak becomes trapped. Good ways to connect toys to cage bars include C-clamps and balls that rest on top of the cage with a hook hanging down for attaching a toy. You can also tie toys in place with pieces of rope or rawhide, but they won't stay put very long.

What toy is bound to light up your bird's face? Unfortunately, no clear-cut answer exists. Toys are a trial-and-error endeavor, a matter of individual preference where only your bird has a vote. Watch your bird. Look for trends in the kind of toys she prefers; those clues can guide you when you're shopping for new ones.

# CHEAP! CHEAP! AND FUN, TOO!

Toys can really break your budget, especially if you have a very destructive parrot. No matter how much you love your bird, you're bound to mutter under your breath the first time you watch him gleefully and quickly destroy a toy you spent $20 on just a few hours before. Keep in mind, though, that aggression toward toys and perches is better than destructiveness directed toward your bird's mental stability, his feathers, or you. Tearing toys up is properly channeled normal behavior for most parrots, and a very good thing. Just keep reminding yourself of that — again, and again, and again.

Fortunately, some alternatives to expensive store-bought toys exist, but you need to rely on creativity to find them.

The cardboard cores of toilet-paper and paper-towel rolls are perfect for shredding, especially for smaller birds. String those tubes together on a thick leather cord and hang them in your bird's cage for his discovery and play. Other cheap options include ball-point pens with the ink tubes removed, Ping-Pong balls, old plastic measuring cups and spoons, and plastic bottle tops.

Toothbrushes are another bargain toy, sturdy and colorful. You can buy them new or give your pet your worn ones — just be sure to run them through a hot, soapy wash and rinse first. Hard plastic keys on a ring for babies or puppies are also a budget-wise buy that birds love, and real keys can be just as fun. Stringing these "jewels" onto leather shoelaces and hanging them in cages provides a very low cost, very big entertainment thrill for your bird.

Keep your eyes and mind open for playthings — you may surprise yourself with the possibilities. Think cardboard boxes, magazines or newspapers inserted with their pages down into the top of the bird's cage, and paper cups or cupcake liners. Use your imagination!

Remember, however, that really none of these items is intended for consumption. If your bird is able to chew them apart and potentially eat them, it may be time to rethink what you offer.

**TIP**

Some birds are apprehensive about new toys. If yours is one of them, try to set the toy outside the cage (but within eye range) for a day or two and then put it on the floor of the cage for another day or two. You also can place desired food items near it, to help your bird learn that yummy stuff accompanies that new thing. If your bird starts to play with the toy, you can hang it up permanently — or at least as permanently as possible with a playful and powerful bird. If he starts screaming and flattening his feathers against his body when the toy is placed at a certain distance, move it back to where he was comfortable with the toy's presence. Wait longer and move more slowly in reintroducing it. Reward your bird with a special treat, a head scratch, or whatever he especially likes any time he doesn't show fear or try to escape from the new item.

Harness and leash getups are a recent invention, geared for larger parrots. With a harness, you can take your parrot along when you're running errands or visiting friends, without worrying about him getting away. (Even a wing-clipped bird can achieve enough loft to escape — it's just harder.) Harnesses can add a lot to a companion bird's life. Just think about it! You can harness up your buddy, let him perch on your shoulder, and go out for a walk. How fabulous is that! Not all birds benefit from this, of course, and no bird should be forced into a harness that he's afraid of or doesn't understand. But it's definitely something to consider when thinking of ways to enrich your bird's life. For more on the basics of harness training, see Chapter 20.

# Clearing the Air

Depending on where you live and what kind of and how many birds you keep, you may want to add an air cleaner or humidifier (or both!) to your shopping list. Paying attention to air quality is good for your bird and for you, too.

First, the pitch on humidifiers: Today's climate-controlled houses are often too dry for birds, some of whom represent species most at home in tropical rain forests. Daily misting is a great idea (see Chapter 7), but so, too, is keeping the moisture content of the air up with a humidifier. If you live in Hawaii, South Florida, or another tropical environment, lack of humidity isn't a concern. In other parts of the country, however, dry air sometimes can be a problem. Remember, too, that when it gets cold outside and the heater is turned on inside the home, the relative humidity of your home drops.

As for air cleaners, the decision whether you need one depends on a couple of factors. Some species of pet birds — the cockatoo is perhaps the best example — give off a lot of *feather dust*, a powdery natural grooming material that originates from the powder-down feathers over the flank and hip areas. (The dust factor is why we don't recommend cockatoos for people with allergies — other particularly dusty species are the cockatiel and the African grey parrot.)

**TECHNICAL STUFF**

Unlike other feathers on a bird's body, powder-down feathers grow continuously and are never molted. They break down and produce the dust we see when birds preen their feathers. Some species, such as cockatoos, cockatiels, and gray parrots have lots of powder down, while others such as Amazons and conures produce little.

One dusty bird can really reduce the air quality of a room. Several can make it downright unbreathable. (Feather dust is not a problem when a bird is in his natural environment outside, but inside your home, it's another story.) The level of dust you're willing to tolerate is a matter of personal preference, of course, but if you're living with one or more dusty birds, we recommend an air filter. You and your birds will breathe better for your decision, and you can look forward to a reduction in your home's dusting requirements. Get an air filter that generates a good amount of air turnover for the room you'll be using it in, and place it near the source of the dust — the bird's cage.

# Cleaning Up

Birds are messy, we admit. They destroy toys, they fling food, and they spread old feathers and dust wherever they go. Keeping things clean isn't all that hard, though, with a plan and the right tools.

## Stocking up on cleaning supplies

For your own sanity and for your bird's health, you need to stock up on basic cleaning supplies. Here's your shopping list:

>> **Brushes:** Assemble an array of brushes with plastic bristles to clean fecal matter off perches, toys, dishes, and cage bars. If your bird drinks from a bottle, you also need a bottle brush. Make sure the brushes you buy can be run through the dishwasher's sanitize setting.

>> **Cleaners and disinfectants:** Plain old soap and water go a long way here and won't cost you very much. For disinfecting, use ½ cup of ordinary bleach to one gallon of water. Do your cleaning away from your bird, of course, and make sure to rinse and air-dry anything you clean before reintroducing items to her living space.

**WARNING**

Although scented cleaners may smell good to you, avoid strongly perfumed products such as those with pine oils. They can damage your bird's delicate respiratory membranes.

>> **Dishwasher:** If you don't have one of these kitchen helpers, bringing a bird into your life and home is a great excuse to invest in a dishwasher. Sure, you can hand-wash in hot, soapy water, but running dishes, perches, toys, and cage grates and skirts through the hottest dishwasher cycle gets them cleaner more easily. For rope toys, your washing machine is a lifesaver, too.

>> **Handheld vacuum:** Great for snarfing up pellets, dust, feathers, shells, seeds . . . and everything else. You gotta have one.

# Preventing messes in the first place

Whatever lands on something you can throw away or wash out is one more battle with mess you can win easily. Newspapers and towels are your main weapons in this war.

Newspaper can line the cage (see the nearby sidebar "All the news that fits the cage") or cover the floor. You can also purchase rolls of butcher paper, packing paper, painter's paper, or newsprint, all available from online or big-box retailers. Avoid anything coated or printed with colored ink. (Plastic mats and dog crate trays are good floor coverings beneath the cage, too.)

Some people prefer to use small-animal bedding under the bottom cage grate, and that's fine. Skip wood shavings and chips, though, and go for bedding made of shredded paper or cardboard. (Care Fresh is one brand we know and recommend.) Wood shavings and chips are dustier and can irritate your bird's airways, especially in the case of aromatic woods such as pine and cedar. Also, remember that one advantage of having newspaper on the bottom of the cage is just that: You can see the mess, which can help you remember to clean it more frequently. Absorbent materials such as shredded paper, wood chips, or other things look less messy and may not prompt you to clean as often as you should.

**WARNING**

Some bedding has fungal spores. Freshly ground materials, including eucalyptus branches and leaves, although they may smell nice, may be introducing things that you really don't want in your bird's living quarters. When dampened and maintained in a warm and humid environment — poof! — you've got fungus among us, which can be a risk to your bird's health. Frequent changing and cleaning keeps the problem at bay.

Towels provide good footing and mess prevention for any areas your bird may explore — and cleanup is as easy as throwing the towels in the wash. Watch for frayed or worn spots that can catch toes, feet, or heads. Towels are also great for covering your clothing when your bird is in a snuggly mood.

**TIP**

Save old towels for bird use, and ask friends and relatives to do the same. You can also look for inexpensive terry-cloth shop towels in the auto section of any discount store. These hold up well to messes and repeated washings.

Towels are also an important tool to help you restrain your bird for grooming or when he's sick. To learn how to "towel" your bird, see Chapter 7.

## ALL THE NEWS THAT FITS THE CAGE

How common are newspapers as poop catchers? So common that many cages are designed to fit the standardized size of an American or Canadian newspaper. (The standardization came about because of advertisers, not bird lovers, of course!)

Newspapers are great cage liners. You're likely to hear some fuss and bother about black ink posing some risks to birds, but we've never seen a problem, and we know of no study to validate that a threat actually exists. Newspaper inks are mostly soy-based, and although they may rub off on your bird (and your hands while you read the paper), they don't present any health issues that we can cite. We recommend plain old black-and-white pages — no color ink, and no glossy paper. (Colors and gloss add chemicals your bird doesn't need to be dealing with.)

# Chapter **5**

# Starting Your Bird Off Right

The day you bring home your bird, the world changes — for both you and your bird. For you, this is the grand moment when all the research, all the reading, all the theories, all the admiring of birds from afar suddenly becomes quite real. Did you choose the right bird? Was the source you selected the right one? Will you really enjoy living with a bird? Are you up to the challenges? The answers to all these questions become evident as you begin to settle in with your new feathered friend.

For your new bird, this momentous day of change can be downright scary. If he has been hand-fed and socialized by a small-scale aviculturist, that person's home may be the only world he has ever known. As trusting as the bird may try to be, his natural instincts will suggest caution. Even if your hand-fed baby bird has spent time in a retail shop and is accustomed to a constant parade of strangers, your home is new to him, and so are you. Just think about the whole new world your bird is being introduced to!

Getting your bird settled in comfortably and setting up your relationship is a two-part process, with each connected to the other:

1. **Ensure that your bird's physical environment is satisfactory.**

2. **Start working on your bird's relationship with you.**

A suitable physical environment helps you work on the gentle training that can turn your bird into a loving companion.

**REMEMBER**

The training exercises in this chapter are for parrots — budgies and cockatiels, as well as those birds more commonly identified as parrots, such as Amazons, cockatoos, and macaws. (They're all parrots, no matter the size!) Finches and canaries usually don't crave the intense interaction that parrots do — they're typically quite content if your only interaction with them is cleaning the cage and maintaining a fresh supply of food and water. If you have a hands-off bird, read the first couple of sections of this chapter on bringing him home safely and setting him up properly, and skip the rest.

# Setting Up the Cage

The cage is your bird's castle, the place where he'll spend much of his time — maybe even all of it, as in the case of finches. A cage not only protects your bird, but also protects your stuff from your bird, who is perfectly capable (if he's a parrot) of reducing prize antiques to toothpicks with his powerful beak.

You want your bird to be safe and to feel secure in his cage, and he should also feel part of the family, even when he's confined. Assuming you have a proper cage (see Chapter 4 for more on selection), proper placement can achieve all these goals.

**TIP**

Choose a location where your bird can be adjacent to family activities, but not in the center of them. Your bird will feel most comfortable if his cage is against a wall, so he can watch the goings-on without having to worry about anyone sneaking up from behind. For the same reason, place the cage where your bird won't be surprised — for example, away from large furniture that may block his view of the room and the comings and goings of people and other pets. Right next to the entryway to a room where there is more traffic would be a bad choice. Birds don't like to be startled any more than humans do!

Position the cage far enough away from a window so your bird doesn't get direct sunlight, at least not for a long period of time. Direct sunlight could cause him to overheat, because he can't escape the warmth. Putting the cage *near* a window so your bird can see outside isn't a bad idea, though, especially if the window overlooks a changing panorama that can help keep him entertained.

Although the kitchen may seem like an ideal place for your bird's cage, think again. The potential for your bird to breathe in deadly fumes, such as those from burning nonstick cookware — is too high to take a chance. (For more on common household hazards, see Chapter 20.)

A good place to situate your bird's home is the family room or any other place (aside from the kitchen) where people hang out in your home. Kim's bird Larry frequently spent time in the home office with her.

After you choose the location, set up the cage. Don't get too enthusiastic about toys — two or three well-chosen ones are good, but more may be overwhelming for your bird. Use a variety of natural and store-bought perches, and position them so they aren't directly over food and water dishes. You don't want to encourage your bird to poop into his dishes. (For more on toys and perches — including using tree branches — see Chapter 4.)

Line the cage bottom with newspaper or any other safe product, and you're ready to introduce your bird to his new home!

Bigger parrots require a couple of cages: a small one for traveling and a large one to call home. That's not the case with little birds such as finches or budgies; one properly sized cage is plenty for them.

The temptation to buy a bird, buy a cage, stuff the former into the latter, and race for home may be inviting, but let it pass. Large or small, your bird will be more comfortable on his trip home if you put him in a small box or carrier, with a towel draped over it to darken the space and help him relax. (Make sure to leave a couple of air holes, though.) Put a towel in the bottom of the box or carrier to provide the bird with secure footing and stop him from sliding around, even if a perch is available. Place the carrier where it won't move around or fall. You can put it on the passenger-side footwell or put the seat belt through the handle to secure it in the seat.

Don't put the carrier in the trunk. Exhaust fumes can kill your bird quickly. Besides, *you* wouldn't want to be stuffed in the trunk of a car, would you? And don't put your small bird in a small carrying box on the dashboard while you are driving home — it would be a bad experience for both you and the bird if you had to slam on the brakes.

## THE SHOCK OF NEW SIGHTS

Predators always consider the possibility that something new in their environment may be edible. Prey animals have to figure the addition is something that could eat them. Is it any wonder, then, that our pet birds, who are considered a tasty mouthful by many creatures in the wild, may not react with enthusiasm to changes in the world around them? Is it any surprise that your pet bird may initially fear new toys, new cages, or new foods?

Even though your bird may be slow to warm up to new things, don't hesitate to introduce him to fresh experiences and variety — just proceed with patience and understanding of *his* perspective, too.

You can help your bird conquer his anxiety by putting the new item close, but not too close. A new cage? Put it next to the old one for a few days so your bird can observe it. Toys, too, are sometimes better accepted if they remain in view on the other side of the cage bars for a while.

When your bird knows and trusts you, you can make use of mimicry to help your bird adapt. Eating meals together may inspire your bird to try different, healthier foods, and chances are, if you play with a toy or demonstrate eating a particular food, your bird will, too. Birds also learn from watching each other, called *social learning.* If you already have one bird with good habits, she can be a role model for new avian additions to the family.

# Settling In

When you get home, put your bird in the cage and *let him be.* He needs time to adjust to his surroundings and sort through a great deal of new information. We don't care how cute he is (very, we know!), how proud you are of him, how much you want to show him off (hard to resist, isn't it?), or how much the kids want to have him perch on their fingers (how many times have they asked now, a hundred?) — *let your bird be.*

**REMEMBER**

Wait three days. That's all we ask. You'll have the rest of your lives together, so laying off for a mere 72 hours really isn't asking a lot.

We're not saying you can't talk to your bird. In fact, we *want* you to communicate with your new family member — gently, and with the utmost respect for how frightened he may be. Sing to him, read to him, make eye contact with him, and take the time to get to know him. What food items does he like or dislike? What can you do to help him *want* to come toward you in his cage? Although telling him that he's beautiful and you love him is nice, you need to respectfully take the time to *get to know* your bird.

As for physical contact, hands off for now, at least until you're more familiar with each other. You have to change the cage liner, clean and refill food and water receptacles, and add and remove fresh foods, but do so slowly, calmly, and deliberately. Don't be insulted if your bird moves as far away from you as possible; your day will come, and your challenge is to earn his trust so that he *wants* to interact with you.

Spend time observing your bird's habits. Most parrots spend their days with "jobs" much like our own: They forage for food, interact with each other, and care for their feathers. Depending on the species, the season, and the environment or living situation, birds have different ways of doing these things or spend different amounts of time on them. The most important thing to know is that these are survival behaviors. Even though your bird is a companion, he still needs to perform these activities for his mental and physical well-being.

**TIP**

Your parrot may need a little help in learning to forage and become good at it. Provide him with puzzle toys that he has to manipulate or chew up in order to obtain food. Help him learn that chewing equals good things by rewarding him when he shreds or chews on appropriate items. Offer some shredded paper or wood toys for him to practice on. When he investigates, even briefly, give him a treat, toy, or something else he likes. When you reinforce his curiosity, he'll want to repeat this fun new behavior!

Techniques to teach foraging include hiding treats in bowls that are half-covered or providing boxes for him to open using that powerful beak. It's natural and healthy for birds to chew and shred things, so don't punish him for those behaviors. Instead, provide him with items that it's okay for him to destroy. If he chews on something you don't want him to chew, distract him and redirect him to an appropriate toy. Increasing your bird's ability to forage can decrease or sometimes even eliminate unwanted behaviors. The result is a bird with a great quality of life!

**REMEMBER**

Most birds are highly social. When yours becomes comfortable in his new home, he'll love spending time, playing, and eating with you. That social interaction is key to his happiness and good health. A bird who's well trained and socialized tends to be less stressed, better nourished, and less likely to become ill.

# Managing Introductions

Living in a multi-species household can be a challenge, even if your house has only two species — yours and your bird's. Add dogs and cats to the mix, and the potential for both delight and danger increases. Pay attention to the danger part, and enjoy all the delights you're bound to encounter!

## Kids

If your new bird will be a young child's treasured pet, we hope you consider investing in one of the hands-off varieties, such as finches and canaries. Young children can enjoy the antics and colors of birds, but they may not all be capable of handling birds safely (for both child and bird).

From the age of 10 or so (with emphasis on the "or so," because all children are individuals, maturing at their own rates), any bird who fits in your family's life-style is an acceptable candidate, although we tend to prefer the smaller ones for kids — budgies, cockatiels, and lovebirds. They're less intimidating, although some kids aren't fazed by even the largest, most raucous macaw! (You can find tips on choosing the perfect feathered friend for your family in Chapter 2.)

REMEMBER

No matter the age of your kids, you need to be sure they respect the three-day settling-in requirement: Leave the new family member unhandled. Do encourage the kids to talk to the bird, though.

When you start handling the bird (more on that later in this chapter), the children can, too, under your supervision and guidance. Some youngsters have a natural affinity with animals, and they do a wonderful job with them. If yours is one of these kids, you can let her take over if you want, just as long as an adult is checking that the bird's needs — fresh food and water, and frequent cage cleanups — are always covered.

## Cats

Cats catch and eat birds. Although many pet cats and birds live together in peace, you should never let such scenes of domestic tranquility lull you into ignoring this basic fact. Although macaws and other large parrots are usually plenty capable of teaching kitty to steer clear, small pet birds are often killed by household cats. This sad event occurs often — in Brian's practice, all the docs see the dire consequences of accidental cat-versus-bird encounters.

Because the teeth, claws, and saliva of a cat can carry bacteria that's potentially deadly to birds, never give your cat a chance to try out his weapons on your bird. If possible, place the cage in an area inaccessible to the cat. And keep your cat out of the bird's room when you aren't there to supervise.

When you are in the room with them, use distraction techniques to teach the cat to stay away from your bird's cage. A laser pointer or dangly toy (not one with feathers, though) can draw your cat's attention away from the bird. When he looks or moves away, say "Yes!" and reward him with an extra-special treat tossed away from the bird cage. This is the time to break out the tuna, steak, or whatever it is your cat will do anything for. Practice this routine frequently, and gradually add the cue "Leave it" as your cat turns away and before you give the treat. You can also reward your cat for calm behavior any time he's in the bird's vicinity and is paying attention to you instead of to his feathered family member.

When Kim acquired her first bird, an African ringneck parakeet named Larry (for his Boston Celtics shade of green), her two cats were intrigued by him. They walked up to his cage — the door was closed, of course — and stuck their noses through the bars. The adolescent Larry, who was going through his biting phase — promptly bit them. They never showed interest in him again. This is a great way for cats to learn that interacting with birds can be painful and that birds are best left alone, but unfortunately, it's not that easy a situation to replicate — nor is it a fair one for the cat to be intentionally subjected to.

If your cat tangles with your bird, head to a veterinarian immediately, even if the bird seems fine at first. Your bird may have internal injuries or be at risk for a deadly infection. Your veterinarian will likely want to start the bird on appropriate antibiotics, just to be safe.

For help with understanding why your cat does what he does, check out *Cats For Dummies,* 3rd Edition, by Gina Spadafori, Dr. Lauren Demos, and Dr. Paul D. Pion (Wiley).

# Dogs

Kim's Cavalier King Charles Spaniels all reacted to her African ringneck in different ways. Darcy liked to sneak up behind Larry's cage and paw at his long tailfeathers that stuck out through the bars. Bella and Harper ignored him. Twyla "tattled" on him any time he jumped off his cage by running to Kim and barking at her. Twyla also learned that parrots, like toddlers, are sources of tasty treats. She enjoyed hanging out beneath Larry's cage so she could feast on any bell peppers or other food that Larry dropped on the floor.

No dog, no matter how gentle, can be fully trusted with a bird. Dogs instinctively chase and bite potential prey, whether it's a rabbit in the field, a tennis ball in the park, or a parrot on the loose. Gina discovered this the hard way. Andy, a Sheltie, put Patrick into the veterinary hospital with a severe bite wound the first week the bird was in Gina's home. It happened in one nightmarish moment: Patrick fell onto Andy, and Andy reacted as a startled old dog sometimes will do — with a bite.

Don't take chances. Your bird should never be out of the cage around dogs unless you're there to supervise — and sometimes not even then.

Your dogs need to know that the cage is off-limits and so is the bird. Teach your dog the "Leave it" cue, just in case. Here's how:

1. **With your dog sitting in front of you, put about ten small pieces of kibble or other low-value treats into one hand and make a fist, positioning it on your thigh.**

    Your dog will likely sniff at your hand.

2. **Wait for your dog to back away. As soon as he does, say "Yes" and, using your other hand, give him a high-value reward such as warm deli turkey or a bite of steak.**

3. **Continue practicing, with the goal of having your dog back away and look at you.**

4. **Gradually add the "Leave it" cue, saying it before you give the treat.**

5. **Offer the treat again, repeating the "Leave it" cue. If she hesitates or turns away, praise her!**

This cue, incidentally, has a million uses, including control of your dog's inclination to snarf up garbage on walks. Use it as often as you can!

You can also cue dogs (and cats) to walk away from the cage when the bird is out of it. One veterinary behaviorist, Dr. Wailani Sung, has taught her dog and cat that when the bird's wings flap, they should move away and go to their places in another part of the house.

Don't offer your bird to your dog to test the "Leave it" cue. Instead, watch your dog's eyes. Say "Leave it" when he's contemplating the bird and provide praise when he averts his eyes.

In addition to teaching your dog to avoid the bird's cage — or the room where the bird's cage is — make use of barriers such as pet gates, an exercise pen surrounding the bird's cage, or a solidly closed door. You can also keep other pets on leash when they're in the same area as the bird, a practice called *tethering*. (If you have a new puppy or newly adopted adult dog, you should do this anyway so you always know where he is and when he's showing signs that he needs to go out for a potty break. It's a great way to build a relationship, as well as knowledge of your home's rules and routines.)

Although you shouldn't trust any dog with birds, some breeds need to be watched even more carefully. Terriers, for example, were developed to kill rodents, and they can be very fast and efficient at dispatching small pets, including birds. Not surprisingly, bird dogs such as retrievers and spaniels may also show intense interest in the family parrot. For more on dog selection, care, and training, check out *Dogs For Dummies*, 2nd Edition, by Gina Spadafori (Wiley).

**WARNING**

A final warning: Never leave a dog alone with your bird, or you may come home to a knocked-over cage and a terrified bird being drooled on by a very attentive dog. Use baby gates, or just close the door, but don't let your dog have access to the cage while you're out.

## Other birds

**WARNING**

For the safety of any pet birds you have already, skip introductions until your new bird has been examined by a veterinarian who's experienced in avian medicine. Even a seemingly healthy bird needs to be quarantined for about six weeks before meeting any other feathered family members. As heartbreaking as it would be to lose your new pet to an infectious disease you didn't know he was carrying, imagine how you would feel if you lost any or all of the birds you already have because you introduced them to a sick bird. You just can't be too careful!

After the quarantine period is up, you can move your new bird's cage near the others and let everyone get used to each other. Eventually, you can invite them out together, as long as you watch to make sure everyone's getting along. Many birds do become friends (and more, but you have to check out Chapter 13 on breeding for that information!).

# Building Trust through Training

After a few days of quiet adjustment, your bird is ready to become a part of your life. Your first interactions with your new bird are extremely important, because they set the tone for the kind of relationship you'll have for life. You need to assure your new bird that you're a wonderful, kind, and fun person, but you also need to remember not to force it. Friendship is earned, not forced.

## THE NAME GAME

Naming a bird is great fun, a chance to really let your imagination go wild!

If you're looking for inspiration, check maps for interesting names of places. Think of literary references for great character names or the names of authors. Or consider names related to your profession or great loves — Gina knows a graphic artist who chose the name Pixel for his Amazon, after the name for the smallest dot on a computer screen. Kim named her Kakariki Spike for his daredevil attitude. In Brian's practice, he doesn't see a whole lot of Polly parrots, but he has more than a few Moluccan cockatoo patients named Peaches.

Although plenty of name-your-pet books are out there — and they're all fun reading — we find that a name-your-baby book is just as useful.

Make naming your bird a family project, and use this opportunity to interest your children in a trip to the library. You don't have that many opportunities in your life to name a family member, so make the most of it!

**REMEMBER**

You become a best friend through consistent, gentle training and vision. Never, *ever* hit your bird. Punishment really has no place in teaching birds a desired behavior, and little value as the sole means for discouraging an undesired behavior. (For more on training your bird, see Chapter 12.)

## Rules for you

Sure, we could've called this section "Rules for your bird," but most of the learning is yours. You need to know how to become the leader, conveying firm, gentle authority in all your dealings with your bird. Here are some guidelines to follow:

» **Know when to leave your bird alone.** Birds have emotions and can be just as moody as humans are. Sometimes it's best just to let them be. As you get to know your bird better, you'll be able to identify the times when he wants to be with you and when he wants to be left alone. (You can also check out Chapter 7 for a primer on bird body language.)

» **Control and guide your bird's comings and goings.** Instead of just leaving the cage door open for your bird to go out and back in when he wants, put some training to work! Some of those key basics such as coming to you on cue or stepping onto your hand when asked can go a long way toward developing a healthy relationship. (Check out Chapter 12 for more on training and problem behaviors.)

» **Keep training sessions short and upbeat.** Most bird species are highly intelligent, but they all tend to have brief attention spans. Several short interactive sessions a day — just a couple of minutes at a time — are better than one or two long ones. And don't worry if you miss a day or two! With good, healthy training methods, your bird will pick right up where you left off! (That's what good friends do.)

» **Read your bird's body language.** If your bird is saying, "No thank you" to what you're asking, that's okay. Make sure there is always something in your request — a fair paycheck — to make your ask worth his while. Your bird will want to repeat things that are enjoyable, but requests that don't make sense, have no value, or are scary certainly won't be on his to-do list. It's not about *making* him do what you command. It's about him *wanting* to do what you ask, because he likes what happens and wants to do it again.

» **Position your bird so you can see what he's doing.** This will allow you to read his behavior and see what he's up to. If you can see what's going on, you have a chance to learn and to change what you're doing to guide his behavior. These simple steps can go a *long* way toward helping the two of you build a solid foundation for your friendship.

» **Talk to your bird.** Make eye contact and say anything or everything that's on your mind. Birds learn by repetition and by mimicry, so start naming things for your bird. Birds also learn that certain words fit in certain contexts and can be associated with what immediately follows. For example, when you're offering to scratch your bird's head and trying to read if he wants you to do that, say something like, "Want a pet?" or "Want a tickle?" or even "Tickle, tickle" while offering your hand and the scratching motion. When your bird makes the connection, he'll drop his head to ask for a scratch — or he may even use the phrase you've chosen!

TIP

Above all, don't ruin any good habits your bird's breeder instilled by failing to be sensitive to your bird's body language. A good relationship is built on two-way communication.

## Teaching the "Step up" cue

"Step up," or just plain "Up," is the most important cue you teach your new bird. When you ask your bird to perform this motion, he should step up onto whatever you're offering, whether that's your finger (for smaller birds), your fist or arm (for larger birds), or a wooden dowel or perch. The "Step up" cue establishes you as the leader and is the basis for all other training.

Although "Step up" — and its sibling, "Step down" — are considered basic behaviors, they're actually quite complex and call for a great deal of trust on your bird's part (and on yours, because he may well decide instead to bend his head down and give you a nip if you move too quickly or he's not ready).

If your new bird was hand-fed and well-socialized, he may already know the "Step up" cue, but even if he doesn't, expect him to pick it up quickly. Teach it to him by following these steps:

1. **Place your hand (if he's friendly) or a T-perch or a dowel (if he's not) gently in front of him, and slightly higher than the perch he's currently on.**

   A T-perch is a perch shaped like the letter *T*. Some trainers don't like using a T-perch or dowel and recommend putting a towel over your hand instead.

2. **Offer a desired food item in your other hand, and say "Step up" in a friendly tone.**

   Not all birds need to hear the verbal cue — they understand what the offered hand means, with time! Keep your hand still. Nobody wants to step onto shaky ground.

3. **Wait until both birdie feet are on your hand before moving it away from the cage. And don't hold onto your bird's feet; many birds dislike this.**

4. **Follow with lots of praise and even a seed treat or two.**

   This behavior should always be fun and worthwhile.

REMEMBER

Every bird is different. Yours may prefer stepping backward onto your hand, or he may show a preference for the left or right hand. Work with him!

Make "Step up" a normal part of everyday life with your bird. You can use the cue many times a day. The request and response not only are convenient in all kinds of situations, but also constantly reinforce your gentle leadership.

## Target training

No, you're not teaching your bird to shoot! In this instance, birds learn to orient a particular part of their body toward a given object in return for a treat reward or other pleasant outcome. It's a way for you and your bird to communicate, which is important for both of you and reinforcing and empowering for your bird. It's also the basis for many other tricks or behaviors you can teach your bird, such as willingly going into the carrier or taking medication from a syringe, and it can come in handy at the veterinary clinic.

Start by teaching him to use his beak to touch a target object such as a chopstick or wooden spoon. Offer the target and see if he investigates it with his beak. If he does, say "Yes!" or "Good!" and give him a treat. After you've done this a few times, gradually begin to move the target away from him so he has to lean forward to touch it and, later, take a step to touch it. Every time he does so, reinforce with praise and a treat. Then start offering the target in a different location, following with praise and treats.

If your bird starts to have difficulty with the activity, back up to when he was previously successful and reevaluate. Do you need to change the frequency or type of reward? Has your training session gone on too long? Many other factors can contribute to his reluctance. Use your observation skills to figure out what they may be.

It's okay for your bird to say — figuratively or literally — "I'm done with this for now." Stop training and try again the next day when you're both fresh.

**REMEMBER**

## WHAT ABOUT THE WILD ONES?

If you follow the advice we offer in Chapter 3, you probably have a hand-fed, socialized parrot, no matter the size. We realize, though, that for a variety of reasons, many budgies and some cockatiels are not really that used to people when you first buy them.

Most of these small birds can learn to interact with you readily — like their larger cousins, they're flock animals, and they want to be part of a family. They just don't know (yet) that you can be trusted and that there can be good value for them in a second (or third, or fourth) date with you. Be patient and gentle, make sure you're respectful of your bird's space and read his behaviors well, and he'll come around.

Think twice about the older approaches of automatically trimming those wings to take away or dramatically limit flight. Force is not the way to create the best-friends relationship you want with your bird. Sometimes, the act of altering a bird's anatomy and flight abilities can make you less sensitive to his feelings and thoughts about the situation. What if you let your bird have flight, and started building a more solid, trusting relationship with the bird in his cage, at a slower pace? What's the rush? Let your bird set the pace!

If you've taken on a really challenging bird, such as a parrot who has been shuttled from home to home and learned to bite first and ask questions later, you need more than getting-to-know-you exercises. See Chapter 12 for advice on dealing with long-term behavior problems and how to build a relationship from broken, distrustful pieces.

# Carrier training

There are many situations in which you can benefit from having a bird who readily goes into a travel carrier. Often, routine trips to the veterinarian are a bird's only experience with riding in a carrier, but emergency evacuations in response to events such as wildfires, floods, hurricanes, and earthquakes are also good reasons to practice with the carrier. Emergencies don't allow for much time to coax your bird into a carrier.

There are tons of ways to teach your bird to enjoy riding in a carrier, as well as to go into and come out of it on request. The following training plan consists of loose guidelines, but we encourage you to reach out to a bird-savvy trainer who uses positive reinforcement techniques if you need more tailored assistance. In our discussion here, we're using a cat carrier, but the method will work for any type of carrier.

1. **Start with only the bottom half of the carrier, with a perch installed.**

   To place the perch in the carrier, you can drill holes in the sides and attach the dowel or other perch material with screws. Place it about one-third of the way into the carrier, which allows your bird to be comfortable inside and leaves plenty of room behind for the tail if necessary.

2. **Place the carrier on a flat surface such as a kitchen table and invite your bird to come play with you.**

   This is a great application for target training. Offer your bird the target stick and give reinforcement for touching it. You can also mark the desired behavior using a clicker or a word such as "Good!" Practice target training in the vicinity of the carrier and gradually begin increasing the distance you ask your bird to move to touch the target.

   Offer the target so your bird is walking toward the carrier and away from it. Remember to give reinforcement each time she touches the target.

3. **When your bird is comfortable around the carrier, offer the target over the threshold and inside the carrier.**

   When your bird comes inside the carrier to touch the target, always allow her to leave if she wants. With more practice, your bird will start to be comfortable inside the carrier, knowing she has the option to leave any time.

4. **When your bird readily moves in and out of the bottom of the carrier, put the top on.**

   For this portion of crate training, tape the door open. This lets your bird know she can still leave any time, and it gives you a physical barrier so you aren't tempted to rush training. You can use the holes in the side of the carrier to position the target and to offer reinforcement when your bird is inside.

5. **When your bird readily enters and exits the carrier, you can start manipulating the door.**

   Offer the target inside the carrier. When the bird has accepted reinforcement, briefly close the door and then open it again.

6. **Gradually increase the length of time the door stays closed.**

   This is a good time to offer other types of reinforcement for the duration of time in the crate. Depending on your bird, that may include paper to shred, access to a favorite foraging toy only while in the carrier, or verbal praise. Of course, treats are fine as well.

   While practicing, any time your bird comes to the door, open it and let her out. Choice is a very important aspect of trust.

REMEMBER

7. **When your bird is comfortable entering the carrier and is calm when the door is closed, try some advanced practice.**

   Lift the carrier off the table, place it back down, then offer reinforcement. As your bird becomes comfortable with this, you can add a quick walk to the living room and back or a brief car ride, always with plenty of reinforcement.

Practicing carrier training outside its usual context helps to build a great reinforcement history and will prepare your feathered friend — and you — in case of emergency.

# Keeping Things Clean: A Basic Regimen

You can live like a slob; we won't stop you. In fact, we aren't exactly in a position to throw the first stone. All three of us have offices that are monuments to clutter, and Gina has the amazing ability to ignore drifts of dog hair when her pack is shedding out in the spring.

Tolerance for mess, to a degree, is a good thing when you share your life with a bird. If you're uptight about things being out of place, about dust, about food crumbs, and, especially, about bird poop, you're going to have a hard time enjoying a bird in your home.

Dogs are messy. Children are messy. Even cats have been known to leave the odd hair — or hairball — about. But birds, oh my, can they make a glorious mess! Food, feathers, all the fun things that have been chewed up over the day, poop — you name it, they fling it, far and wide. Little birds are quite capable of making a big mess, and big birds are even better at it. Cleaning up after birds is a constant duty, but it isn't such a chore after you get the hang of it.

Tolerance is a good thing, to a point. And the point where you need to become concerned is where your bird's health can be affected. Cleaning isn't just about neatness — it's about health, too. Clean, fresh food and water are essential to your bird, and so, too, is keeping his environment as free as possible from the growth and proliferation of bacteria, funguses, and molds — all of which can lead to disease.

**WARNING**

Don't take cleaning for granted. Your bird can become sick and even die if you ignore her surroundings. A messy cage is an invitation to fungal and bacterial growth, as well as food poisoning.

You need basic cleaning tools, of course. Brushes, newspapers, towels, a handheld vacuum, and bleach for disinfecting are basic supplies. We talk more about them in Chapter 4.

## Setting up for cleaning

Getting all your ducks in a row, so to speak, is essential to making cleaning up after your bird easier. If you have to dig under the kitchen sink or through three closets just to find your cleaning supplies, you'll be inclined to let a small mess sit. Put together a kit of bird-friendly cleaning supplies, and keep it handy so even small messes are no fuss to clean up.

**TIP**

Some cages come with shelving or cupboards underneath. These spaces are ideal for storing cleaning basics.

Keep these goods near your bird:

>> **Newspapers:** Make the habit of separating the newspaper as you read it, sending color pages and inserts to the recycling bin and black-and-white papers to the bird area. Having a pet bird means going through a lot of newspaper, so if you don't subscribe for your own sake, do so for your bird's! Other products you can use to line your bird's cage include packing paper, painter's paper, and newsprint, all of which are available online or at office supply stores.

>> **Cloth towels:** Make a collection of towels for your bird — faded or worn towels you're cycling out of your own linen closet. The auto section of discount stores is a good source for inexpensive, plain terrycloth towels; thrift stores and garage sales are another. Cloth towels are great for laying over clothing and for providing solid footing on bird-safe exploration areas.

**WARNING**

Frayed towels are not suitable for use with your bird — she could get a toenail caught and injure herself! Use these towels for drying off wet dogs or muddy feet, but don't let them near your bird.

- **Paper towels:** Keep a roll handy at all times, and consider installing a hanger or using one of those vertical paper towel holders. Buying in bulk is a good idea with paper towels, because you'll go through them fast, trust us!

- **Spray bottle with cleaning solution:** Because birds are sensitive to so many fumes, skip the ammonia, pine-scented cleansers, or any other strong cleansers. Simple soap and water will do for everyday touch-ups.

**WARNING**

Mark the soap-and-water spray bottle clearly so you don't confuse it with the plain-water sprayer you use to mist your bird.

- **Handheld vacuum:** Buy one just for your bird's room, and mount it close to the cage so you can always find it.

A couple of other items don't exactly fall into the category of cleaning supplies, but they're helpful nonetheless:

- **Mat for under the cage:** The heavy, clear plastic mats intended for use under desk chairs and sold at office-supply stores keep the gunk off your floor — especially important if your flooring is carpet.

- **Hamper:** We like to keep the bird towels separate from the others in the household, and a great way to do this is by using a hamper to hold them in one place until you have a load for the washer. Put the hamper near the cage for maximum convenience. (Between bird towels and dog beds, Gina swears she does more loads of pet laundry than people laundry!)

- **Trash bin:** Again, place it right by the cage. Every time you change papers, you won't have to carry them around — just lean over and put them in the trash!

- **Old T-shirts:** Parrots love to nip little holes in cloth, even if the cloth is part of the shirt on your back. Plus, even if you're careful to keep a towel over your clothes when playing with your bird, poop happens, and you're going to get it on your clothes eventually. Wearing clothes you don't mind getting dirty is a good idea.

Finally, you also need brushes for scrubbing and bleach for disinfecting — more on both in our section, "The big clean," later in this chapter.

## Everyday cleanups

Good hygiene is a matter of habit, if you think about it. You're probably in the habit of washing your hands after playing with your pets or before preparing food. Every morning, you get up and brush your teeth, and you do it again before turning in for the night. Do you write these little chores on your calendar so you won't forget them? Of course not — they're part of your routine.

Caring for your bird needs to become part of your daily routine, too. Morning and night, you need to perform some basic cleaning regimen — and keep an eye out for other cleanups throughout the day.

In the morning and evening you should do the following:

>> **Remove and replace soiled cage liners.** You may find it easier to do this chore after you've been awake for a while, so your bird has a chance to get her big morning poop out of the way. Putting newspapers both above and below the grid at the bottom of the cage makes cleaning as you go easier. Put a few layers at the bottom of the cage and remove them layer by layer throughout the day, whenever droppings appear.

Some people insist on keeping cage liners below the bottom grid, in the dropping drawer at the base of the cage, so that their birds don't come in contact with newspaper. Coming into contact with newsprint is fine for your bird, but if you want to avoid it — because the ink rubs off, for example — lightly coat the bottom grid with some nonstick cooking spray to keep droppings from pasting onto the bars. (Don't spray the grid with your bird in the cage, though!)

You can teach your bird to "go" on cue, making cleanups even easier! We tell you how in Chapter 7.

>> **Clean and replace food bowls and water bowls or bottles.** Some birds get food in their water or even droppings in one bowl or another, and you need to constantly check for bowls that need cleaning. If your bird drinks from a water bottle, check every morning to make sure that it isn't clogged by pressing the ball with your finger. (Birds can become seriously dehydrated very quickly.)

>> **Feed your bird.** Many birds usually prefer to eat after dawn and near dusk, so these are great times to introduce fresh fruits and vegetables — just be sure to remove the leftovers before you go to work or bed. Discard leftover pelleted foods every morning and replace with fresh. Birds don't like stale or old food any better than you do! (For more on avian nutrition, see Chapter 6.)

>> **Do a quick cleanup.** Complete your routine by using your cleaning solution, paper towels, and a handheld vacuum to clean up any other messes in the vicinity.

This routine may seem like a lot of work, but it takes only a few minutes each morning and night.

On an as-needed basis, pull out soiled perches and toys. Wood and plastic perches and toys can go right into the dishwasher, as can stiffened rope perches or coils. Throw flexible rope perches in the washing machine along with a load of bird towels.

## The big clean

You need to scrub the whole setup — walls, floors, cage, and all its contents — on a fairly regular basis. How often? It depends on your bird. Big birds are generally messier, if for no other reason than sheer volume of droppings. Some species are real mess-makers, such as the lories and lorikeets. (The mess problem makes lories and lorikeets a poor choice as a pet for some people. Find out more about these birds in Chapter 2.)

If your bird's really good at mess-making, you need to do the big clean on a weekly basis. Neater (and usually smaller) species can usually get by on a monthly scrub-down — provided, of course, you're religious about your daily routines, and you remove, clean, and replace dirty toys on an ongoing basis.

For the big clean, take the cage outside, scrub it with soap and water, and then rinse it well in plain water. Soak everything you can — perches, dropping tray, and so on — in a solution of ½ cup bleach to 1 gallon of water (a bathtub is a good place for soaking) and then leave everything out to air-dry in the sun before setting it in place and putting your bird back in it. Depending on the size of your bird's cage, you can run grates, trays, skirts, and perches through the dishwasher on the sanitize setting. If you don't have a yard, or during cold weather, a shower or bathtub is an option for cage cleaning.

**TIP**

High-pressure nozzles for your hose really help knock the mess off your cage. You can also take the cage to a do-it-yourself car wash, as long as you rinse it well with clear water after getting it soapy.

**REMEMBER**

Cleaning is part of life with birds. Dirty surroundings are more than an eyesore — they're a health risk for your bird! Get into the habit of cleaning as you go, and you'll find it's not so bad.

# Identifying Your Bird in Case He Flies the Coop

Birds fly away and get lost or are stolen. The potential for their loss is a very real concern for many bird lovers. That's why we're really keen on permanent identification, with a leg band or a microchip or, preferably, both. A bird cam in your home is also a good way to monitor your bird's safety and determine if he escaped or was stolen.

# Banding

Banding (also known as *ringing*) is the traditional way of identifying pet birds, and it's still the most common method. Bands can be either open or closed, with a choice of steel or less-expensive aluminum. Identifying information is engraved into the metal. Your veterinarian should record the identification number in your bird's veterinary medical record.

Open bands are put on adult birds with a special tool that crimps the metal around the legs. Closed bands are slipped over the feet of baby birds, who then grow into their IDs. Captive-bred birds may have either kind of band; U.S. rules require that any imported birds have open steel bands, complete with a letter and number code for identification. Make a note of this number — the code is a practical means of identification for your bird.

Either kind of band (open or closed) provides a good means of identification, but open bands require periodic checking to make sure they fit properly, without any gap where the ends meet. A gap poses the potential for the bird to catch a leg, which can result in injury. Closed bands usually aren't the source of problems — if the right size is used to begin with. They probably pose less risk to birds than open bands, but a properly crimped and closed open band is less risky than one that's more open because it was put on incorrectly.

TIP

When in doubt about the safety of any band, ask your veterinarian to make sure the band doesn't pose any significant risk of injury to your bird. Some veterinarians believe all leg bands are inappropriate; others believe they're necessary for the bird's well-being and the owner's peace of mind. We feel that identification, properly and safely applied, is important, and legitimate protection can include microchips, leg bands, or both. Although no form of identification is foolproof, any means of identification is better than none.

# Microchipping

Microchipping is a form of permanent identification that we recommend and encourage. A microchip is important if your bird doesn't have a leg band, has had a leg band removed, or would otherwise benefit from an additional form of identification. Microchips are easy to implant in most birds weighing more than 3½ ounces (100 grams).

The chip, about the size of a grain of rice, is injected into the breast muscle of most birds. It contains a unique number to help match up a missing bird with her person. When the chip is in place, the number on it can be read with a handheld scanner. Anesthesia isn't always required for the injection, but we believe conscious sedation benefits many birds by providing pain management. After all, the needle is big! Your veterinarian will have a record of the chip number, but you should also register it with a service that will contact you if your lost bird is found and scanned. Be sure to keep your contact information up to date with these services.

TIP

If your bird flies out the window and becomes lost or goes up a tree, contact 911 Parrot Alert. This great resource has skilled volunteers who are experienced at retrieving avian escapees. Look for the organization online at www.911parrotalert.com.

TIP

The American Kennel Club (AKC) — yes, the dog people — runs a microchip registration service for all pets. To sign up your bird, contact AKC Reunite at 800-252-7894 or go to www.akcreunite.org. The service matches up pets with owners 24 hours a day, 365 days a year, and costs $19.50 for lifetime enrollment.

Chapter **6**

# The New Art, Science, and Fun of Feeding Birds Right

I f you truly are what you eat, many pet birds would look like turtles, thanks to all the shells they crack off the seeds people insist on giving them.

If you're chuckling in recognition of our little joke, chances are you're one of those bird owners who needs this chapter most. If you take away nothing else from our talk of proteins, carbohydrates, fats, and more, note the following, because your bird's life depends on it:

> Seeds alone are not a proper diet for most pet birds.

We don't care what you've heard or who you heard it from. If your pet bird's diet consists solely of seeds, if he isn't sick now, he will be in time.

But if that seed mix you found on the store shelf isn't the be-all and end-all of avian nutrition, what is?

In a word, nothing. No *one* food is all your pet bird needs to thrive, not even the wide array of commercially prepared food pellets that should make up the largest portion of a typical pet bird's healthy diet. Variety is the name of the game when it comes to feeding your pet bird, and in this chapter you find everything you need to know to select the right combination of foods for your feathered friend.

TIP

If you have a lory or lorikeet, skip to the last section of this chapter.

# Understanding Bird Nutrition

Food provides the energy birds need to survive and thrive. Birds generally expend more energy than mammals, and they need a certain intake of nutrients to support body functioning, regulate their body temperature, and do all those cool things birds do: fly, perch, preen, forage, eat, bathe, vocalize, reproduce, and molt — not to mention use their powerful birdie brains to wrap us around their little claws.

When it comes to their eating requirements, pet birds are more like humans than some people may realize. Birds are *omnivorous*, meaning they can survive on many different kinds of foods — as long as those foods combine to provide them with the balance of nutrients they need.

But birds don't necessarily know or want what's good for them. In study after study, when offered foods that could provide them with balanced nutrition, birds made choices that were deficient in vitamins, minerals, and amino acids, high in fat, low in calcium — we could go on and on. It's up to you, then, to make sure your bird eats right but still takes pleasure from his meals and treats.

WARNING

Don't fall into the trap of believing that if a little bit of whatever is good, a lot must be better. Too much of any nutrient can be just as bad as too little. As always, the goal is *balanced* nutrition.

TIP

We could write a whole book on avian nutrition, but we don't have to — veterinarian Petra M. Burgmann already has. Her book *Feeding Your Pet Bird* (B E S) is a super in-depth work for bird lovers, the best you're going to find without buying a veterinary text. Dr. Burgmann's easy-to-read book includes plenty of pictures of what happens to birds who aren't fed right. Talk about hard to stomach!

REMEMBER

What we know about avian nutrition is always evolving. Working with a veterinarian who has a special interest in or recognized specialist status in bird medicine is the best way we know for you to stay current on avian nutrition.

Nutrients can be divided into two main groups: macronutrients and micronutrients. In the following sections, we walk you through both of these groups and tell you what your bird needs.

# Macronutrients

*Macronutrients* are the things your bird needs in large quantities. Think protein, carbohydrate, fat, and water.

## Protein

Proteins, or rather, the amino acids that combine to create them, are justly called the "building blocks of life." Amino acids make up every part of your bird — from the skeleton to the skin to the organs — and they allow your bird to produce those parts that need to be replaced from time to time, such as feathers.

Your bird's own body produces some amino acids, while others must be acquired from his diet. The amino acids produced by the body are called *nonessential*. (Don't be fooled: Even though the body provides them, they're anything but nonessential!) *Essential* amino acids are the ones your bird gets from food. Birds require 12 essential amino acids, as well as a source of nitrogen so they can synthesize nonessential amino acids.

Your bird's protein requirements vary by life stage. For instance, laying eggs requires extra protein. Young birds need lots of protein to fuel growth and development of feathers and muscle as they move toward maturity. What a bird eats also affects the level of protein she needs. For instance, birds who eat fruit require less protein than birds who eat grain. And size matters — large birds likely have higher protein requirements than smaller birds do.

When you think of protein, you may think of meat, dairy, or eggs, but protein is also found in many other foods, including beans and other vegetables. The difference is that meat, dairy, and eggs are *complete proteins*, meaning they typically contain *all* the essential amino acids. An *incomplete protein*, such as the kind found in beans or corn, is missing one or more of the essential amino acids. As any vegetarian knows, you can get a complete protein by eating certain combinations of incomplete proteins — eating beans with corn is a classic example of combining proteins.

**TECHNICAL STUFF**

You may have heard that too much protein can cause kidney disease or that protein must be restricted in a patient with kidney disease. Not true. Throughout their lives, birds (and humans and dogs and cats) need high-quality protein to maintain good health.

Pelleted foods come with complete or combined proteins already in the mix. You can also give your bird vegetable combinations that offer a complete protein. We recommend you provide complete proteins from time to time — lean poultry, for example, or cooked egg whites. Although you may think that munching on a relative is cannibal behavior, we promise your bird won't give it a second thought.

TIP

Egg substitutes are wonderful for your bird, for the same reason they're recommended for human heart patients — they're low in cholesterol. Scramble up a dish for yourself, and offer your pet bird a spoonful.

## Carbohydrates

Carbohydrates are necessary for the production of energy and heat. You find them in rice, pasta, breads, sugar, and starchy vegetables, such as potatoes. Foods with processed sugar are classified as carbohydrates, but they shouldn't be showing up in your bird's diet very often. The natural sugars found in fruit are far better for the bird who has a beak for sweets. Even then, too much fruit can sometimes lead to dietary imbalances or even obesity.

Carbohydrates form the largest part of commercial animal feeds, whether they're designed for carnivores, such as dogs and cats, or omnivores, such as birds. Carbohydrates also play a large part in the human diet.

## CONCERNS OVER FAT PRESERVATIVES

In the last few years, a lot of controversy has been generated over the use of preservatives — primarily BHT, BHA, and ethoxyquin (eh-THOX-ee-quin) — to protect the necessary fats in pet foods from spoilage caused by bacteria, molds, fungi, or yeast. Preservatives also slow or prevent changes in color, flavor, or texture. But synthetic preservatives have been made the scapegoat for just about every pet health problem you can name.

Many manufacturers have adopted the "If you can't beat 'em, join 'em" approach, which is why you see some products labeled "ethoxyquin-free" or "naturally preserved," usually with vitamins C and E.

No good scientific evidence exists to support the decision to avoid synthetic preservatives, either by manufacturers or consumers. In fact, they may do a better job of preserving high-fat foods. If the issue worries you, choose a pelleted food that doesn't contain these preservatives. But be aware that you've likely fallen prey to marketing strategies and fear rather than scientific fact in that buying decision.

Many carbohydrates are also a source of fiber. Fiber is trumpeted as a good thing in human diets, but experts aren't sure about its usefulness in the diets of pet birds. Interestingly, some birds (such as many geese) need more fiber in their diets than chickens or parrots do. Research in this area is ongoing and is sure to lead to further refinements in commercial bird diets.

## Fats

In our society, we worry endlessly about the amount of fat in our own diets. But the proper amount of fat is an essential part of a good diet — for people and birds both.

The body needs fats, also known as lipids, and essential fatty acids to absorb certain vitamins and move them around the body. Fats serve as a high-octane source of energy and heat. They're also important for cell membrane synthesis, intracellular messaging, and hormone production.

Scientists don't yet know a lot about the specific fatty acid requirements of all bird species, but relatively recent research suggests that omega-3 fatty acids play a significant role in psittacine health and well-being, especially in relation to risk reduction for atherosclerosis.

## TOO MUCH OF A GOOD THING

Obesity is a major concern in pet birds. They're typically less active than their wild counterparts. This lack of exercise, coupled with eating foods such as seeds, which are high in fat, and excessive amounts of otherwise healthy food, has contributed to an epidemic of obesity. Just as with humans, extra weight in birds brings with it the risk of many health problems, including arthritis, fatty liver disease, and heart disease, and it shortens avian life spans. Budgies, cockatiels, and Amazon parrots seem particularly prone to putting on weight.

If you think your budgie is pudgy, talk to your veterinarian about dietary changes that may help. Exercise is also important. One of the better toys for a perch potato, especially a larger parrot such as an Amazon, is a stiff rope coil perch, which forces the bird to work to stay in time with the swings and bounces. It's good for fighting boredom, too!

Teaching your bird to forage for food using puzzle toys (homemade or purchased) is another way to keep your bird in fighting form. In the wild, birds spend up to 90 percent of their time seeking food. Your own bird is adapted for long periods of foraging and feeding. When he doesn't get the opportunity to do so, it's no wonder he puts on weight. You can find out more about foraging and how to encourage it in Chapter 5. For more on the problems with obesity, turn to Chapter 11.

WARNING

As with any nutrient, too much fat is just as risky as too little. Current research in parrots points to animal sources of cholesterol — like that chunk of chicken or cheese he enjoys so much — as very real risk factors for development of *athero-sclerosis* (hardening of the arteries). And it's now known that atherosclerosis is a common cause of illness and death in middle-aged to older parrots and other species as well. Other risk factors include age, sex (females are at greater risk than males), and species. In the order of parrots, grey parrots, cockatiels, and Amazons are the first, second, and third most common species or taxonomic groups with the disease. Other contributing factors are repeated egg laying, high-fat diets, and lack of exercise. Best to avoid those high-fat treats except in tiny amounts on an occasional basis—not every day!

## Water

Do you think of nutrition as being about what your bird eats? Don't forget that what she drinks is just as important to her well-being. Water — clean, fresh, and in ample supplies — is essential to nearly every process of your pet bird's body, which itself is mostly water.

The tiniest cells of living beings can't survive without water. Water carries nutrients throughout the body and removes waste. A bird can go longer without food than without water.

Young birds and large birds have the greatest requirements for water, as do birds living in warm or hot conditions. In general, adult parrots in *thermoneutral conditions* (the temperature range at which birds can easily maintain their core body temperature) need to take in about 2.4 percent of their body weight daily in water. In hot weather, that requirement can increase by as much as 12 times!

TIP

Always make sure your bird has water and encourage her to drink by keeping the dish clean and the water fresh. Check the dish frequently to make sure the water hasn't been fouled by food or droppings or by your bird's enjoyment of splashing around in it.

WARNING

Avoid putting medication in your bird's water dish or water bottle unless specifically directed by your veterinarian. Birds like to play in their water, they may wash their food in it, and they often poop in it, so there's no good way to ensure that your bird is getting all the medication required. Plus, birds can develop *toxicosis* (illness caused by excess amounts of a substance) or a deficiency when vitamins and minerals are added to their water in inappropriate amounts.

Water bottles are fine, but check regularly to make sure they haven't clogged. (Some birds think it's fun to stuff food in the spouts of their water bottles.)

Some people are adamant that their birds have only bottled or filtered water. If you want to take that extra step (and expense), that's fine, but the investment may be unnecessary. If your tap water is okay for you to drink, it's likely okay for your bird to drink, too.

# Micronutrients

*Micronutrients* are the things your birds need in small quantities. Think vitamins and minerals.

## Vitamins

Vitamins, which are found in varying levels in foods, perform several roles in the everyday functioning of your bird's body. They're divided into two categories: *water-soluble* and *fat-soluble.* Both are important to your bird's health, and too little or too much of any of them in your pet's diet can have dire effects.

Water-soluble vitamins include the B vitamins, as well as niacin, pantothenic acid, folic acid, biotin, choline, and vitamin C. The good news about water-soluble vitamins is that if your bird gets too much of them, she'll simply eliminate them in her urine. That means they have minimal potential for toxicity or adverse effects — unless, of course, your bird gets too little of them.

Vitamins A, D, E, and K are fat-soluble. Excess amounts of fat-soluble vitamins can be stored in body tissues, potentially building up to toxic levels if your bird takes in too much. For instance, although vitamin A plays an important role in the immune system, too much of it can cause impaired antibody responses, changes in vocalization, and deterioration of feather quality and muscle mass. Too little vitamin A, often related to all-seed diets, is serious, too, causing signs that include nasal discharge, sneezing, poor feather quality, eye problems, reproductive disease, and more. Not the changes you want to see in your bird!

Vitamin D is another important fat-soluble vitamin for birds. It's critical for calcium metabolism, bone mineralization, and reproduction. Like humans, birds can synthesize vitamin D from the sun, but they can also get it from plant and animal sources.

Although birds appreciate a juicy slice of orange as much as we do, they don't need it for the vitamin C — it's the one vitamin they produce on their own!

## Minerals

Mineral nutrients your bird needs are potassium, magnesium, zinc, calcium, iron, phosphorus, sodium, chloride, and others. Like vitamins, minerals make up a small part of your bird's diet, but in the correct amounts, they're essential for good health. Also like vitamins, minerals aren't something to play with — too much can be as dangerous as too little.

Essential minerals include the macro minerals (calcium and phosphorus), electrolytes (sodium, potassium, magnesium, and chloride), and micro and trace minerals (iron, zinc, copper, manganese, cobalt, and selenium). Birds need high levels of calcium for egg-shell formation and bone development. A calcium deficiency may cause egg binding in females or poor bone development in juveniles.

Levels of calcium vary in different bird diets. Seeds, for example, have low levels of calcium. It's not unusual for parrots who eat mostly seeds to develop calcium metabolism issues. And not every source of calcium is beneficial. Spinach and other plant-based sources of calcium contain oxalic acid, which reduces the bioavailability of that calcium to the bird.

**WARNING**

Zinc is another mineral of concern in birds, but not necessarily because of its presence or absence in the diet. Birds who chew on galvanized cage wire or other foreign bodies containing zinc can develop an excess of the mineral. Birds with zinc poisoning may seem depressed or lethargic, stop eating, and lose weight. Zinc poisoning can be difficult to diagnose because concentrations of the mineral fluctuate throughout the day and vary from species to species.

## WHAT ABOUT VITAMIN AND MINERAL SUPPLEMENTS?

Some pet retailers seem to sell a lot of unnecessary junk, and most vitamin and mineral supplements fall into this category. If your bird isn't getting all the vitamins and minerals he requires, you need to convert him to a diet that can provide him with the true balance of what he needs. Supplementing an already adequate diet can lead to health problems, some of them severe. Adding supplements to a poor diet does nothing good except perhaps ensure that your bird will die younger than he should, but with prettier feathers. Too often, bird owners believe the issues with diet are related to deficiencies and assume that adding supplements is beneficial. These days, however, it's the excess vitamins and minerals that often seem to lead to illness and death.

If you think your bird needs a supplement, discuss your concerns with a veterinarian experienced in treating birds. If you're right, your veterinarian will likely recommend a product that you can add to the soft food component of your bird's diet — at least until you can persuade him to eat a more appropriate type of food.

The bottom line? Adding supplements to a crummy diet doesn't change the big picture: that your bird needs a balanced, species-appropriate diet.

# Knowing What Your Bird Should Be Eating

So how do you make sure your bird manages to take in all the nutrition he needs? By offering a variety of healthy foods to maximize the possibility that every one of those nutrients is a regular part of his diet, and teaching him how to eat as much variety as possible.

**TIP**

We recommend that a bird's diet consist of roughly 80 percent formulated pellet, 20 percent vegetables, and a limited amounts of fruits, seeds, and other treats. But that's only a recommendation. Different birds have different needs based on their species, health, and lifestyle. Talk with your avian veterinarian about what she recommends. If any vet recommends an all-seed diet, find another vet. (See the nearby sidebar for more on all-seed diets and why they're wrong for birds.)

**TIP**

For signs of a reputable retailer, see Chapter 3. For more on choosing the right veterinarian for your pet bird, see Chapter 9.

In the following sections, we walk you through all the components of a healthy bird diet.

## Pelleted diets

Pelleted diets are a blend of foods, such as grains, seeds, vegetables, fruits, and various protein sources. Manufacturers mix the ingredients and then bake and crumble or shape it — ending up with pellets of a proper size for any given species (large pellets for large birds, small pellets for small birds).

This process results in a food with a definite advantage over the "smorgasbord" way of feeding: The bird can't pick out his favorite foods and ignore the rest. With the varying shapes, sizes, and colors of these diets that are available, birds can choose what to eat at any one time. Empowerment is the key! Think about the way you may eat a handful of M&M's: First, you pick out the ones that are your favorite color; then you move on to your next favorite color; and so on, until the only ones left are brown. Birds enjoy making similar choices, and their preferences may change from day to day. That can be so much better than eating the same thing in the same way day in and day out.

Pellets also are convenient for you: These commercially prepared diets are easy to buy, relatively inexpensive to feed (especially when you consider the veterinary trips they prevent), and store nicely in a cool, dry place.

# RAISING GENERATIONS OF JUNK-FOOD JUNKIES: THE ALL-SEED DIET

The idea that birds should eat all-seed diets likely has its roots in two facts:

- Many birds are uniquely adapted to eat seeds and nuts, able to effortlessly crack even the hardest shells and extract the tender insides.

- Birds *love* seeds.

If birds love seeds and are engineered to eat them, doesn't it follow that the bulk of a pet bird's diet should be seeds? Absolutely not.

The nutritional needs of our birds' counterparts in the wild may well be quite different from those of our pet birds, living in luxury in our homes. Also, the nutritional makeup of what they eat in the wild may be quite different from what we feed them in our homes. They're living very different lives!

All-seed diets make most pet birds sick over time, because seeds deny them the nutrients they need for longer-term survival, add nutritional components that are excessive and unhealthy, and ultimately weaken them to the point where other diseases find it easy to take hold. The fact that pet birds can survive *at all* on such diets is a testament to the toughness of birds.

An all-seed diet contributes both directly (through malnutrition) and indirectly (by weakening the bird, making it easier for infectious diseases to take hold) to a serious reduction in the possible life span of any pet bird — by half or more in many cases.

But birds know what's good for themselves, right? After all, parrots are very intelligent. Well, so are you, but we bet that fact hasn't stopped you from enjoying tasty treats that you know aren't good for you. For birds, seeds are the equivalent of a greasy burger: junk food. And it's that high-fat component that tends to get them in trouble. Too many pet birds (and people!) are junk-food junkies.

Pelleted foods are a solid basis for your pet bird's diet, but even pellets, wonderful as they are, probably need to be supplemented with some of the foods we talk about in the following sections — vegetables, fruits, and other such "people food" as bread and pasta. Some birds may even appreciate the addition of a juicy bug now and then — see the nearby sidebar, "A bug's (short) life."

# A BUG'S (SHORT) LIFE

In Brian's and Gina's part of the world — beautiful Northern California — the media always turn up for the annual bug buffet hosted by the UC Davis Bohart Museum of Entomology in an effort to educate people on the nutritional benefits of insects. Entertaining as it is to see kids and adults trying mealworms, ant pancakes, and fried silkworm moth pupae, the menu isn't likely to be turning up in restaurants any time soon.

But the message is on the money: Insects can be good eating, which is why so many birds find them tasty as all get-out. (The early bird gets the worm, remember?) A good pet supply store is likely to have crickets, mealworms, fruit flies, fly larvae (isn't that a better name than maggots?), and other bugs (see the nearby figure). You can also raise these tasty treats on your own. Mealworms are easiest, and your pet-supply store can provide you with larvae and instructions on how to cultivate them. When your insects start reproducing, it's easy to select plump, white larvae to add to the diet of your finches and canaries. Yum!

*Photograph courtesy of D. Davidson Harpur*

A final note on bugs: If you haven't raised them yourself or purchased them from a reputable source, don't feed them to your bird. Backyard bug-hunting may seem like a great idea, until you consider that you have no clue about what pesticides the pests you pick may have been exposed to, or what parasites they may be carrying.

Giving different foods in addition to pellets is a way to replicate the way most psittacines eat in the wild, consuming a wide variety of foods that vary seasonally. Offering these additional foods at the proper dietary ratio recommended by your avian veterinarian offers such nutritional benefits as the moisture from fruits, the balanced vitamin and mineral content of pellets, and the pure fun of manipulating seeds and nuts to get at their tasty interiors.

A properly formulated pelleted diet is only bad if your bird won't eat it — and that can be a common problem in pet birds who've been fed improperly in the past or allowed to become "addicted" to an unsatisfactory diet.

Choose the brand your bird likes best. After you figure out which one that is, you have no reason to switch around. If your bird has been raised on a pelleted diet — and he should have been — the seller can tell you the brand name, so you can continue to feed it. If you have to choose, consider availability; certain brands are hard or nearly impossible to find in certain areas. Other considerations are palat-ability (does the bird really want to eat it?) and cost (you can expect quite a range of costs in the varying products out there on the shelves).

Always make fresh pellets available to your pet bird. Not only are they the main-stay of his diet, but eating them gives him something to do when you can't be with him and toys aren't appealing. Later in this chapter, we explain ways to turn your bird on to pellets.

When you successfully switch your bird to a pelleted diet, you may notice that his droppings are larger and lighter in color than when he was eating seed or that they're the color of the pellet being eaten. So, don't freak out if his feces are red or purple, for instance. However, if you see only scanty, dark-green or black feces, your bird may not be eating. Give him back his original diet right away. Do the same if your bird looks ill, fluffed, or is unusually quiet.

## Fruits and vegetables

Fruits and vegetables are a good source of carbohydrates, vitamins, minerals, and, in some cases, protein. They're a poor source of fat.

Because some people have in their heads that fruits and vegetables are "good for you," they figure that adding them occasionally balances out a seed diet. Not so. Fruits and vegetables are important, but they can't by themselves correct the nutritional problems caused by an all-seed diet.

**REMEMBER**

Too much fruit may be adding too much sugar or otherwise upset your bird's nutritional balance, too. Think about the difference between the plantain banana that tastes pretty bland, as compared to the table banana we typically eat — many neotropical parrots evolved eating the first, not the latter! Not all fruits are the same. Not all vegetables are the same either.

**TIP**

Give your pet bird a wide range of fruits and vegetables, including beans, corn, and such leafy greens as spinach and broccoli. Because these foods also help combat boredom, leave them in as much of an original state as you can — corn on the cob is much more fun to eat than kernels in a dish, as any kid or parrot knows. Besides, each cut you make into a piece of fruit or vegetable shortens the time before it starts to spoil.

Another thing to remember: Be sure to thoroughly wash anything you offer your bird, just as you do for foods you're going to eat yourself.

## A GARDEN FOR YOU ALL

Even the biggest pet birds aren't really that large compared with any human, which means that providing fruits, vegetables, and other healthy foods isn't going to break your budget. Gina attended an avian nutrition lecture where the speaker described shopping for her bird: one green bean, one small carrot, a dozen grapes, broccoli leaves — her shopping cart really raised eyebrows at checkout!

Still, you can save some money and provide fresh food for your whole family by maintaining a garden, including some fruit trees. Invest in a food dehydrator, and you can really go to town, stocking up on a year's supply of healthy treats. Best of all, when you grow your own food, you can be sure it's free of pesticides.

That burn that we get from the capsaicin in peppers doesn't seem to bother parrots at all. Kim and her bird, Larry, shared an affinity for the hot stuff; he loved getting jalapeños — seeds and all. Brian, unfortunately, doesn't handle hot peppers well, so he's totally jealous of what his patients get to eat without consequence.

What to plant? Try peppers of all kinds (even jalapeños!), squash, and corn in the summertime, and broccoli and cauliflower in cooler weather. As far as fruits go, you can't go wrong with apples, blueberries, pears, or oranges. Almonds are good, too. A bonus: The branches of these trees make great perches. (For more on do-it-yourself perches, see Chapter 4.)

Fruits and vegetables are high in water content, which is why they frequently get blamed for causing diarrhea. You can expect an increase in the urine component of your bird's droppings, which is normal for birds who consume a high amount of water. (For more on droppings, see Chapter 8.)

Fruits and vegetables can "turn" very quickly, especially in hot and humid environments. Spoiled food can be as dangerous for your pet bird as it is for you, so be careful to remove uneaten portions before they go bad. If you wouldn't feel comfortable eating the fruits and vegetables you've put before your bird, you should be offering something fresher.

Naturally pigmented red or yellow plant material plays an important role in making canaries colorful. When eaten as new feathers are coming in, these foods help to produce the vibrant colors much admired in these birds. Nothing can help to change the color of a feather that's already grown, though.

## Food for people and other pets

You can offer your pet bird almost any healthy food you fix for yourself — pasta, rice, casseroles, meats, and cereal. Try to keep fatty and sugary foods out of the mix, along with dairy products and large quantities of starches. Birds just don't have the ability to digest regular or large amounts of dairy products, because they're not mammals.

Sharing your meal with your pet bird helps your relationship, too. So knock yourself out fixing fabulous meals you both can enjoy! Just keep your portions separate. Your bird shouldn't eat food that has been in your mouth and vice versa.

Another cross-species surprise: You can *occasionally* add dog kibble to your bird's diet. It's edible and entertaining. But dog food is *not* bird food and should never be fed as a primary diet for your bird.

## Nuts

Nuts are a wonderful treat for birds. Not only are they a good source of protein (although high in fat), but they're also an important source of recreation. Too many nuts, however, is just too much. That is where the excessive fat consumption comes into that issue of balance. When you feed nuts to your bird, try to offer them in limited quantities in their shells, so your bird has to work to get the goodies inside. Even consider raising the bar, and use them as treats that can be earned by foraging, doing things that are requested — not always just free of charge.

**WARNING**

# FOODS AND DRINKS TO AVOID

You know what healthy food is in human terms — fruits and vegetables, beans, rice, whole-grain pastas, eggs, lower-fat meats such as chicken, and whole-grain breads. You can share many of these foods with your budgie, cockatiel, or any of the parrots, within reason. For example, don't go overboard on starchy foods (like pastas). Also, feed egg whites (not yolks), and limit the amount of animal fat (including meat) you feed your bird. The foods you know you really shouldn't be eating — high-fat, high-sugar junk foods — are bad for you *and* your bird, so just knock it off (at least for your bird if not for yourself).

Some foods that are perfectly fine for you (in moderation, of course) are absolutely off-limits to your pet bird. Top of the list: avocado, which of course means not only plain avocado but anything with avocado in it, from guacamole to a California roll at the sushi bar. Persin, a substance found in the seed (pit), bark, and leaves of the avocado plant, is deadly to pet birds such as canaries, cockatiels, parakeets, and parrots (although not to dogs and cats). Eating any part of the avocado can cause breathing difficulty, congestion, and liver and kidney failure. Avocado has also been associated with heart problems in some birds. It's just not worth the risk.

Another potentially deadly food for birds is chocolate, which contains a substance called theobromine that's toxic to them (it's toxic for dogs, too, if they ingest dark chocolate or large quantities of milk chocolate).

Finally, don't share alcoholic or caffeinated beverages with your pet bird. Enough said.

**TIP**

Many bird toys are designed to keep birds busy trying to figure out how to reach the goodies inside (see Figure 6-1). These puzzles are wonderful for engaging curious beaks and minds. For more on the importance of toys, see Chapter 4.

# Seeds

We're so devoted to trashing seeds that you're probably convinced your bird will fall over dead if you offer one. But seeds are okay as a small part of your bird's diet. They're a good source of carbohydrates and a little *too* good a source of fat.

**TIP**

Consider seeds a treat, rather than a dietary mainstay. It's fine to treat your bird now and then, as long as you don't go overboard.

**FIGURE 6-1:**
Having birds work to get their food, such as with puzzle toys, helps keep them busy and entertained.

*Photograph courtesy of Claudia Hunka, Your Basic Bird (Berkeley, California)*

Seeds make wonderful tools for training. Because birds are so nutty about seeds, they make great rewards for reinforcing behaviors you want to see more of, such as coming to you on cue, stepping onto your hand, going into the travel cage when it's time to go, or returning to the cage when asked (see Chapter 5 for more on training).

## BIRD BREAD AND OTHER DELIGHTS

We wonder if baking industry people have any idea how much of their corn muffin mix is purchased to provide nutritious treats for pet birds? Seems like every bird-club newsletter, bird website, or bird book has a recipe that lists a box of corn muffin mix as its first ingredient.

Here's a basic recipe, perfect for experimenting:

1.  **Follow the instructions on a box of corn muffin mix, but add one more egg than the box calls for.**

2.  **Add any or all of the following to the mixture: 1 cup of mixed vegetables (fresh, canned, or frozen) or a 4-ounce jar of vegetable baby food, some hulled**

seeds, some pellets, or the shell of one egg (zap it in the blender to pulverize it).

3. **Bake as directed in either a greased muffin tin or cake pan.**

Bird bread is a great way to convince a confirmed seed eater that maybe other food isn't so bad after all. You can break off pieces of bird bread every day or save it as a special treat (it freezes well). Use 1-inch chunks for small birds and larger chunks for big ones.

Another treat is rice and veggie mix:

1. **Cook 1 cup of brown rice.**

2. **Thaw 1 cup of frozen corn, peas, and carrot mix (a minute in the microwave will do the job).**

3. **Mix the rice and vegetables together and add a couple of finely chopped hard-boiled eggs.**

    What could be easier than that?

You can also can "birdify" French toast by sprinkling the egg-drenched bread with hulled seeds and cooking it as usual. Pancakes can be made better from a bird's point of view with the addition of some hulled seeds, too.

# Converting Your Bird's Diet

Companion bird species often develop neophobia (fear of new things, including foods that are good for them). Birds should be offered a wide variety of foods during the weaning period to reduce or prevent this level of aversion. But if your bird wasn't, don't lose hope!

With patience, you can reform even the most stubborn seed eater. The key is to avoid force — for instance, changing the diet cold turkey. We want you to teach your bird to *love* pellets, not coerce her into eating them.

TIP

The following tips (and did we mention patience?) can help:

>> **Confirm good health.** Before messing with your pet's diet, make sure he's in good health by having your veterinarian give him a thorough exam. Birds can be adept at hiding illness, and the stress of a diet change may be too much for a bird who's sick.

>> **Set a good example.** When you're spending time with your bird at her training perch or favorite spot, eat — or pretend to eat — the yummy pellets yourself. Really show your enjoyment. This is your chance to show off your acting chops! Offer some to your bird but don't force her to take them. If, after a few seconds, she turns up her beak at your gift, keep "eating" the pellets and expressing your pleasure. If your bird tries it, give her a big "Atta bird!" for trying the new food. Make it fun!

>> **Offer several types of pellets for your bird to play with.** Formulated pellets come in many different sizes, shapes, colors, and flavors. The more options you give, the better chance you have of finding one he likes. Offer the pellet buffet two to three times daily for about five minutes at a time. Don't replace your bird's current diet until you're sure he's eating pellets happily.

>> **Feed new foods in the morning or during your mealtimes.** Birds are most hungry when they first wake up, and will be more prompted to eat when their flock members (you) are eating. So, offer your newer pellet diets and vegetables exclusively at the start of the day before adding seed to the mix later in the day.

You can also try some of the following older techniques, but use them judiciously — in combination with the preceding methods:

>> **Combine the old and the new.** Mix what your bird has been eating with the pellets and other foods he should be eating. Remember to feed your bird this mixture out of a single food bowl. Never offer enough seed to fill your bird up, and hold off treats for a while. Vary how much of each component of this mixture is offered at any one time.

>> **If you have one bird on a healthy diet, let your other bird watch her eat.** Birds learn by watching — called *social learning*. And we can't say it enough: Eat in front of your bird. He'll try most anything you're eating, and by that we mean fruits and veggies — we're not suggesting you eat pellets. (But if you really loved your bird. . ..)

>> **Gradually reduce the amount of seeds.** Start with a 50/50 blend of seeds and pellets for two to four weeks and then reduce the percentage of seeds slowly over time. Vary the amounts of pellets, fruits, veggies, and seeds you offer each day. Be inconsistent in what your bird can expect to see in that food bowl the next day — your bird will stay busy checking for the jackpot of food he likes. Even if the offerings aren't all he dreams of, he's at the food bowl, so he may as well eat.

## THE NITTY-GRITTY ON GRIT

The idea that all pet birds need grit is another myth that seems to be taking a long time to die. Some pet birds, such as finches and canaries, can make use of an occasional small amount of grit — but most budgies, cockatiels, and other parrots don't need grit at all.

Why do some retailers persist in pushing ground rock on bird lovers? As with those people who push an all-seed diet, the answer is ignorance. Folks used to believe that grit helped in the grinding organ of the gizzard, assisting in the breakdown of foods. But birds do fine without grit — and grit has been shown to remove vitamins A, K, and $B_2$ from the digestive system.

A tiny amount — as in a couple of grains of grit every couple of months — may be okay for finches and canaries, keeping in mind that no pet bird needs to have access to all the grit they want. For parrots, skip grit entirely. Over-consumption of the stuff has led to many life-threatening problems — grit impaction — in pet parrots, especially young and smaller bird species, such as budgies or cockatiels.

>> **Use a mirror to your advantage.** Smaller birds such as budgies or cockatiels will play with and explore pellets when they're placed on top of a mirror.

>> **Some types of pellets can be soaked in warm water and offered to birds as a treat.** This may work if your bird enjoys receiving warm, soft foods such as hand-feeding formula or lasagna as a treat. When she's eating the moistened pellets, gradually offer pellets that are less soggy until your bird is eating them without requiring the warm-water soak.

>> **When you notice your bird eating pellets, chewing pellets, and passing pellet-colored droppings, you can start to gradually replace the current diet with the pellet of choice.** Each day, add just a tiny bit more of the pelleted diet. *Slowly* is your watchword. Continue practicing these diet conversion techniques until you've completely replaced the old diet with your bird's favorite pellets. Continue checking on your bird on a regular basis to make sure she's eating. Your reward will be a healthier bird, greater potential for strong food reinforcers for training and foraging, and best of all, a deeper bond with your bird.

**WARNING**

Birds can and do starve themselves to death. During the dietary conversion process, make sure you observe your bird eating, make sure he is passing feces of adequate volume and consistency in his droppings, and check the muscle on both sides of his keel bone (which runs right down the middle of his chest) periodically to be sure he's maintaining weight. Purchase a gram scale to monitor your bird's weight. During the new-food journey, you shouldn't see more than a 5 percent to 8 percent drop in body weight. Finally, don't be in a hurry to change your bird's diet. Follow his lead in determining how fast to reduce the amount of seed in his diet.

# Feeding Birds of a (Slightly) Different Feather: Lories and Lorikeets

Although most pet birds commonly kept as pets will do splendidly with the dietary guidelines we put into this chapter, you need to be aware of one notable exception: the diet of the nectar eaters (the lories and lorikeets). These birds do best on a diet of liquids and fruits, although little is known about their actual nutritional requirements.

Many pet lories and lorikeets eat diets prepared by their people using cereal-based ingredients and sugars. People often supplement lory diets with fresh fruit (usually apple). These homemade diets are based on the best guesses of aviculturists, not on any scientific evidence.

Several manufacturers make nectar diets, formulated by nutritionists, or dry powder mixes to which water is added. The liquid doesn't stay fresh long, however — it needs to be changed a couple of times a day. And again, there's no scientific basis for the nutritional composition of these diets.

**WARNING**

The high moisture content of their food means lories and lorikeets must consume a large volume of food daily to meet their energy requirements. That also means that they forcefully eject their primarily liquid droppings, making them among the messiest birds to live with.

Whether homemade or commercial, the high sugar content of these diets can lead to infections of the yeast, fungal, or bacterial kind. Sadly, that often isn't discovered until the bird is dead and undergoes a postmortem.

Wild lorikeets feed primarily on sugar-rich nectar from flowering plants, as well as pollen, their main source of protein. They also eat such items as honeydew, fruits, seeds, greens (such as chickweed, dandelion, and half-ripe seed heads), and the occasional soft-bodied insect. Their dietary protein requirements appear to be lower than those of grain-eating parrots of similar size. Lories and lorikeets have a muscular, extendible tongue with a specialized brush tip and a cluster of threadlike papillae that aids them in extracting nectar and pollen.

Little is known about the role fatty acids and fats — likely obtained from pollen, fruits, and insects — play in their diet. Commercial lorikeet diets contain a minimum of 4 percent crude fat, but their actual requirements are unknown.

When lorikeets eat foods with a high moisture content, they don't drink much water, but when pollen is their main food source, water intake increases.

Pelleted diets for lories and lorikeets are evolving, and some products are currently available on the market. In the future, these birds are likely to have more commercially available diets that are easier for humans to handle and more appropriate for these beautiful and interesting birds.

Chapter **7**

# Beyond Food and Water: Bird Basics

nfatuation can provide a wonderful rush, but the thrill doesn't contribute much toward a lasting relationship. Respect, kindness, consistency, and trust — these are the qualities that can see you through the years.

Do you think we're talking about your relationship with your human life partner? Silly you! We're referring to your relationship with your bird.

Because many pet birds are intelligent and can enjoy long lives, your relationship with your bird may well resemble your connection to other humans, especially with a young child (albeit a child who never grows up). Your bird can become a valued companion, but you're always the one who must provide structure and stability for your pet's life, set guidelines, and make sure he eats properly and sees the doctor when he's sick.

If all that caretaking sounds like a tall order, it is — but you can handle it, in time. If you've ever dealt with a human infant, just remember your nervous awkwardness as you changed that first diaper. Bet it wasn't long before you were changing diapers without a second thought. All it takes is practice and familiarity.

The same anxiety may accompany your initial experiences with most pet birds. The first time you handle a bird or clip wings or nails, you can expect a little uncertainty. But you learn, both from your successes and your mistakes.

No one is born knowing how to care for a child or a bird. But most everyone can develop some comfort and confidence with the responsibility. In either case, the payoff is wonderful.

# Translating Bird Body Language

Because birds aren't born speaking English or knowing how to figure out what we ask of them, the caretaker role revolves around understanding your pet's nature. The task is for you to get to know her, with her learned and natural behaviors, and for her to do the same — to learn yours. It's not always difficult. Parrots, highly intelligent creatures that they are, can seem quite human, although this trait may not always seem desirable. (It's no surprise that many bird lovers compare their companions to 2-year-old humans!) And smarts don't just start and end with parrots. Many other bird species kept as pets, once you get to know them, may actually turn out to be a lot smarter than a number of people you know!

From the tiniest budgie or parrotlet to the largest macaw, from the largest goose to the smallest bantam chicken or pigeon, pet birds can be loving, cuddly, playful, or contemplative one minute and demanding, aloof, manic, or peevish the next. Although all these examples are highly social, their interactions with you require trust and a two-way exchange of thoughts and interactions. Unlike dogs, who seem to almost always be glad to see you, many pet birds don't always want to jump into your lap for a long cuddle. They'll like interacting with you most of the time, but you have to read their body language as to when, and to what degree, you may proceed.

Some of these body language signals are pretty obvious — an Amazon in a rowdy state or a cockatoo who wants to be cuddled isn't hard to figure out. Other times, though, behavior signs may be more subtle, and the failure to appreciate and heed these clues may earn you a nip. Watch for the pinning of those eyes and subtle raising of feathers about the face or head, and pay attention to the stance and posture of the bird. Notice if there is a subtle leaning away from you, or toward you, as you approach. Think about the context and circumstances in which you see these subtle things, and consider what message your bird may be trying to convey to you. Careful interpretation and time help build healthy communication. Always give your bird the option to tell you "No, thank you." Sharing space with a bird is like living with a mate, family members, or roommates — sometimes you just have to pick your moments and know when to back off.

**REMEMBER**

Although some of the body language we talk about in this section applies to all pet birds, we focus primarily on those birds who are routinely handled — the parrots, a broad classification that includes budgies, cockatiels, and lovebirds, all the way up to the giants of the macaw family. Canaries and other finches also can be manic or moody, but because they're primarily hands-off pets, careful observation of their body language isn't quite as urgent.

## The eyes have it

Birds have keen eyesight and often stare at something that fascinates or frightens them, using one eye and tipping the head, or using both eyes for a head-on look. When you see your bird fixated on something, follow that line of vision to see what he's looking at, but also look at your bird's body. A relaxed body posture accompanies a calm, curious bird's staring, and a more defensive or aggressive body language (like that shown in Figure 7-1) demonstrates fright. Most often, a locked-on look is a sign of fascination — like the youngest children, birds can become attracted by something colorful in their environments.

**FIGURE 7-1:** Harley, a 20-year-old red-bellied parrot, has dilated pupils and her feathers are fluffed up. She may be feeling defensive about the camera pointed at her.

*Photograph courtesy of Wailani Sung, DVM*

Birds are able to control their irises, shrinking and enlarging their pupils rapidly in a display that's called *flashing* or *pinning*. Just as you have to translate the meaning of staring, you have to read the whole bird to put the flashing in its proper context. Birds may flash when they're excited or when they're angry. Flashing accompanied by aggressive posturing, such as tail fanning, signifies a bird who's bound to escalate his warnings — and maybe even bite — if not left alone.

Consider flashing to be the physical display of strong emotion — anything from the "I wanna kill you" vibes of an angry or aggressive bird to the "Hey there, cutie" of an infatuated bird. Pinning may even signify intense curiosity directed toward a person or another bird — "Hiya! Whatcha doin'?" When you learn how to read them, those eyes can tell you a lot!

If you could look through the eyes of your bird, what would you see? Do birds see in color? How good is their peripheral vision? You know we're going to tell you — check out Chapter 8 for more.

## Say what?

Even if your bird doesn't talk, she may be trying to tell you something. Most birds are highly vocal, using sounds in the wild to establish and protect territory, attract mates, warn of danger, and maintain social connections. Although screaming is the vocalization that bird owners seem to worry about most, you can figure out a lot about your bird by listening for other sounds.

If you're wishing your screaming bird would just shut up, don't despair — we offer some suggestions in Chapter 12 that may help quiet the clamor.

Here are some of the sounds you may hear coming from your bird:

>> **Talking, singing, and whistling:** Any of these sounds may be a sign of a happy, contented bird. With good talkers, speaking can be more than a matter of parroting words and phrases; your bird is truly capable of having a conversation with you! (See the "Teaching your bird to talk" sidebar for tips.)

Amazon and African grey parrots are widely thought to be the best talkers, but they tend to have totally different personalities when it comes to speaking up or speaking out. Amazons love an audience — these born performers often become more active and vocal when a crowd is watching. African greys often clam up in such circumstances. When they're settled in more secure surroundings, however, the greys really pipe up, and their beeps, bops, boops, and other household sounds are very well known.

>> **Purring:** This lightweight, growly noise can be about contentment, but you really need to consider the whole context; the sound can have a broad meaning that also encompasses displeasure.

>> **Tongue clicking:** This sound resembles the noise you might make to get a horse to move. When parrots click their tongues against their beaks, they're often asking to be picked up or petted. African grey parrots may click or "pop" as a means of self-entertainment, too — completely independent of your presence.

» **Growling:** No ambivalence here: A growling bird is not a happy camper. Growling is most often heard in African parrots, the Congo and Timneh greys, and the Senegal, Meyer's, and other members of the *Poicephalus* club. When Brian hears these sounds in the exam room, he knows it's time to stop and renegotiate that examination experience with his patient. Fear, if being conveyed with these types of sounds or others, is just not a cool thing to ignore, between doctor and patient, or bird owner and bird.

» **Chattering, muttering, and barking:** Often heard at dusk when birds are settling down for sleep, these sounds are about connecting with other birds, touching base with other flock members. Barking can be a mimicking of the sound your dog makes (yes, a parrot can pick that up, too) or may be a louder version of the "Hey, I'm here" chatter. Soft chatter can also be a sign of contentment or the practice exercise of a bird who's learning to talk and practicing (or mumbling) words — just like a toddler getting a feel for words by repeating interesting sounds.

## TEACHING YOUR BIRD TO TALK

Not all parrots talk, not even those from the species known best for their mimicry — the double-yellow-headed and yellow-naped Amazons and the African greys. If you're absolutely set on owning a talking bird, buy one who talks already, make sure you hear the conversation before you plunk down your hard-earned cash.

We suggest that you consider talking a bonus rather than a requirement. Choose a well-socialized bird and love her for her many fine qualities, whether talking is among them or not. Nothing is wrong with trying to teach your bird to talk, though. Some birds end up with incredible vocabularies — and not just the larger parrots. Little parrots, such as budgies, can be great conversationalists!

You can teach your parrot to talk by repeating words clearly or even by using tapes or computer programs that say the same language over and over. You can nurture communication further by using words in their proper context and setting up an association your bird can grasp.

For example, every time your bird lowers his head to request a scratch, ask him, "Wanna scratch?" and then scratch him. When you give him foods or toys, call them by name out loud. Play naming games with him — say "Keys" and then tell him "Good bird!" for taking them from you, and then repeat the exercise.

*(continued)*

*(continued)*

Another way to expand your bird's verbal repertoire is to expand what he can learn as a contact call. A *contact call* is the sound your bird learns to reach out and make verbal contact. This is most often used when they can't see you. Just as you may call someone on your cellphone when you can't see them but rarely would do the same when they're right there in front of you, the contact call is your bird's means of reaching out. If birds learn that the words and sounds you make when you aren't visible to them (for example, in the other room) are likely a good "phone number to dial up," they may be more prone to repeat those words more often, particularly when there seems to be a need to "give you a call."

What about the words or sounds you *don't* want mimicked? The best you can do is ignore them, providing neither positive nor negative reinforcement. And be fair: If you think it's funny for your bird to swear in private, you have to live with the behavior when your parents are over for dinner.

What your bird says can tell people a great deal about your private life, so much so that you may rue the day you dreamed of enjoying the company of a talking bird. Gina has a friend who house-sat for some people with a cockatoo. Every time the microwave timer went off, the bird yelled, "Hey, boys, time for dinner." And the alarm clock's wake-up call was met with a string of four-letter words. Be careful what you say! As children do (ask any parent!), your bird is likely to pick up words and phrases that you'd prefer to keep to yourself, especially if you say them often and with contagious enthusiasm.

## Beak bulletins

Your bird's beak functions as her own multifunctional Swiss Army knife (and we talk about it more in Chapter 8), but the beak can also be part of your pet's body language.

Here are some beak behaviors you may notice:

>> **Grinding:** Characterized by the side-to-side sliding of one jaw, or *mandible,* over the other, this sound may remind you of teeth grinding in humans. Usually this sound attests to a satisfied and secure bird. You're most likely to hear grinding after your pet has a big meal (in which case, the expression is comparable to the belt-loosening utterance — or a less attractive venting of fullness — that some humans share following a big feed). Birds also make grinding noises when they're sort of half-asleep.

>> **Clicking:** Most often seen in cockatoos and cockatiels, the forward-and-backward rubbing of one beak tip over the other is kind of like flipping one fingernail over the other. This motion is a bird's way of staying busy and amused.

>> **Beaking:** Young humans like to put things in their mouths, and so do young birds. In humans (and other animals), we call this tendency *teething*, so *beaking* seems as good a term for the action as any when it comes to birds. The young bird who gently presses his tongue against your finger and puts his jaw around it isn't biting — he's just trying to get an idea of what you feel and taste like.

>> **Biting:** Fear, anger, or territoriality is behind biting, and you need to factor in both the situation and the rest of the body language to figure out what's going on. But observe from a distance, because bites can be nasty.

TIP

Living with a bird who bites is no fun, that's for sure. If your bird seems determined to take a piece out of you, check out our behavior tips in Chapter 12.

>> **Yawning and sneezing:** No big surprises here. Birds yawn and sneeze for the same reasons we do — because they're tired or bored, or because something's irritating their nasal passages. If your bird is snorting up mucus or seems uncomfortable, though, call your veterinarian. Your bird needs to be looked at.

>> **Regurgitating:** When birds bring up half-digested food, they usually don't have a tummy ache — they can be expressing their affection. (We're not making this up, really!) Like many animals, birds feed their young by bringing up food. Bonded breeding pairs do this to each other as well, as a sign of closeness. When your bird brings up food when you're near enough to pet him, he's showing that he considers you a mate or companion and wants you to eat well. Birds bob their heads to bring the food up, and when the behavior is performed between birds, the food is put directly into the other's mouth. Don't try this at home.

>> **Wiping:** You don't like food on your mouth, and neither does your bird. Deprived of napkins, birds wipe their beaks on perches, on the sides of their food dishes, or on your shirt sleeve. Gina's bird, Patrick, used to occasionally catch a ride on the back of Gina's extremely mellow retriever, Benjamin (but only under Gina's close supervision), thanking the dog by smearing food on his ears. Benjamin wasn't amused, but he was tolerant.

TIP

Beak wiping is one of many good reasons to use abrasive perches as part of your bird's environment. The rough texture gives your bird a satisfying wipe and helps keep her beak well-polished and groomed. For more on perches, see Chapter 4.

>> **Jousting:** Birds play with other birds by slapping or grabbing each other's beaks. This frisky behavior is nothing more than playfulness — usually. Sometimes, though, birds can injure each other when playing, especially if there's a big difference in size and strength. Keep an eye on jousting — it's usually harmless, but call your veterinarian if any beak injuries occur.

# Wing things

Wings are for flying, of course, but that's not all. Here's how to interpret what else you may see your bird doing with his wings:

>> **Shoulder hunching or wing flipping:** The bird baby who attracts his parents' attention gets fed first and often fed most. She does this by flipping her wings and hunching her shoulders, accompanied by vocalizing and head bobbing. When done for your benefit, you can chalk this up to attention-getting behavior — usually associated with the need for food or the desire to be fed, especially in a young bird. In a mature bird, however, these juvenile-type movements may mean something's physically or emotionally amiss. Just the wing flips alone, singly or with both wings, can indicate mild annoyance — or an effort to line up the feathers just right.

Always keep in mind that different species have different *innate behaviors*, things that, at least in part, come natural for that species due to the environment to which they're adapted. Examples include the digging in the corner of the cage bottom you may see in your African grey parrot, the raising of their handsome crests to acquire attention that cockatoos do, the "scratch and peck" behaviors of backyard chickens (even when in your living room), and the dabbling in water puddles that pet ducks are fond of. You certainly wouldn't expect to see your macaw dabbling in his water bowl like your duck!

>> **Drooping:** Baby birds need to learn how to fold and tuck in their wings, so drooping in a young bird is nothing to worry about. In an older bird, drooping wings may indicate illness. If you notice the posture right after the bird exerts herself, consider sheer exhaustion as the cause, especially if your pet's a perch potato. Birds who have just been misted or bathed may also let their wings droop as they dry.

Although not a pet species, the anhinga is one bird who knows how to droop wings with style. This waterbird sits in the sun and holds his wings out to let them dry, a behavior that makes the glossy black bird appear like some kind of mystic icon. A great place to see the anhinga (along with more than 100 other species of birds, and quite a few alligators) is Wakulla Springs State Park, near Tallahassee, Florida. The springs are remarkable for their clearness (when conditions are right), their ancient history (mastodon bones were found there), and their less-ancient history (*Creature from the Black Lagoon* was filmed at the site). For us, though, the birds are by far the biggest draw.

>> **Flapping:** Honestly now, if you had wings, wouldn't you flap them? Birds often engage in massive flap-a-thons when they're first released from their cages. Getting some exercise just feels good! They aren't necessarily interested in going anywhere; even birds with unclipped wings can hold on tight to the tops

of their cages and just flap like crazy. They can even do it upside-down! Kim or her husband Jerry often played "elevator" with Larry. As he sat on a finger, they would raise that hand and then bring it down quickly, Larry flapping all the way. He enjoyed doing this in the shower as well.

## Tail tales

Even your bird's tail feathers have a tale to tell, if you're watching:

>> **Wagging:** Some birds wag their tail feathers for the same reason dogs wag their tails: They're glad to see you! The motion is usually not a continuous back-and-forth wag as with a dog, but more like a quick sideways flip and back. Fast back-and-forth flipping can have another meaning, especially in cockatoos: After some wagging, they'll often take a step back and let fly with an impressive dropping. Other parrots do the wag-step-and-poop dance, too, but usually not with the flair of a cockatoo. Watching for this behavior is a step in potty-training your parrot (see the nearby sidebar).

>> **Bobbing:** If your perch potato has just exercised, he's likely breathing hard just to get his wind back, and tail bobbing's part of the package. If your bird's tail is bobbing and he hasn't been active, he may have a breathing problem or infection — see your veterinarian.

>> **Fanning:** Spreading out the tail feathers is one of a collection of behaviors that go along with anger or aggression — we cover others in the upcoming sections. This showy action is quite common in Amazons who want to impress you with how very tough they are, and the wagging is often accompanied by flashing eyes and an erect body posture — not a bird you want to tangle with at that moment!

## CAN YOU POTTY-TRAIN YOUR BIRD? YES!

One of the less pleasant aspects of sharing your life with a bird is dealing with the droppings. When the droppings land on the paper at the bottom of the cage, that's fine, but nobody likes cleaning droppings off the floor (especially if carpeted) or off your shirt if you've been holding your bird when he lets one fly.

With patience and consistency, you can teach your bird to relieve himself on cue, in a place of your choosing. Young birds seem to pick up the skill most quickly and reliably, but you can teach an older bird new tricks, too.

*(continued)*

*(continued)*

Start by observing your bird — the times of day he's most likely to relieve himself and the body language he uses just before, such as tail wagging or stepping back. Pick your desired phrase — "Go potty" or "Hurry up" will do, as will anything, just as long as you're consistent.

When you see your bird getting ready to go or you know it's the usual time he does (such as first thing in the morning), ask him onto your hand (or finger, if he's a small bird) and hold him over a wastebasket, newspaper, toilet, or other "poop zone" (some people use paper plates). Give your potty cue and praise him when he does — even though the response is just a coincidence at first, of course. Praise and stroking are the rewards for desired behavior. Sometimes even better than praise, don't hesitate to pay your bird with a special goodie when he passes that dropping on cue!

The larger the bird, the longer the time he can "hold it." Budgies and cockatiels aren't good for much more than 15 to 20 minutes, tops, while large parrots can wait for several hours or more.

With training, some birds can hold it for a long, long time. A colleague of Brian's had a potty-trained patient whose owners left him with a pet sitter, without sharing the "Go" cue. The bird went a couple of days before the owners were reached on vacation. The sitter held the phone to the bird's ear, the owners gave the cue, and the bird bombed away to a very impressive degree!

Most birds aren't that reliable, so keep paper towels and other cleaning supplies on hand.

## Posture primer

Approaching avian language in bits and pieces is better than not trying to figure out what your bird is attempting to communicate, but you really have to look at the whole bird to get the message right. Some posturing to watch for:

>> **Crouching, head tipped downward:** We can sum this position up in three words: *Scratch me now!* The bird who lowers his body and tips his head forward to offer his neck (as shown in Figure 7-2) is angling for a good scratch. Indulge him!

>> **Crouching, head down, intense stare, eyes pinning or flashing:** This stance is bird talk for "Make my day." This bird is often telling you to stop approaching and to back away. There is a clearly stated promise that if you don't listen to that body language, you're going to get nailed. The body is rigid, with

feathers raised at the hackles, tail feathers flared, and eyes flashing. This early warning is sometimes accompanied by a purposeful lean forward. Make sure you recognize this language and give your bird the benefit of not *having* to use force on you. If they can get you to change your behavior without having to bite and attack, most birds would prefer that.

**FIGURE 7-2:**
Many birds love a good head scratch, but not all! And they have preferences for how they like their scratches, for how long, and from whom.

*Photograph by Brian L. Speer, DVM*

» **Crouching, head down, relaxed body, wings raised or fluttering:** This appearance is another solid statement about a desire for attention. "Hey, babe, I think you're cute. And don't I look cute, too?" In bird lingo, these commonly combined postures attract attention and send a come-hither signal.

» **Body up, head up, relaxed:** The bird's being friendly, especially if she's moving toward you.

» **Body up and rigid, head up, feathers ruffled and flared:** "Alert! Pay attention to what I'm telling you with my body language!" Stop, reassess, and take in the whole message in the context in which it's being relayed to you.

>> **Quivering:** Your bird may be frightened, intimidated, or cold (being cold is common after a good drenching). This can also be seen to acquire attention in some birds, such as in the young Quaker parakeet, so named because of the tendency of their youngsters to "quake" often.

>> **Stretching:** Birds stretch for the same reason we do: It feels good. *Manteling* is one kind of stretch you can see in both birds of prey and pet birds. The manteling bird stretches out a wing and leg on the same side in an impressive show of balance. Think of it as bird ballet or winged warrior pose.

>> **Preening:** Birds keep their feathers in fine form by drawing them through their beaks, cleaning and coating them with oil they draw from a gland at the base of their tails. They also pull off the sheaths on new feathers. Preening is very much a social behavior, too; birds enjoy preening each other and their favorite people.

*TIP*

Don't confuse preening with the destruction of feathers, a deliberate act commonly known as *feather picking.* (See Chapter 12 for more on the vexing problem of birds biting off or plucking out their own feathers.)

>> **Belly up:** When combined with flashing, open beak, general rigidity, and feet up, this display is a sad, sad sight: a bird who is convinced the danger to his life is so great he's prepared to fight to the end, and take a piece or two of his enemy with him. (Sometimes birds, especially baby ones, sleep on their backs, but we know you can tell the difference.) Although some pet parrot species may roll onto their back while playing or relaxing in the company of their favorite humans, make sure that what you see is not in response to what your bird is perceiving as a huge threat.

>> **Head shaking in African greys:** Brian has looked down the ears of lots of African greys whose owners were certain something was hiding inside, because of all the head shaking. He hasn't found anything — yet. Greys also sometimes put their heads down and against something and dig with their feet. Like the head shaking, this behavior usually occurs in young birds only.

# Getting a Handle on Your Bird

No matter how well you and your bird get along, you occasionally may need to do things to him he doesn't particularly appreciate — among them, wing trimming and nail clipping. Because your bird won't always sit still for a procedure he doesn't necessarily like, and because he may decide to bite you in protest, you have to figure out how to safely and securely shape a restraint experience for your bird.

With the hands-off types of birds — canaries and other finches — your first order of business is catching them. A net works fine in some situations such as in a larger aviary setting, but you may be able to catch your bird with your hand, if you darken the room first to "freeze" him. Cup the bird lightly in your hands and don't worry too much about a little nibble from a canary!

Parrots — we're talking about everything from little budgies to big macaws — can be asked up onto your hand first, which saves both of you the stress of capture.

Every pet bird, except the hands-off ones, should know the step-up cue, a basic tool for teaching many other behaviors. If you have a young, well-socialized bird, see Chapter 5 for tips on teaching the step up. If you're blessed with an avian delinquent, see Chapter 12 for techniques to reestablish a good relationship with your bird through a variety of training methods.

**REMEMBER**

When working with your pet bird and trying to shape a restraint experience, take your time, and read her behaviors carefully. It isn't about force or coercion to get your bird to step to your hand; it's all about helping your bird to see value in doing it!

## Meet "Mr. Towel"

For a secure way to restrain your bird that allows you the flexibility to trim nails or handle your bird for other reasons, use a towel. A hand towel is fine for small parrots, such as cockatiels and budgies, while a larger bath towel is better for large parrots, such as cockatoos and macaws.

There are several ways to shape a towel restraint experience for your bird. One method (but far from the only one) is to hold the towel with the ends draped over each hand, make eye contact with your bird, and approach her front the front. Show her "Mr. Towel" and then gently wrap the towel around her, from the front. Regardless of which method you use, the key is to keep it low stress.

When using a towel to restrain your bird (as shown in Figure 7-3), you may not need to keep direct hold of her head, but do expect a few new holes chewed in the towel!

When your bird is gently wrapped up like a mummy (be careful not to inhibit her breathing), *you* are in control and can take care of business. Always remember to handle your bird with respect, but also with authority. Keep in mind that Mr. Towel is supposed to be your bird's friend, not a source of dread, doom, or fear.

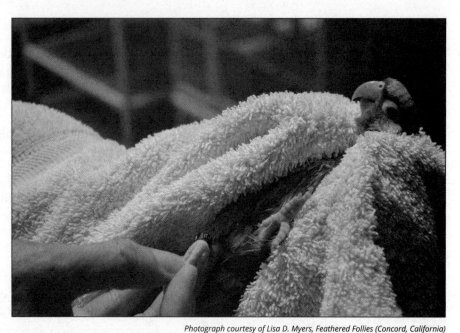

FIGURE 7-3: When correctly introduced, a towel is a safe, kind way to restrain your bird for nail trims or other necessary handling.

*Photograph courtesy of Lisa D. Myers, Feathered Follies (Concord, California)*

**WARNING**

Wrap the towel tightly enough to control wriggling, but not so tight as to restrict breathing. Pet bird species breathe by moving their breast bones forward and back like a bellows, not to the side as we do with our ribs. Be sure to leave the towel wrap loose enough for your bird to draw breath normally.

With your bird secure, you can pull out a wing or a foot for trimming — one person can do this with a towel wrap, but it's still easier if you have a helper.

**TIP**

Toweling doesn't have to be an ordeal for your bird. Play "towel games" with your pet, such as hide-and-seek, and she'll regard Mr. Towel as her friend. To play: Cover your bird with the towel, then flip it off and say "Peek-a-boo" in an animated voice. And repeat. Birds love to play and will soon look forward to this game. When she enjoys the interaction, she won't mind so much being restrained by Mr. Towel from time to time. Consider, however, that a towel your bird is familiar with through play with you at home can be quite different from a towel in a different setting where she's being held by a stranger, in the doctor's office, with memories of scary things that happened there in the past.

Besides attending behavior sessions at veterinary conferences to learn how to interact with avian patients, veterinarians can also acquire training in low-stress or Fear Free handling techniques for birds (`https://fearfreepets.com/fear-free-certification-overview-avian`). Such training includes how to recognize stress in birds, which actions or objects can cause fear in birds, how to design exam rooms for the comfort of birds, ways to help birds enjoy veterinary visits, and how to safely handle, examine, and collect diagnostic samples from birds.

## A MATTER OF RESPECT

When Brian sees a patient at the hospital, he introduces himself to the bird as a pediatrician would meet a child, with eye contact, a smile, and a friendly verbal greeting. As he's talking to the owner, he's constantly watching the bird, getting a feel for the personality and looking for signs of illness or behavior problems. Mr. Towel doesn't come out until he's needed — if he's needed at all. And when Mr. Towel *does* come out, careful attention to what the bird thinks about it is important. Is there fear? In what context? Can Brian do things differently to reduce fear?

Sound reasonable? You'd think so, but too many veterinarians or bird handlers, such as groomers, tend to restrain first and get to know the bird later or not at all. That's the way they were taught, and that's the way they still behave.

When you think about it, fear of Mr. Towel isn't an innate and instinctual behavior. It's learned by past experiences. Someone who as a child had a horrible, frightening experience at the dentist's office can still be quite fearful of going to the dentist 40 years later. Similarly, appreciation of fear that is directed to the towel is important for the short-term and longer-term health and welfare of your bird. When you recognize the fear, you and your vet can start working to help your bird through it.

Your chosen veterinarian, groomer, or other professional should be comfortable with and respectful toward birds. Simply, most parrots should not be struggling, flailing, screaming, or biting when they're subjected to a restraint experience. Most should not require sedation or anesthesia to be handled. Sometimes a problem can arise and sedation may be truly indicated, but it shouldn't be an "always" or "never" kind of thing.

For more on choosing the right veterinarian for your pet bird, see Chapter 9.

# Practicing Good Grooming

A healthy bird will do a good job of keeping her feathers in fine shape by preening them frequently — pulling them through her beak to distribute oils and keep everything neatly aligned. As accomplished as they are, though, pet birds need human help with other necessary grooming tasks.

## Trimming nails

In the wild, birds keep their nail tips blunted by perching on a wide variety of surfaces, some of them quite rough. Few pet birds have such a variety of perching opportunities, so regular pedicures become the owner's responsibility.

You can use either of two techniques in keeping nails short. The one you choose depends on your preference and what your bird deals with best.

The tried-and-true method involves cutting the nails. You can use a human nail trimmer for the task if your bird is small, or the scissors- or guillotine-type tool made for trimming dog nails. Before you start, make sure you have a supply of styptic powder, available at pet stores, to stop bleeding just in case you nick the vein inside the nail.

With your bird restrained, position the cutter to nip off the tip of the nail. Don't go farther back than the tip at first; you can always clip off more later, in tiny increments. If you draw blood, press the powder into the end of the nail until the blood coagulates.

Some bird owners manage nail trims without any restraint at all. Instead of making a big hairy deal out of the process, they clip one nail a night for a week every month (well, eight days actually, a day for each nail). You can trim while playing or watching TV with your bird. A quick clip, and back to the fun and games.

The other method of nail trimming involves the use of a rotary grinding device, such as the electric Dremel tool sold for woodworking and other craft work. The rechargeable version is lightweight and quiet and works well for this purpose. Grinding nails is a two-person job. One person restrains the bird, while the other grinds off the nail tip. (Use a medium-coarse head on the tool.)

Birds can learn to participate voluntarily in a nail-trimming procedure, without restraint required at all! It takes some time and requires good training skills, but it's certainly possible. Work with a bird-savvy trainer, vet tech, or veterinarian to learn how. Birds can also learn to offer a foot, to take medication from a needleless syringe, hold still for an injection, and other skills that come in handy when they need care, either at home or at the veterinary clinic.

To extend the time between nail trims and improve your bird's foot health and emotional outlook, provide a wide variety of perches for him. Use an abrasive perch, with its great texture for wearing down nails. For more on perches, see Chapter 4.

The proper length of your bird's nails depends on the size of your bird — larger birds generally need longer nails. One way to get a handle on nail trims is to have your veterinarian or a bird groomer trim the nails the first couple of times; you can then see the correct length for your pet. Video it if you want a visual aid back at home.

# Clipping wings

When we choose to bring birds into our homes, we must take responsibility for protecting them from hazards. In rare instances, that may mean keeping their wings trimmed, but we believe wing clipping is not in a bird's best interests, either physically or mentally. Flight is a natural bird behavior, and it's important for both their physical and mental well-being.

**WARNING**

Inability to fly because of wing trims can lead to muscle atrophy, decreased bone density from lack of exercise, heart disease, and broken blood feathers when birds crash land. And when birds can't fly, their posture is affected, potentially resulting in pain and orthopedic problems.

Flight — or the lack thereof — also affects a bird's psychological health. The ability to fly is an integral part of being a bird. When birds are unable to perform this most basic of maneuvers, the resulting stress can lead to obsessive behaviors in the form of pacing, rocking, screaming, or self-mutilation such as feather picking. When they can't escape a frightening situation by flying, they may instead respond by biting.

Wing trims are often defended as a way of keeping birds safe. Flighted birds can escape (see the nearby sidebar), and they get injured in more ways than you can imagine (and Brian has seen them all). Birds fly into windows, pots of boiling water, ceiling fans . . . the list goes on and on. But really, wing trimming is more for human convenience than for a bird's benefit. We believe it's better to take safety precautions on our end — like not keeping birds in the kitchen — and teach birds how to navigate their environment safely than it is to restrict an instinctive behavior that is so essential for their well-being.

**TIP**

Still thinking about trimming your bird's wings? First, ask yourself a few simple questions to help decide if and how it should be done:

>> How will this wing trim procedure help my bird? (It's supposed to be mostly about the bird.)

>> Are there alternatives to wing trimming that I could consider?

>> If I decide to trim the wings, how little can be removed to accomplish the desired goal?

>> If the wings have been trimmed in the past, how effective was that approach and the restraint experience required to accomplish it? Were there any adverse consequences noted physically or behaviorally?

If your bird does need a wing trim, observe your veterinarian or bird groomer handling the wing-clip a few times before trying it yourself. Some people always have a professional handle the wing trims, and that's fine, too. We don't recommend a one-sided wing trim, which causes birds to be off balance and at greater risk of falling and injuring themselves.

**TECHNICAL STUFF**

If you must restrict your bird's flight, know that a proper wing trim allows a bird to exercise his wing-flapping muscles, the *pectorals,* which is especially important in young, developing birds. A good trim also gives a bird some coasting ability, so he doesn't fall like a rock when attempting to fly. Birds with no flight ability can injure themselves badly, from beak-tip and chest damage to tail-base, cloacal/vent, and wing-tip damage. Excessively short wing trims can also create psychological issues in your pet — it's scary to think you'll fall like a rock! Properly trimmed, your bird should have no ability to gain altitude, but he should be able to fly horizontally to a safe, easy landing.

With your bird restrained in a towel, pull the wing out and look at the primary flight feathers, the last ten — and longest — feathers on the wing. Using sharp scissors, take the ends off the outer six or seven. Don't get carried away — you can always trim feathers more, but you can't put feathers back on! As long as you're not cutting blood feathers or pin feathers (see our sidebar, "The feathers that bleed"), you're not hurting your bird.

**REMEMBER**

Instead of trimming wings, we think it's better to develop a strong, mutually trusting relationship that will be the foundation of your bird's desire to come to you when you call. Being able to let your bird fly free, as he was meant to, and knowing he'll return on cue, as shown in Figure 7-4, is one of the most wonderful feelings associated with avian companionship. We talk more about safe flight training in the home in Chapter 12.

## THE FEATHERS THAT BLEED

*Blood feathers* or *pin feathers* are new feathers that are starting to grow out. The new feathers are nourished by their own personal blood supply located in the *shaft* (the part you would write with if you were using a quill pen).

After the feathers reach their full growth, that blood supply closes up shop, but until then, developing feathers can be fragile. It's not uncommon for them to break if a bird crashes into a wall, window, or ceiling fan, or takes a Geronimo leap off the cage (all of which are common occurrences in wing-trimmed birds).

If one of these feathers gets accidentally broken, it usually clots on its own, and bleeding stops quickly. Just in case, ask your veterinarian to demonstrate how and where to grasp the blood feather at the base so you can gently pull it out. Jerking it out can damage the wing, but gentle pressure stops bleeding, ensures the least amount of trauma to the feather follicle, and stimulates growth of a new feather to replace the broken one. A little dab of styptic powder from your first-aid kit or even a bit of cornstarch from the pantry will help to stop bleeding. Because pulling out one of these feathers can be quite painful, another option may be to simply tie off the broken feather below its fracture line, which also will stop the bleeding.

A broken pin feather is usually not a life-threatening emergency in an otherwise healthy bird. Sometimes these feathers may be continually re-injured, causing a recurrence of bleeding, but these scenarios are less common than simple clotting. Many birds with internal health problems — usually involving the liver — may have some clotting problems, and these birds may be more predisposed to bleeding problems.

Blood feathers are sensitive and seem to itch as they develop, so many birds love to have their incoming feathers scratched or preened by their owners. However, your pet may jump or complain if you kink or hurt one of these pin feathers. They have a rich nerve supply, which can help explain why your bird may be more sensitive if you touch a pin feather in the wrong way. Appreciation of this sensitivity may be a good guide for you when preening or scratching your bird, or when trying to deal with a broken, bleeding pin feather.

**FIGURE 7-4:**
Companion birds in free flight is a wonderful thing to see, but it can only occur when a bird and human have a close, mutually trusting relationship.

*Photograph courtesy of Chan Quach, The Birdman*

# Raining down with showers, baths, and misting

Birds like to get wet. Water makes them feel good and stimulates normal preening behavior, which is important for their good physical and mental health. And if you compare our homes' dry atmospheres to the moist environs of many birds' rainforest habitats, you can imagine how lovely a nice spritz feels!

You may think that dampening your bird isn't necessary if you live in a humid or rainy place. Remember, though, that it's not the outside environment your bird's dealing with — it's the environment inside your home. Heat and air-conditioning remove moisture from the air, and the indoor environment can be as dry as a desert, especially in winter.

More than that, misting enhances your bird's lifestyle, welfare, and relationship with you. It's a way for you to spend time together. You can mist her outdoors on her training perch if it's a pretty day. That combines social interaction with feather care, two very important activities for your bird.

Probably the easiest way to dampen your bird is to use a squirt bottle set to mist, not spray. A light mist is plenty; there's no need to get him sopping wet. Watch for body language indicating that your bird doesn't like being misted directly — attempts to escape, avoiding the spray bottle, or growling or other vocalizations signaling displeasure. Your bird may prefer some other method of bathing, and that's okay.

Some people shower with their birds, and that's fine, too. You can even purchase a shower-specific perch. For hands-off birds, such as canaries and other finches, you can temporarily add to the cage a shallow bathing dish with an inch or so of water in it.

**WARNING**

Although your bird won't catch a cold if he's wet, avoid misting if your bird isn't in good health. It can add to his stress level and detract from needed energy to deal with his illness.

No rules exist for how often to mist, shower, or bathe your bird. Some birds are misted daily and enjoy it immensely, while others are hardly ever dampened and do just fine. Follow your bird's lead.

Should you blow-dry your bird? That depends on whether she likes the warm rush of air — some really do. If yours doesn't enjoy the sensation, skip it. If you do use a blow-dryer, set it on low and don't concentrate the flow on any one spot for more than a split second so you don't risk burning your bird. Not too hot, though! Brian has seen some birds who have suffered thermal burns from being blow-dried too long and from too closely.

# ESCAPE! WHAT TO DO IF YOUR BIRD GETS LOOSE

Birds are lost every day by people who didn't think twice about opening a window on a fine spring day or who were caught by surprise at just how fast a bird can make it through an open door.

The time to prepare for such a tragedy is *before* it happens. Make sure your bird has identification — a leg band (as shown in the nearby figure), a microchip, or both. Take pictures of your bird and note any unique identifying features. Identification can help reunite you with your bird if someone finds him or help you prove he's yours if the finder is reluctant to give him up, because of real or perceived value or because the finder found your pet as charming as you do.

If your bird escapes, immediately put his cage out in the yard with the door open and a big bowl of his favorite foods on top. After the thrill of being out a day or two wears off, your bird may decide his cage and food dish aren't so boring after all. Keep an eye on the cage to reclaim your wanderer if he reappears.

*Photograph courtesy of Claudia Hunka, Your Basic Bird
(Berkeley, California)*

*(continued)*

*(continued)*

Let people know you've lost your bird. Make flyers with your bird's picture and post them throughout your neighborhood. Don't forget to leave some with nearby veterinarians and with avian veterinarians, pet shops, and shelters in the region. Take out a classified ad in your local newspaper and post information about your bird on websites such as 911 Parrot Alert (www.911parrotalert.com) or Bird HotLine (www.birdhotline.com), which has more than 1,000 volunteers signed up to spot loose pet birds worldwide. Post your missing bird on social media such as Facebook, Twitter, and Instagram to spread the word even further.

Don't give up! Although many birds who are reunited with their owners are gone only a couple of days, some birds have been found after months or even years "on the wing." An African grey named Nigel escaped his Southern California home in 2010. Four years later, Nigel was recovered, thanks to a microchip that enabled him to be tracked to the pet store where he was purchased and then to his original family!

**TIP**

Some birds absolutely don't like getting wet. If yours is among them — or if you're struggling with low humidity in your home — a humidifier is a good investment in your bird's comfort. Another option is to set up a "shower cage" in a sheltered area outside and provide an automatic mister (like those you see at the vegetable counter at the grocery store) that delivers a fine mist periodically as your bird enjoys the sights and sounds of the outdoors. Make sure your bird is supervised constantly so you can intervene if any predator decides to visit.

# Bird Care When You Can't

Before you know it, you and your new pet will be like lovebirds, totally infatuated with each other. You'll quickly become comfortable in a routine that suits you both. Don't get too comfortable, though, because now is the time to plan for those occasions when you can't be with your pet — when you're called away on business or enjoying a vacation.

## Pet sitters

The general title of *pet sitter* encompasses a wide range of services, everything from a reciprocal agreement between friends to care for each other's pets to paying a neighboring teenager or college student to look in or house-sit or hiring a professional pet sitter.

The benefits of having your pet stay in your own home is that he's familiar with the surroundings, which is an important consideration where birds are concerned. And pet sitters can do more than just look in on your pet: They can take in your mail and newspaper, water your houseplants, and turn lights on and off. The best ones are lifesavers and practically become family members.

REMEMBER

Discuss services and prices beforehand. If you're dealing with a service, make sure the business is bonded and insured.

The biggest drawback to pet sitters is that your bird is left alone a great deal of the time, because most pet sitters can't spend their days or nights giving him individual attention. They drop in once or twice a day, make sure everything's in order, and move on to their next client. An arrangement with a young person (especially when school's out) or a house sitter to stay in your home while you're gone may give your bird more opportunities for companionship and ensure greater safety. If your bird becomes ill or manages to escape, a pet sitter may not be there to notice until some time has passed.

WARNING

Informal arrangements for *house-sitting* (actually having the person move in while you're gone) or *pet-sitting* (having the person drop in once or twice a day to check on your pet) can be trickier than hiring a professional service. Just ask the friend of Gina's who left her house and pets in the care of a friend's college-age daughter, only to find out that the young woman had been anything but a quiet resident. She hosted guests and even had a wild party. The house was a bit worse for the wear, but at least the pets were fine. If you're going to go with a young person — and many people do, with no regrets — make sure parental oversight is part of the picture. And then there was Kim's colleague, who was excited to care for Larry while Kim was on vacation. Her bird-sitting activities turned out to include taking Larry outdoors and letting him sit on tree branches because she thought it was cute. Fortunately, nothing went wrong on these expeditions, but Kim made sure future pet sitters were aware that this was *not* acceptable behavior.

TIP

Another approach is to *trade* pet-sitting with a fellow bird lover. Making a deal to cover each other whenever you're gone can work out very well. Trading care is a solution that's both reassuring — if you have friends who share your bird-care knowledge and philosophies, that is — and inexpensive. All the arrangement requires is your own time in return. Just remember that if something goes wrong, even accidentally, it could spoil your friendship. You may decide that paying for a professional is worth the cost.

WARNING

No matter who cares for your bird, make sure they're comfortable with handling your pet, and that your bird is likewise comfortable with the pet sitter. Some people who may be perfectly happy around dogs or cats may find birds intimidating, especially the big parrots.

# HOME-ALONE BIRD

Few of us are able (or willing) to stay home with our pets all the time. Fortunately, birds are quite capable of entertaining themselves while you're off earning the bird food.

When you're away for a few hours or at work for the day, your bird should be left in his cage, of course, but rotate toys regularly for variety, and leave some music on. Birds love many types of music, from serene classical sounds to claw-hammer banjo to pop and rock. Give him some choices and see what he dances to! A bird cam, as shown in the nearby figure, can help you keep an eye on your bird while you're not home.

*Photograph courtesy of Rachel Baden, DVM*

Although it's fine to leave your bird while you're at work, it's *not* okay to leave him alone while you skip out for a few days. How would you like to be left with food growing more stale by the minute, water forming a skin (or worse, if your bird poops in the water dish), and a toilet you can't flush?

Alone overnight is probably fine, but anything more than that, and you should arrange for boarding or call a bird-experienced pet sitter.

# Boarding

Boarding, similar to what's available for dogs or even cats, is an increasingly popular option for birds. Many birds are quite social and can settle in to new environments without difficulty. On the other hand, some birds are happier in familiar surroundings, and putting your pet in the company of strange birds may expose him to heaven-knows-what diseases.

Some veterinarians offer bird boarding, and so, too, do some bird shops. These services are worth checking into, especially if you're already familiar with the provider — for example, if the veterinarian is your own, or if you know the shop is a reputable one, perhaps because it's where you bought your bird.

Most boarding facilities control the amount of exposure birds have with one another, and they have requirements regarding the health of the birds they accept as guests. A facility with health requirements prior to entry is better than one that welcomes any and all birds. Health-screening requirements tend to vary immensely between facilities; some are quite specific, costly, and extensive, while others have no requirements whatsoever.

Realistically, not all required tests are the same, and not all negative test results indicate health and effective reduction of infectious-disease risks. Probably most important is choosing a facility that emphasizes good food, where enrichment is a part of the package and your bird has the possibility of coming home with more skills than he was admitted with, that's clean and well managed, and that's staffed with people who *really* know birds — especially *your* bird — well.

Ask if there's a bird-cam so you can get a glimpse of your bird buddy if you're missing him while you're away or you just want to see how he's doing. Some veterinarians, boarding facilities, or pet sitters may post photos of your pet on social media — with your permission, of course — or text photos to you. Larry was so popular at his veterinarian's office that Kim always jokingly wondered if she would be getting him back when she returned. One time when she was waiting for him to be brought to the front desk, she could hear an audible sigh of disappointment in the back from staff members who were sad to see him go.

**WARNING**

Don't leave boarding decisions to the last minute, if you can avoid it. Check out your choices in advance: Visit the premises and talk to the staff. You can sense the quality of the overall operation. If you don't feel confident and comfortable with the surroundings, don't leave your bird, under any circumstances.

# Harness Training

Exploring the outdoors with your bird is a great way to bond with her and to offer limitless enrichment opportunities. The first step is getting her to accept wearing a harness. This can be a complicated process, with many small behaviors to teach and stimuli to introduce. We always recommend enlisting the help of a trainer who uses positive-reinforcement techniques. A trainer who knows birds can help you tailor a training plan specific to your individual bird. In this section, we offer some tips on harness selection and training.

## Types of harnesses

Each of the many different types of harnesses available for birds has characteristics that you and your bird may or may not like. It's not uncommon to try one type of harness and need to switch to a different style or brand before you find what works well for your bird. When you're considering the type of harness to purchase, keep in mind the following:

>> Is it safe? Will it stay on your bird or will he be able to easily escape it or rip it open?

>> How difficult is it to put on and remove? Be sure you understand how to do so and get comfortable with the process.

There are three main types of harnesses:

>> **Flight suits:** Flight suits tend to cover most of a bird's body. Typically, the leash is attached to the back of the harness with touch fasteners. One benefit of a flight suit is that, like a diaper, it tends to catch droppings. Although this makes cleanup easier, we don't recommend asking your bird to wear the flight suit for long periods of time.

TIP

To put the flight suit on, ask your bird to stand on the harness as it's lying open on the ground and pull the harness up like pants (you'll see openings for the legs). The wings fit through the harness and you secure it over the bird's back with touch fasteners.

>> **Ankle leashes:** Ankle leashes fasten to the bird's leg band or clip around the leg if no band is present. While similar restraints (called *jesses*) are used in falconry, these are typically not suitable for companion birds either inside or outside the home. They can cause injury or even a fractured leg if the bird startles or tries to fly off.

>> **Aviator-type harnesses:** Aviator-type harnesses are usually made of thin, leash-like material or strips of leather and come in several sizes. This type of harness is all one piece, leaving less worry about clever birds unhooking or unclasping the harness or detaching the leash.

TIP

We suggest that you practice tightening and loosening the harness before putting it on the bird. This helps to loosen the adjustors, which can be rigid and difficult to maneuver on new harnesses, and it's just good to be familiar with how it works. The last thing you want during harness training is to have your parrot signal that she wants out of the harness or to panic and you're unable to get the harness off in a timely and easy fashion. The section of the harness that adjusts is the one that fits around the width of the body.

The opening of the harness through which the head fits does not adjust. It can be helpful to order a size up from the one recommended for your bird. A larger opening for the head can make it easier to put on and remove the harness.

Some brands, such as Leathers4Feathers (https://leathers4feathers.com), offer the option of customizing a harness with additional clasps. This allows you to open the section of the harness that goes around the head, avoiding the sometimes-difficult step of asking a bird to put her head through something. Some harnesses have plastic release buckles on either side of the harness that fasten around the body. That may allow less manipulation of the wings.

# Harness-training tips

Most birds, even those who are accepting of the harness, will benefit from training and practice prior to going on adventures with you. Although we recognize — and emphasize! — that there are dozens of different methods for teaching birds to wear a harness, here are a few broad training tips for your consideration:

>> **Wearing the harness should be a good experience.** Show your bird that when the harness is out, good things happen, such as being offered her favorite treats.

>> **Don't rush to put your bird in the harness.** Harness training requires a lot of trust and should be taught at the bird's comfort level and pace.

>> **Keep training sessions short.** You don't want to overwhelm your bird. Don't go longer than one to three minutes — even shorter if your bird loses interest. Stop while she's still having a good time.

>> **Break training into small steps.** If your bird successfully does what you ask, great! Repeat a few times before moving on to the next step.

>> **If your bird is unable to do what you've asked, go back to the drawing board.** Do you need to make the steps smaller, shorter, or easier to complete? Should you offer different reinforcement? Is it time for a break? Listen to what your bird is telling you.

>> **While you're still practicing with the harness, try taking your bird out in a carrier to the park or a cafe.** This will help accustom her to going different places, seeing other people, receiving treats during those experiences, and just enjoying the fresh air and being out of the house. Additionally, it can help prevent you from feeling rushed or pressured to complete the harness-training process because you have a backup plan for outdoor enrichment.

# Taking Your Bird with You

Canaries and other finches are generally best left at home, but other birds may enjoy accompanying you on trips or to work (if you can have your pet at work). The gregarious Amazons may especially relish the chance to show off for strangers, but any healthy parrot — from budgies to macaws — can warm to travel in time, especially if begun at an early age. Of course, check with employers, hosts, or hotels beforehand to make sure your bird will be welcome.

Your bird should have a secure travel carrier with a perch (see Chapter 4 for more details on choosing your travel cage). Be mindful of where you open the carrier door to help prevent escapes.

REMEMBER

Even a bird whose wings are trimmed can sometimes gain enough loft to escape.

## Hitting the beach

You've heard of adventure cats? Well, there are adventure birds, too. In Southern California — and no doubt Florida as well — it's not unheard of to see a macaw, African grey, cockatoo, or other companion bird riding on a shoulder as his person checks out local shops, dines at a restaurant with outdoor seating, or sets up a spot on the sand, as shown in Figure 7-5.

TIP

But before deciding to take your bird on a surfin' safari, be sure he's prepared. This type of outing shouldn't be his first experience in public, especially not if there are crowds, and he should already be accustomed to wearing his harness and leash. Practice with short outings near home and make sure he's comfortable with the experience before you venture out to beaches, parks, or outdoor shopping malls.

WARNING

Taking birds outdoors is fun, but it does have risks. There's a reason California, Florida, Texas, and other states, as well as cities such as New York and Chicago, have numerous populations of wild parrots. According to the California Parrot Project, hundreds of escaped or released parrots have formed colorful and noisy wild breeding flocks.

REMEMBER

Know the behavioral signs of fear, anxiety, and stress so you can cut outings short if your bird isn't having a good time. Those signs include rounded eyes, rapidly dilating and constricting pupils, unwillingness to take treats, feathers held close to the body, or fanned-out tail feathers. Your bird may display these behaviors if he's uncomfortable in a situation or if he's fearful of a predator such as a bigger bird or a barking dog. Speaking of predators, keep your bird close at hand so he doesn't run the risk of being attacked by another bird or animal. Be his advocate if people come up and want to interact with or pet him. Your bird isn't a sideshow act, and he relies on you to protect him from the reaching hands of strangers. But when he's well socialized and comfortable with you, an outing like this can be a wonderful way to spend time with him.

**FIGURE 7-5:** Birds can enjoy outings just as much as the rest of us. Solomon, an African grey, spends a little time on the beach.

*Photograph courtesy of Melody Hennigh, Busy Beaks Academy (Oakley, California)*

## Hitting the road

Lots of people bring pets with them on outdoors vacations, road trips, or boating, and very often those pets include birds. Even more than dogs and cats, they can be ideal traveling companions because of their size and greater ease of care — no need for potty stops or litter boxes, for one thing.

Whether you're tent camping or traveling in an RV, some common-sense precautions will ensure that a good — and safe — time is had by all. Your bird should ride in a carrier (see Chapter 4 for more information about travel carriers) while the vehicle is in motion. No sitting on your shoulder or the headrest, please!

He can enjoy the breeze through his feathers while riding in a pet stroller or backpack bird carrier with a view. This lets him accompany you on hikes or bike rides but protects him from loss or other birds that may attack.

In camp, set up a screened covering with a play gym and a chair for yourself. At night, if you're tent-camping and it's cold, have a blanket you can toss over the cage to hold in warmth.

On a road trip where you'll be staying in a hotel, don't forget to pack a bird-care bag. In addition to food and toys, you'll want to have your birdie first-aid kit, cleaning products and paper towels in case he poops on anything, and a sheet or other covering to toss over his cage so he can nap quietly if you're not in the room. When most hotels and motels say they're pet-friendly, they're referring to dogs, so check to see if birds are permitted when you make your reservation. And get it in writing.

WARNING

Campfires are fun, but not for birds. Leave yours in the tent or RV, safely away from any smoke, fumes, or flames.

TIP

Many manufacturers offer harnesses and light leashes for birds. If you're going to be out and about with your pet, we recommend you look into these accessories. Also be certain that your bird has an ID, in the form of a microchip, leg band, or both. For more on carriers, and harnesses, see Chapter 4; for microchips and leg bands, see Chapter 5.

# Flying with your bird

You can even fly with your bird! Most airlines permit small pets, including birds, in the cabin, which is much safer than putting your bird in the cargo hold — a ride we don't recommend at all.

To travel in the cabin, your bird will need an airline-approved carrier that fits under the seat. Each airline has slightly different rules for pets — some limit the number of animals in the cabin, for example — so call well in advance to secure your bird's reservation and pay the fee for his flight.

Know that you'll have to take your bird out of the carrier to go through security; you can't send him through the X-ray machine. Be prepared to keep hold of him as you walk through the security setup (that's where a bird harness and leash can come in handy), as well as to field questions and comments from admiring and curious security staffers and fellow passengers.

TIP

This process will go best if you have TSA PreCheck so you don't have to take off your shoes or remove your laptop while trying to manage your bird.

# BIRDS IN THE WILD

Ever want to see where your bird comes from? If you're an avid traveler, the continents of Africa, Australia, and South America, as well as other birding hot spots throughout the world, may be high on your bucket list, depending on your species of preference.

East Africa is home to Fischer's and yellow-collared lovebirds, the red-bellied parrot, and the Meyer's parrot. In regions of Central and West Africa, you're likely to spot African greys, red-fronted parrots, rose-ringed parakeets, Senegal parrots, and red-headed lovebirds. Although she went for the predators, Kim came away from her trips to Africa with a vast appreciation for the variety of bird life there and now looks forward to seeing the birds as much as she does the big cats, wild dogs, and elephants. Botswana, Ethiopia, and Tanzania are all draws for birders, no matter what species interest them.

In South America, you'll find macaws, including the stunning hyacinth, blue-and-gold, and scarlet; Amazon parrots; *Pionus* species; monk parakeets; and members of the *Brotogeris* family, to name just a few. The "bird continent" boasts 3,420 species, more than any other, so you can easily spend a lifetime exploring it. Some of the best countries for birding are Brazil, Chile, Colombia, Ecuador, Peru, and Uruguay.

Brian had the opportunity to see blue-and-gold, green-winged, and scarlet macaws at Chuncho Culpa near Tambopata Research Center in the Peruvian Amazon rain forest, and Kim saw hyacinth macaws in Brazil's Pantanal region. To see where and how birds live in their natural habitat is a magical and life-changing experience for most people.

Cockatoos, cockatiels, lorikeets, Eclectus parrots, rosellas, and budgerigars are native to Australia. (Fun fact: The word *budgerigar* is said to translate as "tastes good," but we wouldn't want to find out if that's true.) Brian still gets a thrill remembering his first sight of a flock of red-tailed black cockatoos in the land down under. Among the super-neat locations he has been to and wholeheartedly recommends are Tambopata Research Center in Peru (www.perunature.com/amazon_lodge/tambopata-research-center) and O'Reilly's Rainforest Retreat (https://oreillys.com.au/) in Australia.

If wild birds (not the ones normally seen as companion birds) are your thing, a bird safari in any of these places will leave you staring in wonder and delight at the bright feathers, fantastical nests, and assortment of behaviors, from hunting to mating. Africa has some of the world's most spectacular birds of prey, including the bateleur, crowned eagle, snake eagle, fish eagle, and secretary bird. On the colorful and entertaining side, there are kingfishers, rollers, and bee-eaters with brilliant plumage and aerobatic displays. Beyond hookbills, South America shows off bird life ranging from rheas to toucans, scarlet ibis to pink flamingos, and condors to penguins.

*(continued)*

*(continued)*

Australia, too, ranks high as a birding tour destination, being home to a unique range of bird families, from mound-building megapodes to the crimson rosellas of Kangaroo Island to the iconic cockatoos.

For a trip to a birding destination, consider going with a company that specializes in bird safaris led by professional ornithologists, or at least make sure your guide is well versed in bird life. Her quick eye and in-depth knowledge of local birds will add immensely to your trip.

Bird voyage!

# 3
# Keeping Your Bird Healthy

Discover the secrets of avian anatomy.

Prevent health problems in your feathered friend.

Recognize emergencies and illness.

Understand your senior bird's needs.

# Chapter **8**

# How Birds Work: The Short Course

When you think about what's unique to birds, chances are, you think of their ability to fly. Okay, so maybe some birds don't fly anymore — either by design (such as the ostrich and emu) or by human interference (such as with the clipped wings of pet birds). But the goal of flight is still the basic blueprint of every bird, and the evolutionary choices made to achieve it have dictated the form of the birds you see today — both your pets and the birds you see in the wild.

**TECHNICAL STUFF**

Don't count the penguin on the list of flightless birds. Although the adorable tuxedo-clad birds can't become airborne, they do fly through the water in much the same way as their relatives fly through the air.

What flying demands in real terms is *lightness.* Every detail of a bird must be strong enough to do the job and light enough to allow flight. Flight, after all, is more than a nifty way of getting around: It's the ultimate survival skill for birds, many of which are looked on as tasty hors d'oeuvres by their predatory neighbors. Flying allows for a hasty escape from trouble, and it's a way to easily go where the food supply and climate are more conducive to comfortable living. Would you give up your teeth and a few bones to fly? We would, in a flash.

The change didn't happen that quickly for birds, of course. In 1861, workers splitting slate in a Bavarian quarry came across a fossil that proved the link between reptiles and birds. Named *Archeopteryx*, the Jurassic-period creature was decidedly reptilian, with teeth, a long tail, and hands with fingers. But outlined in the slate were structures that foretold of the beautiful birds that would eventually fill countless environmental niches around the world: *Archeopteryx* had feathers!

More than 150 million years ago, an animal that would become the modern-day bird already demonstrated one of the basic facts of avian survival: A bird's gotta fly, because he doesn't want to become someone else's dinner. The flip side is true for predatory birds, such as eagles, owls, and hawks — without flight, they can't hunt. Understand these basic requirements, and you're already halfway to understanding why your bird is put together as he is and what makes him tick. For the other half — read on!

# The Outside: More than Just Beautiful

To see a macaw in flight (see Figure 8-1) is to view a model of aerodynamics. Embodying one clean, straight, and colorful line from his beak to an elegantly long tail, the macaw, like all flighted birds, has a design that early would-be aviators, from Leonardo da Vinci on, couldn't help but admire and emulate. Look at any plane — from the earliest fabric-covered creations to the *Spirit of St. Louis*, from the latest jet off the assembly line to the Space Shuttle — and you can still see where the designers got their inspiration.

We may think we've conquered the air, with more than a million people airborne at any given time, but we've still got nothing on the bird. Make reservations? Struggle through crowded airports? Sit in unbearably close proximity to people you wouldn't get within a half-mile of in circumstances of your own choosing? That's *flying*? Ha! In numbers uncountable, birds still rule the skies, and they'll continue to, unless we mere humans become able to spread strong, feather-lined wings and be among the treetops with just a few powerful flaps.

All birds, from the tiny vervain hummingbird (0.08 ounce in weight) to the imposing but not overly bright ostrich (275 pounds), belong to a taxonomic class scientists call *Aves*. We honor the bird every time we use words we've chosen to represent our own efforts at flight: *aviation, aviator, avionics*.

Although every feature of the bird has to be compatible with flight, the way these features have developed is pretty interesting, from beaks to toes.

**FIGURE 8-1:**
A green-winged
macaw soars over
the Hollywood
Hills in Southern
California,
demonstrating
free flight.

*Photograph courtesy of Chan Quach, The Birdman*

## Built for versatility: The beak

The beak of a bird is a tool with many features. It's a weapon that can put a serious dent in any enemy and damage the relationship with a friend. It can be a delicate tool for feeding a newly hatched chick in the nest or for grooming and adjusting a bird's feathers so that they're "just right." With their beaks, some birds can pick a lock, crush a walnut, or peel the skin off a grape.

At its most basic, the beak on our parrot pets consists of two hard structures, the upper and lower *mandibles* (bills), and an amazingly agile and strong tongue.

**TIP**

A bird's beak is quite the anatomical marvel — and it's also a common anatomic part that you need to pay attention to when working with birds. Pecks, bites, and other injuries can certainly happen; these are among the many functions of a beak. To shape a restraint experience that is less likely to result in your being bitten or injured, check out Chapter 7 for tips on when and how to restrain your bird, either by hand or with the aid of a towel.

## A tool for all seasons

Beak shapes and sizes vary widely, depending mostly on the kind of food a certain species eats. The short, straight bill of canaries and other finches is ideal for plucking out seeds, grubs, and other edibles. Birds of the parrot family — including budgies, cockatiels, and the larger parrots — are known as *hookbills* because of the shape and function of their beaks.

The beaks of most parrots are remarkably well-designed for one of their most important tasks: cracking, crushing, prying, or otherwise destroying the protective coatings around many of the foods they like to eat. Like everything else on a creature evolved for flight, the beak is surprisingly lightweight considering its strength — a hard shell of constantly growing material (keratin) similar to that found on antlers, over a hollow bony structure. (If the beak were made of solid bone, the weight would probably force a bird to spend his life on the ground, and on his nose!)

The powerful but lightweight beak of the toucan (like the one shown in Figure 8-2) is one-third or more the length of the bird itself. One function of the toucan's beak is to regulate body temperature.

**FIGURE 8-2:** A keel-billed toucan at Omar's Exotic Birds in Lake Forest, California.

*Photograph by Kim Campbell Thornton*

## DON'T BITE THE DOC WHO TREATS YOU

You may think that avian veterinarians are used to getting bitten, almost on a daily basis, because they often need to handle birds who really don't want to be handled. In reality, this is rarely the case, particularly for veterinarians who are comfortable with shaping that restraint experience, reading the bird's behavior, and willing to take the time needed to do things safely for all. When you think about it, there is more risk of a bite when time isn't taken to read the situation properly, when force is always the first choice, and when there is unfamiliarity with the birds being worked with.

Fear of bites may be why some veterinarians insist on towel restraints for every bird before examination, which is the equivalent in many ways of muzzling every dog or cat who comes in. Other arguments for use of towels for restraint during the physical examination are to better control the bird and to provide less risk to the bird, as well as to the examiner in some settings.

This approach, however, is not necessarily fair for all birds, and it certainly can lessen a veterinarian's ability to observe the bird. Brian prefers to give each bird the benefit of the doubt, and he assesses the temperament of each patient before reaching for a towel. Those characters who have learned to bite first and ask questions later tend to reveal themselves pretty quickly. Brian certainly has been bitten plenty of times but almost always can see the fault in what he was doing that allowed the bite to occur. He watches body language — we've put the basics in Chapter 7 — and offers the back of his hand instead of his finger to lessen any damage that may occur.

A hookbill's beak may be lightweight, but it's also strong. Although you need a hammer or nutcracker to get through hard shells to the nut meat, a bird needs only his ridged beak — and perhaps a foot to hold the nut. With small seeds, as well as larger nuts, it's a hands-free operation: Rotate the seed with the tongue to find the seam, apply pressure to crack it at the weak spot, and then rotate it again to slide out the tasty morsel inside.

**REMEMBER**

A parrot has such strength in his beak that owners are often surprised to see even the bars of a metal cage fall victim to a chewing bird. Birds have been known to pick off the welds holding bars together (and get lead or zinc poisoning as a result) and even snap the bars themselves. That's why it's so important to choose the best cage you can, one appropriate for the size and strength of your bird. (For tips on choosing a safe cage, see Chapter 4.)

Parrots also use their beaks as a third foot — they climb with their beaks. You need to remember the third-foot function if your bird grasps your finger with his beak when stepping up onto your hand. Chances are, he's not biting — he's climbing. You'll know when he's biting! Baby birds do more *beaking* than older ones.

Beaking is the bird equivalent of a human toddler wanting to touch and put everything in his mouth.

## Paying attention to beak health

**WARNING**

Depending on the species, beaks grow constantly at a rate of 1 to 3 inches per year, but the beak of a normal pet bird doesn't need to be trimmed. Your bird keeps her beak at the proper length through normal chewing activities. (Chewing is essential for both the physical and emotional health of the typical parrot.)

Overgrowth of the beak is frequently a sign of illness, such as liver disease or malnutrition. It can also happen merely because the bird isn't using the beak in a normal manner and not wearing the keratin surfaces of the beak properly, resulting in overgrowth. In many situations, there may be a *malocclusion* (misalignment of the upper and lower beaks), preventing normal wear from occurring and resulting in beak overgrowth. Contrary to what some bird books still preach, don't accept beak trims as a routine healthcare measure — they're not. A bird who gets routine beak trims instead of proper medical attention may have an attractive beak, but the bird is likely to die of the primary disease that is causing abnormal beak growth in the first place. Many of these malocclusions, nutritional issues, or liver problems can be corrected if diagnosed and addressed early and accurately.

Strong as they are, beaks sometimes break. Common causes of beak fractures include fighting between birds of different sizes (with the smaller one usually getting the worst of it) and excessively short wing trims that offer no gliding ability so a falling bird lands hard on his beak (or on his fanny, which can also be injured). In some species, such as the cockatoos, mate aggression is unfortunately a fairly common and unpleasant event — with the males beating up on their mates, often tearing off their beaks or severely injuring them. Damaged bird beaks can be repaired with dental acrylics, bridges, and even prosthetic beaks.

For optimum beak health, provide your pet bird with lots of things to chew on. Kim's bird Larry enjoyed destroying the wooden chopsticks she brought him from Chinese and Japanese restaurants. Even finches and canaries will often have better beak health if you provide *cuttlebone* (the shell of cuttlefishes, a type of mollusk) or another hard material to work with their beaks in their cage. If you see a beak problem, don't try to deal with it on your own. Your bird probably needs the help of an experienced avian veterinarian to properly diagnose and treat any problem, as well as help to train how to use that beak better and wear it more normally.

## Say "ahhhhhh"

A pretty obvious anatomical difference between humans and birds is apparent when a bird opens her mouth — she doesn't have any teeth. Experts believe teeth were sacrificed on the altar of flight, just another piece of excess baggage whose function could be managed another way. The cutting, grinding, and tearing abilities were taken up by the bird's hard beak, and some of the digestive functions by the *crop,* a space at the base of the neck that expands to allow for food storage. (Heavy-duty grinding happens a little farther along, in the *gizzard.*)

Right in the middle of the mouth is an organ we can recognize, because we have one, too — the tongue. Like our own, a bird's tongue is a model of dexterity and sensitivity, but a few differences exist.

The tongue of most pet birds — the hookbill species — is dry and muscular, made even stronger and more useful by an assembly of supportive bones — yes, bones! — running the length of the organ. The color varies depending on the species: It's black in some, pink in some, or a combination of colors in still others.

**TECHNICAL STUFF**

At the back and base of the tongue, just below the *esophagus* (food canal) is the *glottis* (air passage), the first step on the road to the lungs. At the roof of the mouth is the *choanal slit,* which connects to the nasal cavities. By elevating the base of the tongue and glottis to the choanal slit, a bird can effectively close off the opening of the esophagus and pass air directly from the *nares* (nostrils), through the choana, through the glottis, and directly into the trachea. When food or water is being swallowed, the glottis closes reflexively at the same time the tongue drops to the floor of the mouth, preventing accidental inhalation of food or water into the windpipe, and opening up the esophagus for food to pass through. A bird can breathe through an open mouth, too, by simply opening his mouth and his glottis, and inhaling.

**WARNING**

The closeness of the glottis, esophagus, and choanal slit can sometimes be a real challenge to those just learning to hand-feed baby birds — they can inadvertently get the food down the wrong "pipe," with potentially disastrous results. For tips on feeding babies and other bird breeding challenges, see Chapter 13.

At one time, birds were thought to have only a primitive sense of taste, but that view has changed. Birds are sensitive to the same tastes we are: sweet, salty, sour, bitter, and umami. Sensitivity varies by species, and, as any bird owner will vouch, some birds show a sweet tooth that rivals any human's.

**TECHNICAL STUFF**

In most birds, the taste buds are located at the tip of the tongue. Ducks, however, carry some of their taste buds in their beaks, more commonly called a *bill.* The terms beak and bill can be used interchangeably, although hookbills — birds such as parrots — are generally described as having beaks.

## A bird's-eye view

Birds must be able to see what's safe to land on, find what may be good to eat, or spot a predator before it's too late, so as you may imagine, they have a great sense of vision.

Avian vision is good in both close-up and long-distance categories, and birds can and do see in color. In fact, when it comes to richness of color vision, they beat out cats, dogs, and humans. Birds possess four types of *cones*, the cells that determine visual acuity and color perception. Humans and cats have three types of cones and dogs only two.

TECHNICAL
STUFF

How do we know what birds see? Part of the answer is simple deduction, Watson. What good would all those vibrant feather colors be if birds couldn't see them? Some experts believe birds see even more colors than we do, which may explain why mating continues unhindered in species in which we can't see any difference between male and female — what looks the same to us may not look the same to birds. Good color vision may even be helpful when it comes to finding food. The ability to see some ultraviolet wavelengths allows birds to pick out fruits and flowers, which reflect this light better than do the surrounding leaves.

The eyes in most birds are positioned on either side of the head, not side by side as in humans, dogs, or cats. Although this means birds haven't as much range of *binocular vision* (objects seen simultaneously with both eyes), their range of monocular vision approaches 360 degrees, and they can achieve full monocular vision with a simple twist of the neck. The owl, on the other hand, has eyes positioned more in the front of the head, allowing for better binocular vision and accuracy for successful hunting, but also making it more important to really turn the head around in order to see the full 360-degree spectrum. And, no, they can't turn their heads around all the way!

When a bird wants to get a really good look at something, he cocks his head and focuses one of his eyes. In some birds, the eyes can move independently of each other — most clearly seen in toucans, but also in parrots, to a lesser degree.

Like dogs and cats, birds have a third eyelid, a semitransparent sheet that helps to protect the eye and keep it moist — it's even thought to function as a "windshield" while birds are in flight. Another interesting avian feature is the bird's ability to voluntarily adjust the size of her pupils, usually in a moment of excitement, in a display called *pinning* or *flashing*.

# The better to ear you with

You can't see the ears on your bird — birds have no external ear, as humans do — but they certainly do have ears, and they work very well. Protected by a soft swirl of feathers, the avian ear, like the human one, has three sections:

>> **Outer:** The outer ear is a short funnel that directs sound toward the eardrum.

>> **Middle:** The middle ear is where sound vibrations are picked up, amplified, and transmitted to the inner ear.

>> **Inner:** The inner ear transmits the impulses to the brain for decoding and handles balance, with the aid of semicircular canals.

Birds don't hear high- and low-pitched noises as well as we do, but within the range they do hear, they can discern more details. The song of a finch would have to be played ten times more slowly for us to be able to hear the richness and detail of sound a bird can.

Many parrots, especially cockatoos, cockatiels, macaws, and the African parrot species, love to have the area around their ear canal scratched (the ear covert feathers). Most also flip for a scratching of their soft facial areas and their armpits, too. (Or should we call them "wingpits"?)

# Beautiful, functional feathers

The crowning glory of any bird — and a contributor to extinction for a few species — are the feathers. These gloriously modified reptilian scales protect birds from the elements, keep them warm, attract mates, help put on impressive displays of territoriality, and, in most species, make flight possible.

It's hard to say which of these unique avian characteristics we, as humans, have appreciated more — flight or beauty. Every single feather is the embodiment of both, which is perhaps why humankind has coveted, collected, and worn feathers for as long as birds have had them.

Although less technological cultures may have made do with found feathers or feathers from the birds used for food, in the last couple of centuries society raised the pursuit of feathers to a brutal level, killing birds by the millions so ladies could have decorative feathers on their hats.

Fashionable feathers were big business at the turn of the 20th century. We found one vintage advertisement for a Southern California farm selling ostrich plumes for $2 to $5. Nowadays, though, the Migratory Bird Treaty Act makes it illegal to possess feathers of native species, even if you simply find them in your yard. Collecting or purchasing feathers isn't worth risking a fine of up to $15,000. (Because the ostrich is not a native species, ostrich feathers are still okay, and you can find them for sale in some locations or even order them directly from commercial ostrich farms.)

In Native American culture, eagle feathers are powerful symbols given to mark important milestones or to honor people for achievements. The U.S. Fish & Wildlife Service maintains the National Eagle Repository to provide eagle feathers to Native Americans who have a permit for use of feathers — for making religious or cultural objects, for instance — and proof of tribal enrollment.

## Variety

The feather (shown in Figure 8-3) is one of nature's most stupendous feats of engineering. Not only are feathers strong and lightweight, but they're also constantly being replaced. Imagine a modern aircraft with an automatic maintenance and part-replacement system — that's the only way to fully appreciate the seemingly effortless cycle of replacing worn or damaged feathers with new ones. Quite an incredible system, isn't it?

**FIGURE 8-3:**
Different feathers have different jobs: Some provide insulation, while others provide protection or the ability to fly.

*Photograph courtesy of Lisa D. Myers, Feathered Follies (Concord, California)*

Although feathers vary from species to species — compare the feathers of a penguin with the plumes of an ostrich to see how much — the birds we keep as pets have three basic feather types:

>> **Down feathers:** The soft, short down feathers, usually closest to a bird's skin, serve to keep the bird warm. Down feathers are the first feathers a baby bird has, and they keep him warm as he grows. That down feathers keep birds warm should come as no surprise: Humans have used the down feathers of birds, especially geese, in any number of stay-warm products, from comforters to jackets. On some species, a few of the down feathers are made to crumble: These *powderdown feathers* break into fine dust to aid in the bird's grooming.

>> **Contour feathers:** These feathers have down "puffs" at their base and are stiffer toward the end. Contour feathers cover most of the body, including the down feathers. Dr. T. J. Lafeber, a pioneering avian veterinarian, describes the relationship of the down feathers to the contours as similar to a lined windbreaker: The down feathers keep warmth in, while the contours keep wind and rain at bay.

Unlike the fur of mammals, which grows pretty evenly over the entire body, contour feathers are arranged in tracts, called *pterylae.* Between these tracts are areas of bare skin called *apteria.*

>> **Flight feathers:** The longest and stiffest feathers are those used for flight, and they're found both on the wings (where they're called *remiges*) and on the tail (where they're called *rectrices*). The flight feathers are really modified contour feathers — specifically evolved to get the bird up into the air and help keep him there. These feathers have little or no down at the base, and the wing feathers are shaped unevenly, with longer crosspieces, called *barbs,* on the backward edge, called the *inner vane.* (The forward-facing side is called the *outer vane.*) The shaft running through the center of the feather is called the *rachis* (pronounced *ray*-kiss). Tail feathers, for the most part, have even lengths of their barbs on the right and left side of the vane. If you look at a flight feather closely, you'll notice threads (called *barbules*) protruding from the barbs. On each barb, the barbules on the upper edge have *hooklets,* and the ones on the lower edge have ridges for catching the hooklets. The result is a strong, smooth, interwoven surface perfect for supporting flight.

A feather may contain up to a million tiny barbules. When you watch your bird grooming his feathers, you see him rearranging the location of the feather, as well as pulling the feathers through his beak gently, to help relock hooklets that may have popped loose — kind of like Velcro that came unattached and that needs attention.

The number of flight feathers a bird has depends on the species, as does the number and shape of the tail feathers. A macaw, for example, has 22 flight feathers on each wing (10 primary, as counted from the end of the wing inward, and 12 secondary), along with a dozen long tail feathers. Compare those long feathers with the short, square tail of the African grey, which would be nearly obscured when his wings are folded if it weren't for the bright red color contrasting with the gray plumage of the rest of the bird.

The color of a bird's feathers doesn't come entirely from pigment, such as melanin, which is what colors the skin and hair of humans and other mammals. In birds, some color is determined by the physical makeup of the feathers. *Melanosomes*, cells that produce pigment, affect color based on the way light bounces off of them. The layers of keratin that make up feathers also reflect light in certain ways. Both melanosomes and keratin make the difference between feathers that look dull or flat and feathers with a high-gloss appearance.

New research suggests that feathers arose 100 million years before the existence of birds. They may even have been present on the very first dinosaurs. That means feathers originated at least 250 million years ago, well before birds were a twinkle in Mother Nature's eye. This was a time when life on land was recovering from the most devastating mass extinction ever. The new reptiles differed from previous ones in that they walked upright instead of sprawling; they had bone structure suggesting rapid growth and possibly warm-bloodedness; and on the mammal side, hair had developed. The advent of feathers may have occurred to provide insulation for their new physiology and ecology. Interestingly, a single genome regulatory network drives the development of reptile scales, bird feathers, and mammal hairs.

## Maintenance

The gift of flight doesn't come without a price, and for birds that means a large part of their time is spent keeping feathers in fine shape, a behavior called *preening* (see Figure 8-4). Birds are so dedicated to keeping every one of the couple of thousand feathers they have in good order that they make even the neatest human seem like a slob by comparison. Preening is an essential maintenance behavior, and is such a large part of a bird's life that it's even part of socializing — when they're done with their own feathers, they work on those of their mates, often in a most loving fashion.

**TECHNICAL STUFF**

Birds use their beaks to tend their feathers, but they also get help from an oil gland, called the *preen gland,* and from a specialized feather called a *wick feather,* which helps bring out the gland's oils to an accessible location for grooming and preening purposes. The preen gland is located at the base of the tail in most birds but is absent in the hyacinth macaw and the Amazon parrots. The grooming and preening behavior produces powder and dust, too — as they groom and preen their powderdown feathers, the ends of those feathers crumble into chalklike white powder, which is distributed over the body. The *powderdown* feathers are typically located on the flanks and over the hips of most birds. The oils from the preen gland and the powder produced from the down feathers help to keep all of the bird's feathers well-groomed and clean.

**FIGURE 8-4:**
Preening is both a grooming activity and a social behavior.

*Photograph courtesy of Melody Hennigh, Busy Beaks Academy (Oakley, California)*

Birds from more arid environments — such as some parts of Africa and central Australia — are often "dustier" than rain-forest birds such as Amazons, conures, and macaws. Some cockatoos are so dusty that snuggling them for a couple of minutes against your chest can turn a dark shirt nearly white with powder residue. This fine dust is the reason people with allergies (especially to feather dust and dander) or asthma should think twice about acquiring these species as household residents.

It's not enough to merely go over every feather individually — it's also important that each feather be nudged into its proper place, to ensure the smooth lines needed for flight.

No matter how fastidiously a bird cares for his feathers, they do eventually become worn or damaged. The bird's body then switches into replacement mode, and the damaged feathers drop, or *molt*. Molting happens typically once or twice a year, generally in spring and fall, when the rapid lengthening or shortening of the days triggers the change.

TECHNICAL
STUFF

The words *sitting duck* apply perfectly to a bird who has lost all his flight feathers at once — which is why nature doesn't work it that way. Flight feathers are usually molted only one or two at a time. Feathers are even molted in many species symmetrically; that is, the same one or two flight feathers that are missing on one wing will be missing on the other, to keep the bird on an even keel when flying. You can often see this when you look up at a turkey vulture flying overhead. Pretty nifty design, if you ask us!

WARNING

*Feather-picking* (feather-damaging behavior), a bird's destruction of his own feathers, isn't a disease, but a clinical sign. This vexing problem could signal poor health or diet or be a response to stress or other behavioral factors. In some situations where it has been present for a long period of time, it can be an established behavior of value for an individual bird — it's just a thing that they like to do. (For the latest on feather-damaging behavior, see Chapter 12.)

## A leg to stand on, times two

As magnificent a gift as flight is, it's easy to overlook the interesting and well-developed structures supporting a grounded bird — legs and feet. And that's a mistake, because those limbs and their appendages are especially interesting and useful in many birds.

## UP, UP, AND AWAY

Birds are able to fly for the same reason planes do, and that should come as no surprise, because plane designers have always drawn inspiration from birds. Wings are shaped in what's called an *airfoil,* with the surface more curved on the top edge than the bottom. Air flows faster over the top than under the bottom, and the difference is what creates *lift* and draws the wings (and the bird or plane) upward.

By adjusting their wings (in much the same way flaps are adjusted on planes), birds are able to control the amount of lift and move higher or lower as they need to.

Members of the parrot family — and that includes both the tiniest budgie or parrotlet and the largest macaws — have not one but two pairs of opposable toes, a setup called *zygodactyl* (see Figure 8-5). Bird toes are numbered from the inner to outer, and parrots have numbers 1 and 4 pointing backward, and numbers 2 and 3 pointing forward. This design is ideal for climbing and grasping, allowing parrots to use their feet like a hand. Because so much is made of the opposable thumb of our species, maybe we should be wondering why such smart birds as the zygodactyl parrots aren't making pets out of *us!* (Truthfully, this does seem to occur in many households, where the parrot truly has successfully "trained" his owner exactly how, when, where, and why to obey his every desire.)

**FIGURE 8-5:**
A parrot's opposable toes are invaluable when it comes to perching, climbing, and grasping objects.

*Photograph courtesy of Lisa D. Myers, Feathered Follies (Concord, California)*

Canaries, other finches, and pigeons have a foot designed strictly for perching and walking. Called an *anisodactyl foot,* their number 1 toe is pointed backward, with the other three pointing forward. Ducks and geese are also anisodactyl, but they have webbing between their second, third and fourth digits. (The latter type of foot is called *palmate,* meaning that the front toes are united by the webbing, giving them the appearance of an outspread hand.)

With no feathers on their feet, wouldn't birds like a nice pair of slippers? Not really, because they would interfere with another of the many functions of the feet: temperature control. In cold weather, birds decrease the amount of blood circulation to their legs and feet to preserve body heat. In warm weather, they increase blood circulation to their feet and legs (and beaks, too), making them feel quite warm to our touch and allowing the excess heat to be released. The core body temperature of most birds ranges from 103°F to as high as 105°F or more — so it's not surprising that the beak and feet of our birds feel hot or warm to us from time to time.

The nails of pet birds are more like a dog's than a cat's — designed for traction and gripping, not for defense.

Nails (also known as *claws* or, in birds of prey, *talons*) wear down naturally in the wild because of the variety of perches and high levels of activity — neither of which are part of most pet birds' lives. Abrasive perches help to blunt the nails of pet birds, but most still need to have nails shortened from time to time. (For more on perches, see Chapter 4; nail-trimming details are in Chapter 7.)

# Finding Your Inner Bird

To the casual observer, the outer bird most clearly reflects changes made to enable flight — smooth lines; strong, lightweight feathers; and a beak to replace the heavy teeth of mammals. But inside, just as many adjustments have evolved to meet the unique demands of the avian lifestyle.

## Them bones, them bones

Perhaps no part of the amazing creatures we call birds has adapted more rigidly to the demands of flight than the skeleton and the bones that form it. So restrictive are the anatomical requirements of flight that the structure of birds is pretty much the same, from the smallest flit-about finches to the largest flightless ostrich.

Strangely enough, it's that rigid adherence to the demands of flight that led to the diversity of birds — with flight, birds could (and did) end up everywhere, continents and isolated islands alike. And after they were there, they changed to better fit the niche in which they found themselves. Beaks show perhaps the greatest diversity, with each species adapting over time to develop a beak that made eating what was available easier. Some birds — such as the ostrich, emu, and cassowary — adapted to their new homes so much that they gave up flying entirely, while penguins adapted the movements of flight to swim through water. Fascinating bunch, the birds!

### A tiny bit of history

The original model for birds was *Archeopteryx*, a reptile with teeth, a long tail, a short spinal column, hands at the ends of the wings, and the feathers that would remain as standard issue on all the birds to follow. The creature already featured some skeletal developments — a wishbone on which to center wings and a foot for perching, with the opposable toe (called the *hallux*) seen in many birds today, such as canaries and other finches.

Time improved on this bird blueprint, with key changes that would reduce weight and increase maneuverability. Gone were the teeth, the tail, and the hand (although their skeletal reminders would remain). The age of the modern bird had begun.

## Modern improvements

Two main skeletal improvements can be seen in the modern bird's bones — there are fewer of them, and they're lighter in weight.

The old song that goes, "The hip bone's connected to the thigh bone . . ." would have to be modified if you were singing it about birds. That's because in many places, the bones aren't connected so much as fused together. Although the hip bone is still connected to the thigh bone of birds, you can find single bones where two or more bones once were in the legs, as well as in the spinal column and pelvis, producing new arrangements that had to be given new names.

**TECHNICAL STUFF**

One example of this fusing is in the legs, where the *tibia* (lower leg) bone has fused with the upper collection of *tarsal* (ankle) bones. The name for the resulting assembly: the *tibiotarsus*. Farther down the leg, the lower layer of tarsal bones (two horizontal rows of bones in human ankles) have been fused with the *metatarsal*, producing the *tarsometatarsus*. The bird's ankle joint technically would be called the tibiotarsal-tarsometatarsal (or intertarsal) joint. Is that a mouthful, or what?

The fusing of some bones may have occurred just to decrease weight, but the combined bones of the spinal column have another purpose as well. Although the spine of the bird isn't as flexible as ours — you won't see birds bending at the waist to do lateral toe-touches — what they lost in movement they more than made up for in strength. Their modified shoulders and spine are perfect for withstanding the strains of flying.

The strength of the bird's skeleton is even more remarkable when you realize that many of the bones are *pneumatized* (filled with air). This adaptation lightens the weight of the skeleton, increasing the mobility and flight potential of the bird — without sacrificing strength.

The skeletons of baby birds grow rapidly, another necessary adaptation in a creature who must become mobile quickly. A typical blue-and-gold macaw hatches weighing less than an ounce, and in about ten weeks weighs just over 2 pounds. This incredible increase in weight (a 50-fold growth) is supported in part because of the rapid growth of the skeleton.

# Live and breathe: The cardiopulmonary system

The breathing and circulatory system of the bird is another model of ultralight efficiency — one so good at what it does that it can sometimes get a bird into trouble.

The respiratory tract starts with the *nares* (nostrils) and sinus cavities, and proceeds deeper into the bird with the *trachea* (windpipe), lungs, and air sacs. Whereas human lungs have dead-end areas in the lungs for passing oxygen into the blood through the *alveoli* (air sacs in the lungs), birds have evolved to allow a continual circuit of air flow through their respiratory tracts.

Birds have a four-chambered heart — similar to the human heart — but it beats a heck of a lot faster, which is why taking a pulse isn't typically part of a bird's physical exam by the veterinarian. The heart rate of birds can reach as high as 1,000 beats per minute (in the case of hummingbirds), with the typical heart rate of the budgerigar at 675 beats per minute and the Amazon parrot at about 390 beats per minute. Their arterial blood pressure is also much higher than what we may wish for ourselves — two to four times the human norm. Compared to our own, the respiratory and circulatory systems of the bird are strong, efficient, and supercharged — and it's all an adaptation to allow for maximal absorption and delivery of oxygen to meet the demands of flight.

**WARNING**

The mechanisms that allow birds to collect oxygen so efficiently can also put them at risk in our home environments. Fumes from such common household products as nonstick cookware or cleaning supplies can kill a bird who inhales them — and death can come quickly. (For more on fumes and other household hazards, see Chapter 20.)

# Ya gotta eat: The gastrointestinal system

Like everything else having to do with the bird, the digestive system is lightweight, highly efficient, and designed for maximum mobility.

The first difference you notice is the lack of teeth. Birds don't have time to chew food, nor do they need the extra weight that teeth represent. They swallow their food rapidly, just in case danger requires a quick exit from the feeding site.

From the beak, the food moves down a tube called the *esophagus* and into an organ at the base of the throat called the *crop*. Crops are particularly obvious in babies being hand-fed (because they have fewer feathers to hide them and because crops are larger on baby birds than on adults, relatively speaking) or in birds who have really pigged out on a big meal.

Noted for their intelligence and friendliness, Welsummers, like this rooster, are named for the Dutch village where they were developed.

This scarlet macaw is preening, a grooming behavior that involves using the beak to straighten and clean the feathers and distribute protective oils.

Because male and female Eclectus parrots are so different in appearance, it was once thought that they were different species. The finely textured feathers are bright green on males; females are a rich red with a violet-colored belly and a black beak.

Gouldian finches, native to Australia, are widely admired for their colorful plumage. Both sexes are brightly colored, with red, black, or yellow heads, but males have a purple chest while females have a paler mauve chest.

The strikingly beautiful blue-and-gold macaw hails from South and Central America. With proper care, they can live 70 years or more.

A single glance is enough to see how the rainbow lorikeet got its name. They're medium-size parrots with bright, multicolored plumage

Don't let the parrotlet's small size fool you — these are bold and spirited parrots, just as much fun to live with as their larger cousins. Parrotlets are affectionate but feisty and will demand to have their own way if you aren't good at negotiating with them.

Strikingly beautiful galahs, also known as rose-breasted cockatoos or pink-and-gray cockatoos, are intelligent and affectionate, bonding closely to their people. With good care and proper nutrition, they can live into their seventies.

Budgerigars, also known as budgies or parakeets, originated in Australia and are known for their good looks and charm. They're among the most popular pet birds in the world.

Named for the rosy patch of coloring on their faces, peach-faced lovebirds are amusing, active, and pleasant friends who love attention. A single one will love you, but a pair will give all their attention to each other.

The hyacinth macaw, dressed in a stunning array of cobalt-blue feathers, is the largest of the parrot species, with an equally large personality. They're rarely seen as companions because of the expense of acquiring and keeping them. These two were photographed in the wild in Brazil.

The Maximilian's Pionus, the largest of the *Pionus* species, can live 40 years or more. They are fun-loving and affectionate, enjoy learning tricks, and can become good talkers.

Canaries come in hundreds of types but are best known for their singing ability — at least in the male of the species.

When first born, baby parrots, such as this parrotlet, are naked, blind, and helpless, but being lovingly handled by humans helps prepare them for their eventual families.

Domestic pigeons are smart, friendly, and beautiful and can thrive as family pets or in aviaries with doves or other pigeons for companionship.

This Sebastopol goose stands out for its long, white, curly feathers.

The crop functions as a temporary storage organ and is where the initial phases of digestion begin. When your bird regurgitates food for you to share — because he loves you so — this is where the food comes from.

Not all birds have crops. Some who don't include the *ratites* (ostriches and emus), penguins and many other fish-eating species, and owls. All parrots — from budgies and cockatiels through macaws — have crops, as do canaries and other finches. However, the crop may not be so obvious on the small birds in the latter group.

The crop empties slowly, sending food to the *proventriculus* (glandular stomach). Right behind the proventriculus is the *ventriculus* (gizzard), which does the grinding work teeth would do — if birds had teeth. The small and large intestines are where digestion is completed and nutrients are absorbed, in pretty much the same way as the human system works.

One long-lived myth is that birds need to be fed *grit* (particles of rock or minerals) to help their gizzards do the grinding. Not so! In fact, grit can cause problems in birds who ingest too much of it. (For the nitty-gritty details, see Chapter 6.)

Most birds prefer to eat a bit at a time, although some (like some people) would rather eat a ton at one sitting, or just eat all the time. (And yes, like people, birds get fat, as we discuss in Chapter 11.) A condor, on the other hand, will settle down on a yummy carcass, gorge until he can barely fly, and may not eat again for a few days. The difference is that most birds have a constant supply of food, whereas scavengers like condors must eat when they can.

The end result of the digestive system is the part bird lovers like least — the elimination of *droppings* (waste), which are released (as are eggs in female birds) from a single organ called the *cloaca* (vent). The cloaca is another example of design efficiency — why have two or three openings when one will do?

Not surprisingly for a creature who needs to stay light, waste products are constantly dumped without regard to where they fall (as anyone familiar with pigeons or seagulls will vouch). A bird's capacity varies according to size — a budgie may pass dozens of small droppings a day, whereas the largest birds hold it longer, producing larger droppings less frequently.

Their wild cousins may not care where or when the bombs fall, but pet birds can be choosy about where they go. Larger parrots, with their increased holding capacity, can learn to go on cue in a place of your choosing, such as in a wastebasket or on a paper plate. (For training tips, see Chapter 7.)

Bird droppings may look like a mixed-up mess to us, but they have three distinct components: feces (from the gastrointestinal tract), urine (clear liquid from the kidneys), and the white *urates* (concentrated uric acid from the kidneys). Birds do urinate without defecating and defecate without urinating.

Many times, what bird lovers interpret as diarrhea is really just droppings with a high volume of urine in the mix — the result, perhaps, of eating a food with high water content, such as fruit. On the other hand, excessive urinary output can also be seen in birds with diabetes or kidney disease. If your bird is truly urinating in excessive amounts, he needs to see a veterinarian. True diarrhea warrants a veterinarian visit, too.

## IS ANYTHING BUGGING YOUR BIRD?

Worms, mites, lice — how much should you worry about the effect of parasites on your pet bird? The answer: Not too much, overall. Parasites are not only a lot less common a problem than most people think, but the actions some bird lovers take to get rid of pests that don't exist in their birds in the first place can also put their pets at risk.

Birds who come from reputable sources (see Chapter 3 for more on that topic) are very unlikely to arrive in your hands with parasites, either internal (such as worms) or external (such as mites and lice).

For the most part, as long as your healthy bird isn't exposed to other birds whose health is unknown, he realistically shouldn't be picking up parasites. Mites, lice, and worms don't just materialize out of thin air.

Regular deworming, use of lice sprays, or exposing pet birds to inhaled toxins for their "protection" from mites can be bad news for your bird. Brian sees more pet birds with problems caused from over-the-counter parasite treatments than he sees birds who actually have or had parasite infestations.

Yes, birds can and do get parasites on occasion. If you suspect your bird has them, don't scattershot a "fix" with some over-the-counter concoction. See your veterinarian for proper diagnosis and treatment, as well as advice on how to prevent reinfestation. There are different types of lice, different types of mites, and different types of intestinal parasites — and there are different types of treatments for these problems, too. An accurate diagnosis, combined with accurate treatment and accurate prevention, should not only safely eliminate the problem but also prevent a reappearance of the pests.

Chapter **9**

# A Preventive Care Approach to Your Bird's Health

I n recent years, the emphasis in human health care has increasingly moved toward preventive care — starting healthy, getting healthy, and staying healthy. That means eating right, being fit, and taking care of little problems before they become big ones. This approach is universally recognized as the better way to go, enhancing quality of life and saving time, misery, and money along the way.

Veterinarians also know the value of preventive care. In dogs and cats, vaccinations against infectious disease have long been standard, and obesity prevention and regular dental care, including professional teeth cleanings, are increasingly recognized by pet lovers for their long-term health benefits to pets.

But what about birds? In the avian world, preventive health care is also a priority: It's good medicine and common sense, asked for by savvy bird lovers and practiced by the veterinarians who share their clients' love of winged companions. Preventive care is proper care, for all the reasons named for humans, dogs, and cats, and for some reasons that pertain to birds alone.

In this chapter, we offer the basic rules of preventive medicine for your pet bird and fill you in on your role and your veterinarian's role in preventive health care. An ounce of prevention truly is worth a pound of cure — and then some.

REMEMBER

Preventive care sometimes requires a change of mindset. If you tend to get help only when you notice your bird is ill — or even wait a day or two to "see if he gets better" — we strongly encourage you to review the basic tenets in this chapter and take them to heart. Over the course of your bird's lifetime — a longer one, most likely, with preventive care — you'll enjoy your bird more, improve his quality of life, and probably save money. Is this a deal, or what?

REMEMBER

Although this chapter focuses primarily on preventive medicine, a preventive-care approach to keeping a bird physically and mentally sound reaches into every page of this book. We touch on some of the most basic strategies in this chapter, such as nutrition, but we urge you to also look at specific chapters for more detailed information. More nutrition information, for example, is in Chapter 6. Getting the right bird from the right source is the most basic of preventive-care measures, and we cover that topic in Chapters 2 and 3.

# Understanding Why Preventive Care Is the Best Care

Preventive care is important for everyone, humans and animals alike, but for pet birds, it's downright essential. Intelligent as they are, as human as they may seem to us, pet birds are different from us in some very important ways. Not only are they *not* human, they're not even mammals, like many of our other pets. Animals who are preyed upon often can react differently, and may be less prone to visibly display signs of illness in the manner you're used to seeing.

You may have heard that prey animal species tend to hide signs of illness, but Brian would argue a little differently. Although many birds do show signs of illness differently, they still show signs — if you know the bird well. It's really no different from when your best friend says she's fine, but you *know* she's not, so you press her for more information. If you really *know* your bird well, subtle changes you observe can take on much greater meaning. In a nutshell, a key component of early recognition of problems requires a healthy and mutual relationship between you and your bird. Good friends just know one another well!

REMEMBER

How do birds fly? How do they eat? What can they see, hear, and taste? Why don't they have teeth? If you want to know more about how your bird's body operates, check out Chapter 8 for a quick-and-easy guide to the basic bird.

# What your bird won't tell you — and why

"I don't know what happened — he was fine yesterday" is one of the saddest comments Brian hears in his practice, usually said over a pet bird who's dead — or soon will be. Death or deadly illness is plenty sad, but many of these tragedies are often made worse because they could've been prevented. The crucial point we need to impress on you is that a bird who's dead or dying today probably *wasn't* fine yesterday. Yesterday, he was most likely showing subtle signs of illness, and these signs may not have been recognized. Although hiding signs of illness can and does occur, the key lies in the details. The goal is to pick up subtle signs early, which you can do if you're familiar with your bird and know when things just aren't right.

Humans don't typically have a habit of hiding signs of illness. Any parent can tell in an instant when a child is starting to get sick, and many of us live with mates for whom even an ingrown toenail is cause for much moaning. Dogs don't see much need to hide how they feel, either: Whining is a trait known to both canine and human sufferers alike.

Whining is fine when you're a social animal and at the top of the food chain. When you're closer to the bottom, though, outwardly evident signs of illness may draw attention you surely don't want. This difference is what some folks mean when they refer to the tendency of prey species to mask or hide their illnesses.

**TECHNICAL STUFF**

Yes, this is a bird book, but we can hear the more curious among you wondering where cats fit in. Cats can also be adept at hiding illness, for the same reasons as birds: Although cats are predators, they're also small enough to be prey. For more on cats and dogs, you can't go wrong with *Cats For Dummies*, 3rd Edition, by Gina Spadafori, Dr. Lauren Demos, and Dr. Paul D. Pion (Wiley), and *Dogs For Dummies*, 2nd Edition, by Gina Spadafori (Wiley).

At least in principle, if you're a prey animal species (or a smaller predator species), showing signs of illness is sure to capture the keen-eyed attention of something with big teeth and a hearty appetite. In some social groups of prey animals — such as herd animals — signs of illness will also get you kicked out of your peer group. Your friends and family know you're destined to be someone's dinner, and they don't want any part of *that*. Been nice to know you. *Hasta la vista,* baby. Survival of the fittest? Don't you doubt it for a second.

Sure, it makes more sense for pet birds to communicate their health problems to their largely clueless human caretakers, but that's not the way the world works. Most pet birds are only a few generations removed from the wild — often not even that — and their survival instincts don't become rewired just because they're now living in a cozy home with humans. The difference, however, is that when you really *know* your bird, and when your bird recognizes that he's a part of your flock at home, you can and will come to realize that birds convey a lot more than we used to think. Brian can recall many clients who had presented their bird because they just *knew* something was wrong, even though there was nothing outwardly apparent. One client was convinced that his grey parrot was ill, merely because the morning social routine of having a bit of oatmeal was suddenly no longer appealing. And he was right! His bird was just entering the critical phase of right-sided heart failure.

REMEMBER

Birds will do anything to hide their illness, particularly during social interactions or in social settings. They can't help it — such secrecy has been a key survival skill for eons, and we humans can't change it. The difference will appear when they're at rest or one-on-one with you, if you have a good and healthy relationship with them. Too often when a bird is obviously sick, even to people who don't know her, she is *very* sick — so much so that she can't hide it anymore, and it's going to be a hard, expensive fight to save her, if she can be saved at all.

## More arguments for preventive care

Your bird's subtle early signs of weakness are among the most important arguments for preventive care, but they're surely not the only ones. Let us list a few more, just in case you're not yet convinced.

### Scarcity of urgent care

A veterinarian with more than the most basic knowledge of avian medicine is not always available. Emergency clinics are mostly geared toward dog and cat care. If you happen upon a veterinarian in an emergency clinic who's well qualified to handle an avian medical crisis, you can count yourself lucky, because it's not the norm. Even if you develop an excellent relationship with an avian-savvy veterinarian, she won't always be available for emergency response. And trust us, if you let a health problem simmer, Murphy's Law dictates that it will come to a boiling point at night, on a holiday, on a weekend, or when your veterinarian is on vacation.

### Cost savings

Preventive care costs both time and money, we grant you that. Although it costs no more to feed a bird properly than to feed him poorly, other aspects of preventive care can ding your bank account. Proper husbandry, from the start-up costs of a safe cage to the time or money spent keeping your bird's environment clean, isn't cheap, nor are annual well-bird exams with necessary diagnostic or screening laboratory tests. Still, a good veterinarian can, in some ways, share the same motto as a car mechanic: "You can pay me a little now or pay me more later." Heading off illness is less expensive in the long run than trying to save the life of a bird in crisis. And besides, would you rather pay to keep your bird healthy and happy — and confirm that he is — or wait to pay to manage a medical crisis that may kill him (and your budget)?

High levels of veterinary care are also available for birds, from CT scans (as shown in Figure 9-1) to surgery to remove a foreign body from the gastrointestinal tract. That costs money.

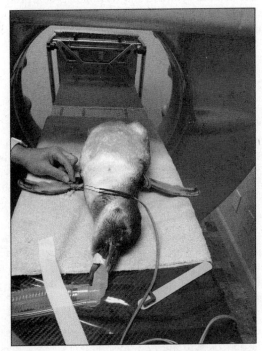

**FIGURE 9-1:** Birds can receive high levels of veterinary medicine. Here, a penguin gets a CT scan.

*Photograph by Brian L. Speer, DVM*

Humans have health insurance to help cover the cost of expensive surgeries or unexpected illness. Pet health insurance for dogs and cats has been around for at least 30 years, but it's only recently that coverage has been available for birds and other exotic pets. In January 2020, Nationwide introduced a plan to cover veterinary care for birds and exotic pets, reimbursing up to 90 percent of eligible expenses, plus an option for reimbursement of preventive care expenses. We hope other pet health insurance companies follow suit. We think pet health insurance is a must if you never want to face the choice between your money and your bird's life.

TIP

Check to see if pet health insurance is one of the benefits offered by your employer.

## Quality of life

If you have a chronic illness or deal with constant pain, you're well aware how those conditions can take the joy out of life. Just because a bird is hiding his illness doesn't mean he isn't feeling dreadful. It may be days, weeks, months, or even years before your bird finally gets so sick that he stops caring what happens to him and reveals the more obvious symptoms of illness. Misery has been his companion for a long time at that point — and we can think of no stronger argument for early medical recognition and intervention. Common and very manageable problems Brian sees in his practice include painful arthritis, circulatory disease, and a number of behavioral problems that can become problematic in terms of a bird's health and well-being.

**TECHNICAL STUFF**

## CAUSE OF DEATH: UNKNOWN

The Internet has turbocharged the good old rumor mill. Not a day goes by when we don't hear about the latest "bird-toxic" product. Although plenty of items in common household use, from cleaning supplies to cookware, can do your bird in (we cover the most common in Chapter 20), many times what a pet owner thinks has killed a bird is merely a coincidence. Nonetheless, the incorrect cause of death is too often reported as fact — and spread and spread — on the Internet.

This misinformation often starts when a bird owner doesn't realize she has a sick bird on her hands, because the pet is doing his best to behave "normally," a survival strategy as old as birds themselves. Something new is introduced to the household, and the bird is found dead. "Aha!" thinks the owner, "My bird was fine yesterday, and now he's gone. It must have been that new thing."

But what seems like a closed case is still a mystery, and detective work is the only way to solve it. Some people don't want to know why their birds are gone, others want to know, and some — like breeders or those with many birds — *need* to know in order to protect the rest of their flock.

If you want or need to know what killed your bird (and we strongly advise this), you need your veterinarian's help. A *necropsy* is an examination of the bird's body, an attempt to figure out what happened and why. Gruesome as it may seem, the procedure, also called an *autopsy* (in humans) or *postmortem examination,* is an important educational tool for you (you don't want to lose another bird in the same way) and possibly even an important new finding for the future of avian medicine.

If you don't want to know what happened, that's fine. But if you don't know, don't spread your assumptions — you could be wrong. Moreover, having that knowledge will bring you peace of mind, closure, and understanding that can help you avoid those haunting thoughts about what you could have done differently or better for your bird.

### Bottom-line pragmatism

Birds can be expensive to acquire, especially the larger parrots, with prices that can range into the thousands of dollars. If you've paid a couple grand for a Moluccan cockatoo or ten times that for a palm cockatoo, the cost of preventive care is relatively cheap insurance protecting your investment. Of course, the purchase cost of many of our pet birds pales when compared to the value of these birds to our families and our hearts. Considering the outstanding companionship even an inexpensive-to-buy budgie can provide, we'd like to think you wouldn't place your emphasis solely on the bottom line. But some people do — especially those for whom birds are a livelihood and who must be pragmatic to stay in business.

# Following a Three-Part Plan for Preventive Care

Here's some great news: Preventive care is easy, or should we say easier than the alternative — treating the effects of a full-blown illness. After you learn the basics, your bird is set — for life! Starting birds off right and keeping them healthy may seem a little boring, but it's far easier than fixing what's broken.

How easy? Real easy. In fact, we've boiled preventive care down to three easy-to-remember basic areas, outlined in the following sections.

Although the last part — "Working with the pros" — does entail seeking outside help, the first two parts are pretty much do-it-yourself. Learn what's right, set up a routine, and stick to it.

**WARNING**

Because we're telling you what preventive care *is*, we'd like to put in a word or two about what it *isn't*. Good preventive care does *not* include any attempts to treat or prevent illnesses that your bird may or may not have. A couple of examples: The all-too-common practice of adding vitamins, antibiotics, or pest-control products willy-nilly to your pet's daily rations or environment. Vitamins are no substitute for balanced and proper nutrition, and the indiscriminate use of antibiotics is never a good idea. As for pest-control products, breathing in toxins isn't a healthy way to live. Talk to your veterinarian about the concerns making you consider such measures, and work to get your bird on the right track to health.

## Starting with a healthy bird

Birds sold with price tags at the low end of the normal range for their species or free-to-a-good-home, "fixer-upper" birds are not always the bargain they seem to be. That doesn't necessarily mean you should avoid them, but it does mean that if you go forward with a purchase, do so with your eyes wide open. Ask yourself: *Why* is this bird a "bargain"?

Maybe because the seller cut too many corners to get that price down. Breeding and selling healthy birds is no small feat — it takes knowledge, proper facilities, attention to detail, and plenty of time, all of which are reflected in the price tag.

Healthy birds come from breeding facilities that practice good flock management, including strict adherence to the *closed aviary concept* (CAC). Briefly stated, the CAC dictates that no birds of unknown health status be introduced to healthy birds. New birds must be quarantined, and they must be screened for health problems — as the other birds already have been. It makes good, simple sense — if you have a group of birds of known, sound health and only bring in others just as healthy, the risks of infectious disease are significantly less.

When birds are transferred from the breeder to the retailer, it falls to the pet store to ensure that no new health challenges are introduced. All birds for sale should come from known, traceable, and reputable sources, and the birds should not be exposed to others who may be sick, such as those brought in for grooming or boarding (these birds must be kept separately from birds for sale). This procedure is easiest to accomplish in stores that acquire birds for resale from a controlled and limited number of sources — not just any person who wants to sell them a bird.

**WARNING**

Birds who don't come from such health-oriented, controlled, and documented higher-quality sources are much more likely to be ill (physically or mentally), even if they don't look sick at the time of purchase. Many of these birds are mass-produced pet birds of the more inexpensive species — budgies, finches, and cockatiels. Maybe you're figuring you can just replace a cheap bird who dies. You may even have bought from a store that encourages that practice — for them, replacing a sick or dead bird may be less expensive than the effort and costs required to sell healthy birds in the first place. We think it's particularly sad to consider that many of these little birds are purchased as children's pets and will die long before their wonderful potential as companions is recognized.

**REMEMBER**

Because birds are so good at concealing any sign of illness, your best bet for getting a healthy bird to start with is to buy or adopt from a store, rescue group, or person who has healthy birds, is committed to keeping it that way, and is willing to back up what they sell. Save yourself (or your child) the heartbreak by insisting on a healthy and higher-quality bird from the get-go. Be prepared to pay more for this bird — realistically, he'll be a bargain in the long run.

**TIP**

More on buying a healthy bird — including tips on getting one who's also well-socialized and friendly — is in Chapter 3. You can find our checklist of questions to ask when buying a bird in Chapter 17.

## HEALTH ISN'T THE ONLY ISSUE IN BIRD BUYING

Another reason to deal with the most reputable sources you can find is for the birds themselves. Bird-breeding establishments comparable to the much maligned puppy mills most certainly exist. In these puppy-mill equivalents, progressive health practices may be virtually nonexistent, leaving birds appearing healthy but primed for illness after being subjected to the stresses of shipping and handling. We have no quarrel with reputable commercial breeders producing birds for the pet trade, as long as the birds are treated with proper care and respect. And we encourage pet stores that carry birds to promote responsible breeding, adoption, nutrition, and care of them, and to support the same for reptiles, ferrets, and other small pets.

Remember that as a consumer, you wield the power of the dollar. Money talks! Deal only with those who share your love of birds by selling healthy, well-cared-for animals. The others will have to change to remain in business.

## Providing proper care and nutrition

Good routine care and proper nutrition help a healthy bird stay that way. And it's not hard to provide your bird with either one.

**TECHNICAL STUFF**

Good care is what the experts call *husbandry*. Husbandry involves setting up a safe and secure environment for your bird, one enriched by toys, food, and other materials to keep his mind and body busy. It also involves keeping everything clean — changing cage papers or bedding material, scrubbing perches regularly, and keeping food and water containers clean. Good husbandry involves good food and good care. Cleanliness is important, just like mom always taught you! Good husbandry practices promote good welfare for birds.

**TIP**

Everything you need to know about what to buy for your bird — what you need and what you don't — is covered in Chapter 4. How often and how to clean is covered in Chapter 5.

Feeding your pet bird properly is another essential part of husbandry, and it's one that is finally getting better, with more people every day getting the message about the best way to feed their birds. We can sum it up for you and for most of our pet parrot species: To a basic diet of primarily pellets from a reputable manufacturer, add fresh fruits and vegetable. Seeds are a treat, not a dietary staple.

TIP

The myth that seeds are the best diets for birds is one we debunk in Chapter 15. You'll want to read the other nine common bird myths, too — check your knowledge! And for a thorough look at avian nutrition, don't forget to visit Chapter 6.

## Working with the pros

Too often, veterinarians see birds only when the animals are sick. We can't stress enough that a reactive approach to medicine serves your bird poorly.

Developing a relationship with your veterinarian entails an initial well-bird examination, which will likely include a recommendation for some diagnostic tests. Such screening is intended not only to catch health or behavioral problems that can't be seen (but that can more easily be treated if diagnosed early) but also to establish a baseline for your bird's health, against which future changes can be measured. Good health, however, is *far* more than a barrage of negative or normal test results. Diagnostic tests are merely questions — they have to be asked at the right time, in the right manner, to answer the right question; all of that needs to be balanced with what the veterinarian notes when examining the bird and after talking with you, the new owner.

Your veterinarian is more than a "bird mechanic" — or at least he should be. He should also be a consultant on setting up and maintaining your bird's environment and on proper nutrition. He should be the person you start with when you need basic behavior advice. And he should be right on the spot to tell you the good things you're doing and to compliment and celebrate the health of your bird with you.

TIP

As you've no doubt guessed, Brian's a true believer in preventive care. With every client, he goes over a checklist of items, including obvious signs of good or poor health, as well as nutrition, behavior, training, enrichment, and general husbandry. His preventive-care checklist forms the foundation for Chapter 16.

TIP

A veterinarian who is experienced and up to date in avian care is one of the most important professionals in your bird's life, but there are others. A good trainer can be an asset, too. Some veterinary practices, such as Brian's, work regularly with trainers to make sure all their doctors and veterinary technicians have a good foundational understanding of the science of behavior. We talk about these professionals in Chapter 12. For those who prefer to avoid toenail trimming and, if necessary, wing clipping, the services of a bird-experienced groomer can be a lifesaver. Where to find one? We tell you in Chapter 7, along with providing tips for do-it-yourselfers. And finally, don't forget about pet sitters! Advice on finding the right one for your bird is also in Chapter 7.

# Finding the Right Veterinarian

Choosing the right veterinarian for a dog or cat can be a challenge. Selecting one for your bird, though somewhat more of a challenge, is less difficult than it was 20 years ago. Avian medicine is in many ways still growing, but there are now numerous veterinarians practicing in this specialized field.

Here a guide to the designations to look for after a veterinarian's name:

» Approximately 135 avian veterinarians are board-certified through the American Board of Veterinary Practitioners. They carry the designation ABVP (Avian practice).

» Approximately 35 avian veterinarians are certified through the European College of Zoological Medicine. They hold the designation ECZM (Avian).

» About 10 veterinarians down under are certified as fellows of the Australian and New Zealand College of Veterinary Scientists. They carry the FANZCVS (Avian Medicine) designation.

» A number of veterinarians are certified as zoological species specialists, which includes avian species, through the American College of Zoological Medicine. They carry the ACZM designation.

Veterinarians with these credentials have been recognized through a rigorous training and examination process as true specialists. The body of information available to them is growing and evolving, and what was considered standard practice even a few years ago may be outdated tomorrow. These specialists are in an excellent position to be most current. Other veterinarians may have a special interest in bird medicine and may actually be quite skilled and current in their knowledge; they just lack the recognized formal certification.

**REMEMBER**

Birds are vastly different from dogs and cats, and their health needs are, too. They need a veterinarian who stays current and who is dedicated to providing the very best in care for the birds she sees — and the very best in advice for the owner. To do so requires time — always in short supply — and commitment. You need a veterinarian who has dedicated a good portion of her time and energy to increasing her knowledge of avian medicine — and who knows that education is a process that never ends.

## Why "any veterinarian" may not be right for your bird

Think of veterinary school as a buffet line — a lot of courses on the menu, from which you choose enough dishes to get a well-rounded meal. On that buffet, canine and feline medicine are, in many ways, the meat and potatoes. Students interested in companion-animal species need to know a great deal about dogs and cats, because for most veterinarians, the majority of the patients they see either bark or meow. Specialties such as cardiology, dermatology, or avian medicine are side dishes, really. The pursuit of more knowledge in these areas is usually done in an internship or residency after a student earns a veterinary degree. Your basic veterinary graduates come out of school knowing a decent amount about dogs and cats (or horses, if they went the large-animal route), but they usually don't have more than beginners' knowledge of how to treat birds, reptiles, or other small pets, unless they specifically pushed hard for additional exposure beyond what's normally offered.

This limited education is not itself a problem — you can only fit so much into four years of veterinary schooling, after all. And good veterinarians soon realize that their time in veterinary school is only the beginning of a lifetime of learning. A sound basic education is the foundation upon which veterinarians can build their specialty practice, if desired.

TECHNICAL
STUFF

After graduation, veterinarians may choose to work with more experienced practitioners and expand their learning with continuing education courses. Some opt to continue their formal education, seeking to become what's called a *board-certified* or *boarded* specialist in a particular area of veterinary medicine (more on this in a bit). An informal way to improve knowledge: Many veterinarians discuss cases with more experienced or board-certified colleagues, including those well-known for their expertise, some of whom may teach at veterinary schools or colleges. All these choices build on the basic knowledge a veterinarian learns in school.

Despite the efforts of a good veterinarian to keep up with everything, even the most dedicated veterinarians don't have time to learn it all. They have to pick and choose, and if they don't see a lot of birds in their practice, avian medicine may be one of the areas in which they're less well-versed.

The situation is changing, fortunately. Because of the increasing popularity of birds and other exotic pets, such as reptiles, ferrets, rabbits, and hedgehogs, more veterinarians are becoming interested in providing the most up-to-date care possible for these pets.

For the bird owner, though, the situation can be hard to figure out — how do you really know what they know? Is the veterinarian who says he treats birds keeping up on current trends? Is he interested in keeping up?

## THE VETERINARY INFORMATION NETWORK

An increasing amount of the advanced learning your veterinarian is doing these days is online, such as that offered by the Veterinary Information Network (VIN), at www.vin.com. VIN is the first and still the largest online service for veterinary professionals, offering its subscribers searches of journal articles, electronic continuing education, and access to specialists and other colleagues who can help with tough cases. Brian serves as an avian medicine consultant for VIN. We admit to being proud of VIN (which was co-founded by Gina's *Cats For Dummies* writing partner, Dr. Paul D. Pion); we think the more than 73,000 veterinarians who are members show an understanding of the importance of keeping current with advances in their profession.

**REMEMBER**

A successful relationship with your veterinarian isn't the same for everyone. We like to measure it in a veterinarian's ability to engender confidence, engage in open discussion, and be willing to consult other colleagues or refer clients elsewhere for special treatment if necessary. Combined, these are the basics to building a powerful relationship between you and your bird's veterinarian.

The limitations of the human mind being what they are, Brian stopped seeing dogs and cats years ago because he felt he couldn't do right by them — he had become a "featherbrain." The condition is serious, in his case: He once couldn't remember off the top of his head how long dogs are pregnant, and when he did remember, he called it an "incubation period," as if dogs came from eggs. Brian's a great doctor for birds, but to help ensure the best for his clients who also have dogs, he encourages them to see a colleague with day-to-day experience in good canine medicine. When his family dogs or cats become ill, he takes them to see their own doctors!

## Special care for a special pet

The body of knowledge in avian medicine is sufficiently large and different enough from canine and feline medicine that we believe you must seek out a veterinarian who has made the commitment to care for avian patients properly, in a way that meshes best with your own ideas.

No consensus exists on what makes a "good" veterinarian, as far as pet owners are concerned. Some people choose a veterinarian based only on price and convenience, without considering the quality of care their pets receive. Other pet owners want their animals to be treated as they want themselves to be cared for, using all that modern medicine has available — no matter what the cost. And, of course, many other people are somewhere in between — they want to know all the options, even those they may not choose to pursue.

No matter what you're looking for in a veterinarian, we encourage you to find one who'll be willing to look beyond the symptoms — what veterinarians call *clinical signs*, or those that can be observed — and offer to help you to get to the bottom of your bird's health problems so an accurate course of treatment can be found. This kind of medicine is especially important with birds because symptoms can sometimes be misleading. A scattershot treatment of clinical signs may not be the best thing for your bird in the long run, and we encourage you to find a veterinarian who understands this and advises you of the same.

Does it seem as if we're pushing diagnostic tests? Perhaps, but given the nature of birds, these tests are sometimes all you can count on to figure out what's going on inside. Do all birds need all diagnostic tests, both for the diagnosis and the prevention of illness? Not necessarily. Good avian medical care is about common sense, judging relative risk factors, and, perhaps most important, tailoring care to best serve both you and your bird. Good avian medical care is *not* defined by the number of tests that have been ordered.

REMEMBER

What we're trying to emphasize: Be *proactive*, not *reactive*, and understand the lengths to which birds will go to appear healthy until it may be too late.

We also want to point out that proper care isn't just for top-dollar parrots: Less-expensive birds, such as finches or budgies, are sometimes considered second-class citizens when it comes to proper veterinary care, but we believe even less-expensive birds, like the pigeon in Figure 9-2, deserve appropriate medical attention.

REMEMBER

Time and convenience are important, and money, especially, is always a factor in veterinary care, which is still largely unsupported by any form of pet health insurance. But many times, preventive care from a knowledgeable and thorough veterinarian turns out to be a better bargain in the long run, and that's especially true when it comes to pet birds.

## Who's out there, and what are they offering?

If you accept the not-so-radical idea that the veterinarian caring for your bird should know more than the rock-bottom basics of avian medicine, then you're going to be looking for one of two types of practitioners — the person who sees a lot of birds and cares for them well, and the person who does all that and has extra certification to show for the time spent learning about birds.

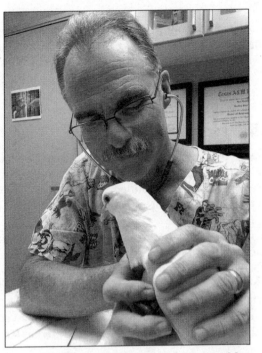

**FIGURE 9-2:**
This pigeon
needs the same
kind of preventive
medical care as a
more costly bird.

*Photograph courtesy of Elizabeth Young, Palomacy Pigeon & Dove Adoptions*

## TESTS? AW, DO WE HAVE TO?

What is all this diagnostic testing we keep mentioning? It's a revolution in avian medicine. Diagnostic tests include blood analyses and bacteria- or virus-identifying tests. They're essential in helping a veterinarian find out what a bird will do his best not to reveal — that he's sick with an illness that may, in time, kill him.

As part of a preventive-care regimen, laboratory diagnostic tests are constantly being refined and expanded, to improve their ability to catch diseases that cause so many problems among birds — and that are currently the focus of intense, ongoing research.

As important as diagnostic tests are to avian medicine — and to preventive medicine, in particular — they are just one part of the puzzle. He who does the most tests doesn't necessarily win: Preventive care for any pet has never been as simple as a vaccine or a test result. Your part in providing proper daily care and good nutrition, and your veterinarian's part in providing you with expertise, guidance, and "fine-tuning" of what you're doing to care for your bird is the heart and soul of preventive care.

Here's a shortcut for narrowing your list of possible candidates: Seek the advice and recommendations of the person you got your bird from, assuming he's a reputable and knowledgeable breeder or retailer in your area. These folks know very well who practices good avian medicine and are happy to steer you in the right direction.

## Board-certified specialists

*Board-certified specialists* of any kind are comparatively rare birds, indeed, especially if you don't live in a large urban area or near a college of veterinary medicine. Even more rare are board-certified *avian specialists*, especially those like Brian who limit their practice exclusively to the care of birds.

To become a specialist and to be entitled to add letters behind the DVM (Doctor of Veterinary Medicine), VMD (Veterinary Medical Doctor), or the comparable titles in use around the world, a veterinarian must do more than what was required to graduate from a veterinary college. Specialists are called *board-certified* because testing for specialty knowledge is handled and those extra letters given out by what are called *review boards,* such as the American Board of Veterinary Practitioners (ABVP) or the American College of Veterinary Internal Medical Practitioners (ACVIM).

In the case of a board-certified avian specialist in the United States, the managing entity is the ABVP, which grants titles in Avian Practice along with comparable ones in Canine and Feline Practice, Feline Practice, Dairy Practice, and other areas of expertise.

To become board-certified by the ABVP, a veterinarian must have been in practice for five years and must pass a rigorous credentialing process and then study for and pass a test on a species specialty area. "System" specialists, such as *cardiologists* (heart specialists) or *oncologists* (cancer specialists), work with all species, and earn their ACVIM letters after serving residencies and then passing their test. Only veterinarians who have been board-certified are allowed to call themselves "specialists." Currently, there are approximately 180 avian specialists around the world.

Brian is one of those specialists, and he has the extra letters after his name to prove it: Brian L. Speer, DVM, Diplomate, ABVP (Avian Practice), ECZM (Avian). What does all that mean? Board-certified individuals are awarded *Diplomate* status by whatever credentialing body is identified after the word — in this case, the American Board of Veterinary Practitioners (in the Avian Practice category), and also the European College of Zoological Medicine (Avian specialty).

## Other practitioners of avian medicine

If you can find a board-certified avian practitioner, is that the best choice for your bird? Not necessarily. Brian knows a great many non-boarded veterinarians who are marvelous with birds, up to date on their knowledge, and completely enamored of them as patients. And he knows a specialist or two whose "book learning" may be top-notch, but who aren't necessarily all that hot with the hands-on work.

So, how can you find the right veterinarian? Referrals from other bird lovers, breeders, or pet stores are grand, but even if you're just doing a web search for veterinarians in your town, veterinarians who see birds usually mention it on their websites or in their advertisements. If they're board-certified specialists, you'll see the letters after their name; if not, they can express a special interest in birds but should not claim to be a "specialist."

WARNING

Occasionally, you may come across an ad that seems to suggest credentials a veterinarian may or may not possess. "Special interest in the treatment of birds" doesn't say "specialist," but it gives that impression, doesn't it? The way to figure out what you're dealing with? Ask! There may be nothing at all sneaky intended — some veterinarians may be wonderful with birds whether or not they're board-certified avian specialists.

TIP

Call up a prospective animal hospital and ask how many birds are treated there and whether the veterinarian is a member of the Association of Avian Veterinarians (AAV). Membership in the AAV at least conveys a professional interest in keeping current on avian medicine. If a veterinarian is not an AAV member, does this mean that she doesn't know her stuff? Not necessarily, but it's sure an indication. The Association of Avian Veterinarians is one of our featured websites in Chapter 17, and the organization has a Facebook page.

REMEMBER

The veterinarian you choose should be comfortable with handling birds in a way that won't stress them unduly (for instance, by being sensitive to their body language, having a bird-friendly exam room, and offering favorite treats or toys to help them associate the veterinary visit with good things). She should see them routinely enough to be well-versed in their needs, and should be interested in keeping current on developments in avian medicine. One more trait we feel is important: willingness to discuss difficult cases with more experienced avian veterinarians.

## The cooperative approach: Vet to vet

In a perfect world, every local area would have at least one board-certified avian specialist, but that day will never come. In place of such a dream has sprung up a cooperative approach to avian medicine, where specialists like Brian spend a great deal of their time as consultants, helping colleagues with tough cases. It's a way of spreading the knowledge, and it saves a lot of feathered lives.

Some of Brian's workdays consist of nothing but telephone and Internet consultations with other veterinarians or with breeders or retailers — he may see only one patient "in the feathers." Although he's based in the San Francisco Bay Area, his clients and patients live all over the world.

REMEMBER

Because of the rapid pace of growth and change in avian medicine, perhaps the most important feature of the veterinarian you choose is that she be willing to reach out for help when she needs it. The help is out there — online veterinary services, board-certified specialists, telehealth, and more. Get a sense from any veterinarian you're considering as to whether she's willing to do the legwork for the sake of your bird's health.

# Chapter **10**

# Your Bird in Sickness — and Back to Health

lthough veterinarians have always tried to do their best for pet birds — relieving suffering is their job and their passion, after all — only in recent decades has the body of knowledge of avian medicine grown large enough to start being available and useful for the average pet bird owner out there. What a difference it's making in the lives of birds and those who love them! Species-specific details of medical treatments and diagnoses continue to become more commonplace, making what had been generic "bird tests and treatments" much more detailed and accurate. The old saying that "A sick bird is a dead bird" doesn't hold as firmly as it used to. Now, that saying is one of the myths we're happy to debunk in Chapter 15. Veterinarians knowledgeable about and experienced in bird care are saving birds who wouldn't have had a chance even a few years ago. And the revolution has just begun! Advancements in our knowledge of avian medicine, nutrition, and behavior continue to grow, promising an ever-brighter future for our avian companions.

**REMEMBER**

Although all practicing veterinarians are qualified to treat birds by virtue of the degrees granted to them by their alma maters and their governmental licenses, many — if not most — in general practice really don't have enough experience or detailed avian medical knowledge to provide the best medical care available for your bird. You need a veterinarian who is truly experienced and interested in avian care to ensure your bird benefits from the advanced knowledge now available. We explain who these bird veterinarians are and how to find one in Chapter 9.

Preventing illness is the best way to go — and you can find plenty about that in Chapter 9 — but illness and accidents happen even to the best-cared-for birds and the most vigilant of bird keepers. To give your bird a fighting chance, you must know a few first-aid basics and have a decent knowledge of the signs of illness. We cover most of the basics in this chapter, along with giving you an idea of where avian medicine is heading.

TIP

We've put other health problems in the chapters that seem to fit them best. Maladies of older birds such as arthritis and chronic malnutrition are in Chapter 11. Feather picking can have both medical and behavioral aspects to it, and we put our discussion of it and ways to approach that problem in Chapter 12.

# Remembering That Birds Are Birds — Not People, Not Dogs

Even though humans and animals have been companions for countless generations, the focus on the medical needs of *pets* is, to a certain extent, a modern development. Our priorities in centuries past were keeping ourselves alive and healthy, and then caring for those animals who worked for us. Few had the luxury of worrying about animals whose job was to keep us company — we needed to care for those animals whose job was to keep us alive.

Our farming ancestors worried about the horse who pulled the plow and took the family to town or to church; the dog who hunted, herded, or protected; or large livestock such as cows, sheep, or pigs who provided food, wool, and leather. The history of medical care for these animals — especially horses and dogs — is a long one.

Today many animals live with us as companions and are valued family members. Modern veterinary medicine reflects the changes in our perceptions of animals.

When Gina was researching the first edition of *Cats For Dummies* (which she coauthored with top veterinary cardiologist Dr. Paul D. Pion), she discovered that cats in the past had been given short shrift by the veterinary establishment. Cats were important for catching vermin, but they reproduced quickly, and one cat was considered pretty much the same as another. (Some people still hold this view, unfortunately, dumping cats with health or behavior problems in favor of a fuzzy kitten face.)

When cats came into their own as cherished companions, not much was really known about their medical needs — they were treated like "little dogs," without much regard to their distinctiveness. Cat lovers and veterinarians demanded better, and now a great deal of research is conducted on understanding and improving feline health and behavior. A growing number of veterinarians study further to become board-certified feline specialists, and no competent veterinarian these days would make the mistake of treating a cat like a dog.

This same scenario is playing out now in avian medicine. Although the veterinary community — along with behaviorists, retailers, manufacturers of supplies and food, and, of course, bird lovers — are busy keeping up (or catching up) with the changing information about bird care, some folks just aren't hearing the news.

## TRADITIONAL VERSUS COMPLEMENTARY MEDICINE

Call it anything you like — including "alternative," "Eastern," or "holistic" — *complementary medicine* is hot in both human and veterinary medicine. The growth of complementary medicine is in part a backlash against high-tech, impersonal, and often expensive care that sometimes seems more focused on the disease than the patient, but it's also about getting back to the basics of sound preventive care. Complementary medicine includes a wide range of treatment options, including acupuncture, traditional Chinese medicine, chiropractic, massage, and magnetic therapy.

In holistic medicine, the whole patient is the focus, rather than the specific disease. "Western" medicine tends to do better with acute illness, such as a bacterial infection, or with trauma, such as a broken leg. "Eastern" medicine's strength is in looking at the big picture of the pet's health, as well as helping to manage chronic conditions such as arthritis using such practices as acupuncture or Chinese herbal medicines.

Some veterinarians now embrace integrative care, combining conventional and complementary approaches. Brian is one of those who believes a healthy mix of both kinds of medicine is best. He's a firm believer in good nutrition, "whole-bird" preventive care, and behavioral counseling, but he's also quite capable with a scalpel or appropriate antibiotic when it's called for.

The American Holistic Veterinary Medical Association (AHVMA) is perhaps the best place to start finding out more about alternative veterinary medicine. You can learn more about the AHVMA at www.ahvma.org.

**REMEMBER**

As a bird owner and as a consumer of veterinary care and bird-related products and services, keep in mind one important concept. We put it large at the beginning of this section, but it bears repeating: Birds are birds, not people, not dogs (or cats, or iguanas, or any other creature you care to name). They react differently than other creatures do, both emotionally and physically. You have to think about them differently, too.

What does this mean in real terms? Don't expect illness to be the same in birds as it is in yourself or your other pets. Don't treat their signs with medicines meant for humans or other pets — you could be reading the symptoms entirely wrong, and even if you guess right, the medicine may not affect a bird in the way you hope it will.

**TIP**

Seek out the latest knowledge from experienced and up-to-date veterinarians, behaviorists, aviculturists, and even some specialized retailers. And keep learning!

# Understanding the Role of Home Care

We hope we've prepared you for the "bad news" of this chapter: We're not going to present a list of illnesses and their "cures." To do so would be irresponsible on our part. The correct diagnosis and treatment of disease is a job for someone who knows what he or she is doing, and that person is a veterinarian trained and experienced in avian medicine. As a bird owner you should be informed, and you should demand the best care for your bird and have all your questions answered. But you can't diagnose and treat avian illness from a book, from a phone call to your local pet shop, or from a website.

The role of home care — your role — is to recognize not only that your bird is ill but also *how* ill, and to act with appropriate speed. And after your bird has seen your veterinarian, you need to provide supportive care to help your pet regain his health.

**REMEMBER**

We're not trying to drum up business for veterinarians. But any person who dedicates years to studying how to identify disease and treat avian patients is going to be better at it than someone who was hired to ring up dog toys, cat food, and bird cages at a pet store or even someone who has bred birds for years and has picked up a body of knowledge that may be out of date or not as balanced in current medical fact as they think. Your bird's health relies on a partnership between you and the right veterinarian. Although any veterinarian who is willing to see birds could be called an avian veterinarian, as we mention earlier, not all are the same. Scrambling to find someone — anyone — willing to see your bird in an urgent situation is not where you want to be. Make sure you have your options thought out well before an emergency hits, and have those contacts available when you need them.

# Knowing First-Aid Basics

First aid is about saving a life, reacting in such a way as to remove the patient from immediate danger, and then getting more experienced help — a doctor, in the case of a human patient; a veterinarian, in the case of an animal one.

That old scout motto, "Be prepared," is the most important concept in first aid. Here are the basics of preparedness:

>> Keep the supplies you need on hand (see the nearby sidebar for the contents of an avian first aid kit).

>> Know what's life-threatening and what's not.

>> Know who to call, where to go, and how to get your bird there safely.

>> Know how to help stabilize your bird.

Seem like a lot to remember? It's not, really. If you find out what you need to know before you're called to act — and review it from time to time — you can react instinctively when you need to, and you may well be the difference between life and death for your bird.

## What qualifies as an emergency

One of Gina's veterinarian friends works in an emergency care clinic, and he's constantly amazed at the non-emergencies he's asked to treat at 2 a.m. He's even more astounded by the people who call about a genuine medical crisis and decide to see how their pet is doing in the morning instead of taking the time or spending the extra money for emergency care. Although it may — or may not! — be okay to wait a few hours on a dog or cat who "just doesn't seem right," waiting is probably not a good idea when your pet is a bird: If a bird is sick enough to look sick, he's probably very, very sick indeed.

**TIP**

The rule is: When in doubt, call.

Call your regular avian veterinarian or, if she's not available, an emergency clinic with experience in handling birds. (Be sure you've done your homework and have the numbers to call before you need to. We offer guidance in the section, "Who to call, where to go" later in this chapter.)

# THE HOME FIRST-AID KIT

The role of first aid is to stabilize your bird enough to get help, and to do that, you need to keep some basic supplies on hand. Many different containers will work for holding your supplies, including a sewing kit or small tackle box. Just make sure whatever you choose is easily portable — a handle is convenient, too.

The first thing to put in the kit is a first-aid book. We recommend *First Aid for Birds: An Owner's Guide to a Happy, Healthy Pet,* by Julie Rach and Gary A. Gallerstein, DVM (Howell). It's a small, inexpensive book that's easy to navigate and understand.

Tape the name and phone number of your veterinarian and of the emergency clinic inside the lid of your first aid box. Here's what else to keep inside:

- **An old towel:** Use this for restraining your bird (even well-mannered birds can become unmanageable when hurt).
- **Basic bandaging supplies:** Include an assortment of gauze pads and rolls. Instead of regular first-aid tape (which sticks to feathers), use bandaging tape such as Vetrap, paper tape, or masking tape.
- **Cornstarch or styptic powder:** Use to stop minor bleeding.
- **Needle-nose pliers, square-tipped tweezers, scissors:** Use needle-nose pliers to pull broken blood feathers if indicated (more on blood feathers in Chapter 8). Tweezers come in handy for all sorts of problems.
- **Cotton swabs and cotton balls**
- **Betadine:** This is both a soap and a disinfectant. Use it for cleaning and treating wounds.
- **Hydrogen peroxide:** Use this for cleaning wounds.
- **Heating pad**
- **Syringes with the needles removed and an eye dropper:** You can get syringes without needles from your veterinarian. Use both of these for irrigating wounds or administering fluids or medication.
- **High-energy liquid:** Try Pedialyte or a ready-to-mix glucose solution for feeding and restoring fluids.

You also need a carrier or travel cage for transporting your bird to the veterinarian. For more on cages and carriers, see Chapter 4.

That said, we have some general guidelines on what constitutes a life-threatening emergency, an urgent situation, or one that can wait until your regular avian veterinarian is available:

>> **Life-threatening emergencies** need to be dealt with immediately by a veterinarian. They include

- Bites or deep cuts

- Bleeding that can't be stopped

- Burns

- Poisoning

- Difficulty breathing

- Collapse

- Blood in droppings

- Straining to defecate or pass an egg

In these situations, you usually can't get help fast enough.

>> **Urgent situations** that should be seen by a veterinarian within a few hours of your noticing them include

- Eye injury

- Lack of interest in eating, especially if your bird also seems "puffed up"

- Sudden swellings

- Broken bones

- Diarrhea

- Direct contact with dog or cat saliva, regardless of whether the skin was broken

>> **Situations** that can wait until the next day or after the weekend include

- Undesirable behavior problems

- Feather picking

- Lameness unrelated to an obvious fracture

- Droppings with an abnormal color

- Excessive egg laying

**REMEMBER**

Watery droppings are not necessarily diarrhea. True diarrhea is droppings with poorly formed or loose feces in them. Watery droppings that aren't diarrheal are often the result of increased urine production, which can happen for perfectly healthy reasons such as eating foods with high water content, such as fruit. High urine output can also be a sign of disease, such as diabetes or kidney problems. If your bird's droppings always seem to have a high amount of urine in them, your bird needs to be checked out. For the lowdown on droppings — what goes into them, what's normal, and what's not — see Chapter 8.

» **Not-so-urgent situations** such as undesired behavior problems, feather picking, and lameness in the absence of an obvious fracture can wait until the next day or the end of the weekend. Remember, though, to watch your bird carefully. Because birds are so adept at hiding the signs of illness, your bird may be quite ill by the time you notice. If any of the more urgent symptoms we note earlier in this list pop up, get help. No matter what, bear in mind that a "wait and see" attitude is not appropriate for a sick bird. Call your veterinarian for guidance, at the very least. Kim's avian-expert veterinarian told her that if he wasn't available, local veterinary emergency hospitals would have him on speed-dial for late-night emergencies. If veterinary ERs don't have a bird veterinarian on staff or on call, ask them to keep your bird warm, quiet, and hydrated until you can get expert assistance. It's probably unfair to expect or demand focused bird medical expertise in most of these emergency clinics, but an interest in helping and a willingness to stop pain, stabilize fractures, and provide oxygen and other basic supportive care if needed could be the difference between life and death. After your bird is stabilized, she can be transferred for more detailed diagnosis and treatment as needed.

## Who to call, where to go

The wrong time to try to find veterinary care is when your bird is seriously sick or injured. After you have a veterinarian experienced in regular avian healthcare (see Chapter 9 for tips in finding one), you need to find out what arrangements are available with that veterinarian for emergency care.

**TIP**

Subtle clues that your bird may be sick include fluffed feathers, inactivity, talking or vocalizing less than usual, or sitting on the bottom of her cage. If your bird is shivering, sniffling, seems off balance, or is having trouble breathing, she needs help fast!

Some veterinarians take after-hours calls, some don't. Some trade coverage with colleagues the way many human doctors do — this week and weekend Dr. A is on call; next week, it's Dr. B.

Ask your veterinarian what arrangements he recommends, and if he — or a colleague — will not be available for after-hours care, ask him where you should go to find it.

Although emergency clinics are prepared to do their best for whatever furred, feathered, or scaly creature comes in, wild or tame, some are up front about the fact that they prefer to stick to dogs and cats. Finding this out in advance is obviously a very good idea.

Call your regular veterinarian and discuss the situation. If you need to choose an emergency clinic for a backup, call around if more than one exists in your area to find out how they feel about treating birds — and working with your regular veterinarian.

Gina's "dog veterinarians" worked hand-in-hand with Brian in a bird emergency, when one of Gina's dogs bit Patrick. The teamwork was admirable, with excellent care at the emergency hospital augmented by Brian's specialized expertise on the phone.

**TIP**

When you know who'll be able to treat your bird in an emergency, make sure you know how to get where you're going. The route to your regular veterinarian you surely know well, but how about to the emergency clinic? A dry run probably isn't necessary — unless you're new to the area and don't know your way around — but it's a good idea to know what streets will get you there quickly and without getting lost.

## What to do, in what order

When a pet is injured or ill, the first thing to do is take a deep breath. This is no time to panic!

Using the guidelines in this chapter, figure out the severity of the problem — whether it's immediately life-threatening. If you're by yourself, attend to first aid and then call your veterinarian to let her know what you're dealing with and that you're on your way. If you're not alone, one person can handle the first aid while the other calls the veterinarian.

Tell the receptionist you have an emergency and explain the problem as calmly and clearly as you can: the symptoms, the source of the problem (such as swallowing a lead weight or flying into a pot of boiling water), and the first-aid measures you've taken, if any. Calling ahead allows office staff to confirm that a veterinarian is available and able to see you — bumping you ahead of patients who aren't in as much danger as your pet — and will be prepared to deal with the specific problem endangering your bird's life.

**WARNING**

If possible, we suggest stabilizing your bird before calling or having someone else call as you do so, but this is just a basic guideline. You know what you can and can't handle and should adjust your response accordingly. If you don't know what you're doing in handling a sick or injured bird or aren't comfortable doing it — if you pass out at the sight of blood, for example — call your veterinarian *first*. She — or one of her staff — can help talk you through what you need to do.

**TIP**

Before treating or evaluating a sick or injured bird, you need to be able to properly restrain her in a towel. Become familiar with the steps for restraining your bird now by reviewing them in Chapter 7 and practicing a time or two. You simply can't count on your bird's cooperation when she's sick and scared.

**REMEMBER**

In general, you need to restrain your bird, offer first aid, put her in her carrier with as little handling as possible, and keep her warm as you head for the veterinarian's. Always provide comfort. Your bird likely knows you well, and this is what good friends do for one another in times of crisis.

**TIP**

Every bird should have a travel cage or carrier for emergencies. For help in choosing one, see Chapter 4. Kim used a small plastic cat carrier lined with a towel for her African ringneck, Larry. In a pinch, however, a cardboard box with a few air holes will do, as will a paper grocery bag for small birds. Brian has seen all these "carriers" — and a few more. Whatever you use, remove the perches and put a towel on the bottom to give your bird firm footing and a degree of cushion and warmth. Put another towel over the cage or carrier — darkness helps to keep the bird calm.

The following is the basic first-aid regimen for various emergencies. Do what you can — as long as you're not making matters worse, of course — and get your bird the help he needs right away.

>> **Bites:** Bite or claw wounds by the family cat or dog are always a potentially deadly situation, even if it doesn't seem so at first. Dogs and cats are able predators, and their jaws are quite capable not only of piercing the skin of a bird but also of crushing internal organs and breaking bones. Birds can bite each other, too. A young Larry once bit Kim's other bird, a kakariki named Spike, on the wing, an incident that required a veterinary visit. Even a bird who seems to have escaped an attack with "only" a small bite or scratch can fall victim to infection, as can birds with no visible signs of injury at all. If your bird is attacked, try to control the bleeding and contact your veterinarian. Your bird may need to be treated for shock, infection, or internal injuries, and she very likely should be started on antibiotics as soon as possible.

>> **Bleeding:** Restrain your bird and try to figure out the source of the bleeding. Apply direct pressure with a cool towel or your finger (thoroughly wash your hands first, of course). For bleeding from a toenail clipped too short or that has

been broken, apply a *styptic,* or blood-stop, powder to help with clotting (cornstarch or flour works fine in a pinch). For bleeding from a *blood feather* (a budding feather still in its clear protective sheath), you may need to get your needle-nose pliers and grip the feather as close to the base as possible, pulling it out smoothly. Apply pressure to the place where the feather was. Keep in mind that a broken pin feather hurts, and that pulling one out also hurts. Alternatively, you may be able to tie off a bleeding and broken pinfeather with thread and stop the bleeding that way. (If you don't feel comfortable pulling the feather yourself, get your pet to your veterinarian right away and allow him to handle it.) Many bleeding pinfeathers will clot and stop bleeding if your bird is merely placed in a dark carrier and rested, allowing heart rate and blood pressure to drop. Keep an eye out to make sure it does, though.

Although we don't believe a healthy bird is likely to bleed to death from an injured blood feather, you can stop the bleeding faster in most cases by pulling the broken feather and washing the wound with hydrogen peroxide. We do not recommend use of a styptic powder on pinfeathers — only on beak tips and toenails.

» **Breathing difficulty:** This is a life-threatening emergency. Restrain your bird as gently and calmly as you can and place him in his travel carrier, with a towel over it to keep him as still and quiet as possible. Call the veterinarian and get going. Causes for breathing difficulties can be the inhaling of deadly fumes — such as from cleaning products or burning nonstick cookware — or symptoms of respiratory tract, reproductive tract, or even heart problems. In any case, time is of the essence.

» **Broken bones:** Although usually not immediately life-threatening, a bird with a broken bone is in enough pain to warrant urgent treatment. Another problem with a broken bone: Any accident severe enough to break a bone could also have caused internal damage. Call right away and ask for guidance.

» **Burns:** First aid depends on what substance burned your bird. For boiling water burns, cool water, whether in a mist, a flood, or immersion (for a wing or leg) calms the situation. If grease has caused a burn, flour or cornstarch helps to absorb the still-dangerous material. Household chemicals can burn, too, and they fall into two categories — acid and alkali — both of which must be treated differently. Drain cleaner, an example of an acid, should be treated with lots of cool water to dilute the chemical, followed by application of a baking soda and water paste to neutralize the chemical. Treat a burn with an alkali chemical, such as ammonia, by diluting with cool water and neutralizing with household vinegar. Let the veterinarian take matters from there.

**WARNING**

Don't use topical cortisone products to treat burns or any injury in your bird.

>> **Eye injury:** Not usually immediately life-threatening, but still urgent. Restrain your bird and place in the carrier with a towel over it to keep your pet calm — and get to the veterinarian.

>> **Eating or drinking problems:** A bird who's not eating or drinking can go downhill in a hurry. Don't wait to see whether he "gets better" in a day or so — call to see whether your bird can get in right away for proper diagnosis and treatment.

>> **Fanny problems:** Any tissue sticking out from your bird's fanny, or *vent,* suggests a serious problem that needs to be dealt with fairly quickly. A veterinarian needs to determine the cause of the protrusion and treat accordingly. Call your veterinarian for guidance and keep your pet warm and calm until he can be seen.

>> **Heatstroke:** An overheated bird holds his wings down and pants, and he may be listless, weak, or unable to keep his balance. Cool — not cold — water from a misting bottle helps bring your bird's temperature down, as does moving him to a cooler part of the house. Offer a little water or electrolyte solution and contact your veterinarian for guidance.

**TIP**

Overweight birds may be particularly prone to overheating. For more on obesity and other forms of chronic malnutrition, see Chapter 11.

>> **Poisoning:** Birds like to get their beaks on things that aren't good for them — including many that are poisonous. Some common poisons include lead (from paint, welds on poor-quality cages, or even fishing weights), zinc (from galvanized items that have been chewed and swallowed), houseplants, medications meant for humans or other pets, and even good food gone bad. Bloody droppings, vomiting or regurgitation, diarrhea, convulsions or paralysis, or irritated skin around the mouth are some signs of possible poisoning. Call your veterinarian and hit the road. Your veterinarian needs to know what your bird got into — bring the suspect substance along, if you can.

>> **Seizures:** A bird having a seizure needs immediate attention to figure out and treat the underlying cause. Call your veterinarian and get your bird to the clinic right away.

>> **Swallowing or inhaling a dangerous object:** Birds enjoy destroying things, but some of the items they dig their beaks into can elicit a measure of revenge. Toys that are flimsy or not sized properly for your bird are one such source of danger (see Chapter 4 for more on choosing toys). Supervise your bird! Sometimes pieces go down the throat; other times they go up or down the nostrils. If you see or suspect that your bird has a problem with any foreign object, call an experienced avian veterinarian for guidance. The problem needs to be evaluated and may require surgery.

>> **Trauma:** Birds can get into so much trouble! Flying into a pot of boiling water is one kind of trouble; flying into a window, ceiling fan, or wall is another. They can also jump or fall onto the floor. You can't do much at home for your bird besides restrain, provide what comfort you can, allow your bird to settle into a carrier, and head for your veterinarian's office.

It's not unusual for birds to experience traumas when they fly into a wall, ceiling fan, mirror, window, or other object. Sometimes they jump off their cages and the skin splits on impact, revealing the two large muscles that hold the tail up. People often think their bird has developed a tumor, but fortunately the injury is simple to suture up. Although this injury can happen potentially to all pet birds, it is generally more often seen in birds that have had their wings clipped, altering the way they land after trying to fly and how they land. And large, heavy birds such as African greys, Amazons, and Eclectus parrots may split the skin on their chest if they fall and hit the ground. This type of injury may also be seen more frequently in wing-clipped birds as opposed to those that have full flight ability and skills. The injury can be sutured or may be treated topically. Often, good pain management will help keep the discomfort of the wound off of the bird's mind, and most will not even damage their stitches. On occasion, however, your veterinarian may put a bird-size collar in place to keep your pet from bending his head down.

**TIP**

Common sense dictates that the best way to deal with emergencies is by working to prevent them whenever possible. Check out Chapter 20 for some dangers you can help your bird avoid.

**REMEMBER**

No number of pages in a book can make up for years of study and hands-on experience. Birds can and do die from any number of specific diseases and injuries, including infectious ones that can typically be prevented by keeping your healthy bird away from others of questionable health status — but generally not cured. Cancers, heart disease, and diabetes often can be treated, as in human medicine, and catching illness early gives your bird the best shot at survival.

## Emergency! The veterinarian's role

If you get on the phone with your veterinarian or an emergency clinic to discuss your bird — and we recommend you do call first — the staff is as prepared as possible for the kind of care your bird needs.

That doesn't necessarily mean your bird gets treated first, especially at an emergency clinic. When you arrive, the staff determines the level of emergency and ranks your bird against other pets, with the most seriously ill or injured pets being treated first. The veterinarian may choose to stabilize your bird with warmth and extra oxygen before proceeding, either because other cases are more urgent or because your bird needs to be settled before being further stressed.

# DEALING WITH A BROKEN BLOOD FEATHER

After years of living with her, Larry Bird developed a strange fascination with Bella, Kim's senior Cavalier. He always watched her and frequently flew off his cage to walk over to her. Once when he did this and Kim picked him up to return him to his perch, she noticed blood dripping onto the floor. She guessed he had broken a blood feather when he landed, but she didn't know what to do for it since Larry was her most trouble-free pet. Off they went to the veterinarian, Kim celebrating that for once a pet emergency was on a weekday instead of late at night on a weekend.

When birds *molt* (lose their old feathers), the new feathers coming in have a blood supply that provides nutrients while the feather is growing. The developing feathers can be fragile, so a broken blood feather is a common problem in pet birds. Common precipitating events are flying into a wall, window, or ceiling fan or, as in Larry's case, a hard landing on the floor.

If this happens to your bird, you can grasp the blood feather at its base and gently pull it until it pops out of the socket it's growing out of on the wing. Jerking it out can hurt the wing but putting gentle pressure on it for a moment or two first will usually stop the bleeding. That offers the least trauma to the feather follicle and stimulates growth of a new feather.

Be careful not to apply too much pressure. If the blood isn't able to circulate, it can't bring new clotting factors and platelets to the wounded area to stop the bleeding.

Diagnostic tests are an important part of figuring out what's going on with your pet. Depending on what's going on, your veterinarian may need to conduct some of these tests before determining the best course of treatment. Asking what the tests are meant to accomplish is reasonable, as is expecting thorough answers to your questions — although not when a pet's life is hanging by a thread. Your veterinarian should be busy with your bird!

**REMEMBER**

Although the staff of the hospital or clinic do their best to keep you informed, their priority in the case of an emergency is helping your pet. Be patient and cooperative, answering their questions and giving them time and space to do their jobs. You can expect them to discuss testing and treatment options with you along the way, as well as give you an idea of the expense involved.

If the veterinarians at the emergency clinic aren't experienced at treating birds, they can at least place him in a quiet, covered cage and give him oxygen, pain relief, and fluids until your bird's regular veterinarian can take over his care.

**REMEMBER**

A life-threatening emergency is just that — an illness or injury that puts your bird's life at risk. Sometimes, despite the best efforts of everyone involved, a pet doesn't make it. You may be asked to make the decision to end your pet's suffering. For more information on euthanasia and resources to help you cope with the loss of your bird, see Chapter 11.

# Looking at Infectious Diseases That Panic Parrot Lovers

The diseases that give parrot lovers nightmares have big names — most starting with the letter *P* for no reason in particular. You need to know they're out there, and how serious they are, so you can understand how important it is to do your very best to prevent them.

We don't want you to read this section and come away with an idea that your bird is doomed to catch some dreadful, incurable disease — we're not trying to turn you into a *birdochondriac.* Your bird's best protection against any infectious diseases is preventive health care, good nutrition, cleanliness, and keeping clear of birds who may be sick. Review our chapters on basic husbandry (Chapter 5), nutrition (Chapter 6), preventive health (Chapter 9), and multi-bird households (Chapter 13); there you find the sections that help you keep disease at bay.

## Tiny beings, big problems

Some of the deadliest things in our environment are so small that you need a powerful microscope to see what they look like. Infectious agents or germs — veterinarians call them *pathogens* — are everywhere. These troublemakers fall into three categories:

>> **Bacteria:** These single-celled life forms can be found inside and outside your bird, and most live in happy coexistence. Some bacteria, called *normal bacterial flora,* are beneficial to your bird, serving as "squatters" that keep dangerous bacteria from settling. Bacteria that are no challenge to some creatures can be dangerous to others, which is why we caution against sharing food that has been in your mouth with your bird — the normal bacteria in your mouth can be bad news to your bird. The sharing of bacteria is also why dog and cat bites are so dangerous — even if the injury is minor, a resulting infection may not be. When properly diagnosed, bacterial infections can usually be fought with antibiotics. In large part, bacterial infections tend to

happen for a reason. If your bird repeatedly develop bacterial infections, you may want to ask your veterinarian to help you find out why.

Bacteria multiply both inside living things and on surfaces such as food and water dishes, countertops, and toys. An example of a disorder caused by bacterial contamination is food poisoning.

>> **Viruses:** Viruses are only "sort of" alive, and they rely on the cells of their bird hosts to reproduce — most cannot survive for long exposed to open air. Antibiotics have no effect on viruses, as do few other medications — although the scene is changing, thanks to research into viral diseases that affect other species, such as HIV in humans and feline infectious peritonitis in cats. The fight against viruses is basically a preventive one: Some can be thwarted by vaccination, while others are best fought by preventive care — a bird in good health is more likely to withstand an assault by a virus.

>> **Fungi:** Primitive plant-like life forms, fungi flourish in moist, warm environments and shed spores that can be inhaled. Fungi are opportunists: They typically prey on birds already weakened by disease or with less-than-normal immune function. Long-term or inappropriate antibiotic treatment also gives them an edge, by killing healthy normal bacteria that can keep fungal infections out. Antifungal medications, not antibiotics, are designed to fight fungal infections.

We provide information on a handful of the more worrisome infectious diseases in the following sections.

## Psittacine beak and feather disease

Tell-tale signs of this viral disease include abnormalities in the feathers or beak, hence the name *psittacine beak and feather disease* (PBFD). Although the disease is often thought of as one affecting all parrots, not all parrot species are equally susceptible. Parrots of old-world origin (Australasia, Africa) tend to be more susceptible to infection and disease than those of South American origins. More often a disease of youngsters and *sub-adults* (birds who haven't yet reached sexual maturity), PBFD is less often acquired by adults. In young birds, PBFD can be rapidly fatal; in older parrots, the disease can take up to several years after infection for signs to develop, and a bird in a weakened state may succumb to other infections.

Your veterinarian will diagnose PBFD infection based on observation, as well as a few laboratory tests, and will caution you against "doom and gloom" if your otherwise healthy-appearing bird tests positive for the presence of the virus on a single pass. Not all birds who become infected are destined to develop the disease. Currently no cure or vaccine exists for PBFD, and individual pet birds with the disease should be isolated from other parrots for the rest of their lives to prevent the further spread of the disease.

# CAN YOUR BIRD MAKE YOU SICK?

Every animal we share our lives with has the potential to pass on infectious diseases to us, whether rabies, parasites, or salmonella. Illnesses that can be passed between animals and humans are called *zoonotic*.

Like any companion animal, pet birds can share illness with their human keepers. *Chlamydia psittaci*, the organism that causes avian chlamydiosis (also known as *psittacosis*), is probably the best known, and offers arguably the highest degree of risk to some individuals from an infected bird. People in higher-risk groups should be especially careful when choosing an avian companion, dealing only with those breeders and shops maintaining the highest level of disease-prevention strategies and working with their veterinarian to best ensure the health of their bird. Some experts go further, and suggest avoiding birds (and other pets, such as reptiles and even cats) altogether. Considering the importance of companionship, especially to someone who's struggling with chronic illness, we wouldn't go that far, but we do recommend good education, good husbandry, good veterinary preventive health measures, and plenty of basic common sense when it comes to hygiene.

Allergies are another human health problem in relation to birds. If you have allergies or asthma, especially if you are allergic to feathers and feather dust, you probably should consider avoiding certain species of pet birds. We tell you which ones in Chapter 2.

Can you make your bird sick? Although it's commonly thought that birds can get sick from human colds, that's one of the myths we debunk in Chapter 15.

## Psittacid herpesvirus and Pacheco's parrot disease

First documented in parrots in the 1930s, *Pacheco's disease* is caused by a herpes virus. While some species and individuals seem able to fight off the disease, all parrots are capable of being infected. Although psittacid herpesviral infection can also cause other conditions such as *papillomatosis* (the growth of wartlike lesions inside the gastrointestinal tract) and pancreatic and bile duct cancers, the immediate and most dramatic version of infection is Pacheco's disease.

Pacheco's is brutal to its victims, with death often the first clinical sign a bird owner notices. Disease can develop in as little as two days from the time of exposure, with death coming in as few as five days or as long as several weeks. Sadly, most diagnoses are made at the examination of the infected bird's dead body. Although a vaccine is available, it's usually given to birds deemed to be in comparatively high-risk environments only, such as birds constantly exposed to new birds or to those of unknown health status. If caught early enough, some antiviral medications may help.

Pacheco's disease is best handled preventively, through proper cleanliness, vaccination, and rapid action if the disease pops up in a household or aviary. Sick, dying, or dead birds must be quickly removed, and your bird's living areas must be disinfected.

## Avian polyomavirus

Young budgies were the first diagnosed victims of polyomavirus, once known as *budgerigar fledgling disease.* The virus has been found in adult parrots but primarily remains a problem with all young pet birds, including canaries and other finches.

Signs of disease may include depression, bleeding, loss of appetite, weight loss, regurgitation, diarrhea, dehydration, and difficulty breathing. Polyomavirus can kill young birds quickly — within 12 to 48 hours after the first signs are noticed. Virtually nothing can be done for infected birds to help rid them of this viral infection.

The good news is a vaccine exists that can, in conjunction with good husbandry and isolation of new birds, help to eliminate infection and the disease from the birds of a home or aviary. The vaccine series starts at the minimum age of 21 days, with the second shot at the minimum age of 35 days. Breeding birds and adult pet birds can also be vaccinated — two shots 14 days apart, and then booster shots annually.

**TIP**

When you see your veterinarian with your bird, ask what testing and preventive measures are most appropriate for your bird.

## Proventricular dilation disease

"Wasting away" used to be the classic sign of *proventricular dilation disease* (PDD), which was once known as the *macaw wasting syndrome* or *macaw fading syndrome.* Now it's starting to become known as *avian ganglioneuritis,* a more descriptive term that is likely to replace PDD in the future. Since it was first discovered, this condition has been diagnosed in many species of birds, not just macaws. The cause is now known to be linked to infection with avian bornavirus. One of the catches, however, is that many asymptomatic birds are now known to be infected with this virus and do not always develop the disease. A number of birds with the disease also may test negative. With this virus and its disease, somewhat similar to beak and feather disease virus, distinction between infection and disease is key.

**TECHNICAL STUFF**

PDD often affects the *proventriculus*, which is the first section of the bird's stomach. Unable to perform its job of secreting digestive enzymes that mix with food before it moves on to the gizzard, the proventriculus becomes a place where food just rots, sometimes resulting in bacterial infections that can be fatal, as well as simply failing to move food normally to allow digestion to properly occur. Other birds with this disease may develop neurological signs.

The good news is that there may be a variety of treatment options for disease, if it's diagnosed in a timely manner.

## Psittacosis

Enough with the viruses! *Psittacosis* — also known as *chlamydiosis* — is caused by a bacterium. It causes a disease similar to a serious flu, affecting the breathing or digestive systems.

Psittacosis can be a serious killer of pet birds, but it doesn't have to be. If diagnosed early and appropriately treated with the right course of antibiotics, psittacosis can be beaten. Read those key words again: *if diagnosed early and appropriately treated.* Those actions could save your bird's life.

Veterinarians find the disease to be often devilish and hard to diagnose because of the wide range of symptoms. A wide variety of tests are available to support or confirm their suspicions.

## Aspergillosis and candidiasis

Fungi and their relatives, the molds, are a significant threat to pet birds. They're in large part not contagious — one bird can't catch a fungal disease from another. Instead, they're the result of poor hygiene and overall weak or poor health — a healthy bird is usually able to fight off a fungal infection.

Although countless kinds of fungus and molds exist, the two diseases that worry parrot keepers most cause aspergillosis and candidiasis. Both are more of a concern to bird lovers in warm, humid places, such as Florida or Hawaii.

Fungal diseases come in many forms, affecting the nose, the *trachea* (windpipe), lungs, or air sacs. Your veterinarian makes her tentative diagnosis based on the symptoms she sees and backs up her hunch with laboratory tests.

Antifungal medications and supportive care can be effective against aspergillus infections, but they often take a while to work and involve periodic rechecks to assess progress.

# THE ANTIBIOTIC SHOTGUN AND OTHER DISASTERS

Antibiotics are one of the outstanding contributions of modern medicine and have saved countless lives of both the human and animal variety. But we have become so comfortable with these medicines and their frequent usage that we sometimes forget they are powerful drugs that should be used with care.

And yet, many pet owners respond to any sign of illness by dosing — and often, overdosing — their pets with the couple of antibiotics that used to be more commonly available at pet-supply stores (and often labeled for other pets, such as fish). This sort of treatment for your sick bird is a spectacularly bad idea, for a few reasons:

- **If your bird has a viral or fungal infection, an antibiotic doesn't help.** Particularly in the case of a fungal infection, an antibiotic may even worsen your bird's condition.

- **Not all antibiotics are the same.** Each antibiotic has a target bacteria and may have little effect on bacteria that it's not designed to combat or bacteria that are resistant to their effects.

- **Regular use of antibiotics may affect both your bird's immune system and the bacteria trying to beat it.** This can lead to the development of antibiotic-resistant strains of bacteria that are hard to stamp out even with the "right" medication.

When you buy an antibiotic at a pet-supply store, you're often wasting your money, and you're certainly losing time — time that should be spent taking your bird to your veterinarian for an accurate diagnosis and targeted treatment.

**TIP**

Because fungal spores are everywhere, good hygiene is the only way to help prevent the disease — keeping your bird's living area clean to minimize the amount of infectious elements.

Another, relatively newer disease that is in this same fungal category is macrorhabdosis, caused by infection with *Macrorhabdus ornithogaster*. This is a unique type of yeast that likes to infect the inner lining of the stomach. Although it has been recognized in a number of bird species, infection and disease seems to be more commonly noted in smaller species such as budgerigars, cockatiels, and canaries. The organism may be identified in infected birds by testing the feces, and some birds may be able to be treated and cleared of infection with specific antifungals.

# Offering Supportive Care

Your bird may not be out of the woods for a while even after your veterinarian treats him. During recuperation, you and your veterinarian need to weigh many factors in determining what's best for your bird. Your bird's condition is an important consideration, of course, but so, too, is your skill and comfort in dealing with a sick pet, as well as your ability to monitor your bird closely.

## The hospital stay

A severely ill bird usually needs to be hospitalized. In reality, this is no different from what is needed when humans are ill. Your bird may need tube feeding or injectable fluids to keep him fed and hydrated, as well as the warmth and oxygen a birdy intensive care unit (ICU) can provide. Perhaps most important, because a sick bird's status can change rapidly, he needs to be under observation by people who can evaluate his status regularly and react quickly to give him the care he needs.

At what point your bird can go home is something you need to discuss with your veterinarian. Some questions she may ask include the following:

>> **How can we help make sure you're comfortable taking over treatments, when your bird goes home?** Even though recuperating birds need plenty of rest and should, for the most part, be left alone, you need to be comfortable with what needs to be done and how to do it. If you're working long hours away from home, that may not be possible.

>> **Will your schedule allow you to give your bird medications as required?** If you're not proficient at toweling your bird or if injecting medicine (see the section, "Giving medication," later in this chapter) leaves you cold, your bird may be better off with a longer hospital stay. If you have vast experience, on the other hand, your bird may be able to go home even if he needs to be hand-fed. Regardless, you and the doc will need to discuss the criteria that will determine when your bird is stable enough to go home.

**TIP**

Be honest about what you can and can't do for your bird — honest with yourself and honest with your veterinarian. Some people just aren't comfortable with nursing sick family members, whether two-legged or four-legged. If you're up front with your veterinarian, you can work out a solution that is good for you and your bird.

Many veterinary hospitals don't have staff on-site 24 hours a day. You and your veterinarian should discuss plans for your bird after-hours. In Brian's practice, critically ill birds may come home with him or his staff so they can be monitored. In other cases, a calm night in the hospital is often just what the doctor ordered. Although transporting your pet to a 24-hour clinic may be possible, doing so may not necessarily be the best course of action because of stress considerations.

## Home care

If you're able to care for your bird at home, you'll need to make some adjustments to provide him with as quiet and stress-free an environment as possible.

» **Use a smaller cage, if you can.** If your bird has a travel cage, use it while he's healing. The smaller space keeps him less active and feeling more secure. Even better, many birds will recuperate best if housed in clear plastic storage bins that have plenty of holes for ventilation. This provides easy visibility for you, and protected rest and comfort for your bird.

» **Lower or remove perches.** Folded towels make excellent "beds" for sick birds, providing a degree of insulation and softness and a good texture for secure footing. Plus, they can be changed and laundered when soiled. Low perches — 1 inch off the towel — can make a big difference for your bird, making him feel better but not having to work too hard to get up onto them.

» **Keep food and water close by.** If your bird's food and water bowls are attached to higher parts of the cage, take them out of their holders and put them on the floor of the cage. Feed your bird his favorite foods to keep him eating, especially those with high water content, such as fruits (within reason, of course). For the short term, don't worry about complete and balanced nutrition.

» **Maintain a warm environment.** You can choose among several ways to provide extra heat. Heating pads, wrapped in towels and with the cord safely hidden, are fine when kept on a low temperature. Microwaveable "hot packs" are fine, too, as long as they're not too hot to begin with. You can also use a heat lamp or drape an electric blanket over the cage. Whatever source you choose, check frequently on the heat level — warm, not hot! Generally, around 75°F to 85°F is a target to shoot for.

» **Strive for peace and quiet.** Try to keep the household as low-key as possible and place your bird's cage in a spot removed from family activities. Because birds relax in low-light conditions, partially covering the cage or dimming room lights helps. Don't turn lights off completely, though! When your bird decides he wants to eat, make sure he can see and find the food you have available for him.

>> **Keep handling to a minimum.** Your bird needs to rest. Don't be a worrier and check on him constantly, or stress him with frequent handling. Have you ever been in the hospital and been annoyed at how often you're bothered for medications, blood draws, or blood pressure checks? Wouldn't resting be nice? You bet! So, leave your bird alone!

# Giving medication

If you've ever struggled with getting a pill down the throat of a dog or cat, the good news is that you can't practically or easily pill a parrot or canary, so you aren't expected to do so. The bad news is it isn't really any easier to get medication in them. You can get medicine inside pet birds in four basic ways. Each approach has pros and cons, although the last two are usually what your veterinarian recommends:

>> **Water-soluble medications in drinking water:** Many of the over-the-counter medications we discourage you from wasting your money on are added to drinking water. Adding medication to water is the easiest approach, but it has drawbacks: You have little control over dosage because you can't count on your bird to drink any set amount of water. Some species drink little water at all, and other birds may not feel up to drinking when they're ill. For these reasons, putting medicine in drinking water is probably not the route your veterinarian recommends, except in some very specific circumstances.

>> **Medicated feeds:** These have the same pros and cons as medicated water. It's easy to offer medicated feed, but you have no way of making sure any of it gets inside your bird. Plus, many medicated feeds taste awful, so even if your bird feels like eating, he may not touch the stuff with medicine in it.

>> **Oral dosage:** Accuracy of dosage is a benefit of giving your bird medication orally — assuming you get the stuff in him instead of dribbling it everywhere but down his throat. You get the appropriate amount in an eyedropper or a syringe with the needle removed and slide the tip into the side of your bird's mouth. The downside you've probably already guessed: Your bird isn't likely to sit still for this procedure, so you have to restrain him with a towel. After he's restrained, a bird who has been hand-fed as a baby will usually go along — the sight of a plastic tip nearing his mouth often causes him to open up in hopes of a meal.

You can, however, use target training (see Chapter 5) to teach your bird to willingly take orally administered medications in exchange for payment with something desirable. This technique is commonly employed at Brian's practice, and many birds have learned this skill by the time they go home from the hospital.

Also, liquid medications can be placed inside a *food vehicle* (an absorbent favorite food item that your bird will consume rapidly and readily).

>> **Injections:** This approach gets high marks for accuracy and, after you're used to injecting your bird, high marks for ease as well. As with oral medications, though, you'll likely need to restrain your bird with a towel to inject his medication. Some people get really good at injecting their birds, even after initial reluctance. Those with diabetic birds, for example, may need to inject their birds every day — and it's no big deal for either bird or person.

TIP

Discuss with your veterinarian which method of medicating your bird is right for you — and for your bird — and make sure you're comfortable with whatever method you choose. Medication won't do your bird any good if little or none of it gets in him. Ask all the questions you need to, watch your veterinarian demonstrate, and then practice under his tutelage before you go. If you run into problems at home, call.

WARNING

Whatever you do, don't skip any medication sent home with your bird, and don't stop giving it because your bird seems to feel better. Administer the medication exactly as prescribed and call your veterinarian if you have any problems.

Chapter **11**

# Lifelong Care for Your Bird

M any of the bird species we keep as pets, such as the large parrots, have the potential to live nearly as long as we can — up to 70 years or more. Even the smaller parrots, such as cockatiels, are capable of outliving almost any dog or cat. This reality is dramatically changing our ideas of planning for a lifetime of care.

And yet, until recently, relatively few pet birds achieved the life span of which they were capable, many dying in a fraction of the potential time they should have enjoyed on this earth. We just didn't know enough to provide them with what they needed to achieve a long and healthy life. Things are different now, and they're getting better by the day.

In just the last two decades, since the first edition of this book, great advances in our knowledge of bird care and medicine have continued to percolate through to the entire avian world — veterinarians, breeders, pet stores, and bird owners. The result: healthier, happier birds who can be our companions for years.

These changes can't come soon enough or fast enough, given our growing appreciation of birds as companions. The next decade and beyond promises even more for those who love sharing their lives with birds.

In this chapter, we share the latest on health concerns for aging birds, along with the help you need to cope if your bird dies. Because basic good care and preventive medicine have no age limits, we strongly encourage you to review the information on those topics in Chapters 5 and 9, along with proper nutrition in Chapter 6.

# Why Birds Are Living Longer

So, what's behind the increasing life span among pet birds? The same forces that contribute to our own healthier lives make a notable difference in the bird world — the knowledge of how a life lived well can be a life lived long. In the case of pet birds, though, serendipity (or just plain luck) has also played a role.

## Domestically raised versus wild caught

More pet birds in the United States, as well as in many other parts of the world, are domestically raised — more than ever before. This fact is, in large part, a response to large-scale bans by many countries (including the United States) on importing wild-caught birds for the pet trade. Laws that were introduced to protect birds in the wild — and to fight the cruelty that was, at times, involved in their capture and transportation — ended up creating demand for domestically bred and raised pet birds and an appreciation for those already in our care.

The best of these aviculturists have changed the very nature of the birds available as pets. Healthier, better socialized, and comfortable in a human environment, these birds are solid citizens from the start, spared the stresses of capture and exposure to infectious disease that were so common in wild-caught birds. Although the infectious-disease problems of those previous days of importation of wild-caught birds is significantly less common, they're still around. Good aviculturists are well aware of this situation and have practices in place to maintain the safety and health of those birds in their stewardship.

**WARNING**

Although the growth and refinement of bird breeding, or *aviculture,* has been a boon to the pet bird trade, not all breeders do their part to ensure that the birds they produce are healthy, well-socialized pets. And they sell to retailers who are likewise sometimes in the dark about the right way to do things. The bird-supply business is full of opinions. You may hear advice that may not be what's right for your bird. We can't stress enough the importance of getting a healthy bird to begin with. For the ins and outs of bird buying, see Chapters 3 and 16.

# New views on nutrition

When pressed for one — and only one — reason for the increased health and longevity of birds, Brian starts out by saying he honestly can't choose one. And then he picks nutrition. A close second, he says, is how birds eat — foraging, enrichment, and the use of food for reinforcement during training all tie into good nutrition.

And then he backtracks into bird breeding because of the aviculturist's massively important role in getting baby birds started on good foods, which comes back to . . . nutrition. Good nutrition is another area with a strong parallel to what we know in our own lives. When you're young, you can get away with a junk-food diet — or, at least, it seems as if you can. High-fat foods, few fruits and vegetables, and an emphasis on some food groups over others are all things we seem to muddle through when we're young, but bad habits catch up to us as we age. The same truth applies to birds. High-fat, seed-only diets may seem to be fine for young birds, even for years, but they do take a toll in the end. And a lot of the predictable problems that we experience when we eat an inappropriately high-fat, imbalanced diet are pretty much the same as what is seen in birds: obesity, increased vulnerability to infections, some cancers, and cardiovascular disease, to name a few.

## THE IMPORTANCE OF RESEARCH

Because avian medicine is still evolving, we encourage all bird lovers to support continued research into bird health. The contributions can be monetary — we offer a couple of worthy funds in the appendix at the back of this book — but you can give an even more personal gift.

When you lose a bird, talk to your veterinarian about allowing her to perform a post-mortem examination, which is the only way to determine an accurate cause of death — and perhaps find a key that can help other birds survive. This knowledge can have direct value for you and other birds you have or may have in the future. *Morti vivos docent* — the dead teach the living — is as true in avian medicine as it has always been in human medicine.

Even living birds can help to advance medical knowledge. Brian likes to share the stories of birds afflicted with a deadly disease who ultimately became critical to understanding how their disease was acquired and spread to others. Owners of these birds donated them to a qualified university researcher, who figured out and then disseminated information that has since saved the lives of countless birds.

Making such a selfless decision can, of course, be difficult, but for some people, the realization that they're helping to save lives can help them cope with a loss.

The advent of nutritionally balanced, formulated diets has been perhaps the single greatest leap forward in bird care. The selection of high-quality commercial diets is astonishing, especially when compared with what was available just a decade ago. Even more promising is the continued education of the bird-owning public about feeding these foods, along with fresh, healthy human food.

For a thorough overview of what your bird should and shouldn't be eating, check out Chapter 6.

## The veterinary contribution

When Brian was studying to be a veterinarian, "avian medicine" — what little there was of it — was primarily dedicated to keeping poultry alive and healthy long enough to become somebody's dinner. Few veterinary schools taught students the basics of pet bird medicine and surgery. Back in the day, veterinarians treating family pets weren't well equipped with the knowledge they needed to care for pet birds — little information was actually available for sharing — so pet birds pretty much lived or died. Even the best veterinarians had limited ability to make a positive difference in the pet bird population.

Fortunately, Dr. Murray Fowler had a single elective course on caged bird medicine when Brian was in veterinary school. Today's veterinary students at UC Davis, where Brian went, receive a much more comprehensive introductory course to bird care. Some other veterinary schools in the United States and abroad have also developed excellent coursework to help bring new graduates on board with better knowledge of avian healthcare.

In the last 30 years or so, and especially in the last two decades, the body of medical knowledge about pet birds has grown significantly, and continues to do so at a greater pace.

The development of focused avian healthcare specialists like Brian and groups like the Association of Avian Veterinarians signal these changes. More is known today about how pet birds should be cared for, why and how they get sick, and how to treat them. And while the need for new and insightful information is ongoing, more veterinarians than ever are interested in exploring the subject of pet bird care — and that means an even brighter future for our avian companions.

# Health and the Older Bird

The problems of "older birds" don't necessarily start at an advanced age. For the purpose of this chapter, we define birds as "older" when they're past the age of sexual maturity, which differs from one species to another. Many behavior problems present themselves at this stage — we cover those challenges in Chapter 12. This is also the point in your bird's life when bad health habits start coming home to roost.

**REMEMBER**

Although we put the most common problems in this section, keep in mind that the information you find here isn't and can't be all encompassing. A good relationship with a well-qualified veterinarian is key to keeping your pet bird healthy as he ages.

## Chronic malnutrition

In medical terms, a *chronic* condition is one that develops over time, as opposed to an *acute* condition, which occurs suddenly. An acute condition — a bite, say, or poisoning — puts your bird's life at risk immediately. A chronic condition can be just as deadly, but it steals life away in little chunks over time. *Chronic malnutrition,* which simply means continued bad eating habits, is one of the more insidious problems shortening the lives of birds, and it comes in at least two varieties — too much and too little.

**TECHNICAL STUFF**

Can a bird be both overnourished and undernourished at the same time? However unfair, the answer is *yes.* Improper diets can cause both obesity and nutritional deficiencies, resulting in a fat bird who's still starving for the vitamin, mineral, or protein components of a healthy diet.

### Obesity

Fat birds are everywhere, and the problems they suffer because they're overweight are fairly similar to those caused by excess weight in our own lives. Obesity puts stress on bones, joints, and internal organ systems. The list of health problems associated with obesity is a long one, and it includes liver problems, heart and lung problems, diabetes and other pancreatic disorders, fatty tumors, thyroid problems, and added stress to the skeletal system, especially the feet. Overweight birds are also at higher risk during surgery or stressful handling.

Seed-heavy diets (which are high in fat) are often to blame for obesity, but some birds (like some people) eat such large quantities of even a perfectly balanced diet that they put on weight. Add in boredom, lack of exercise, and even overfeeding as a chick, and you can figure out why veterinarians see a lot of pudgy birds like the one in Figure 11-1.

**FIGURE 11-1:**
This budgie suffers from obesity, which can severely affect the quality and length of her life.

*Photograph by Brian L. Speer, DVM*

**TECHNICAL STUFF**

Genetics and species differences play a role in determining a predisposition to obesity in pet birds. Amazon parrots, some of the large cockatoos, cockatiels, and budgies seem to pork up much more frequently than other pet birds. Elderly birds and breeding hens of all pet species are also at a higher risk. Backyard chickens and some pet duck and goose breeds can get pretty chubby if what and how much they eat is not attended to.

**TIP**

Because those nifty height/weight charts for humans don't exist for birds, you need to rely on your powers of observation — and those of your veterinarian — to determine whether your bird is overweight. Here are some signs to watch for:

>> **Rolls of fat around the abdomen and hip areas, along with cleavage on the abdomen or breast area.**

>> **Visible fat under the skin, which Brian calls the "broiler chicken look."** The skin of most normal pet birds is typically very thin and quite transparent. When the skin is wet with rubbing alcohol, you should be able to see dark pink or red muscle underneath. In overweight birds, you see yellowish fat under the skin instead.

>> **Breathing difficulty, such as labored breathing, especially after physical exertion.**

>> **Heat intolerance, shown by excessive wing drooping or openmouthed breathing in a hot environment.**

>> **Overgrown upper beaks.** The beaks of some birds grow excessively long if they're obese or have fatty-liver disease. This trait is particularly true in Amazon parrots and budgies, but it can also be seen in other parrot species.

If you suspect your bird is fat — and especially if you *know* your bird is fat — see your veterinarian right away for nutritional counseling and other ways to attack the problem. Restricting your bird's calorie intake is only one aspect of dealing with obesity. It's important to provide him with play or activities that challenge his brain to replace the time he would otherwise spend eating or foraging.

Because lack of activity is one of the factors contributing to obesity, look for ways to motivate your bird to move around more. A great bird toy that inspires exercise is a stiff rope coil perch, which moves as the bird moves, promoting balance and coordination and strengthening muscles. These perches are great fun, and they really burn calories! For more on outfitting your bird, see Chapter 4.

## Undernutrition

The lack of critical nutrients in a bird's diet — known as *undernutrition* — can make birds seem old and fragile before their time. Here are the most common nutrients missing in poor diets:

>> **Vitamin A:** Vitamin A has an important role in maintaining healthy vision, helps maintain the integrity of the skin and mucous membranes, is involved in the function of the immune system, contributes to normal reproduction and proper growth of bones, and likely has a role in the maintenance of healthy cells. Some forms of cancer, specifically skin cancers, may be predisposed by chronic lack of adequate vitamin A in the diet.

>> **Vitamin D:** Vitamin D helps to absorb calcium from the gut and to regulate blood calcium levels in the body. Without vitamin D, bones grow weak and fragile, prone to easy breaking.

>> **Calcium:** Calcium deficiencies may appear similarly to vitamin D deficiencies, but they're linked directly to dietary calcium levels and the calcium–phosphorus balance of the diet. Calcium nutritional deficiencies can also lead to osteoporosis in female birds, the result of chronic egg laying that forces birds to pull calcium reserves from their bones, weakening them as a result. We talk about reproductive health concerns in Chapter 13.

A proper diet of commercial pellets supplemented by fruits, vegetables, and other healthy human food is the best way to address these deficiencies before they become health problems.

**WARNING**

Although you may entertain thoughts of throwing vitamins at your bird to make sure he gets enough vitamin A, vitamin D, and calcium, we urge you to forget any such idea. Balanced nutrition comes from a balanced diet. If you add what you think your bird may be lacking, you may end up substituting one problem for another — or adding one problem on top of another. Your veterinarian is your most reliable source of knowledge about whether your bird needs vitamin supplements, in the short or long term.

## Cataracts

Weakening vision is a problem in aging birds, just as it is in aging humans and other animals, and one of the main problems is cataracts (an increased density of the lens of the eye). Although cataracts are often an old-age problem, they aren't always. The cause needs to be sorted out, and surgical options do exist that can restore vision in some older birds.

**REMEMBER**

Although you may feel sad for your bird if she goes blind, in Brian's experience, blind birds who are otherwise healthy can get along just fine — as long as you don't rearrange the furniture or the cage and you take extra care to let them know when you're approaching them so they don't bite out of fear. Just speak to them or whistle so they know you're there.

## Arthritis

Old bones and joints become a little less functional with age, as you may have come to find out with your own body. *Arthritis* is defined as any inflammatory problem within a joint, and the condition may have several causes. If you notice your bird is consistently lame or you see swelling at the joints, have your veterinarian check out the problem. Caught early and properly diagnosed, arthritis may be treatable, sparing your bird years of misery.

Another reason to see your veterinarian: Some forms of arthritis, such as gout or infection in the joints, can even be life threatening. Kim's bird, Larry, an African ringneck parakeet, developed arthritis. Fortunately, his veterinarian was able to prescribe medication to keep it under control.

## Heart disease

Birds, especially sedentary ones on high-fat diets, can fall prey to many cardiovascular problems, such as *atherosclerosis* (hardening of the arteries). Although early heart disease is now more manageable than ever before, the best recommendation for prevention is still diet, exercise, and early diagnosis and treatment of any problems that do erupt. Signs of heart disease may include a shortness of breath, fainting spells, weakness of the legs or periodic falling from the perch, seizures, stroke-like symptoms (such as weakness of one or both legs or one-sided problems such as head tilts), enlargement of the abdomen — or sudden death, with no warning signs whatsoever. Another good argument for preventive care, wouldn't you say?

**TECHNICAL STUFF**

Atherosclerosis is commonly seen in birds, although its prevalence varies by species. Contributing factors include age (older than 20 years), body size (it's more common in large birds than small ones), sex (females are more prone to it than males), and species (African greys, cockatiels, and Amazons have a higher incidence of the disease). Nutritional risk factors include diets low in polyunsaturated fatty acids (PUFAs) and high in saturated fatty acids and cholesterol.

## Chronic pain

Have you ever wondered if your bird is in pain? Like other animals and humans, birds undoubtedly experience *pain* (the sensory and emotional response to tissue damage caused by traumatic injuries such as a beak, leg, or wing fracture; surgery; or joint degeneration). Other conditions that can be painful include egg binding, feather picking, or gastrointestinal or respiratory conditions. A good question to ask yourself is: "If I had experienced this injury or procedure, would I be in pain?" If the answer is yes for you, it's likely yes for your bird as well.

It's not always easy for humans to recognize pain in birds. As prey animals, they may be reluctant to exhibit signs of pain. In the wild, showing signs of pain is the kiss of death. It's also difficult to read avian facial expressions, which are often a way that we know a person or animal is in pain. And birds can't tell us verbally how they feel. Even if they can talk, they don't have the words to tell us that they hurt. For these reasons, it's not unusual for chronic pain to be underrecognized in birds.

Although a bird's pain signals can be subtle, good observation skills can help you realize that she doesn't feel well. Behavioral changes are often the earliest sign that something is wrong. Behavior varies widely from species to species, so you need to be familiar with the full range of normal behaviors for the species you live with, as well as for your individual bird. That knowledge will help you identify changes that could signal illness or pain.

Many different types of behaviors can indicate pain, including the following:

>> Loss or abandonment of normal activities

>> Increased or decreased vocalizations

>> Perching or sleeping away from other birds in the cage or aviary

>> Decreased preening or social grooming behavior

>> Overgrooming or feather picking

>> Eating or drinking more or less than usual

>> Reduced interest in spending time with you (especially if your bird is normally sociable or enjoys physical contact) or even trying to escape from you

>> Letting you handle her when normally she doesn't like being held

>> Less interest in her surroundings

>> Biting or other aggressive behaviors that are unusual for your bird

There are some species-specific things, too. For example, chickens experiencing chronic pain may be more likely to abandon dust-bathing behaviors, and pigeons may demonstrate wing trembling.

**REMEMBER**

Keep in mind that you may actually *like* the behavior change — not screaming while you're on the phone, for instance, or no longer incessantly ringing the bell in her cage — without stopping to consider whether it has a deeper meaning. The absence of those annoying behaviors should send a message about your bird's health, welfare, and pain level. Any time your bird stops exhibiting what are normal behaviors for her, it's cause for a veterinary exam to make sure everything is okay.

More obvious behavior changes can be physical. Birds in pain may appear hunched over or miserable, squint or close their eyes, look fluffed up, move more slowly, fall or stumble, or be less confident as they move around or fly. If you know that your bird has an injury in a certain area, you may notice protective behaviors, such as positioning herself with the injured area away from you. Restlessness, anxiety, or fear can also be signs of pain.

In diagnosing pain, your veterinarian may use a pain scale or score sheet. Usually, these tools rate pain on a simple numeric scale of 1 to 10. Your veterinarian may also detect physiologic signs such as *hypertension* (high blood pressure) and *tachycardia* (rapid heart rate), which can signal pain. When appropriate pain relief is provided, an obvious change in posture or behaviors can be seen.

Different types of pain travel through different pathways in the body. Whether birds have experienced an injury, have undergone surgery, or are suffering arthritis pain, they can be helped by several different types of analgesia: nonsteroidal anti-inflammatory drugs (NSAIDs), opiates (no, you don't have to worry that they'll become addicted), local anesthetics for certain procedures, and combinations of different types of drugs to manage pain along different pathways (known as *multimodal treatment*).

Depending on the problem, these drugs reduce painful inflammation, improve the anesthesia experience for birds undergoing surgery, and decrease pain in general. The better the pain relief, the more quickly your bird will recover and return to normal.

You can't give your bird your own Tylenol, Aleve, or aspirin, but a number of NSAIDs have been developed for use in birds and other animals, such as meloxicam and carprofen, both widely used in avian practices. Your veterinarian will know which NSAID is safest and most effective for your particular bird.

Local anesthetics may be used to prevent pain during procedures such as biopsies, microchip injection, or blood draws. Local anesthetics may also be given before surgery or in conjunction with anesthesia to improve a bird's comfort with handling and reduce postoperative pain. That's important because it's a lot easier to prevent pain than it is to reduce pain after the fact.

**TECHNICAL STUFF**

Every avian species is different, so in many cases, little is known about how or why certain drugs perform in individual species. One example is buprenorphine, an opioid that works well in a few species but has little effect in African greys, even in large doses.

If they need surgery, birds require general anesthesia. Although there is always some risk with anesthesia, birds are commonly anesthetized for surgical procedures with good results. Advances in monitoring and other types of equipment have greatly increased safety. Combining opioids, NSAIDs, and sometimes local anesthetics — known as *balanced anesthesia* — ensures that pain and inflammation are blocked in different ways, maximizing pain relief and minimizing the risk of side effects.

**REMEMBER**

Any drug has the potential for adverse side effects, but in weighing your bird's comfort versus a possible adverse effect, we think pain relief should tip the balance.

# Knowing When It's Time to Say Goodbye

*Euthanasia*, the technical term for "putting an animal to sleep," is one of the hardest decisions you must ever make, and the choice doesn't get any easier, no matter how many times you face it over the years. Your veterinarian can offer you advice and your friends can offer you support, but no one can make the decision for you. If you live with an elderly or terminally ill bird, you look in her eyes every morning and ask yourself: Is this the day I help my friend to the other side?

To know *for sure* that you're making the right decision is impossible. Asking guidance from your friends, family, and veterinarian is appropriate, but only you can make the final decision. After others share their empathetic "If it were my companion . . ." advice, they need to respect your decision without question.

Some owners choose euthanasia before their bird's discomfort becomes pain, which is sooner than many people are able to come to grips with their pet's condition. Some owners use a pet's appetite as the guide — if an old or ill bird is no longer interested in eating, they reason, he's not interested in anything. Other owners wait until no doubt remains that the time is at hand and they know their bird is hurting.

Each guideline is the right one for some birds and some owners at some times. You do the best you can, and then you try to put the decision behind you and deal with the grief.

TIP

The origins of the word *euthanasia* mean "a good death." In the larger picture of this definition, pain, fear and suffering should not be allowed to be a part of the experience.

The incredible progress in veterinary medicine in the past couple of decades has made the decision even more difficult for many people. Not too long ago, the best you could do for a seriously ill pet was to make her comfortable until that wasn't possible anymore. Advances in avian medicine — and more are on the way — keep alive birds who wouldn't have had a chance even a few years ago.

If you have a realistic expectation that veterinary care can improve your aged or chronically ill bird's life — instead of simply prolonging that life, sometimes in misery — then treatment is a reasonable option. But don't allow guilt or wishful thinking to push you into making a decision that doesn't feel right to you.

REMEMBER

Euthanasia is a kindness extended to a treasured bird, a decision we make at a great emotional cost to ourselves. It's a final act of love, nothing less.

WARNING

Horrifying as it seems to us, books and other references exist that provide a how-to approach to DIY euthanasia. Frankly, the suffering such approaches inflict makes our stomachs turn, and they suggest that birds are somehow less deserving of a peaceful death than dogs and cats are. They're not. The gentle easing from life a veterinarian can offer is your final gift to your bird. If euthanasia is necessary, please make compassion the last act your bird knows.

# Euthanasia options

Should you be with your pet at the end? What should you do with the remains? These questions are difficult, and there are no wrong answers.

As performed by a veterinarian, euthanasia is a quick and peaceful process. The bird is often sedated or even anesthetized prior to the final injection, which ultimately stops breathing and heart function. The euphemism "put to sleep" is a perfect description. Those who attend the procedure come away reassured that their pets felt no fear or pain.

**REMEMBER**

If you're bringing your bird in — as opposed to making the decision for a sick bird already in the veterinarian's care — call ahead to set the appointment and make clear to the receptionist what you're coming for. That way, the staff can ensure that you won't sit in the waiting room — you, your bird, and your grief. Your veterinarian will do her best to answer all your questions and ensure that you're comfortable with everything before proceeding. Brian used to discourage bird lovers from staying with their pets at the end, but staying with a bird has become much more common in recent years. Through the use of sedatives, sometimes followed by gas anesthesia, euthanasia can be quiet, peaceful, and free of fear and anxiety. Not all veterinarians may be familiar with these methods, so be sure to discuss things beforehand with your veterinarian. Make sure your veterinarian prepares you for what you'll see and experience.

Crying is normal, and your veterinarian understands. So, too, we believe, does your bird.

You may want to spend a few minutes with your bird afterward, and your veterinarian will understand that, as well, and will give you all the time you need alone to begin the process of dealing with your loss. (If your pet dies while in the veterinarian's care, you may also choose to view the body to give yourself closure and let the healing begin.)

You may be more comfortable with having your bird euthanized at home. If so, talk to your veterinarian about this possibility. Many veterinarians extend this special service to long-time clients. If yours doesn't, you may ask him to recommend a colleague who offers house calls.

**REMEMBER**

Just make sure the veterinarian you choose is familiar with proper euthanasia technique in birds. This makes the process as stress-free as possible for both you and your bird.

After your pet's death, most veterinarians will discuss the value of conducting a postmortem examination (known as a *necropsy* in animals and an *autopsy* in humans), to confirm the diagnosis and to make sure that you or your other birds at home are not potentially at risk of any infection that may have been present. The postmortem is a much more common event in birds than it is in dogs and cats, and it's important to consider the potential value of this examination. Understanding what you can about why death occurred, and knowing that you're potentially help save the lives of other birds in the future, can be helpful for many people.

You can handle your bird's remains in many ways, and doing so is easier on you overall if you make this decision beforehand. Your veterinarian has the information you need on your options, which may include having your local animal control department pick up the body, burying the pet in your backyard or at another site (where it's legal and with the landowner's permission, of course), arranging for cremation, or contracting with a pet cemetery for full services and burial. Again, no choice is wrong. Whatever feels right to you and comforts you best is what you should do.

**TIP**

Several manufacturers offer tasteful and attractive memorial markers that you can place in your yard or at a pet cemetery if you choose to go that route. Other choices include large rocks or slabs of stone or a tree or rose bush. Even if you choose not to have your bird's body or ashes returned, placing a memorial in a special spot may soothe you.

Another way to celebrate the memory of your bird is to make a donation to your local humane society, regional school of veterinary medicine, bird health or rescue foundation, or other favorite animal charity. A donation in a beloved companion's name is a wonderful thing to do for a friend who has lost a pet as well.

The major greeting card companies now market pet sentiments, and among the items available are some elegant sympathy cards. We see these cards as further proof that society recognizes the strength of the bond we share with our pets. Don't be surprised to receive a card from your veterinarian, friends, and family, and know, too, that a card, call, or note is always appreciated when you know someone who is dealing with the loss of a pet.

## Dealing with loss

Many people are surprised at the powerful emotions that spill over after a bird's death, and they're embarrassed by their grief. Remembering that pets have meaning in our lives beyond the love we feel for the animal alone may help. Often, we don't realize that we're grieving not only for the pet we loved, but also for the special time and the ties to other people the animal represented in our lives. Considering the potentially long lifespan of many pet birds, you may be dealing with the loss of a companion you've known longer than any other. Is it any surprise you're grieving?

# YOU'RE NOT ALONE

You may find comfort in talking to others about your bird's death. Ask your veterinarian about pet loss support groups. Almost unheard of a couple decades of ago, these groups now exist in many communities. You may also want to see a counselor; this, too, can be helpful.

Veterinary schools and colleges and humane organizations are among the leaders in creating programs to help pet lovers deal with loss. Some operate pet loss hotlines staffed by veterinary students trained to answer questions, have regular counseling groups, offer materials that may help you (including guidelines for helping children with loss), and just plain listen.

Here are some resources for those coping with the loss of a pet:

- **UC Davis School of Veterinary Medicine:** www.vetmed.ucdavis.edu/grief-counseling/pet-loss-resources

- **Colorado State University Veterinary Teaching Hospital:** http://csu-cvmbs.colostate.edu/vth/diagnostic-and-support/argus/Pages/resources.aspx

- **University of Florida College of Veterinary Medicine Small Animal Hospital:** https://smallanimal.vethospital.ufl.edu/resources/pet-loss-support

- **Iowa State University Lloyd Veterinary Medical Center:** https://vetmed.iastate.edu/sites/default/files/LVMC/SmallAnimal/Specialties/Oncology/ClientResources/ISU%20LVMC%20Oncology%20Pet%20Loss%20Support%20Flyer.pdf

- **Louisiana State University Veterinary Teaching Hospital:** www.lsu.edu/vetmed/veterinary_hospital/services/counseling_services.php

- **Tufts University Cummings School of Veterinary Medicine:** https://vet.tufts.edu/petloss

- **Michigan State University College of Veterinary Medicine Pet Loss Support Group:** https://cvm.msu.edu/hospital/services/social-work/pet-loss-support-group

- **Cornell University College of Veterinary Medicine Pet Loss Support Hotline:** https://www.vet.cornell.edu/about-us/outreach/pet-loss-support-hotline

- **The Ohio State University Veterinary Medical Center Pet Loss Hotlines and Online Resources:** https://vet.osu.edu/vmc/companion/our-services/honoring-bond-support-animal-owners/pet-loss-support-hotlines

*(continued)*

*(continued)*

- **University of Pennsylvania Penn Vet:** www.vet.upenn.edu/veterinary-hospitals/ryan-veterinary-hospital/services/grief-support-social-services

- **University of Tennessee College of Veterinary Medicine:** http://vetsocialwork.utk.edu/grief-and-bereavement/

- **Utah State University School of Veterinary Medicine Pet Loss Hotline:** Call 435-757-4540 Monday through Thursday 5 to 7 p.m. Mountain time (7 to 9 p.m. Eastern time) or email petloss@usu.edu. Voicemail and email can be left 24/7 and will be responded to as quickly as possible.

- **Virginia-Maryland Regional College of Veterinary Medicine:** Call 540-231-8038 Tuesday and Thursday 6 to 9 p.m. Eastern time.

- **Lap of Love:** https://www.lapoflove.com/community/Pet-Loss-Support or call 855-352-5683 Monday through Friday 10 a.m. to 9 p.m. Eastern time.

Adding to the sadness of loss is the fact that for some bird owners, the pet they lose may have been in the family for a generation — or more! Not that longevity is the key to a bird's value — Brian has helped many clients through the loss of charming budgie companions, who have passed on after a lifespan that was a fraction of what a macaw may enjoy.

**TIP**

Taking care of yourself is important at this difficult time. Some people — the "It's just a bird" crowd — don't understand your feelings and may shrug off your grief as foolish. Even those who may understand the emotion over the loss of a dog may not be so empathetic when a bird is gone — many people just don't get the "bird thing" like we do. The company of other bird lovers is very important. Seek them out to share your feelings. Social media sites are a great place to post memorials and share memories with others who understand.

A difficult time, no doubt, but remember: In time, the memories become a source of pleasure, not pain. You're not on any set timetable, but healing happens. We promise.

**TIP**

A handful of books and one really fine video may help you help your child with the loss of a pet. From Fred Rogers (yes, Mister Rogers of Neighborhood fame) comes the book *When a Pet Dies* (Putnam), a classic after more than 20 years, and the episode "Death of a Goldfish" from *Mister Rogers Neighborhood,* which you can find online (https://vimeo.com/153417661). Rachel Biale's *My Pet Died* (Tricycle Press) not only provides pages that children can fill in, but also offers special pages of advice that parents can refer to and save. Finally, Judith Viorst's *The Tenth*

*Good Thing About Barney* (Aladdin) is a book that experts in pet loss have recommended for many years. Although not specifically about birds, these resources can still help.

# What If You Go First?

Some birds have lifespans nearly as long as humans, so if you get your bird when he's young and you're a young adult (or older), he may outlive you. Thinking about how you'll provide for your bird after you're gone is an essential part of taking care of him.

TIP

You can set up a trust to ensure that your bird will be cared for in the event of your death. A trust allows you to specify exactly how you want your bird cared for, such as the type of diet he eats or the frequency or reason for veterinary visits.

Each state has different laws pertaining to pet trusts, so consult an attorney in your state who specializes in estate planning. Some states put a limit on the lifetime of a pet trust. The trust may last for 21 years or expire on the death of the last covered pet, but Minnesota and Tennessee allow pet trusts for up to 90 years and Washington for up to 150 years, so bird owners don't need to worry about their pets' lengthy life spans in those states.

Although you'll need to consult your attorney about the legalities of providing for your bird in the event of your death, talking about the subject with friends and family is even more important, because you have to identify one of them as a potential caretaker. You must leave your avian "property" to that person, along with enough money to provide for the bird's care for life. You have no real control over the outcome, which is why you need to choose someone you trust and then hope, for your bird's sake, that things turn out okay.

No one likes to think about dying. But you have a responsibility to those you leave behind, and that includes your pets, especially when you're talking about a bird who may potentially outlive you for decades. Talk to your friends, family, and even your veterinarian. Call an attorney. Just don't rely on the kindness of strangers to care for your pets if something happens to you. Your bird deserves better than that.

TIP

The ASPCA has a Pet Trust Primer at https://www.aspca.org/pet-care/pet-planning/pet-trust-primer.

# 4

# Living Happily with Your Bird

**IN THIS PART . . .**

Develop good bird behavior habits.

Decide whether to breed your bird.

Get to know chickens and other poultry species.

» Dealing with specific problems

» Knowing what to do if you can't solve the problem

# Chapter **12**

# Behavior 101: Getting to "Good Bird!"

Perfection is overrated, in our experience. We don't expect it from our families. We don't expect it from our friends. We know better than to expect it from ourselves. And we certainly don't expect it from our pets. After all, if we have a hard time getting along — or even communicating well — with our own kind, how can we expect to have an easy time of it with another species?

From the smallest budgie or lovebird to the largest macaw or cockatoo, chickens, ducks, and geese included, the birds we talk about in this chapter are intelligent, generous, territorial, sometimes sex-crazed, affectionate, distant, talkative, uncommunicative . . . we could go on, but we bet you're getting the picture. Birds are a lot like humans!

Human as they may seem, though, birds are still birds. And you have to be understanding both of their needs and of their motivation for doing the things they do. What you see as "bad" behavior may well be perfectly normal for a bird, and you have to think like a bird to alter the behavior you don't want — if you can.

And there's the rub. With some birds, "bad" — really, normal — behavior can't be changed, and for others, the road to change is a long one. The quick fix isn't all that common when it comes to behavior, and we want to emphasize that fact going in. Still, if you're ready and willing to work with your bird, chances are, you'll end up with a companion who's easier to live with.

**REMEMBER**

Don't be discouraged by the prospect of working with a bird who's making you crazy. Seemingly miraculous turnarounds are possible with companion birds. Hard work, patience, understanding, and commitment can make almost any relationship work.

**TIP**

No matter what else you take out of this chapter, remember this concept: The first step in dealing with a behavior problem is to make sure it doesn't have its roots in an underlying health problem.

**TIP**

Take a look at nutrition in Chapter 6 and basic bird health problems in Chapter 10. You also need a veterinarian skilled in avian medicine to help your bird regain health — we help you find one of those in Chapter 9.

# Setting the Stage for Good Behavior

Changing a behavior in a bird is rarely a matter of reacting only to the problem — whether it's biting, screaming, or feather picking. Good behavior builds from within, and that's especially true with creatures as intelligent as birds. Show us a bird who's a well-behaved member of the family, and chances are, we're looking at a bird who gets plenty of positive attention, eats properly, is in good health, is well-trained, and gets a good amount of exercise.

**TIP**

Preventing a problem is always easier than fixing one, which is why we stress prevention in this book. Chapter 5, with its emphasis on starting a bird out right, complements this chapter, which focuses on getting a bird back on track.

**REMEMBER**

Yes, we know your bird is driving you crazy, and maybe it doesn't make sense to you to worry about, say, your pet's diet when his screaming is damaging your eardrum. But a relationship is kind of like a house: A sturdy one always starts with a good foundation. With your bird, the time is right to bolster the groundwork.

## Ensuring your bird's health

You're doomed before you start if you try to work on undesirable behaviors of a bird who's sick, for two primary reasons:

>> A bird who's sick — and remember, a bird can be very sick without showing any signs of illness — is hardly interested in you and what you want from her. She's fighting for her life, and that's where her energies must be focused.

>> Whatever is wrong with your bird may be causing the behavior problem. Feather picking or even self-mutilation, for example, can be an outward sign of any number of internal medical conditions. Another possibility: Your bird may be in pain. Consider how unhappy a bird with a undiagnosed arthritic knees — yes, it happens! — is going to be about being asked to step up on your hand. Wouldn't you bite if it meant you'd be left alone?

If you have a bird with a behavior problem, the veterinary hospital is your first stop. Your veterinarian can not only work to restore your pet to good health or document that baseline health is sound, but also offer some good, solid behavior intervention advice or help you find someone who can.

Making sure a bird is healthy before working on behavior issues is so important that most trainers and veterinarians will not even take a case unless and until the pet has been thoroughly examined by a veterinarian who has experience with birds. This is not to say that you can't start working on behavior while getting the medical side of things in order — Brian strongly recommends that *both* occur simultaneously if at all possible! (See the "Calling for help" sidebar, later in this chapter, for information on trainers.)

## Being fair to your bird

Look around your home. Does it bear any resemblance that you can see to an Amazon rain forest, an African jungle, or the Australian outback? Likely not. And yet, these environs are your bird's natural habitat. When your bird is falling asleep at night, is he dreaming of some jungle he may never have known? Most pet birds are wild at heart — a fact you need to keep in mind when trying to deal with what, to you, are behavior problems. Even a bird born into domestication and lovingly raised by human hands is still not more than a few generations — and sometimes far less — from the wild life. Even domestic poultry, although domesticated for centuries, still are quite different from household dogs.

Domestic life is a trade-off for birds — a bargain, we must point out, they had no say about making. Sure, their lives may be longer in captivity, and maybe they don't have to worry so much about food (it's provided) and predators (they're discouraged). But they also don't have the pleasure of living in a huge flock of their kind, of flying for miles a day, of landing on anything they fancy and tearing it apart just for the sheer joy of it (and then pooping all over it before they fly somewhere clean and new).

To put it bluntly: No wild bird lives in a cage.

You can't turn your home into a rain forest or other natural environment, but you can manage some substitutions that help make up for what your bird is missing.

## Creating a suitable environment

Although many of today's zoos go to great effort to keep animals happy, this situation wasn't always the norm. With little more than bare enclosures and food, many zoo animals in years past slowly went mad or got sick and died from the stress of captivity. Compare that existence to the rich environments the better zoos provide for their animals today — as close to wild as you can get. Even when building a massive, natural-like habitat isn't possible, good zookeepers today do their best to enrich the environment of their charges. Toys, training, food that's more challenging to find and eat — all these and more are part of a good zoo today, and the animals are better for it.

We encourage you to consider following the example of these zoos and improve the space your bird calls home. Although zoo birds aren't pets — they're generally not handled as often, and they don't have to be a human companion — you can still learn from the zoos and their tricks of the trade.

**TIP**

If you're looking for a well-researched, engrossing, and sometimes eye-opening book on how zoos work today, pick up a copy of *The Modern Ark: The Story of Zoos, Past, Present and Future,* by Vicki Croke (Scribner). The way zoos deal with the issues of captivity help you gain a new perspective on the challenges that face you and your bird.

When you think animal welfare, what comes to mind? Being kind to them? Making sure they have enough food? Shelters that take them in if their families can't keep them? You may be surprised to learn that animal welfare has a specific definition. Good welfare, according to the World Organization for Animal Health, is being healthy, comfortable, well nourished, and safe. The definition also includes psychological well-being, meaning that animals — including birds — should be able to express innate behaviors and be free from pain, fear, distress, and suffering. Those standards of what the bird should be free of are known as the Five Freedoms.

Specific avian welfare principles state that birds need food, water, proper handling, health care, and environments appropriate to their species. We think it's important to focus not just on satisfying their physical needs but also on ensuring that they have positive experiences. Companion birds should have the ability and opportunity to experience vitality, companionship, contentment, satiety, happiness, curiosity, exploration, foraging, and play. When you provide these things for your bird, you're contributing to his physical and mental health.

In a nutshell, good welfare is not just the absence of bad things, it requires that a number of activities, foods, and behaviors that are important to your bird be provided and enriched. And your bird is the one who dictates what he likes, not you. A bird's welfare belongs to the bird.

**REMEMBER**

Not all zoos hear the message of better care for their captive creatures — and many birds and other animals suffer as a result. We encourage you to make your voice heard and support the efforts of zoos to modernize for the sake of the animals. Zoos in North America accredited by the Association of Zoos and Aquariums must meet certain standards of animal care and management. Vote with your feet — and dollars — on second-raters that show no interest in improving: Don't patronize them!

**TIP**

Check out Chapter 4 for information on buying a cage and accessories and Chapter 5 for tips on setting up your bird's home.

## Investing time in positive interaction

Have you ever had a teacher or boss who never had anything nice to say about anything you did but came down hard on you if you made a mistake? Did you find that person likable? Did you enjoy being around that person, or were you stressed out waiting for the boom to fall?

We're not sure why so many people are quick to criticize and slow to praise, but we do know this all-too-human tendency can have an undesirable effect on your bird. Instead of waiting to catch your bird doing something wrong, look for opportunities to praise him for doing something right. A few sweet words, a favorite treat, or a neck scratch — your bird deserves these signs of respect for being the kind of companion you want him to be, however briefly he's managing to pull it off. One of the reasons punishment works is that (for a while) you see it working. This can reinforce you to do more of it, and you forget to reinforce the behaviors you want to see. Watch out for that trap! If you use punishment as a primary strategy, you may see increased escape and avoidance behaviors, increased aggression, increased or generalized fear, and apathy.

Is your bird playing quietly with a toy? Staying on his play gym? Show him you approve! Spend time with your bird every day, working on helping to build and reinforce good behaviors such as the step-up cue (more on this later in this chapter, as well as in Chapter 5), playing with toys together, and just plain hanging out. Talk to your bird, snuggle your bird, if he likes that sort of thing (not all do), and take time to figure out your bird's favorite places to be scratched.

If the only time you deal with your bird is to (occasionally) clean up the cage, change the food and water, and yell at him for screaming, you're not holding up your end of the bargain. Your pet bird should be a member of your family. Make him one, and always keep an eye out for opportunities to let your bird know he's appreciated. He'll appreciate you back!

## Getting that bird a job!

Find something for your bird to do, or you can count on him finding something on his own. Give him lots of things to destroy, puzzle toys to figure out, and treats that take some effort to eat — like an occasional almond or other nut in the shell, a bit of corn on the cob, or even more complicated foraging-type items.

Be creative! Try using tree branches as perches — we list the safe kinds in Chapter 4 — and recycle old ballpoint pens into chew toys (remove the ink cartridge). Celebrate when your bird makes mincemeat of something you've provided him for just that purpose. Bird can be seriously destructive and providing an outlet for those tendencies is a wonderful way to give your bird a "job."

## Giving your bird choices

Birds living in a bland cage with minimal opportunities for interaction don't have a lot of choice in their lives. They don't choose to come live with you, they don't choose their cages or toys, they don't choose the food they want to eat (and if they did it would probably be junk food). That lack of choice can be a source of stress in their lives, even if you don't see it.

Signs of stress in birds include appetite loss, vocalizing more or less frequently than normal, feather picking, sudden aggression, development of repetitive behaviors, or fear — sometimes of something new in the environment. Pay attention to changes in your bird's behavior; they're important clues to how he's feeling.

To help your bird live his best life, let him make choices whenever possible. He should be able to choose if or when he wants to interact with you. Provide him with an assortment of toys so he can choose which ones he wants to play with when he wants to play with them. Pay attention to the types of fresh foods he likes so he can have a little birdie buffet and pick out his faves. Training gives your bird choices, too. It gives him the opportunity to perform a behavior you ask for and receive a reward or to say, "Not right now; not interested." There are all kinds of ways you can provide your bird with choices in his life, and we bet that if he had the words, he'd thank you for it.

# Being consistent with your bird

Children may fuss about house rules, but it's pretty well accepted by parenting experts that children like the security of having limits set for them and knowing those restrictions are consistently and fairly enforced.

Birds like being treated the same way, and perhaps that's not surprising, considering how many bird lovers say their parrots are like 2-year-olds.

Another human–bird parallel: Like some people, some birds are opportunists — if you're not going to provide the framework for how social interaction happens in your home, they may be more than willing to take on the job, whether you want them to or not. Not all birds are bucking for a promotion to upper management, but even the most easygoing pet birds enjoy the security of knowing that they live in a home where there is a framework built on mutual trust and that is worth being a part of.

**REMEMBER**

Being an effective bird "parent" doesn't mean being a dictator. If you teach your bird to do what works best for him and that behavior also fits best in your home, you can have a winner!

# Becoming your bird's life coach

Guiding your bird's decisions is a big part of being his friend and companion. Parrots and many other birds are highly social, so forming a friendship with you is natural to them — if you go about it the right way. That doesn't mean teaching him that you're "the boss"; it's more like negotiating any other type of relationship. Think about what behaviors are acceptable to you, the ways you expect to interact with your bird, and what activities the two of you can do together, whether that's going to the beach, being road-trip buddies, making therapy-animal visits, or simply hanging out at home enjoying each other's company. To do any of those things, you'll want to teach — and continually reinforce — certain behaviors that will be the foundation of your life together. That will help you build other, more complex, behaviors to allow your bird to confidently and successfully navigate any situation, whether it's a visit to the veterinarian or a trip to Grandma's house.

You can't sit your bird down and explain to him that you're in charge, and you can't write the house rules and post them on your refrigerator for him to read. You have to explain your expectations in a way your bird understands. You have to show him what you want to see and make sure it's worth your bird's time to do it, because it pays well for him.

First things first: When teaching your bird, we recommend always using positive reinforcement as the driving principle to guide behavior. That's the addition of something your bird likes — a favorite treat, a head scratch, a word of praise, a fun activity — after he gives you a desired behavior. For instance, if you offer your hand and your bird steps up, you reward him with a pine nut or whatever he especially likes. If your bird's favorite treat is pine nuts, he'll be more willing to step up in the future because he knows it means good things will happen.

Some people confuse positive reinforcement with bribery. They're not the same at all! For one thing, bribery is intended to benefit the person offering the bribe, while positive reinforcement is meant to benefit the *receiver*. You can separate them this way: A bribe is offered *before* a behavior while positive reinforcement comes *after* a behavior. Positive reinforcement is a way of communicating with our birds: "Hey, I liked that!" Birds are smart — they get the message that stepping up, touching a target, or pottying in a specific area brings rewards. Bonus: You become more observant of your bird's behaviors, which in turn deepens your ability to communicate.

**REMEMBER**

## SAYING NO TO PUNISHMENT

What about punishment? Is that a good way to communicate with your bird? We say an emphatic no! Certainly not as the only approach to bring about change. Punishment doesn't tell or show your bird what you want him to do. The main thing it teaches a bird is that sometimes you act like a crazy person. Worse, it can damage the relationship between you.

Yelling at your bird doesn't solve a problem. If anything, your shouts are usually a negative reinforcement of a behavior such as screaming. Your bird wanted attention, any kind of attention, and he got it — he won. You, on the other hand, have just taught him to scream for what he wants.

Beyond not solving a problem, hitting almost always makes the problem worse. **You should never, ever strike your bird.**

Physical punishment doesn't work because your bird has no frame of reference for understanding it. Birds aren't hardwired to understand physical discipline. Punishing your bird makes him think you're an unpredictable jerk at best and a dangerous lunatic or predator at worst. If you were a parrot living with someone who popped you for reasons you didn't understand, wouldn't you be inclined to protect yourself by biting?

Striking a bird can do more than injure your relationship. Physical violence can injure his body. Even the largest birds are much smaller than humans, and they can be hurt easily by a physical correction.

**TIP**

Here are the guidelines you need to know well and introduce to your bird:

>> **Your pace, your call:** Now that you know a bit more about reading your bird's behaviors (see Chapters 5 and 7), you can make a promise to him: It's okay for him to say, "No." When you see signs of aggression, hesitance, or apprehension, make sure your bird understands you're willing to stop and renegotiate. No need for outright combat — just make sure your negotiation skills are good and your expectations are appropriate. This promise is huge and positions you to be viewed much more favorably by your bird. With lots of deposits into the "bank of trust," your bird can begin to see more value in interacting differently with you.

Achieving this goal may mean you need to make sure your bird is in a location where you can more easily see what he's doing and interpret/respond appropriately. It may be hard to read behavior when your bird is at the top of his play stand or cage, or on your shoulder, or in other hard-to-see places. Remove the rooftop play gym your bird's cage may have come with if it offers you a better vantage point to interact from, and lower portable play gyms and perches. Cancel shoulder rides; carry your bird on your hand and keep your arm down. Always remember that your bird has the right to say, "No, thank you," when you ask him to step onto your hand or arm. The task for you will be to develop the skills to ask, "Are you sure?" The ability to offer something he values may help him rethink his response.

>> **Time out!** Although we may think that time-out refers to a disciplinary action — "Go stand in that corner and think about what you have done" kind of thing — it really isn't. When your bird is used to getting treats and rewards for things he does with you and adds in a behavior you don't want to see, stop the rewards for a moment. Give him time to connect the dots that that last behavior resulted in a stop of the flow of what he wanted. Give him the opportunity to do a behavior for which you can again reward him. This is the principle of *positive reinforcement* (giving rewards for behaviors you want) and *negative punishment* (taking away rewards in response to behaviors you do not want). It is an ethical and effective means to bring about behavior change if put together well.

>> **Follow the leader:** Teach your bird the step-up cue — we explain how in Chapter 5 — and practice, practice, practice. This is an important skill for your bird to have and allows you to move him and interact more efficiently and easily. That said, not all pet birds must learn the step up, and not all birds with problems (particularly with trusting you) should have this lesson as their first.

>> **Go where I ask you to; I'll make it worth your effort:** Most birds appreciate and enjoy lots of time out of their cages. But letting them out, if they don't know how to come to you or go where asked, can lead to problems — lots of them. By employing target-training methods and expanding into recall training, the fun can really begin. Coming to you and going where asked requires a mutual relationship and perceived value for doing so.

# CALLING FOR HELP

When you're dealing with bird behaviors that are painful to you or destructive to your home or belongings — especially if the situation is long-standing, and even more if it's causing strife in the family — you can easily get sidetracked by the frustration and anger you feel. A one-on-one consultation with an avian behaviorist or a veterinarian skilled in behavioral medicine and training can really help put you and your bird back on track, leading to a healthier and happier interactive lifestyle. With guidance, you can establish — or reestablish — a true bond.

Finding someone qualified to help you understand your bird's behavior and develop a better relationship calls for attention to experience and expertise. Credentials are a tricky business. Although they're important to consider, they don't necessarily guarantee that the holder is compassionate or up to date in her thinking. Ask questions to make sure you're in philosophical agreement.

Some behaviorists are veterinarians with extra study in the field of animal behavior and the credentials to back that up; others are people with degrees in animal behavior, psychology, or a related field. Some well-respected animal behaviorists, however, acquired their "degrees" by learning on the job — and they've been doing great work for years. Others, however, rely on experience without challenging their interpretations of it. They can end up out of date, out of touch, and a bit dangerous with their methods.

A veterinarian experienced in avian medicine is a good place to start when your bird is exhibiting a behavior you don't like. Many, such as Brian, are pretty good with behavior advice, while others prefer to make sure your bird is physically healthy and then refer you to someone else for behavior help.

Some behaviorists make home visits. Others do telephone consultations, in part because many clients are too far away to visit. Usually, a consultation with a follow-up or two can bring you relief and deliver enough information to keep you headed in a positive direction. Rates vary widely but can cost up to $200 per consultation — expensive, perhaps, but not when compared with the price of living with a bird you find intolerable.

These skills will take you a long way toward a fun, healthy, and long-lasting friendship.

You can distract a bird and redirect undesirable behavior, but you can't punish him for it. If your bird is chewing the edge of a piece of furniture, you can get his attention and then approach him, ask him to step up, and find him something more appropriate to destroy. But don't hit him, yell at him, or (as is sometimes suggested) shoot him with water from a spray bottle or water gun. These strategies, known as "positive punishment" because they involve adding an aversive consequence to the situation, won't help, and they usually make behavior problems much worse in the long run.

# Problem-Solving Unwanted Behaviors

If your bird is healthy, and if you've fussed with his environment and your attitude, you can start to work with the individual behaviors you can't stand.

Sometimes, simply returning your bird to good health improves his attitude. Other times, adjustments take a little more work. And sometimes, what bothers you can't be fixed. Sorry, but it's the truth. Doesn't mean you should stop learning and trying, though.

## Feather picking

If we had to pick one problem that has bird lovers, behaviorists, and veterinarians alike pulling their hair out in frustration, we'd have to choose *feather picking*, a bird's willful destruction of his own plumage, as shown in Figure 12-1.

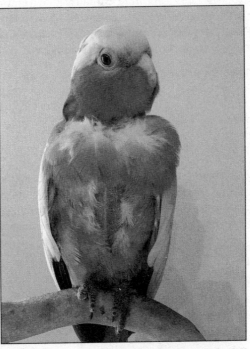

**FIGURE 12-1:** Feather-damaging behavior can leave birds partially or fully naked.

*Photograph courtesy of Rachel Baden, DVM*

**REMEMBER**

The first thing you need to know about this problem: Feather picking is a sign of something wrong with your bird or that was wrong in the past and has set the stage for learning the behavior for future or continual use. The only hope you have of reducing or eliminating feather picking is finding out and addressing what's behind the behavior.

## What causes it

Frequently, feather picking is attributed to boredom, but it can relate to a staggering variety of problems; any one or any combination of the following scenarios can be the source of your bird's plucking:

>> **Health problems:** Medical conditions behind feather picking include allergies, parasitic infections, bacterial infections, abnormal growths (cysts) in the feather follicle, internal health problems, and hormone-associated problems. And that's the short list!

>> **Vitamin deficiencies:** Deficiencies of certain nutrients, such as vitamin A, niacin, zinc, and more can lead to feather-damaging behavior. For instance, birds who get too little vitamin A can develop dermatological problems such as rough, scaly skin or poor feather quality. In turn, those can cause birds to groom themselves excessively and the destructive behavior becomes a habit.

>> **Low humidity:** Many birds come from extremely humid environments, and our houses can't hope to duplicate the conditions of a rain forest (we'd be miserable). The dry air of most houses can be a factor in feather picking and can set the stage for some secondary medical problems.

>> **Boredom and pent-up energy:** Birds are active and intelligent, and they don't always handle the strain of being forced to sit around in a cage all day. Birds with no opportunity to forage (read more about this natural behavior in Chapter 5) can develop feather-picking behavior. Without things to play with and stuff to destroy, and without being able to get out of the cage and exercise, birds may direct all their energy toward self-mutilation.

>> **Psychological problems:** A bad wing trim — too short, with no allowance for an "easy landing" — can upset a bird so badly that she starts tearing at herself. True phobias can and do exist in parrots, as well as other obsessive-compulsive behavioral disorders — all of which can result in feather-damaging behavior.

>> **Attention-seeking:** You love how your bird looks. He starts tugging at feathers and you freak out, imagining your beautiful bird with the broiler-chicken look. Every time he touches his feathers — even for normal preening behavior — you rush over. See how this works? "Aha!" thinks your bird. "All I have to do to get attention is pull a feather!"

>> **A means of alleviating stress:** Although this category may seem vague, it's pretty huge in Brian's mind. You may remember being under stress in the past (while studying for final exams, for instance, or preparing a presentation for work). Maybe you got into the habit of biting your fingernails or twirling your hair as a sort of outlet for your stress. This type of displacement behavior is common in humans *and* animals, and in both cases excessive instances of it can lead to actual injury, whether that's fingernails gnawed to the quick or feathers pulled out.

**TIP**

## PREVENTING FEATHER PICKING

There are a number of ways to enrich a bird's environment and reduce the risk of problems such as feather picking. One is *foraging* (the ability to search for food). Foraging is essential to a bird's well-being, but it's a behavior that many companion birds don't get much of a chance to carry out. Just setting a bowl of pellets in front of them isn't enough. They need to be able to carry out that natural function of seeking food, through puzzle boxes or toys, hiding food in a container for them to find, or providing paper, cardboard, or other items they can chew or shred to bits. Providing opportunities for foraging is an important way to head off, lessen, or eliminate unwanted behaviors and give your bird a great quality of life.

Start changing things up, in small increments. A gentle daily misting with a spray bottle (very different from using the hard spray setting) and the addition of a room humidifier may be part of the solution. Also consider different toys, especially those that encourage foraging or that are fun to destroy, a smaller cage or a larger one, a new cage location, keeping a radio playing during the day or playing nature sounds, and other things that may redirect your bird or provide alternate activities. Observe carefully what happens. Are the changes helping to redirect your bird to alternative activities? Can you see at least a decrease in the amount of feather damage that is occurring?

You may have heard that birds need a certain number of hours of sleep per day and that you should cover their cage for that period of time to ensure it. Not necessarily so. Some birds like having a cage cover; some birds don't. Some birds sleep more or less than others and do just fine. Watch out for these generic recommendations and let your bird guide you. He's just as individual as you are!

In short, it's essential to provide your bird with a clean, appropriate — as much as possible, anyway — environment and real opportunities to express normal behaviors such as play, seeking food, and interaction with either yourself or other birds.

## What can be done about it

So, what can be done with the feather picker? Call your veterinarian, *as soon as the problem appears.* You need to rule out (or if necessary treat) medical or nutritional problems before you proceed exclusively along a behavioral intervention pathway. That should take place sooner, rather than later. In general, the longer your bird has been picking, the greater the probability of a habit or unresolvable pattern of behavior being set. Don't wait a few years before addressing a picking problem — when it starts, you need to start looking for a solution.

Even before your bird receives a clean bill of physical health, you can start seeking and addressing other things that may be signaling it for your bird. First, realize that feather picking could well be an environmental problem. That is, your bird's environment isn't stimulating enough, or is providing stress that leads to the need for your bird to find a way to deal with that stress. Feather picking is not commonly seen in birds in the wild, compared to those who live in homes as companions.

Try making environmental adjustments to see whether you can ward off the picking. Prepare for the project to be a long one! Start a diary to record changes you notice and any effects they may have on your bird's behavior. If your veterinarian is knowledgeable about bird behavior — not all are, and that's not a knock on them — talk to him about behavior modification techniques (such as desensitization and counterconditioning; see the nearby sidebar, "Modifying your bird's behavior") or providing positive reinforcement when your bird is doing something other than feather picking.

**WARNING**

Avoid the feather-picking "cures" you may see in stores or on the Internet. This condition is a complex one with many potential causes that are often interrelated. There's no quick fix for it, much as we all wish for one. A real and effective resolution to the problem calls for establishment of a diagnosis — which in and of itself can take time — followed by corrective action, time, and if needed, reevaluation of and alterations in treatment. There's no such thing as a single-visit diagnosis, definitive treatment plan, or overnight cure.

**REMEMBER**

We know: You want a definitive cure. Alas, one doesn't exist. The best we can suggest is to be patient, work with your veterinarian, and be prepared to love your bird no matter what he looks like. In some cases, feather picking is for life. In others, the problem is only occasional. Yes, some birds do become full-feathered again, but not every pet bird is bound for complete redress in the plumage department.

# MODIFYING YOUR BIRD'S BEHAVIOR

*Desensitization* is the process of gradually and safely exposing your bird to a situation or stimulus that scares him, starting at a distance or sound level that doesn't evoke fear or undesirable behavior. The sight, sound, or distance is gradually increased so that the bird has a chance to become accustomed to the stimulus and it no longer seems threatening. *Counterconditioning,* which often goes hand in claw with desensitization, is the act of associating a scary sound or object with something the bird likes.

Maybe your bird is really afraid of the vacuum cleaner — that long hose does sort of resemble a snake — but he loves pine nuts or blueberries. To desensitize and countercondition your bird to the sight or sound of the vacuum cleaner, you might run it in another room, where he can hear it but not see it. If even that's too loud, maybe you play a recording of it at low volume, so low that your bird doesn't notice or respond to it. Gradually, you increase the volume or the nearness to the object, at the same time offering your bird an extra-special treat so that eventually he starts to associate the sound of the vacuum cleaner with good things and no longer exhibits a fear response. The most important thing is to increase exposure slowly so your bird never gets to the point of feeling frightened. It's all too easy to rush birds and set back their progress. Also, make sure the reward is something your bird really, *really* wants, not something he gets every day.

Beyond a physical exam and baseline laboratory tests, you and your veterinarian may find yourselves working through the A, B, Cs of behavior: antecedents, behavior, consequences. Using careful observation, you may be able to determine the events and conditions that occur prior to a specific behavior such as feather-picking (those are the *antecedents*) and identify the results following the *behavior,* the *consequences.* By looking at the circumstances surrounding a behavior, you're better able to work with your bird to change old behaviors or teach new ones.

Here's an important thing to keep in mind: The more activities you add to your bird's behavioral inventory, the more things he'll have to do and the more alternatives he'll have to feather-destructive behavior. Even if your bird still prefers to clip off a wing feather or two (or more) from time to time, he'll have more life skills and an overall improved quality of life and welfare. Simply put, if you keep your eye on the prize of your bird's happiness and engagement, you can't lose!

Strategies that *don't work* for feather picking include all manner of over-the-counter sprays and pesticide treatments for mites that probably don't exist on your bird. In general, you're wasting your money trying these concoctions, and you may be risking your bird's life. When you recognize that the main goal is to teach your bird alternative behaviors and activities, you can see how those types of "magic potions" fail; they don't teach your bird a darn thing! Their "goals," if you read the label are simply aimed at stopping the behavior, not at changing your bird's lifestyle, happiness, and welfare.

**TECHNICAL STUFF**

## PROZAC FOR BIRDY?

With dogs on Prozac and cats on Xanax to help moderate their behavior, you may naturally wonder: Can a medication stop my bird from ripping himself to pieces? Many medications, from mood adjusters such as Prozac to tranquilizers such as Valium, have been tried on feather pickers, with discouraging or extremely variable results.

Believe us, Brian would like nothing better than to say yes and to write a prescription for a medication to cure the frustration of feather picking. At times, these types of psychotropic medications are certainly used. They aren't employed as a first-choice treatment plan; at best, they come into play to aid in an overall behavior modification plan that is specifically designed for an individual patient. However, no drug therapy is available that works on its own to treat feather picking. Just like those magic feather-picking potions, psychotropic drugs don't teach your bird anything. They may, however, help speed up the ability to teach key lifestyle changes, in some specific patients and circumstances.

Usually, however, these medications have been used outside the framework of an overall behavior-change strategy, often with little reassessment or adjustment of the treatment plan over time. Research continues, of course, but you can expect to wait a long time for that "miracle drug," if it ever comes at all. Any drug that's intended to help has the best chance of working when it's directed to the underlying problem. ***Remember:*** Feather picking isn't a disease — it's a clinical sign and, more important, a behavior.

## Biting and other forms of aggression

Birds bite. That's the first rule of Bird Club.

Any parrot is capable of delivering a powerful punch with his sharp, strong beak. Birds bite for any number of reasons, including the following:

» **Fear:** Who doesn't feel the need to become much more forceful if they feel afraid or cornered?

» **Territorial protection:** Stay away from my place, or else!

» **Redirected aggression:** They can't bite what they want to, so they bite who's at hand.

What's important to know is that biting is a form of communication for birds. None of us likes to be bitten, especially when those powerful beaks draw blood, but sometimes a bite is the only way a bird has of delivering a message.

Sometimes she's saying, "No, I don't like that!" and sometimes she's startled because she wasn't expecting whatever you did. In either case, it's your job to figure out the cause and determine a better way for the two of you to "discuss" your problems.

**REMEMBER**

Avoid using emotional or interpretive words to describe your bird's behavior — instead of saying, "He's vicious," say, "He bites." Saying that he bites is a clear description of what he does; saying that he's "vicious" doesn't provide any useful information as far as describing or determining the cause of the problem. When you can describe the behavior ("He bit me"), you can begin to think about the context in which it occurred ("When I startled him by approaching too quickly to ask him to step up, he bit me to get me to back away").

**REMEMBER**

Sometimes your bird isn't biting — at least, not in anger. He may be using his beak as a third leg or to steady himself as he steps onto your hand. If he's not showing signs such as pinning his eyes (see Chapter 7) or fluffing his feathers, stay calm, don't jerk your hand away, and give him a chance to be gentle. You may be surprised! That's how trust is built between you.

When your bird does bite, swallow your anger and remind yourself that striking back at a biting bird makes matters worse. Your bird needs the security of understanding that you really are his friend and that he can learn other ways to interact with you. What you learn in this chapter is key to developing a trustworthy bird from the inside out.

**TIP**

Even the sweetest bird can have an off day. Learn to read your bird's body language — we cover the topic in Chapter 7 — and give your bird space when he needs it.

## Screaming

Enduring a certain amount of loud vocalizing goes with living with a parrot. Some species are worse than others. Some bird lovers have kiddingly said that if you really don't like someone, give him a cockatoo (like the ones shown in Figure 12-2) — they're world-class screamers.

Even relatively quiet birds pipe up at dawn and dusk — the time in nature when they'd be using their voices to "touch base" with the rest of their flock. Birds also scream for some of the reasons they feather-pick: They're bored, they're stressed, and they want attention.

**FIGURE 12-2:**
Cockatoo species in general are a common group of pet parrots with screaming issues.

*Photograph courtesy of Lisa D. Myers, Feathered Follies (Concord, California)*

To quell the noise, put in place a framework for good behavior (see the "Setting the Stage for Good Behavior" section, earlier in this chapter). Try to avoid reinforcement of screaming; don't rush to pick up your bird every time he pipes up, and don't go over to yell at him. Either action on your part *rewards* the screaming behavior. Instead, wait for a time when he's quiet and reward him verbally — "Good quiet!" — and with a treat or some interaction that he likes. Be consistent about this so he learns what gets rewards and what you walk away from. More important, try to figure out what your bird is getting out of making all that ruckus — or what's making him want to continue doing it. This can help you understand how to diminish the payoff and set up a plan to preempt unwanted screaming before it gets started.

**TIP**

You can "adjust" sunrise and sunset by covering your bird's cage, but be fair — you can't keep your bird in the dark all the time. Use the cover maneuver for those times when you just have to sleep in or when you think your head will explode if you hear one more scream. Cover the cage and take a couple of aspirin — you're having one of those days, and the best thing you can do is just get through it. Covering your bird is *not* a permanent solution to screaming, however. Alternatively, you can move the bird's cage to another room and quietly close the door. Or you can redirect your bird's behavior to a favorite foraging toy when you know he's likely to scream.

# SEX AND THE SINGLE BIRD

Bees may do it, and even educated fleas do it, but when your bird wants to do it, you may find it a little disturbing. Small parrots like budgies come into sexual maturity under a year of age, while bigger parrots, such as the large macaws, may not reach maturity until they're 7 or older.

When those hormones surge, though, you'll know it; particularly in birds such as Amazon parrots or some cockatoos. A lot of behavior problems can surface when birds become sexually active — and we talk about them in this chapter (feather picking, biting, screaming) — but one of the behaviors caused by sexual maturity is . . . sex.

Some birds go in for self-pleasuring, rubbing against perches or toys. Some birds start eyeing their owners as prospective mates, putting on grand "come hither" displays by lifting their tails and screaming for their owners to pet them . . . just so. Your bird may lay eggs, which settles the question of gender once and for all (she's a she!). The eggs won't hatch — without a male, they can't be fertile — so just put them in the trash after she has finished laying her clutch. Some birds simply won't quit laying, and for those, you may need help changing their behavior and redirecting those urges properly. In some specific circumstances, there may be a need for hormonal or even surgical help from your veterinarian. Keep in mind that reproductive hormones cycle normally in birds, but unlike what we know with many mammals, the things that help signal that "it's time" come from their environment rather than from an intrinsic internal cycle. What this means is that because our companion birds live in an environment that we control pretty well, we should be able to control and redirect those hormonal urges. Reproductive hormones do not "cause" most behavior problems, even though this is a popular generic message out there. They can, however, certainly contribute to the problem.

Key things that tell your bird that it's time to mate include their perception that they have a mate (that may be another bird in the home, you, their reflection in the mirror, or even their favorite toy in the cage); their perception that their mate is telling them that they want to start a family (this can easily be related to how you may interact with your bird if you're "the one"); their perception that they have a nesting site; their ability to obtain high-energy foods with little effort; and their perception that it's springtime. Most of these things can be analyzed, understood, and modified to send your bird a clear signal: "Not now; I have other things to do."

Can you spay or neuter your bird to avoid hormonal problems? Not really. Since those gonads and their hormones rarely function as the sole cause of most behavioral problems, removing them is almost never a solution. Those procedures can be done, but they aren't simple and aren't done by most veterinarians — and they aren't nearly as commonly done in birds as they are in cats and dogs.

Be realistic. Your goals are to decrease the frequency, duration, and volume of the screaming, not to immediately extinguish it. This may require keeping a log of when screaming occurs, how often, and how loud it is. Even though it's frustrating to hear, if the log shows it's reducing, you're making progress!

REMEMBER

Covering your bird's cage to help with a behavior problem is really the only reason you need a cage cover at all, in most indoor settings. Contrary to popular belief, your bird doesn't need his cage routinely covered at night, either to get enough sleep or to stay warm. He's perfectly capable of managing both without a cover.

And no, you can't have your bird devocalized surgically. The alteration doesn't work with their anatomy — plus, most veterinarians consider it an unethical procedure. Success in the screaming category comes from behavior modification, not from the surgeon's scalpel.

# Deciding What to Do If You Can't Solve a Big Problem

Some relationships just aren't meant to be, no matter how hard you try to make them work. Although we do not believe you should "get rid of" — oh, how we *hate* that phrase — your bird at the first, second, or even third sign of problems, we do realize that in some cases your bird may be better off in a new home.

By "new home," we do not mean placing an ad in paper — "Parrot and cage, $800" — and handing your bird over to the first person who shows up with the dough. You need to be up front about your bird's problems and honest with both yourself and any prospective new owners in discussing the difficulties. Someone with more experience may well be able to handle a bird who's just too high-powered for your taste.

TIP

Ask your veterinarian for help if you need to find a home for a bird. Brian often has a bird or two on the bulletin board at his hospital who's looking for a new address. Rather than euthanize a bird for behavioral problems or have the bird go into an unsuitable situation, Brian would rather help find the right home for the "problem child."

Rescue and placement groups — we list a number of them in the appendix at the back of this book — are another option.

**REMEMBER**

Pull out all the stops when it comes to working with your bird's behavior problem. But even if you decide to place your bird with someone else, you have a responsibility to do right by him.

## BEHAVIOR RESOURCES WORTH TRACKING DOWN

People can most certainly have a lot of problems with their birds, so you can expect to find a lot of advice on the market. Here are some resources we like:

- At Busy Beaks Academy, Melody Hennigh, a registered veterinary technician who has studied with top avian behavior experts, works in-house with patients at Brian's practice, the Medical Center for Birds in Oakley, California, and offers outpatient consulting, online training classes, and webinars.

- Dr. Susan Friedman, a psychology professor at Utah State University, has contributed chapters on learning and behavior to five veterinary texts, has presented seminars to the Association of Avian Veterinarians, and offers the online course Living and Learning With Parrots for Caregivers. Learn more at www.behaviorworks.org.

- Animal trainer and behavior consultant Barbara Heidenreich is president of Good Bird, Inc. (www.goodbirdinc.com), and author of parrot-training e-books that include video, audio, and written advice on parrot behavior problems.

- Lara Joseph at www.theanimalbehaviorcenter.com/meet-lara-joseph is another good source of behavior information through lectures, workshops, and live-streaming events.

- Steve Martin (not the comedian) provides bird and animal training and consulting through Natural Encounters, Inc., at https://naturalencounters.com.

- Kris Porter, an enrichment specialist for the World Parrot Trust, offers books and other sources of information on parrot enrichment, training, activities, and more at www.parrotenrichment.com.

- The Lafeber Company does more than make bird food. Its website has a compendium of articles written by experts on many aspects of living with a bird, including behavior. Go to https://lafeber.com/pet-birds/avian-expert-articles/.

- Mattie Sue Athan's *Guide to a Well-Behaved Parrot,* 3rd Edition (Barron's Educational Series), provides book-length treatment of the points we make in this chapter, with some good stories to heighten the interest.

Giving up your bird doesn't necessarily mean you're not meant for an avian companion. You may have chosen the wrong species for the life you lead — a bird too loud, for instance, or you may have purchased a bird who was a behavioral train wreck (or at least well on the way to disaster) when you got him.

TIP

Before you even consider falling in love with another feathered face, do your homework. We recommend reading Chapters 2 and 20 on bird species and Chapter 3 on choosing a reputable source. If you made mistakes, be sure you learn from them!

# Chapter **13**

# Living in a Multiple-Bird Household

The joy of having a pet bird brings with it one small problem: After you've given your heart to an avian companion, a little seed takes root in your soul, an idea that's likely to spring vigorously to life at the slightest provocation. Then you may do something crazy. In fact, you may already be at risk!

Have you ever been to the bird shop for supplies and found yourself looking at a particularly charming bird, wondering if your credit line (or mate) would tolerate the addition of a new pet, along with a cage and other paraphernalia? Have you ever seen a bird on social media, one quite different from your own — bigger, smaller, more talkative, more mellow, and always, so beautiful — and thought, "I wonder what it would be like to live with one of *those* birds?" And finally, have you ever gone so far as to act on these thoughts, bringing home a second, third, or even seventh bird?

If so, congratulations! You have a condition known as NEB: Never Enough Birds. Don't worry — NEB is normal enough and usually poses no health risk to either you or your birds (see the nearby sidebar "How many birds are too many?" for the exceptions), although it may put a dent in your wallet.

We know many people who happily share their lives with ten or more pet birds. And we know other people for whom one bird is really more than they should have.

Some well-meaning people get in over their heads with too many cats and dogs, but with birds, the "collector" mentality seems to be an even more common problem. Some people end up with more birds than they can manage. Infectious diseases can overwhelm these households if proper husbandry isn't practiced, especially if corners have been cut on good veterinary care as well.

Multiple-bird households — whether the birds are pets or breeders — are a good thing, in our opinion, but only if the birds are well cared for. If you have one bird, you're familiar with the noise, the mess, and the amount of time it takes to attend to your pet's emotional and physical needs. Ask yourself if you're really in a position to take on more responsibility.

How many birds are too many? Simply put: one more than the number you can care for properly. You owe it to your birds and to yourself to know your limits and to stay within them.

Whether you're interested in having plenty of feathered pets or you're planning to start breeding, you may find that being a flock parent is a very rewarding experience.

**TIP**

Because you don't want to make any mistakes in choosing additional birds, we recommend you visit Chapters 2 and 3 on choosing the right kind of bird and the right place to get him.

# Deciding Between Companion Birds and Breeders

Before you add another bird, ask yourself what relationship you hope to have with the new bird. The answer can help you decide the next step to take.

Do you want another pet bird, or are you thinking of a breeding partner for a bird you already have? You usually can't have it both ways. When most birds pair up to breed, they bond tightly to their mates, and you're not going to be of much interest to them anymore. If you can't stand the thought of losing your bird's companionship, you should probably pass on the idea of breeding. You can, however, have multiple birds living (mostly) in harmony with each other and with you, as a non-breeding flock.

## Choosing birds for companionship

Statistics don't really exist to support our theory, but our experiences tell us that when you're a "birdbrain," one pet bird soon becomes two — or more. And no real reason exists to fight the urge to let your flock grow. As long as you have the desire, time, energy, and money to care for each bird properly, you may discover what many people already know: More birds can bring even more pleasure and beauty to your life.

Birds are naturals at living together. In the wild, they live in groups called *flocks*, and their social nature is part of the reason they make such great companions for people — they're able to make us a member of their family, even as we make them a member of ours. As happy as you can be with more than one bird — and as happy as your birds can be with each other — you may hear people cautioning that you can expect to be ignored when birds have each other for company.

Will the pet bird you have now ignore you if you get another? It depends on if there's a chance they could mate up. Pair-bonded birds usually have eyes only for each other, but birds who are "just friends" can live happily and sociably as part of a blended human-bird family. They won't cut you out of their lives as long as you give them the attention and handling they crave. Most flocks in their wild habitats are made up of pair-bonded ("married") couples, family units, and unpaired individuals, and the same kinds of possibilities can be true in your home, too.

**WARNING**

A bird who's not getting enough attention may go nuts when her owner finally has time for her. If this is the kind of relationship you have with your bird, proceed with caution before adding another pet bird. If you don't have time for one bird, you probably don't have time for two. Plus, your neglected bird will likely glom onto a new bird like a piece of driftwood after a shipwreck — and then who needs *you* anymore? Two birds who have eyes for each other are the ideal if you're looking to breed them, but if you want companions, you're sure to feel left out. If you really don't have a healthy interactive relationship with one bird, it'll be even harder to have an improved relationship with two (or more).

**TIP**

To avoid the problem of your birds excluding you, make sure you have a solid relationship with the bird(s) or birds you already have before adding any others. Give all your birds — new and old alike — quality time alone with you.

# Deciding whether breeding is right for you

Instead of imagining more pet birds, you may be thinking about adding birds for breeding to your household. There are some good reasons to breed birds. One is to provide companion birds with nice temperaments and good health who have been bred in captivity. Breeding birds is farming, and farming can be good for the soul. There are immense benefits both to the aviculturist (farmer) and to those birds who are reared. They include healthy, happy young ones who have value to the aviculturist, to the public, and to the bird's ability to fit into our culture and society as companions. They can contribute to endangered species management programs and zoologic exhibits, and educate and entertain as performing animals. These are all good things.

But the jump into bird breeding is a big one, and you need to think carefully before making the leap. Cats and dogs seem to do pretty well on their own as parents — handling mating, feeding, and early training quite well — but birds are different. You may have a hard time getting them to mate at all, much less produce fertile eggs and hatch babies. And not all birds should be bred; there are plenty of birds out there who are already looking for homes, as we know from the many bird rescue organizations in existence.

You also need to have a plan for what to do with the chicks that come along. Will you keep them or sell them? Is there a market for them? Will you be able to give them up to new homes or will you find yourself living with more birds than you had planned — or budgeted — for?

Additionally, human intervention — that's you — may be required anywhere from the earliest stages, as soon as the egg appears, to anywhere along the developmental phases for those chicks. Although a dog or cat mother happily handles the midnight, 2 a.m., and 4 a.m. feedings, if you plan to hand-feed your baby birds, you should expect to handle these tasks — and more! Hand-fed birds are raised by humans sometimes even from the moment they're hatched — fed around the clock, kept warm, cleaned, and ultimately weaned. Because you're not naturally or instinctively equipped for being a bird parent, you need more than just good intentions. You need a great deal of time and dedication. You also need to invest in some pretty pricey equipment, including incubators, brooders, scales, and more.

REMEMBER

Although birds can be expensive to purchase, they're often not very profitable to breed. Raising healthy, well-socialized, hand-fed babies is labor-intensive, as is purchasing, maintaining, and replacing necessary equipment.

Money and time are prerequisites for bird breeding, but you may need emotional strength, because you're going to lose some babies along the way. What you may see as a tragedy is merely nature's way — some babies aren't meant to make it.

And odds are, someday you'll have one of those doomed ones. Although losing babies is not a common event, it does occur, and the more you breed, the greater your odds of experiencing this loss, which can be emotionally rough for some folks.

Have we put you off breeding? That's not our intent. Brian has been breeding birds for more than four decades, and although Kim and Gina have only kept companion birds, they admire and respect the work of good aviculturists. Breeding birds can be incredibly rewarding. Working with bird babies, and watching them develop into loving, well-adjusted companions and self-confident individuals is exciting. Aviculturists have helped prevent some species from becoming extinct, and they've created interesting and beautiful color and feather variations in species such as canaries, cockatiels, and lovebirds.

**REMEMBER**

Breeding birds is a challenging calling, with many rewards for those who can handle the demands. A hobby for some, a profession for others, aviculture requires an astounding investment in time, emotion, and money. The task of raising healthy, well-socialized pets is not for every bird keeper, but those people who do the job well find raising birds to be a pleasure.

**TIP**

For more information on breeding, check out "Recognizing the Joys and Challenges of Breeding," later in this chapter.

# Understanding the Closed Aviary Concept: Rules to Live By

Whether you're considering adding birds to your household for companionship or for breeding, you need to follow some important rules to ensure the health of both the birds you have and the birds you're adding to your flock. Aviculturists call these rules the *closed aviary concept* (CAC), and disregarding the CAC puts your birds' health at risk.

At its most basic level, the CAC is a strategy for developing a healthy collection of birds — and keeping them that way. The basic rules are as follows:

>> **Make sure the birds you already have are in good health.** Because of the nature of birds, you can't just eyeball one — nor can a veterinarian — and figure that because he *looks* healthy, he *is* healthy. Your bird(s) need to be thoroughly examined by a veterinarian who is experienced in working with avian patients, and the birds may require some forms of diagnostic testing to ensure they're not carrying an infectious disease risk. (For more on preventive care, see Chapter 9).

>> **Never, ever introduce a bird without determining that he's healthy.**
A bird can look completely normal and still be incubating an infectious-disease-causing agent that may take his life — and the lives of birds you already have if you expose them to him. An experienced avian veterinarian should examine your new bird and give him a clean bill of health before you bring him home.

>> **Isolate the new bird(s) for at least six weeks.** The temptation is to take a new bird straight from the veterinary clinic into the flock — but resist temptation. Screening tests are a help, but they're not perfect. A quarantine period allows time for diseases to appear without putting the rest of your birds at risk. The separation also gives your new bird time to settle in and time for you to get to know her on a one-on-one basis. Be sure that you're not a "link" between a bird in quarantine and the other birds. Don't swap dishes, toys, perches, and so on, and wash your hands before and after handling any new birds.

**WARNING**

Don't take the CAC lightly, and don't cut any corners in implementing it. Imagine your heartbreak if a bird you just brought home harbored a disease that ended up killing a bird you've cherished for years.

**REMEMBER**

Infectious diseases (we cover some of the worst ones in Chapter 10) can kill your bird. If you're careful about introducing new birds and follow CAC precautions, you can rest assured you're doing the best you can to keep these killers from spreading into your home.

# Choosing Compatible Birds

Unless you're planning to house your birds in different rooms, they're going to have to be compatible with each other, as well as with your own personality and lifestyle. Fortunately, ending up with a happy flock is pretty easy. We offer a few guidelines to choosing companions who are likely to get along with each other and with you as well. Exceptions exist to every rule, these included, but following them gives you your best shot at peaceable coexistence.

**TIP**

One way to help birds behave compatibly toward one another is to keep their living quarters at the same height. In the bird mind, "Height equals comfort and security." By keeping everyone on the same level, you can level out the psychological advantage of any one bird.

## Species and gender issues

If you're choosing birds for companionship, not breeding, don't give any of your birds the opportunity for pair-bonding if you can help it. Because you don't always know whether your birds are male or female, you may be adding, say, a female blue-and-gold macaw to a household with a male of the same species. Mixing species makes for a much better plan. If you have a macaw and want another large parrot, consider a cockatoo. If you have an Amazon, perhaps a conure would be a good addition.

**TECHNICAL STUFF**

Parrots are mainly monogamous and, in the case of larger species at least, pair for life. The bond between pairs is constantly reinforced by a variety of behaviors, such as allopreening and feeding. This strategy is perhaps adaptive, because of the high proportion of learned (as compared to instinctive) behavior exhibited in parrots: Pairs who know each other well and have experience of one another breed more successfully.

Pair-bonding exists in male–male and female–female couples — although the combinations produce no offspring, of course. The situation is common enough that when a happy pair of breeding birds aren't producing fertile eggs, an avian veterinarian is likely to suggest confirming that the pair actually is made up of one male and one female.

**TECHNICAL STUFF**

Many birds, both male and female, look the same to us, particularly among the parrot species. When we can't tell them apart, we need a little help from science to do so. The gender of birds is generally determined either by DNA testing of a blood sample or by surgical examination of internal sex organs (which are, of course, the only kind of sex organs the aerodynamically efficient bird has). For companion birds, DNA is probably the more popular way of determining gender. For a breeding bird, though, the surgical option may be preferred, because the procedure not only determines what kind of "equipment" a bird has, but also reveals the stage of maturity and any problems that may be visually identifiable.

## Size and temperament issues

Although we know of bird lovers whose budgies, lovebirds, or parrotlets get along famously with their larger cousins, as a rule you're probably better off sticking to birds of about the same size, if you expect to allow them contact with each other.

Learn about the temperament of the species you have in mind (we offer insights into many of them in Chapters 2 and 19). Although every bird has individual characteristics, some species tend to be more aggressive than others. Birds who can't get along (see the nearby sidebar, "You talkin' to me? You talkin' to *me*?") can injure each other severely — with bites, broken beaks, and more. You may think the damage typically goes only one way, with the bigger birds hurting the little ones. But some little guys really know how to get their licks in — they've even bitten toes off their larger avian companions!

Despite your best planning, if you end up with incompatible birds, they're better off living separate lives, or at least in separate cages or rooms within your home.

# Recognizing the Joys and Challenges of Breeding

When you decide to become an aviculturist, you can look forward to an exciting time — and a lot of learning and hard work.

Although we touch on some of the basics here, breeding is one area of bird keeping that requires you to seek some one-on-one help. A veterinarian with experience in avian care can serve as your mentor, but so, too, can a reputable and experienced breeder. In fact, a reputable breeder may be a better choice as a mentor, because not all avian veterinarians have experienced the "joy" of 2 a.m. handfeedings for weeks at a time and of wondering hourly whether an egg is developing properly. Breeders have experienced these dubious pleasures, and the best ones are happy to share their expertise with a dedicated novice.

## PET TO BREEDER TO PET: A UNIQUE CONCEPT

Sure, dogs and cats are better pets when they're spayed or neutered, but even those animals who remain intact for breeding usually are people-friendly their whole lives. The same is not typically true for birds. Bonded breeding pairs generally are interested only in each other, not in humans, and they need to be left alone together to produce offspring.

Because birds are now living longer, healthier lives than ever before, we're seeing the concept of "life stages" taking hold with some bird keepers. Young birds are raised and cherished as pets until sexual maturity or beyond, and then paired for breeding. After their breeding time is past, these birds reclaim their roles as members of a human household.

Such an idea may be hard to get your arms around if you're in a dog-and-cat frame of mind, but consider that the potential life span of a parrot is far longer than that of most other common household pets. Many parrots have life spans comparable to our own. We go through different stages in our lives, some of them involving children, others not. Is it so hard to imagine a similar life for a long-lived pet bird?

Many of the birds being born today will always know the benefits of preventive care and good nutrition. When these birds are past their reproductive years, they'll be healthy and happy enough to retire and spend their golden years as a cherished companion.

**WARNING**

In all phases of breeding birds, we encourage you to find a mentor. Particularly in one aspect, hand-feeding, we can't *in any way* condone a "learn-it-yourself" approach. If you try to figure out hand-feeding baby birds on your own, you're very likely to have sick or dead babies on your hands. Spare the babies — and yourself — the misery: Find an experienced veterinarian or breeder who's willing to show you the ropes with this delicate procedure.

## Pair bonding: 'Til death do us part

Finding a suitable mate for your bird may not be as easy as you think. Although cats and dogs are perfectly content to engage in "one-night-stands" with partners they'll never see again, parrots must form strong bonds before they're interested in reproducing. And they just don't fall in love with the first feathered face they see.

**TECHNICAL STUFF**

Some species, such as the blue-and-gold macaw, are fairly easy to match up, forming pair bonds with relative ease. Other species are pretty picky. The African grey parrot is one of the more selective birds. You can introduce a pair of greys and get an immediate "Wow, that's the one for me" reaction — or you can have two birds together for a decade, and they'll always stay on opposite ends of the perch!

When they're compatible, parrots mate for life, but the "life" in question is not the birds' lives, but rather the life of the relationship. As long as the two birds remain together, they'll usually remain bonded, but if one dies or disappears, the other will try to form a new pair bond with another bird.

Bonded pairs of parrots are pretty solidly attached to their mates, but straying isn't unheard of. Brian likes to tell of one aviary where two pairs of birds "divorced" their mates and spent their time lusting after the birds next door. After the humans moved the birds around to put compatible couples together, everyone settled down and made babies! Other variations are possible, too. For example, a male canary may happily take two or more mates, flitting back and forth between his families — and the females don't seem to mind.

## Setting up your birds' love nest

Even if you have a pair of birds making eyes at each other, don't expect any babies until you establish the right environment. Breeding birds need the following:

- » **Proper housing:** Breeding pairs don't get the out-of-cage freedom that pet birds should get because they're usually no longer responsive enough to humans to be let out safely — and because they'd rather be left alone with each other. As a result, they need a cage with plenty of room for two birds to move about comfortably, along with the usual items that are part of every good setup — lots of toys and enrichments, and a variety of healthy perches.

- » **Plenty of privacy:** Breeding birds need to be spared the distractions of human life. Set up your birds where they can be alone together — and leave them be, as much as possible. Give them the opportunity to choose if you'll be able to see them or not.

- » **Plenty of food:** An abundance of food is one of the triggers for reproduction in many species. Birds instinctively avoid bringing babies into a world where food supplies are questionable. Regularly feed your birds a high-quality commercial diet, supplemented with lots of fresh fruits and vegetables.

- » **A nesting area:** The kind of nesting box depends on the species. Talk to your veterinarian or a breeder experienced with your bird's particular species about an appropriate nesting setup.

Given the right (or wrong) circumstances, some parrot species can fall for abnormal "mates." These can include an owner or other human, some items within the cage, and toys. Another bird housed in the same cage, the same room, or even simply within hearing distance may strongly stimulate reproductive drive.

Even with seemingly perfect conditions for breeding, you may not have the formula "just right" for your birds. Rely on your veterinarian and other breeders for insight and information. Health problems may be at fault, or maybe your breeding setup needs some fine-tuning. Or maybe you're just expecting too much, too soon. Good things come to those who wait!

Most pet birds "do the deed" through a process called the *cloacal kiss.* The female pushes her cloaca partially through her vent, and the male rubs his vent against it to deposit sperm, which the female can store for a few days to fertilize her eggs when she ovulates. Just because birds are actively mating doesn't mean babies are on the way, though. Birds just like to mate! You won't find any birds who are members of the Mile High Club, though — it's not possible for them to mate while in flight.

## Taking care of eggs

The egg is one of nature's most amazing creations, and the story of how it's produced is even more awesome. The female houses an "assembly line" called the *oviduct,* where in just slightly more than a day, the brand-new avian life is produced, set up with nourishment, wrapped in protective membranes and, finally, surrounded by the hard casing that most of us visualize when we hear the word *egg.*

Bird mating rituals go well beyond shaking a tail feather at a desirable love partner. Beyond mating dances, they may add sound effects (red-capped manakins), walk on water (Western grebes), or build an elaborate love nest (bowerbirds).

### Natural incubation

Fertilization occurs high in the oviduct of the hen, shortly after the *ovum* (the female's contribution to a new life) is produced. As the yolk (ovum) traverses the oviduct, yolk membranes, dense *albumen* (the egg white), two shell membranes, and the eggshell are all added on in a period of a little over one day.

At egg-laying time, a fertile egg's embryo is roughly the equivalent of a very early pregnancy in mammals, which makes it easier to understand why some eggs never hatch. Just as many human pregnancies are lost before a woman even knows she's pregnant, many eggs contain defects that prevent their development, even under seemingly perfect conditions.

## TOBY AND TILLY: A LOVE STORY

Hello, Hollywood! Here's a love story that isn't your usual boy-meets-girl, boy-loses-girl, boy-gets-girl yawner. Try this one on for size: Boy meets bird. Bird falls in love with another bird. Bird cuts boy out of his life.

Well, maybe we won't hold our breath waiting for the contract to write the screenplay, but we like the story of Toby and Tilly anyway.

Toby was Brian's first bird, a blue-and-gold macaw brought into his hospital in a lidded plastic garbage can by a man who wanted some cash to get his "bird problem" off his hands. Love at first sight happened between Brian and Toby, and soon the bird was Brian's constant companion, even riding to and from work on Brian's shoulder.

And then came Tilly.

Tilly was to be a companion for Brian's wife, Denise, but the two birds had eyes only for each other. Brian set up the pair in an aviary and was rewarded with several healthy, happy babies the first year they were together.

Toby passed away of a heart condition at the age of 45 (Brian had the privilege of living with him for 34 years). Tilly has a new flame, Tyler. Brian will be forever grateful to Toby, who helped open his eyes to how richly rewarding the keeping of these birds, their care, breeding, and successful rearing of their offspring truly can be.

Eggs don't start their development into hatchlings until the warmth of a parent is applied, and for good reason. If each egg started developing as soon as it left the mother, the babies of a *clutch*, or group of eggs, would hatch at different times, leaving the last babies to hatch at a significant disadvantage when it comes to survival. By having eggs develop and hatch more or less simultaneously, more hatchlings have a chance at survival.

**TECHNICAL STUFF**

Chronic egg laying is when a hen repeatedly lays clutches or produces larger-than-normal clutches without regard to the presence of a normal mate. The behavior can lead to myriad health problems. Functional exhaustion of the reproductive tract can be a metabolic and physiological drain on the bird, particularly on calcium and energy stores, and can predispose the hen to egg binding, cloacal prolapse, osteoporosis, and many other physical problems. Although chronic egg laying occurs in many companion bird species, it's most commonly seen in smaller species, including budgerigars, cockatiels, lovebirds, and finches. Intervention may include environmental management such as removing shredded papers or boxes that can serve as nests, frequently changing cage location to make it seem as if the environment is not stable enough for safe reproduction, encouraging "flock" interactions instead of single "mate" encounters, and avoiding petting the bird in areas that can stimulate reproductive behaviors. If those environmental changes fail, your veterinarian may recommend counter-hormonal therapies, or as a last resort, surgery.

## Artificial incubation

Humans get involved in incubation of eggs for a couple of reasons:

>> **Under the artificial conditions of a human-made environment, some pairs of birds are simply not capable of hatching their own eggs.** They won't incubate them, and they may even destroy them, refuse to feed their chicks after they hatch, or kill their young hatchlings.

>> **Humans can use a bird's own species survival mechanisms to produce more babies than would be normal.** Eggs are good eating, which is why many predators love to raid bird nests for eggs (and for young birds, too). A suddenly empty nest triggers a bird to produce another clutch of eggs to replace those that are gone. This procedure, called *double-clutching,* enables an aviculturist to incubate one set of eggs while the birds incubate the others.

Artificial incubation involves an *incubator* (a machine that keeps the eggs at optimum temperature and humidity for the species) turning the eggs at regular intervals as the birds themselves would.

TECHNICAL
STUFF

The amount of time between when an egg starts to develop and when a chick hatches (the *incubation period*) depends on the species, just as the gestation period between different species of mammals varies. Budgie eggs, for example, develop for 16 days, cockatiels and lovebirds for 18 days, and larger parrots, such as Amazons, for about 24 days. Other species of parrots may spend as much as 34 days in the shell.

TIP

You can tell whether an egg is fertile and developing by a procedure called *candling.* Shine a bright light — such as a penlight — though the egg from behind. A living, developing egg shows a web of red veins.

# Raising babies

The moment a baby starts poking his way out of the shell is when the real fun begins.

The babies of more common pet birds — all parrots, canaries, and other finches — are born with their eyes shut and completely naked, unable to retain heat or moisture without the help of attentive parents — or of humans acting as parents. If you're going to hand-feed your babies, this is the moment you change from one piece of equipment to another — from the incubator, designed for the warming and turning of eggs, to the *brooder*, a place where baby birds (who don't need turning) are maintained at the proper temperature and humidity for their species as they grow.

TECHNICAL STUFF

The naked babies of common pet bird species are described as *altricial*, requiring care and feeding by parents, as opposed to the *precocial* babies of chickens, pheasants, and ostriches, born fully fuzzed, eyes open, and mobile, able to feed themselves almost immediately.

## Hand-feeding and socializing

Bird parents feed their young by regurgitating food from their *crops* (a food storage organ at the base of the neck) directly into the babies' mouths. Humans aren't really equipped to barf for baby birds, so we raise them through hand-feeding.

WARNING

Hand-feeding is not a learn-as-you-go skill. You need to practice under the watchful eye of an experienced person, working with his help until you can hand-feed as naturally as shifting the gears of a car.

Although different methods exist for getting food into baby birds (we recommend using a commercial preparation for complete nutrition), syringes and spoons are perhaps the most common methods among small or hobby breeders. To start out, you feed hatchlings around the clock, in two-hour intervals. The length of time spent hand-feeding — weeks, even months — and the intervals between feedings depend on the species, and to some extent the individuals themselves.

REMEMBER

Raising several clutches of babies can be stressful and exhausting. These all-too-human problems factor into the diseases or even death of babies, especially at the end of a breeding season. Brian has been known to take in an exhausted client's babies at the bird hospital for a day or two so the person can get some sleep — a lifesaver to both the babies and the hand-feeder!

Careful daily record-keeping is as important as proper feeding. You must weigh babies daily and record their weights to ensure that they're developing normally.

TIP

You need help to learn how to be a good hand-feeder, but if you've ever cared for a human baby or successfully bottle-fed a puppy or kitten, you probably have what it takes. The basics of hand-raising are the same with any infant: Keep them warm, keep them clean, and feed them when they're hungry.

Hand-fed babies need to learn an array of normal behaviors. Many young parrots sold as companions learn only one form of social interactive skills (known as *pair-bond enrichment behaviors*) from their new owners, as opposed to the typical social skills that would've been taught by the parents of their wild counterparts. It's not uncommon for them to lack knowledge of normal social interactions and foraging activities, or to learn inappropriate pair-bonding behaviors. To ensure that they learn those important skills, you need to enrich their environment (especially the cage), provide positive-reinforcement training to help guide interactive behaviors, and offer foraging opportunities. See Chapters 5 and 12 to learn more about enrichment and foraging.

One final parallel to raising a human infant you need to remember: The most important ingredient to add is love.

REMEMBER

A baby bird needs to be socialized to human beings. Talk to your babies. Handle them gently and lovingly. Sing to them, play the radio, and just be with them. Every touch the baby bird feels and every sound he hears is making him more comfortable with people, and that makes him a better future companion. Raising the bodies of baby birds with good and regular food and raising their minds and hearts with love is a powerful combination.

## Weaning and fledging

*Weaning* is the stage where baby birds go from hand-feeding to free-feeding, eating a healthy diet on their own. The key concept: Weaning isn't something you do *to* a baby bird; it's something a baby bird does on his own. You don't have to train a bird to eat like a "grown-up," and you most certainly don't schedule a set age at which to wean the bird. At whatever time is right for that bird — different species wean at different times, and so, too, do individual birds — he'll start to pick at and play with grown-up food, soft foods such as soaked pellets and bananas to begin with and then harder food, such as commercial pellets and hard vegetables and fruits.

WARNING

Don't complicate the weaning process by continuing to hand-feed babies without really giving them the opportunity to wean themselves. Let them use their natural instincts and curiosity to teach themselves about new foods.

Instead of offering to hand-feed first, provide your baby with a wide variety of healthy foods, commercial pellets soaked in water, and easy-to-eat fruits and vegetables, such as bananas and corn cut off the cob. Remove toys from the cage, so the baby is inclined to play with and learn to eat the food.

Wait a half-hour or so beyond the regular hand-feeding time and then offer the syringe or spoon with hand-feeding formula. If your baby still wants to be hand-fed, feed him. If your baby isn't too interested in the syringe and even turns his head away from you — perhaps busy playing with a banana or some other exciting new thing that is fun to chew up — skip that feeding.

TIP

Put the grown-up food in a shallow, wide dish, such as a pie pan, and make sure the container is on the baby's level — babies are a little clumsy at this age. A shallow pan gives the baby the opportunity to eyeball everything that's offered and even climb in the pan for play, if desired.

**WARNING**

Don't force weaning on a schedule. Continue to offer grown-up foods before hand-feeding, and be patient. Your baby will come around in time. And don't panic if your careful record-keeping reveals weight loss — most babies lose some weight during their weaning phase, up to 15 percent of their peak weight in some cases. Usually, that's just baby fat disappearing, nothing more.

Along with starting to eat adult food, your baby will begin practicing and learning another grown-up skill, flying. We feel that even though many pet birds spend their lives with their wings trimmed for safety, the babies need to be able to *fledge*, or learn to fly. Let them. They aren't too coordinated at this age, and any help in that area, such as leaving their wings unclipped, is usually much appreciated on their part!

## FLYING THE NEST

After you've poured your heart and soul into raising your bird babies, you want them to go to homes where they'll be loved and properly cared for. Some breeders prefer to sell their babies to a reputable bird shop instead of dealing with pet buyers directly. They may sell unweaned babies to the shop and have shop employees continue to feed and then wean the birds, or they may sell the babies weaned and ready to be sold.

No matter how you choose to sell your babies, pay attention to the same kinds of details we suggest when you're on the other side of the fence as a buyer. Check out Chapter 3 to remind yourself of the hallmarks of a reputable bird shop, and don't let your babies go to any retailer who won't take proper care of them or make sure they go to an educated buyer.

If you're selling your babies through a good-quality retailer, expect to be quizzed and "tested" — they want to know that they're bringing healthy, good-quality babies into their store. And not all stores bring in outside birds for resale — some sell only birds they have bred and raised themselves.

If you're letting your babies go directly to the public, you need to assume the role of educator as well as seller. With all you know from buying, caring for, and breeding your birds, you're in an excellent position to educate prospective buyers — and to turn away those who won't be good caretakers of your special babies.

Visit Chapter 17, with its questions to ask when buying a bird, and consider how you'd answer those questions as a seller. Above all, remember that your babies have value beyond the money you can get for them — they represent countless hours of your time, and they leave your custody with a piece of your heart. Make sure they go with someone who understands how very special they are.

Chapter **14**

# Caring for Chickens and Other Backyard Poultry

Chickens? As pets? You bet! Chickens have been popular in cooking pots for 2,000 years or more, but today, many people keep the cuddly cluckers as companions. Not only are chickens useful for laying eggs, but they're as entertaining and friendly to have around as a feathered Golden Retriever would be.

The craze for chickens as companion birds really took off approximately 20 years ago. Thousands of homeowners in the United States and around the world flocked toward keeping chickens because they wanted to be more self-sufficient and also get fresh eggs from chickens raised humanely and fed organically. Soon they discovered that chickens were not only egg-laying experts but just plain fun to have around.

Chickens are social, smart, and surprisingly soft. They can be clicker-trained to play a xylophone, tell one color from another, ring a bell, or complete an obstacle course. More practically, they can learn to enter or exit a carrier or coop, fly onto an arm or shoulder, and come when called. Their interactions are fun to watch. It's no surprise that there's an Instagram page devoted to drinking with chickens (not serving them drinks, but enjoying a cocktail while watching them — check out www.instagram.com/drinkingwithchickens). Plenty of people refer to their chicken-watching habit as "chicken TV," and there are numerous "chicken TV" videos on YouTube. Chickens follow their people around, roost on their shoulders, snuggle in their laps, and — bonus! — produce tasty eggs for breakfast and baking. When these birds are kept as companions, the bond people develop with them can be strong, and chickens are increasingly presented for veterinary care just like any other companion animal.

But before you run out and order a dozen chicks online (yes, they come in the mail!) with visions of omelets dancing in your head, it's important to consider every facet of keeping chickens. Living with any kind of animal means that you have to deal with noise, smell, and waste. Early-morning crowing means most municipalities prohibit roosters within city limits. (After you've been awakened at 3 a.m. for three days running by a rooster with a poor sense of time, you can understand why.) Even if your area allows chickens, check with neighbors beforehand to make sure they don't have any objection to the soft, soothing sound of clucking. Of course, bribing your neighbors with the promise of fresh eggs and — for avid gardeners — a ready source of high-quality manure is a time-honored method of gaining buy-in from the folks on the other side of the property line.

TIP

If you want to make sure you don't get roosters, buy older birds or *sex-link birds,* whose sex can be identified at hatching. You may also want to consider adopting a flock from someone who is downsizing and placing hens in new homes.

Choosing the right breed of chicken is another important factor. You'll need to take into account the climate where you live (some chicken breeds are more suited to hot or cold temperatures than others), frequency of egg laying, and of course, size, personality, and appearance. If you live in the Midwest, for instance, you'll want chickens who are winter-hardy. And having a diversity of breeds can help you tell your chickens apart when you're just getting started. A buff Orpington, a silverlaced Wyandotte, and a partridge rock all look very different. That can make it easier to get to know them individually — part of the fun of having chickens!

In this chapter, we introduce you to the joys and cautions of chicken keeping, the many different chicken breeds, chicken care and maintenance, and what to know about interactions between chickens and other pets. We also cover other kinds of poultry you may want to add to your flock.

**TECHNICAL STUFF**

The United States Department of Agriculture recognizes six categories of poultry: chickens, ducks, geese, guineas, pigeons, and turkeys. For our purposes, we also include peafowl — better known as peacocks — and game birds such as quail and pheasants.

**TIP**

Throughout this book, we talk about the different types of birds and their suitability as companions. You can read more about chickens and their popularity in Chapters 2 and 19.

# Chickens with Benefits: Seeing What Chickens Have to Offer

There are many great reasons to keep chickens. As far as companion animals go, they're relatively simple and inexpensive to care for after you've provided for their housing needs. In so many ways, chickens can be fun and educational pets for children and affectionate companions for adults.

Chickens even provide lawn care — their "services" include chemical-free bug and weed control and excellent lawn fertilization.

Eggs from home-kept chickens fed a high-quality diet are fresh, flavorful, and nutritious. They're also beautiful, coming in multiple colors such as blue, green, and pinky-brown, in addition to the traditional white.

Chickens are beautiful. Many of them are what are known as *ornamental breeds*, prized for their fancy spangled, speckled, barred, and laced feather patterns; outrageous topknots, combs, wattles, and earlobes; rich gemstone colors of topaz, ruby, and emerald; fluffy beards; ruffled leggings; and jaunty tails.

The first poultry shows, like the first dog and cat shows, originated in the Victorian era and attracted large crowds of spectators. Queen Victoria loved animals of all kinds, and she had a special poultry barn at Windsor Castle to house the chickens from the far reaches of her empire — among them Cochins and Langshans from China and Brahmas from India. We wonder if she kept Scots Grey chickens at her Highland hideout of Balmoral. . . .

# WORDS ABOUT BIRDS

Chicken-related terminology is a language unto itself. Here is some chicken lingo you should know:

- **Alektorophobia:** Fear of chickens (we hope you don't suffer from this!).
- **Capon:** A castrated male chicken.
- **Chook:** A popular Australian term for chickens.
- **Clean-legged:** Used to refer to chickens with no feathers growing from their shanks.
- **Clutch:** A batch of eggs hatched together, either in a nest or in an incubator. The term *clutch* is used with other birds, too, such as parrots and pigeons.
- **Cockerel:** A young male chick.
- **Comb:** The fleshy protuberance on the top of the head, larger on roosters than on hens.
- **Crest:** The puff of feathers on the heads of such breeds as Houdan, Silkie, and Polish chickens. Also known as a topknot.
- **Feather-legged:** Used to refer to chickens with feathers growing from their shanks.
- **Frizzle:** Feathers that curl rather than lie flat. A frizzle is also a common breed of chicken.
- **Hackles:** Feathers at the top and lower portion of the neck, which can be raised to make roosters look more intimidating. The phrases *getting your hackles up* and *ruffled feathers* both originate with chickens (or at least humans talking about chickens — the chickens themselves don't have a word for it!). Chickens also shake and readjust their feathers as a part of normal grooming.
- **Pecking order:** The hierarchical social order of chickens.
- **Pullet:** A young female chick.
- **Saddle:** The part of a chicken's back just before the tail.
- **Sex feather:** A hackle, saddle, or tail feather that is rounded in a hen but usually pointed in a rooster.
- **Shank:** The part of a chicken's leg between the foot and the ankle (formally known as the tarsometatarsus).
- **Sickle:** The long, curved tail feathers of some roosters.

# Considering Different Chicken Breeds

There are multiple types of chickens, from the small bantam varieties to the egg and meat-production breeds to the fancy show chickens, which have fine feathers, indeed. Just like show dogs and cats, there is a standard for each chicken breed. Produced by the American Poultry Association (APA), it's called the American Standard of Perfection (ASP), and it classifies and describes the physical appearance, coloring, and temperament for all recognized breeds of poultry, including chickens, ducks, turkeys, and geese. Judges at sanctioned poultry shows use the ASP to determine which birds are the best of the best.

**TECHNICAL STUFF**

Beyond the regular types, chickens can also be cross-bred. *Sex-links* are cross-bred chickens whose color at hatching is differentiated by sex, making gender determination easier. Two common varieties are the black sex-link and the red sex-link. Black sex-links are a cross between a Rhode Island Red or New Hampshire rooster and a Barred Rock hen. Red sex-links are a cross between a Rhode Island Red or New Hampshire rooster and a White Rock, Silver Laced Wyandotte, Rhode Island White, or Delaware hen.

The APA recognizes 11 classes, or types, of chickens: six large types and five bantams. Standard classes are American, Asiatic, Continental, English, Mediterranean, and All Other Standard Breeds. Bantam classes include Single Comb Clean Legged, Rose Comb Clean Legged, Feather-Legged, Game Bantam, and All Other Comb Clean Legged. Within each class are a number of different breeds. For instance, the American class — breeds that originated in the United States or Canada — includes Plymouth Rocks, Rhode Island Reds, and Wyandottes. Some members of the Continental class (from Northern Europe) are Favorelles, Houdans, and Welsummers. Orpingtons belong to the English class and Sicilian Buttercups to the Mediterranean class.

**TIP**

Did you ever imagine there were so many different types of chickens? You can find descriptions of popular chicken breeds at www.mypetchicken.com/chicken-breeds/breed-list.aspx. You can search for them by friendliness, size, egg color, rarity, and more.

Before you choose a chicken breed, consider your lifestyle and what you're looking for from your chickens. Do you want chickens just for their eggs? Will your kids be caring for them? If so, you want a "kind" breed, such as an Orpington or Cochin. Do you want a "house chicken" who wears a diaper and lives indoors? (Yes, they exist.) You also need to think about what the chickens are bred for. Those intended to be "meat birds," such as Cornish or Cornish crosses, will eventually become too large for their legs to support them.

To get you started, here are some of our favorite chickens for beginners:

>> **Australorp (see Figure 14-1):** These stately chickens with shiny black plumage are Orpingtons from Australia. They're calm, friendly, and dependable egg layers.

>> **Barred Rock:** People new to chickens can't go wrong with these steady and reliable birds. Friendly and smart, they have a reputation for being easy keepers.

>> **Belgian Bearded d'Uccle (see Figure 14-1):** Bantam-size with feathered legs and a sweet but sassy nature, these ornamental chickens aren't the greatest layers, but they stand out for their attractive colors (millefleur is most popular, but they also come in black, porcelain, golden neck, mottled, self-blue, and white).

**FIGURE 14-1:**
Pictured are an Australorp (black) and a millefleur Belgian Bearded d'Uccle.

Photograph courtesy of D. Davidson Harpur

>> **Cochin:** This large and lovely breed from China entered the spotlight in the 19th century when Queen Victoria received some and fell in love with them (as she did with most animals). Cochins come in a variety of colors (as well as bantam size) and live life with a peaceful, easy feeling.

>> **Orpington:** Large, friendly, and fluffy, Orps, as they're nicknamed, are highly popular, especially in the buff coloration. Less commonly seen are black and blue Orpingtons.

>> **Silkie Bantam:** Bantams often aren't recommended as companion chickens because of their tendency toward flightiness, but Silkies are the exception. Beloved for their soft, fluffy feathers and often compared to kittens, they're entertaining and sweet, as well as being excellent mothers — even to other species, such as baby ducks.

**TECHNICAL STUFF**

Silkies are unusual in having black skin and bones and five toes instead of the four that other chickens have.

## GREAT EGGSPECTATIONS: CHICKENS THAT LAY DIFFERENT-COLORED EGGS

Leghorns are the standard for laying white eggs. The chickens themselves come in white, brown, *exchequer* (white with black spots), black, and *millefleur* (multicolored), but they all lay white eggs.

Sex-link chickens often produce brown eggs. Other chickens known for brown eggs are the following:

- Barred Rocks
- Black Australorps
- Marans (which lay some of the darkest-brown eggs)
- New Hampshires
- Rhode Island Reds
- Salmon Favorelles (which lay light-brown eggs that sometimes look pink)
- Welsummers (which lay speckled brown eggs)

Easter Eggers are named for the blue or green eggs they lay. Other breeds that lay blue eggs are the following:

- Ameraucanas
- Araucanas
- Cream Legbars

Isbars lay a mossy-colored green egg that is sometimes speckled. Olive-Eggers are cross-bred chickens that lay olive-colored or dark-green eggs.

>> **Sussex:** These friendly and sturdy chickens are great egg layers, even when it's cold out. They're curious and easy to handle, not prone to flying off, so they make good backyard denizens. For beauty, the spangled silver Sussex can't be beat, with long tailfeathers, a jaunty comb resembling a pirate's hat, and large, expressive eyes.

>> **Wyandotte:** Favorites for their easygoing nature, variety of feather patterns (especially the gorgeous silver-laced look), and dependability as egg layers, these large, hardy chickens are calm and docile with humans but pushy toward other chicken breeds.

# Buying Chicks or Chickens

Baby chicks are usually available throughout the year, but you'll have the greatest choice of breeds in the spring. That's also a good time to purchase chicks because the weather is warm, making it easier to care for them. Baby ducks and other types of poultry are also best purchased in spring and are less likely to be available at other times of the year.

## SHIPPING CHICKS

Young poultry can be purchased locally from feed stores or breeders or by mail from hatcheries. Chicks have been sent through the mail for decades with little problem, but U.S. Postal Service slowdowns at the time of this writing have resulted in many dying before delivery. Be cautious, and make sure delivery delays are not an issue before you order. It's also smart to avoid buying in the heat of summer or the depths of winter so that chicks aren't subject to temperature extremes that could kill them.

Many hatcheries sell a variety of chickens and other types of poultry. The advantage of buying from a hatchery is that they're more likely to have the unusual breeds you have your heart set on. Some have a minimum order of 15 to 25 chicks, though, which may be more than you want. If you have friends who are also interested in chicken keeping, you could split an order, or you can ask if the hatchery has a "city chicken" package with fewer chicks.

Look for hatcheries online. If possible, choose one in the same region so your day-old chicks aren't going all the way across country, making their journey less stressful. Some hatcheries also sell young adult or adult birds if you don't want to raise baby chicks.

If you have friends with chickens, ask where they got them and if they were happy with their choice. You can also do a web search to find breeders in your area. Even if they don't have the type of chicken you want, they may be able to refer you to someone who does.

If you'd rather start with less-fragile birds than baby chicks, look for *pullets* (young hens less than a year old) or adult hens from local breeders. You may also find someone with too many chickens who would like to place a few in a new home. Make "chicken friends" on social media to stay on top of such offers, check with your veterinarian about availability (if she frequently treats birds, she may know), or look at local feed stores. Some online hatcheries also sell older birds in addition to day-old chicks.

# Poultry Keeping 101

There's more to keeping chickens and other poultry than simply having a big enough backyard and maybe a pond if you're looking to have ducks or geese. They need appropriate housing — more than just the cute but usually too-small plastic coops often seen advertised — including plenty of shade and fresh water. Protection from predators is a must. And your lovely lawn or garden needs protection from these very destructive birds, too. Chickens can dig holes bigger than the ones your terrier excavates, and water-loving ducks are extremely messy. Although chicken manure is great for your garden, it stinks to high heaven. You'll also need to move their grazing area periodically to allow grass to recover from nitrogen burns left by chicken poop and from chickens scratching at the ground.

How many chickens should you have? Three is a good starter number, especially if you're an urban or suburban dweller. The more space, the more chickens you can have, but you don't want so many that you can't have a fun relationship with them or that caring for them becomes a chore instead of charming. And if you're in the city, remember that chickens produce a lot of poop and stir up a lot of dust. Fewer chickens can be less stinky and messy. In general, a flock of three to six hens is a good number, but some people enjoy keeping many different types, not only for their distinctive appearance but also because they like getting different colors of eggs.

**REMEMBER**

Before you put up the scratch to purchase chickens and a coop, make sure city ordinances, zoning or health regulations, or homeowner's association rules don't prohibit the keeping of poultry. A surprising number of cities and towns permit citizens to keep chickens or other poultry, including New York City, Portland (Oregon), San Francisco, and Seattle, but plenty of others don't, citing noise, odor, health concerns, and predator problems.

TIP

Not sure you're ready for chickens? Look for a chicken co-op. It's like a garden co-op, except you share the work and rewards of having chickens. Member families rotate cleaning and feeding and split the expenses. On the day that a family cleans and feeds, they collect and keep the eggs. Some businesses rent out hens and coops, providing training before handing over chickens. That can be a good way to experiment with chicken keeping before making a commitment. And chickens are a commitment. They typically live five to ten years, although one, Matilda, made the *Guinness World Records* for her astounding 16-year lifespan.

TIP

The National Association of Professional Pet Sitters offers a certification course on chicken care, which covers feeding, housing, flock health, and more. This can be something to look for if you're planning a trip and need someone to care for your chickens while you're away or even a course you might want to take yourself.

## Setting your chickens up with a proper coop

Chicken coops, sometimes called *henhouses,* must not only offer plenty of space where their feathered inhabitants can roost at night but also protect them from extreme temperatures and other animals who want to eat them. A good henhouse is constructed so as to conserve heat in winter and allow cooling during summer. Good ventilation by way of windows, roof vents, or exhaust fans is a must. An appropriate temperature range throughout the year is 40°F to 85°F.

A chicken coop also needs to keep chickens dry to help them stay healthy. Other important factors are easy access for cleaning, good drainage, and water sources and feeding equipment. And some ordinances require that coops be placed at least 20 feet away from any dwelling. There's a lot to consider as you plan your chicken domicile.

TIP

Bantams may seem like a good choice for beginners because of their small size, but they're highly destructive and are typically less calm than larger chickens. They also aren't known for being good layers, if a regular egg supply is important to you.

Outdoors, chickens need a good grazing area where they can dig and scratch for worms and bugs and bathe by rolling in the dust. Although they enjoy warming themselves in the sun, they also need to be able to gather in a shady area when it gets too hot. It's not unusual for chicken caretakers to install fans on top of the coop or water down the yard at night. In winter, a light in the coop can provide some extra warmth.

**TIP**

We touch on the basics here, but there's more to caring for chickens than we can provide in a single chapter. You can learn more about chicken keeping in *Raising Chickens For Dummies,* by Kimberley Willis and Robert T. Ludlow (Wiley). It covers choosing and purchasing chickens, coop construction, nutrition, pest and predator control, health, and more.

A coop should be easy for you and your chickens to access, but not easy at all for predators to enter. Equip doors with metal locking systems. Chickens also need a nest box (one large single box or multiple individual boxes) and places to perch with enough room that they can snuggle next to each other to generate heat. Elevated roosts offer safe perching.

For bedding, you can line the coop with straw or hay, pine shavings, or builder's sand from a home-improvement store. You can also use straw, hay, or shavings as bedding material in nest boxes. Chickens will also love having a run or other outdoor space filled with sand for their bathing pleasure. A removable tray makes cleanup easy.

**TIP**

Plan on a minimum of 2 to 3 square feet per chicken inside the coop for nighttime roosting (don't expect them to live in it all the time). Be sure you don't have too few chickens in too large a space, though. Chickens use body heat to help stay warm, and if they're too spread out, they can get cold.

Outdoors, chickens need space, too. Count on at least 15 square feet per chicken for roaming space during the day. The more room you can give them, the happier they'll be. Besides grassy spaces where they can peck for bugs, they need an area where they can dig up dirt and roll in it for a nice cooling dust bath.

## Keeping predators at bay

Keeping chickens and their eggs safe from foxes, coyotes, raccoons, opossums, skunks, weasels, dogs, cats, rats, snakes, and aerial predators such as hawks and crows is one of the primary challenges of chicken keeping. It seems that everyone loves the taste of chicken. (In a case of "turnabout is fair play," some chickens will kill and eat small snakes.) All these animals are found in urban and suburban areas, as well as in the country, so don't assume your chickens are safe from them just because your home isn't rural. Bantam breeds, chicks, and eggs are at greatest risk.

Having a predator-proof coop and safe outdoor roaming space is a must from the get-go. Think Fort Klux. If they think your chickens are easy pickings, predators will return to the scene of the crime over and over again.

Chicken wire won't do the trick. Coops should be protected with sturdy wire fencing, and doors need metal locking systems complex enough to thwart the manual dexterity of raccoons.

Use hardware cloth, not screens, to cover windows and secure other access points, and use screws, not staples, to hold it in place. Digging predators can be deterred by a 12-inch-deep trench surrounding the coop lined with wire or hardware cloth. Secure hardware cloth at least a foot beneath dirt floors, too.

If hawks, eagles, owls, and other birds of prey soar your skies, your chickens may also need a covered run to prevent fly-by predation. This can also help to protect them from climbing critters. A solid roof is best; strong wire or netting can help, but it's not as good as something predators can't see through or grab through. For free-range chickens, provide safety in the form of bushes, boxes, gazebo- or teepee-style covered areas, and other places where they can run and hide when they hear the whoosh of wings overhead.

Technology can be your friend, too. Put up a chicken cam with night-vision capability so you know what types of predators patrol your yard in search of a chicken dinner and when they're likely to come around. Motion-sensor or blinking lights can help to startle away approaching predators. Place an inexpensive baby monitor in the henhouse to alert you to sounds of agitation or attack.

Biosecurity is just as important as physical security. Any time you bring in new birds, isolate them for three weeks to make sure they don't bring in any diseases or parasites such as scaly mites.

Battery- or electric powered poultry doors with timers and light sensors can be set to open and close at specific times. That gives you more freedom to sleep in without being wakened by chickens wanting out or to come home after dark, knowing that your chickens are safely inside with a door that closes at dusk.

Check coops to make sure no predators have snuck in during the day to lie in wait for your flock. You may also want to consider protecting your poultry with a dog or other guardian animal such as a donkey or llama.

## Feeding your chickens what they need

First things first: Make sure chickens always have access to fresh water. Over a short period of time, they're much more likely to suffer from lack of water than lack of food.

Chickens are omnivores but that doesn't mean they don't need a balanced diet. They should eat a commercial food supplemented with worms, insects, vegetables, and leafy greens. Calcium supplementation can be given in the form of oyster shells or recycled eggshells. You're not turning your chickens into cannibals if you give them eggshells, but some chickens are known to eat their own eggs or the eggs of other chickens, and that habit is referred to as *cannibalism*.

TECHNICAL STUFF

Chickens have simple digestive systems that rely on acid and enzymatic secretions to break down food for the body's use. For that reason, only foods that can be digested by the enzymes secreted are useful as food.

Chicken diets typically come in such formulations as starter, grower, maintenance, and layer. They're available in different forms: mash, crumbles, and pellets, each of which has advantages and disadvantages.

Pelleted feeds are compacted so poultry can consume and metabolize a greater amount of feed. Birds also aren't able to pick out their preferred ingredients from pellets so they're more likely to get balanced nutrition from them. Pellets also easier to handle than mash feeds, which can be dusty.

TIP

Many people prefer to give their chickens organic feed. After all, whatever your chickens eat, you eat as well — in the form of the eggs they produce. High-quality eggs have firm, round yolks and thick whites. A deep golden yolk is desirable, and many people believe yolks with that deep color are tastier.

For chicks, though, mashes and crumbles can be easier to eat. Young, growing chicks need to eat feed formulated especially for their needs. Avoid giving them layer mashes and crumbles.

Chickens love greens but it's important not to give them large amounts of spinach and chard. Those greens contain high levels of oxalic acid, which can bind available calcium in the gut. They'll enjoy kale, arugula, and lettuce, though. Just don't give them your leftover salad with dressing on it!

TIP

Keeping chickens is not a guarantee that you'll save money on eggs. Depending on their laying ability, with five chickens you may be lucky to get three eggs a week. Chickens don't lay when they're molting, and they usually lay seasonally, stopping in the winter. They may also cease laying when it's hot outside, because they need to conserve their energy for keeping cool. And not every breed lays an egg a day; some lay eggs only every other day.

WARNING

Poultry get protein from hunting bugs, worms, spiders, other insects, and sometimes even frogs and lizards. Whatever you do, avoid feeding only table scraps. That's a recipe for depleted calcium stores and other nutritional and metabolic diseases.

**TIP**

You may have heard that chickens need grit to aid in digestion, but they generally find all the grit they need outdoors in the form of tiny pebbles or coarse sand. When ingested with whatever else they're pecking at, grit helps to grind their food and break it down in the gizzard.

## Protecting your lawn and garden

Protecting poultry from predators is important, but it's equally important to protect your lawn and garden from the predations of poultry. Chickens are destructive of lawns in general. Rethink keeping them if your lawn is your pride and joy. They'll fly into trees to eat the fruit. And they'll eat up your garden fast if given half a chance. Cover pots with chicken wire after planting seedlings.

Erect a sturdy fence around your garden (and be aware that chickens may be more adept at fence hopping than you expect). You may need to place netting over your garden to prevent chickens from flying over the fence and feasting on your plants. (These precautions can also help ward off raiders such as bunnies and deer.) On the plus side, if you pluck tomato worms off your plants and hand them over, your chickens will be very happy! Don't be surprised if they follow you around as you garden to keep tabs on whether you turn up a juicy bug or worm.

You don't have to move your chicken run around, but doing so has some benefits. It prevents development of bare spots in your grass and ensures fertilization of the entire lawn. This can be done by means of a portable run, known as a *chicken tractor*. Move chickens to a different area every two to three days to give grass a chance to spring back up after being trampled on and clawed by chickens. The chickens are happy because they have fresh grass and new bugs to find. One resource that can provide more in-depth information is *Chicken Tractor: The Permaculture Guide to Happy Hens and Healthy Soil*, Homestead (3rd) Edition, by Andy Lee and Patricia Foreman (Good Earth Publications).

## Controlling waste

Chickens are (mostly) vegetarians, and although they're not very big, they still produce plenty of manure that's strongly scented with ammonia. It will be in your yard and inside the coop. All that chicken manure has to go somewhere.

Pathogens can grow in bird droppings, so plan on spending time weekly scooping and raking. It's just as much a necessity as picking up after a dog or scooping a cat's litter box. Add more hay, shavings, or sand as bedding starts to get low or require freshening. At least twice a year, toss out all old bedding and provide new. You should also routinely clean ceilings, walls, nests, and floors of coops with a disinfectant that is safe for use around poultry. Ask your veterinarian for a recommendation.

TIP

If you have a large compost system, you can add shavings and manure to it and let it "cook" for six months to a year before using. It's probably best to avoid putting chicken manure into backyard compost spinners or other small systems.

## Keeping your chickens healthy

What kind of veterinary care do pet chickens need? They can suffer broken bones, broken beaks, severed toes, and injuries from fights when they don't get along. (Chickens can be downright mean to each other — the term *hen-pecked* isn't just a figure of speech.) They can also develop a number of medical conditions, both from infections as well as noninfectious disease processes. Horrible, incurable viral diseases and the cancers that they cause, such as Marek's disease and lymphoid leukosis, are both common problems in chickens on a global scale. Although there is no vaccine available for lymphoid leukosis, there is for Marek's disease.

TIP

Make sure you purchase chicks vaccinated at the hatchery for Marek's disease to reduce your risk of that heartbreak.

Bacterial infections with organisms such as *Mycoplasma, Pasteurella, Avibacterium*, and others are contagious among birds and can seriously threaten not only the life of an infected bird, but also be transferred to others. Noninfectious types of problems Brian often sees include ovarian cancer, oviductal impactions, trauma, foreign-body ingestions (yes, if allowed, chickens can and often will eat lots of things that they shouldn't), and others. Although not all these problems are possible to treat, many can be treated with reasonable success if diagnosed early enough.

Be prepared for illness or injury by setting up a chicken infirmary. A large dog kennel or crate can serve as a "hospital room" where you can quarantine a sick or injured chicken until you can get her to the veterinarian. If you need to segregate a chicken — either because she's being picked on by the others or because she has an illness — you don't want to have to scramble for a place to put her. Isolating a chicken who is taking medication is a good idea as well — you won't be able to eat her eggs, and this way you know which ones to throw away.

REMEMBER

We discuss what to include in a bird first-aid kit in Chapter 10.

You'll also need separate food and water dishes for your sickened chicken. If your veterinarian recommends putting medication in the chicken's water or feed, this is a hassle-free way to make sure she's the only one getting the medication. Other supplies that can be useful include plastic gloves and K-Y Jelly if you need to reach in and see if a hen is *eggbound* (when an egg is lodged inside the hen's oviduct).

# HUMAN HEALTH-CARE TIPS

Raising chickens isn't risk-free when it comes to your family's health. Chickens and other poultry can carry foodborne bacterial infections such as salmonellosis and campylobacteriosis, which can cause intestinal disease in humans. Because their immune systems either aren't fully developed or have become weaker with age, those most at risk are children younger than 5 years old and seniors, as well as women who are pregnant and people with compromised immune systems.

Exposure occurs when people come in contact with chicken feces or pet or carry chickens without thoroughly washing their hands afterward. It's one of the reasons that some ordinances require chicken coops to be a certain distance away from human households. Most of the poultry-related *zoonotic* (transmissible between animals and humans) diseases are transmitted by inhalation of contaminated fecal dust or ingestion of food or water contaminated by fecal matter.

To keep yourself and your family safe, follow these tips:

- Wash your hands thoroughly after caring for or handling chickens.

- Supervise youngsters when they interact with chickens.

- Follow good coop hygiene standards, such as appropriate location and waste control.

- Avoid eating or drinking while you're in the chickenyard.

- Wear a mask, a coverup, and boots or shoes that are limited to the chickenyard when cleaning the coop or raking litter. Remove them before entering your home and wash fabric items in hot water to kill pathogens.

- Cook eggs thoroughly to prevent diseases transmitted by eggs, such as salmonella.

Any time you see your physician for illness, mention that you keep chickens or other poultry. This information could play a role in your diagnosis.

**TIP**

Keep tabs on news about epidemics that could affect your backyard flock, such as avian influenza or Newcastle disease. Talk to your veterinarian about the measures to take to prevent members of your flock from becoming infected.

Some diseases aren't directly transmitted by backyard poultry, but they are related to the keeping of them. Poultry attract rodents and their associated diseases. Think leptospirosis, rat bite fever, and hantavirus. Standing water left out for chickens can attract mosquitoes and the diseases they spread, such as West Nile fever. Consider giving chickens water through an automatic watering system that isn't accessible by mosquitoes or rodents. Putting feed in a covered automatic feeder is also a good idea.

## Providing your chicken with enrichment and training

Yes, you can train chickens — and it's fun! Chickens learn quickly, so training them requires good coordination and timing. They can fly away if they don't like your training techniques, so it's important to use positive reinforcement to gain their cooperation.

Training is one important way to enrich a chicken's life, as well as improve your relationship with your bird. Teaching a chicken to differentiate between different shapes or colors, push a lever to release a treat or food, or play a game such as tic-tac-toe is fun for you and your bird.

**TIP**

Because chickens learn quickly and are easy to train, behavior specialists and trainers often run "chicken camps" to teach good habits to dog trainers. Training a chicken enhances hand-eye coordination and observation skills. The theory is that if you can train a chicken, you can train anything. You can find out more about training techniques (whether for a chicken or a dog) in *Dog Training For Dummies*, 4th Edition, by Wendy Volhard and Mary Ann Rombold Zeigenfuse, LVT (Wiley).

Beyond training, pet chickens also need enrichment — in other words, an interesting environment. Chickens are social birds who appreciate the company of other chickens, as well as the mental stimulation that prevents boredom.

**REMEMBER**

Whenever possible, chickens should have some chicken buddies — or maybe other poultry such as ducks. We've even heard of chickens being friends with other animals, such as dogs or horses. Social isolation isn't pleasant for them.

Foraging, which we also discuss in Chapters 6 and 12, is an important part of a chicken's daily routine. Chickens are motivated to search for food, and you can provide them with that opportunity in lots of ways. In addition to giving them the opportunity to range over your yard in search of bugs, you can put out a treat garland for chickens to peck at; make or purchase food puzzles that distribute food or treats when the chicken pushes them; or hang a piece of corn on the cob, a head of lettuce, or a slice of melon for them to peck at. In summer, freeze some pieces of fruit or vegetables in ice for them to peck at.

Visual stimulation is also important for chickens. They like looking at things, and they like what they look at to change once in a while. Rotate the images you put out for them. Hang a mirror so they can look at themselves or see the reflections of other objects. Some chickens enjoy pecking at a pinwheel or watching it turn.

We don't think of chickens as having powerful senses of smell or hearing, but olfactory and auditory enrichment are important for them, too. Certain odors can contribute to a sense of security or familiarity or simply be interesting to chickens. For instance, if you're moving chickens to a new coop or yard, placing some used bedding from the previous area can indicate "home" to them. The scents of vanilla and lavender may have calming effects. So can playing classical music or a radio show such as *Wait Wait . . . Don't Tell Me!* or *A Prairie Home Companion*.

Chickens also enjoy things like colorful soft toys (choose something they can't swallow), ladders to climb on, balls they can push and peck at, cardboard boxes to hide in, hay bales to climb on, and swings to sit and rock on. Different ground surfaces can be interesting to chickens, too. Try gravel, grass, mulch, sand, and leaf litter.

REMEMBER

Swap things around occasionally to offer them a change of environment.

## Outfitting your chicken with diapers, sweaters, dresses, and more

If you search the web, you can find lots of chicken diapers and other fun sorts of attire. You can even find chicken fashion shows! One retailer sells a soft, snuggly pouch in the shape of a flower for holding baby chicks safely and comfortably. Tutus and dresses are just for fun — as long as your chicken doesn't mind wearing one.

But chickenwear is about more than just dressing up your fashionista fowl. For house chickens, diapers prevent accidents that could mar flooring or furniture. Sweaters or dresses can keep chickens warm if they're molting or the weather is colder than normal and prevent them from pecking at their own exposed skin or that of other chickens. An apron (like the one shown in Figure 14-2) protects a hen's backside and the top of her wings from damage by frisky roosters. Without aprons, hens can develop bald spots on their lower backs. Rescued battery hens who have lost a lot of feathers may benefit from clothing until they regain their plumage. If your chickens are normally feathered, though, they probably don't need any help staying warm; it's natural for them to snuggle together to generate body heat.

If you're crafty, you can find patterns to knit or sew clothing for your pampered poultry. You can also purchase chicken clothing from sellers on Etsy (www.etsy.com) or online retailers such as www.pamperyourpoultry.com.

**FIGURE 14-2:**
A chicken wearing an apron — it's not just about looking good.

*Photograph courtesy of D. Davidson Harpur*

# Keeping Your Chickens Safe around Other Family Pets

Dogs and chickens go together like bacon and eggs — except when they don't. Here's what you should know about ensuring safe and peaceful coexistence between chickens, dogs, and cats.

Dogs, cats, and chickens are not exactly a match made in heaven. Too often, the relationship between predators (dogs and cats) and chickens (prey) can go wrong. But when you introduce and supervise them properly, they can get along and sometimes even become friends. Some people have dogs and cats who protect their chickens from wild predators and who help round them up as needed, whether that's to send them to the coop at dusk or to find a lost chicken. And the presence of a dog (or in some instances a barn cat) can deter other predators. Some are even vigilant about hawks, owls, and other raptors. And sometimes dogs or cats are rightfully respectful of and even intimidated by bold chickens.

Introductions are important. No matter how sweet, small, or friendly your dog or cat is, never turn them loose with chickens the first time they meet. That's true even if your chickens or other poultry are already used to dogs or cats. They don't know this particular animal, and the dog or cat doesn't know your birds.

The age and experience of the chickens matters, too. Baby chicks, which most people start with, move rapidly and frequently, all the while making high-pitched squeaky sounds. And adult chickens who aren't used to dogs may panic, flutter, and run. To a hunter such as a cat or dog, these sounds and actions say one word: "Prey!"

The average cat will go after smaller prey than adult standard-size chickens, which are able to protect themselves with their beaks and claws. And there are plenty of barn cats who protect "their" chickens from other predators. But baby chicks and bantam chickens are likely to be attractive hunting targets to certain cats and dogs. When you have a predatory animal, the best thing you can do is to keep chickens in a run that offers them protection from a stalking feline or canine. If your chicken and other pets live indoors, follow the advice in Chapter 5 and keep them separated.

**WARNING**

Without any training or acclimation, expecting a dog or cat to leave chickens alone isn't reasonable. Most normal dogs and cats, without guidance to the contrary, will take the opportunity to kill and eat your chickens. Take the time and make the effort to make introductions and ensure that your four-footed pets know how to behave around chickens. If that's not possible, you need to do all you can to keep your chickens safe, and that means supervision, supervision, supervision.

To teach dogs and cats how to behave toward their feathered brethren, hold baby chicks, one at a time, and give the dog or cat an opportunity for a sniff. Make the words *gentle, babies,* and *mine* your mantras. Reward gentle behavior with verbal praise. When your dog or cat and chicks are used to each other's presence and your furry companion isn't showing any strong interest in the chicks, you can put the chicks in an exercise pen and allow the dog or cat to see them, still never leaving them alone together. Offer rewards for calm, relaxed behavior and distractions if you notice any predatory staring or stalking. Gradually allow your dog or cat to come into the exercise pen or coop with you as you clean or feed. Repeat your mantra. At first, keep the dog or cat on leash to control any sudden lunges. With cats and dogs, it can be a good idea to have someone else with you whose sole job is to supervise animal interactions until you're sure everyone is getting along.

One thing your dog must learn is that chickens can be out of their coop and roaming on their own. Some types of dogs, such as herding or guardian breeds, have definite ideas about how their charges should behave. To them, roaming may seem like alarming behavior on the part of the chickens.

Some dogs are more suited to safe interactions with chickens than others. For instance, guardian and working breeds such as Anatolian Shepherds, Mastiffs, and Rottweilers can learn that poultry is to protect, not to eat. Sporting dogs such as Golden Retrievers, Labrador Retrievers, Pointers, and the various spaniels may be attracted by a chicken's feathers, but they're also highly trainable and often friendly toward other animals.

Many toy dog breeds are not much bigger than chickens, but they have the same instincts as bigger dogs, especially if they're mini versions of terrier or sighthound breeds. Give them the same training and supervision you would any other dog.

Non-sporting dogs are a mixed bag. A miniature Poodle or an American Eskimo (which used to be a common farm dog) may do quite well with chickens, but always consider the dog's temperament and heritage when planning introductions.

Herding breeds may seem to be naturals, but without training and supervision, they can be just as aggressive toward poultry as any other dog.

Cats also have varying personalities. Bengals and Savannahs may like nothing better than to hunt chickens, while Persians will probably yawn and turn away from them. Every cat is an individual, though, so study yours thoroughly before deciding whether introducing her to chickens is really a good idea.

TIP

Go on chicken forums such as www.communitychickens.com or www.backyardchickens.com and ask about the types of dogs or cats people have and whether they tend to be chicken-safe. The important thing to remember, though, is that every animal is an individual and you may not have the same experience with your own dog or cat.

REMEMBER

In order for your dog to learn to be good with chickens, he must already have a foundation in training and a good relationship with you. Practice sit/stays in the chickenyard. Your dog can't chase chickens if she's sitting or doing a down. Dogs with more advanced education can practice off-leash heeling. If she's a wild child who has never received consistent training, though, your best bet is to keep her well separated from your chickens with sturdy fencing and gates.

TIP

Not every dog can learn to safely be around chickens. (More predatory types include northern or spitz breeds, sighthounds, and terriers. They all have high prey drive and are best kept away from chickens.) Similarly, not all chickens are good with dogs. If you want chickens who are dog-compatible, avoid flighty types such as bantams, Leghorns, and other small, light types. Chickens with feathered heads may startle easily around dogs because their topknots can impair their vision. Instead, choose calm, friendly birds such as Orpingtons, Barred Rocks, Hampshires, and Ameracaunas.

# Keeping Other Kinds of Poultry

Beyond chickens, other types of poultry can also be entertaining and interesting to keep. They have many of the same benefits as chickens — bug control and egg production, for instance — but there are a number of differences as well. In the following sections, take a brief look at what to consider for some of these other species.

## Ducks

Beatrix Potter's children's classic *The Tale of Jemima Puddle-Duck* may well be the motivation for many people who acquire ducks. Gardeners admire them for their hasty dispatch of slugs and snails in the garden. Bakers say their eggs make fluffier, richer baked goods. And some people keep them as training animals for their competitive herding dogs to practice rounding up without harming them. Whatever the case, ducks are social and can be enjoyable to keep — with a few precautions.

REMEMBER

The average duck lifespan is 8 to 12 years, although Brian certainly has seen some 14- to 18-year-old ducks and even older geese over the years. So, be prepared to enjoy (and commit to) a long-term relationship.

Ducks are messy — all that mucking about in water makes for a muddy yard. Male ducks display aggressive mating behavior toward females. And keeping too many ducks for the amount of space you have can lead to injuries and illness. But keeping a few females (two or three is a good number to start with) can be fun, and not all duck breeds require access to a lake or pond. They can be happy with a kiddie pool to paddle about in, but you'll need to refresh the water daily. Ducks love to be clean, and they require a good source of fresh water, like that in Figure 14-3, where they can dip and clean their bills as they eat.

Even though the areas are harder to keep clean, ducks do best on grass or dirt. Expect to re-sod grass or turn over dirt at least once or twice a month. Avoid hard surfaces such as concrete, which can cause foot sores.

Feed ducks a pelleted diet, such as one for game birds, supplemented with material they forage themselves: vegetation, grasses, worms, and insects. Laying ducks need a game-bird-laying diet that is higher in protein and calcium than maintenance pellets. Corn, bread, crackers, and other high-carb foods are not good for ducks and can lead to health problems, but they enjoy treats such as greens and peas. Toss peas in water so your duck can bob for them!

**FIGURE 14-3:**
Ducks don't need a large pond or lake, but they do need a source of fresh, clean water.

*Photograph courtesy of Lorraine Aubert, Pacific Waterfowl Rescue*

Enclosures should have areas for both foraging and hiding — think hollow logs, platforms, and some tall grasses. If you have an artificial pond for them, it should be easy to drain and clean, with a water aerator or filtration system to prevent ammonia buildup.

Enclosing ponds with netting can protect ducks from predators and limit their exposure to wild ducks, which can spread disease. Not all locales allow domestic ducks to have free flight. Your veterinarian can alert you to any ordinances regarding duck keeping. And speaking of veterinary care, ducks can be prone to foot, respiratory, and intestinal issues, so a duck–savvy veterinarian is important.

Here are our recommendations on duck breeds you may want to look into:

>> **Indian Runners:** Indian Runners are among the breeds satisfied with a bucket for the occasional splash. They have a comical nature, are good layers, and come in an assortment of colors, including black, fawn, chocolate, and silver. Their upright stance calls for a taller-than-normal duck house.

>> **Campbell:** Friendly Campbell ducks have a reputation as prolific layers. They do well sharing space with chickens, don't require large bodies of water, and have striking plumage in shades of khaki, apricot, and blue, to name a few.

>> **Muscovy:** Muscovy ducks can also be easy keepers. These large waterfowl tend to be calm and quieter than other ducks, and they're useful for eating bugs and other small pests. Their size makes them unafraid of predators and may help to keep hawks away from your chickens or baby ducks. They're affectionate and hardy, and they take well to training.

>> **Aylesbury:** For *Jemima Puddle-Duck* fans, large, snow-white Aylesbury ducks are just the ticket. Because of their size, plan on having more space for them — and keep your neighbors in mind before getting them. They can have a loud quack! One reason to consider keeping Aylesburys is for preservation purposes; the Livestock Conservancy rates their status as "critical."

There are many other duck breeds to consider as well. Do your homework to choose the ones best suited to your environment and needs.

## Geese

These larger waterfowl sometimes have a reputation for being aggressive but anyone who has raised them from goslings or read the work of naturalist Konrad Lorenz (including *The Year of the Greylag Goose*) knows that young geese will "imprint" on humans or other animals shortly after hatching, following them around like friendly pups. Geese are smart and social, and they can make excellent "watch" animals, protective of their territory and the other animals in it. If you don't have a dog to protect your chickens or ducks, a goose may well be an excellent alternative.

In addition to their protective nature, geese are attractive and entertaining to watch. They're easy keepers, primarily feeding themselves through grazing on grass. Different breeds have different personalities, so some may be better at "watch-goose" duty than those that are more friendly and laid back.

TIP

Start with a pair of goslings if you want geese who will enjoy your company and be easy to handle.

Brian has always been impressed by the dignity and composure of many of his goose patients over the years. Their composure, behavior, mannerisms, and unique character is simply beguiling! One of his favorite goose friends of all time was Gordy the Wonder Goose, simply one of the most fabulous and wonderful feathered souls anyone could ever hope to have waddle into their lives and hearts.

Among the breeds to consider keeping are the following:

>> **Toulouse:** A French goose with a placid disposition.

>> **Emden:** A tall and heavy German goose who is calm and gentle.

>> **Pilgrim:** Personable and known for being sexually dimorphic — males are mostly white and females are dove-gray.

TIP

One good resource for keeping geese is *The Book of Geese: A Complete Guide to Raising the Home Flock*, by Dave Holderread (Hen House Publishing), which you may be able to find in used-book stores or on sites like eBay. Beware: There is a section of the book on butchering, which you'll probably want to avoid.

With good care and protection from predators, geese can live 20 years or more. According to *Guinness World Records*, a gander named George lived to be almost 50 years old!

## Turkeys

You've probably never thought of turkeys as companion birds, but if you live in a rural area and have the space to provide them with roomy housing (such as a small shed with good ventilation and a sturdy perch), heritage turkeys raised from *poults* (young fowl) can make inquisitive, docile, friendly pets. Heritage turkey breeds that can be interesting to keep include the ornamental Royal Palm, the rare Midget White, and the large and attractive Bourbon Red. Others to consider are the Auburn, Buff, Black, Narragansett, and Standard Bronze.

TECHNICAL
STUFF

Heritage poultry breeds are those in danger of extinction because they are no longer considered to be commercially viable. That can mean the loss of important genetic lines and traits. There are heritage breeds of chickens, ducks, turkeys, and more. You may also hear these breeds described as "heirloom," "antique," or "old-fashioned." Keeping heritage birds is like stepping back in time and helps to support poultry genetic diversity and disease resistance.

A male turkey in full display is a sight to behold. Like roosters, male turkeys (known as *stags*) need behavioral boundaries, but if they imprint on you as a youngster and receive good guidance and training, they can be fun to have around. Just be aware that during adolescence, their level of vandalism can be breathtaking. Hens are smaller and gentler, but not as impressive in appearance. If you're planning on keeping a turkey (or two or three) as pets, make sure to choose the smaller breeds that don't get too heavy. Their excessive weight is a huge problem for many of the large broad-breasted breeds of turkeys that are being kept as pets.

Turkeys can live as long as 10 years but it's rare for them to go much beyond that.

**TIP**

Young turkeys need a high-protein diet. Basic poultry feed is generally not appropriate for them.

Farmers have been presenting turkeys to the White House since at least the 1940s. Occasionally, presidents gave the turkeys a reprieve from the dinner table, but it wasn't until the administration of George H. W. Bush that the turkey pardon became a tradition. Over the years, the turkeys have been retired to various petting zoos; theme parks; historic homes such as Morven Park in Leesburg, Virginia; and currently, to Virginia Tech University, known for its poultry science program.

## Guineafowl

Like geese, guineafowl (shown in Figure 14-4) have a reputation as "guard birds," keeping a close eye on their territory and setting off a loud alarm if a predator makes an attempt to enter (or if they're just angry because you haven't fed them yet). Their noise level can make them poor choices for people with nearby neighbors, but in more rural areas, their gregarious nature, speckled plumage, and tasty eggs can make them welcome.

**FIGURE 14-4:** Guineafowl are endemic to Africa, but the helmeted variety, pictured here, has been widely disseminated around the world.

*Photograph courtesy of Jerry M. Thornton*

Seen in large flocks in the wild on their home continent of Africa, they're perhaps best suited to larger properties where they have room to roam. When introduced gradually, they can get along well with other types of poultry.

Guineafowl typically live 10 to 15 years.

# Game birds

If you read Margaret Stanger's classic book *That Quail, Robert,* you were probably charmed by the story of the foundling raised as a family companion. Like Robert (who turned out to be Roberta), quail are lovely aviary birds with funny, interesting personalities. They're members of the family *Phasianidae,* which also includes chickens, grouse, guineafowl, partridges, pheasants, and turkeys. Quail breeds to consider are the Chinese painted, Japanese, and Harlequin. They usually have short lifespans of two to four years.

Some bird lovers like having quail in aviaries because they're good at cleaning up feed other birds drop, although they can also eat specialty quail food.

Domestic pheasants, admired for their colorful plumage, can also be pleasant additions to aviaries— albeit loud in the case of males. They can get along with other poultry, but they can also be lured away by wild pheasants if allowed to roam free. Like any poultry, pheasants need warm, dry shelter at night and for protection from the elements. Outdoor runs should be on grass, with dust for bathing, and shrubs and boxes for hiding. Muddy areas can contribute to foot problems. Indoor spaces need high perches. Hardy breeds for beginners are Golden, Silver, or Lady Amherst's pheasants, and with good care they can live as long as 18 years.

# Peafowl

Everyone loves to look at peacocks (the term for male peafowl), but no one enjoys hearing them scream. If you decide to keep them, however, know that they're social birds. Your male will need at least two peahens (females) to cast him admiring glances as he unfurls his tail and struts about.

Screams notwithstanding, peafowl are relatively easy keepers. They eat a wide variety of foods and can do well on chicken or commercial game bird feed, supplemented by their own foraging for insects and plants. They need access to warm, dry shelter, and although you may never have seen them do so, they enjoy roosting in trees, flying up for a branch with a view. A barn with a hayloft is a good alternative and provides the spacious accommodation needed by those tails.

These sturdy and beautiful birds can live 20 to 50 years so stock up on earplugs!

# 5

# The Part of Tens

# Chapter **15**

# Ten Bird Myths Debunked

Humans have kept close company with birds for thousands of years — and admired them from afar for even longer — but only recently have we gained a true understanding of how to help our winged friends be healthy and happy in our households. Even so, we've hardly scratched the surface. Recent advances in health and behavior knowledge will continue, even as our appreciation for birds moves, as they say, to higher levels.

And yet, misinformation is everywhere — in books (even new ones); in veterinary, bird club, or bird shop handouts; and certainly on the Internet. Most of the information is well-meaning, based on what was thought to be true even a few years ago.

To help you separate the seeds (which your bird doesn't need, as you can see if you read on) from the hulls (which at least provide exercise for your bird), we've assembled some of the more common myths and taken them apart, one by one.

# Birds Are Low-Maintenance Pets

In a rare departure from a life of writing about pets, Gina once took an assignment to write about a talented interior designer, hoping in some small way to pick up some wisdom regarding her own home — to this day, decorated in Early Thrift Store. She met the designer at a house he was working on and listened eagerly to his (expensive) plans for the place.

"And here," he said, waving his arm at one wall, "I see an aviary. Those blue parrots. . . . What do you call them? Macaws? Perfect colors!"

Even the suggestion that birds are "things" to enhance the decor of a room reveals a great deal of ignorance about the nature of these intelligent pets. Unfortunately, the designer's views are not uncommon. Too many people see a bird as little more than a beautiful, colorful addition to a room, a low-maintenance pet you just set on a perch and be done with.

REMEMBER

Birds *are* beautiful. They *do* add color to our lives. But if you go into your relationship with a bird thinking that all you need to do is throw a little seed at him now and then, you'll discover the error of your ways — and quickly. Plus, you're sure to miss out on the great pleasure of living with what can be an intelligent, affectionate, and challenging companion.

TIP

Figure on spending time every day on basic cleaning, as well as time on the weekends for more of the same, with extra scrubbing and disinfecting thrown in. You'll spend time preparing nutritious meals, with vegetables and fruit. And you'll spend time, most of all, enjoying your bird's company and letting him enjoy yours.

WARNING

Without effort on your part, you're going to have a sick bird or one who's bored, lonely, and unhappy — a feather picker (so much for all that beautiful plumage) or even an empty cage.

You want low-maintenance? Get a stuffed animal. Even fish tanks take some effort. But if you're willing to make the personal investment in your relationship with your bird, you can expect to receive wonderful rewards.

# Birds Are High-Maintenance Companions

You can't just throw your bird in a cage and forget her, but neither do you have to center your whole life around caring for your bird. And yet, some people do. Some bird owners disinfect their birds' quarters three times a day — scrubbing cages, cleaning dishes, soaking perches in a bleach solution. Overdoing tidiness isn't necessary, no matter what you may have heard.

Good husbandry requires cleanliness, make no mistake. But the work some bird lovers put into keeping their birds squeaky-clean borders on obsessive.

You don't have to pick up every food crumb as it falls. Sterilization is not necessary on a daily basis, as long as you make fresh food and water available in clean dishes and change cage papers once or twice a day.

TIP

Make life easier on yourself: Invest in a handheld vacuum, a seed-catching bib for the cage, and anything else that can help keep things neater.

Beyond those basics, relax. Use the time you have for your bird for togetherness, snuggling, training, and play. You'll both get more out of the experience.

So, how much cleaning is too much and how much is not enough? Check out Chapters 5 and 7. For tips on what you need to buy to make your life easier, see Chapter 4.

# Birds Are Fragile

Some folks in this world — and you may be among them — believe that birds are so delicate that a cold breeze is enough to do them in. In fact, birds are among the hardiest and most successful creatures on Earth, adapted to many different ecological niches — including the one that brings them into our homes as pets. With bodies designed for the rigors of flight, birds are very tough — so much so that were we possessed of their powers, we might seem like superheroes. Brian often tells his clients that he aspires to be half as tough as a parrot, chicken, or pigeon!

Birds fight illness with tenacity, endure temperature variations with no effect, and live for years on the equivalent of junk food that many owners insist on giving them. They're survivors! With proper husbandry, nutrition, and medical attention that focuses on disease prevention, your bird may well outlive you.

REMEMBER

Because of the potentially long life span of some birds — up to 70 years or more for larger parrots such as macaws — planning for care if something happens to you is very important. (For information on how to ensure that your bird's long-term care is covered, see Chapter 11.)

# A Hand-Fed Bird Makes a Better Pet

Among the feathered pet population, improvements in the art of successfully breeding birds and socializing them into the world of humans is one of the bigger developments over the last couple of decades. The advancements are good news for birds in the wild — whose populations came close to being demolished by the pet trade — and a positive move for people who want to share their lives with an avian companion. Captive-bred birds make the best pets.

Captive-bred doesn't necessarily mean hand-fed, however, although in many cases, birds come from both backgrounds. The keys are somewhat in the process of the feeding of baby birds, as well as their socialization. Natural parents can do a decent job of feeding, and as long as human caretakers ensure that the babies are handled and exposed to loving human care, captive-bred birds benefit from the best of both worlds.

Hand-feeding can be fine, and we most certainly don't want to knock those breeders who do it. But no matter how birds are fed — by their parents or by human hands — gentle, patient socialization is the way to build the trust in humans that is so essential in a good pet.

**TIP**

We share some tips for building trust in your birds — along with a strong bond between you and your pet — in Chapter 5.

# Seed Is the Best Diet for Birds

How pervasive is this myth? You can find out by asking any child, "What do birds eat?" The answer you're likely to hear: "Seeds!" Wrong, wrong, wrong.

**WARNING**

Pet birds fed a diet of only seeds eventually become malnourished and may develop serious illnesses or even die.

So, why does this "Birds eat seeds" idea stick with us? The myth is perpetuated by so-called experts who have kept birds for years but who haven't kept up with current research trends, as well as by pet product manufacturers and retailers who want to keep less useful or antiquated merchandise selling, either because they don't know any better or because they don't care.

Although we talk about specific nutrition in Chapter 6, know before you turn there that for most pet birds — and certainly for parrots — seeds are the equivalent of junk food, high in fat and low in balanced nutrition.

You can find the foundation of proper nutrition for your pet bird in a box or bag of nutritionally complete pelleted diets available from high-quality pet stores or veterinarians. Add healthy "people food," and even some seed, to this basic diet, and your bird is on the way to healthy eating for life.

**TIP**

Unfortunately, some birds (just like some people) vastly prefer junk food to a well-balanced diet and will resist their owners' efforts to switch them. If your bird is a seed junkie, check out Chapter 6 for help in converting him to healthier habits.

## Birds Get Mites and Lice Easily

Here we have another bit of nonsense that sells a lot of useless junk at pet stores. People are appalled when their pets start chewing off their own feathers, and they seek help, preferably something easy. They're far too happy to hear (incorrectly) that their pet most probably has mites or lice, and they buy a pesticide to eliminate what isn't really there.

In truth, Brian rarely sees mites or lice on companion parrots in his practice — but he does see a whole lot of birds with unrelated feather-damaging behaviors. The problem is a complicated one and usually suggests something is wrong with the bird's behavioral health as much as her physical health.

**TIP**

The best way to have your bird's maladies correctly diagnosed and treated is by having a good relationship with an avian veterinarian. Otherwise, you may be throwing money away on useless products — and endangering your bird's life. (See Chapter 12 for more about the causes and treatments of feather picking.)

## Birds Catch Colds from People

Although birds may become infected with human influenza-type viruses, those bugs rarely make a bird ill. Human colds and flus come and go, so it's easy to imagine people thinking what looks the same in people and birds is, in fact, the same illness, but it's usually not.

If your bird is sick with what appears to be cold- or flulike symptoms, chances are, something else is going on and you need to call your veterinarian.

Don't blame yourself for passing on your own cold. You couldn't have, realistically.

**REMEMBER**

As with all pets, birds are capable of passing some diseases to humans. These diseases, called *zoonoses*, don't represent much of a concern as long as you're careful to engage in good habits such as washing your hands before and after handling pets and making sure your bird remains in good health.

# A Sick Bird Is a Dead Bird

Before birds earned their just place as welcome and respected pets, veterinary care wasn't very advanced. The nature of illness in birds was misunderstood, and signs of illness were usually missed. By the time a pet bird appeared sick, he was usually too sick to be helped.

The good news is, a lot can be done for a sick bird today. Birds are fighters, and when they're given the help they need from modern avian medicine, they can pull through injuries and diseases that once may have done them in.

**REMEMBER**

Don't give up on your bird! Learn to recognize what's normal and what's not and how to get help when you spot changes (see Chapter 10). Even a very sick bird may well survive with modern antibiotics and supportive care from a knowledgeable veterinarian.

# Lovebirds Will Die of Loneliness If Not Kept in Pairs

If you want to keep a pair of lovebirds, we're not going to stop you — their affectionate behavior toward one another is inspiring to watch. But don't complain to us when you start feeling like an in-law on a honeymoon: Neither bird is likely to be very interested in you, because they have each other.

A single lovebird (like the one shown in Figure 15-1) is a great bird for beginners. Lovebirds aren't too big, too loud, or too hard to care for — and they're very affectionate. If you decide to invite a lovebird into your life, you can expect to share company with a wonderful companion, one who will not miss having a lovebird mate.

FIGURE 15-1:
Lovebirds can be
happy with you
as a companion;
they don't have to
be kept in pairs.

*Photograph courtesy of Lisa D. Myers, Feathered Follies*
*(Concord, California)*

# All Parrots Talk

Most parrot species, from budgies to macaws, are capable of mimicking sounds, words, or phrases, but not all individuals learn to talk. Patient, clear repetition helps your parrot learn to pipe up, but don't be disappointed if your bird never develops this skill.

Male cockatiels are better at talking (whistling, too) than their female counterparts, but most larger parrot species have no obvious difference in talking ability between the genders. Your best chance at finding a talker is to adopt one with proven ability or to choose from those species best known for talking. Two to consider: the African grey (like the one shown in Figure 15-2) or the Amazon (especially the double-yellow-headed or yellow-naped varieties). These birds are so known for their speech abilities that we don't recommend them to folks who love to swear — the birds rapidly pick up words and phrases they overhear, and they don't hesitate to gleefully pepper their chatter with them.

*Photograph courtesy of Lisa D. Myers, Feathered Follies
(Concord, California)*

# Chapter **16**

# Ten Steps to a Healthy Bird

Birds are hardy creatures, capable of living well for years, even decades, when provided with a good diet and proper care and handling. But for them to reach their true pet potential, they have to start out right — and far too many don't. Some birds pick up infectious disease from less-than-ideal origins, while others may contract illness when exposed to other birds during shipping or when waiting to be sold. Many birds aren't taught to eat an optimal diet and come to their new owners on a nutritional road to nowhere good.

Even when a bird gets off to a great start, the wrong care or handling can quickly turn a situation sour. Screening for infectious diseases and practicing proper *husbandry* (the care of animals) is the best preventive-care medicine you can provide for your bird.

In Brian's hospital, preventive care and education go hand-in-hand, in the form of a checklist he uses to ensure that a new patient receives the best treatment from the beginning. We share the items on his list in this chapter, so you can check them off yourself with your own veterinarian. They don't all have to be done in the same visit, but working through the list is a good way to set the stage for continued good care. With luck, every check will confirm good health, but if it doesn't, you can feel good about catching a problem before it becomes potentially deadly.

More detailed information on nutrition is in Chapter 6, and you can find help with equipment in Chapter 4 and behavior in Chapter 12. See Chapter 13 for tips on maintaining more than one bird, and don't forget our other health chapters — Part 3 is dedicated to the topic!

REMEMBER

What better time to ask questions than when you have your veterinarian cornered in an exam room? A good veterinarian never minds taking time to educate a client — the better educated you are about your bird, the better client you'll be, and the healthier your bird will become. In so many ways, education and knowledge are truly the best medicine. You and your veterinarian are partners in ensuring your bird's good health, and you must be comfortable enough with each other to accomplish this goal.

# The Physical Examination

An experienced veterinarian isn't usually in a hurry to get her hands on your bird. Quiet observation, in fact, should be the first stage of any expert examination. Visual observation of the bird in her cage or on a perch when relaxed can reveal a great deal. Through patient attention, your veterinarian can determine whether the bird's breathing is easy or labored, and size up density and quality of plumage and ease of movement. The vet will be able to look out for and note any fear of certain things — such as a towel or unfamiliar surroundings.

This first stage also allows the veterinarian to start evaluating the relationship you have with your bird and the potential problems. For example, are you tentative or frightened when handling your bird? During this portion of the exam, your doctor speaks to both you and your bird, collects a history, and asks you appropriate questions about your bird.

In the second part of the examination, your veterinarian actually handles your bird. A towel wrapped around the bird often serves as a safe and comfortable restraint. If you don't already know how to restrain your bird in a low-stress manner, now is a good time to ask your vet to demonstrate. (We also show you how in Chapter 7.) Restraining makes it possible to do procedures that may concern your bird, such as having blood samples drawn or toenails clipped. The hands-on examination should be as short as possible to keep the bird's stress level down — and yours, too!

REMEMBER

A veterinarian can learn a great deal just by letting a bird relax. Gordy the Wonder Goose, shown in Figure 16-1, always enjoyed his many visits with Brian, who treated him for a number of injuries and ailments.

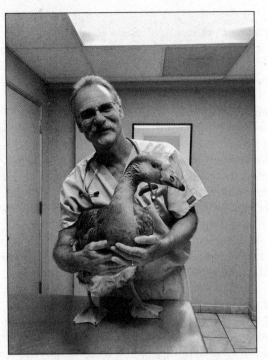

**FIGURE 16-1:**
Gordy the
Wonder Goose
with Brian.

*Photograph courtesy of Lorraine Aubert, Pacific Waterfowl Rescue*

Low-stress handling methods help to preserve a bird's emotional well-being. Veterinarians or technicians may use techniques such as positive reinforcement, counterconditioning, and desensitization to teach birds to be comfortable with procedures involved in veterinary exams — from listening to the heart and lungs with a stethoscope to drawing blood — and even to willingly participate in them.

**TECHNICAL STUFF**

*Positive reinforcement* is the act of rewarding a bird who performs a desired behavior. The bird associates her action with the reward and then wants to do it more often. The reward — which can be a treat, toy, or attention — is what is known as a *reinforcing stimulus. Counterconditioning* involves pairing a desired stimulus with something the bird avoids or fears, with the goal of changing the feared object — a stethoscope, for instance — into something the bird welcomes. If your bird enjoys a bite of pizza, for instance, or getting a head scratch, pairing that special treat with the presence of the stethoscope can eventually override her fear response. *Desensitization* is the process of gradually exposing the bird to something she's afraid of without going so far as to cause her to show fear or try to escape. At first, the frightening object may be 10 feet away. If the bird doesn't show a fear response, she's given a reward. Over time, the object is brought closer to the bird, who's rewarded whenever she doesn't show fear. Eventually, the bird is able to be near the object without fear because she has learned to associate it with things she likes.

**TIP**

Many folks argue that positive reinforcement is nothing more than bribery. Not so! There's an important distinction between the two. With bribery, the reward is given *before* the bird has engaged in the desired behavior. With positive reinforcement, the reward comes *after* the bird has engaged in the desired behavior.

Veterinary professionals trained in these techniques avoid the old "capture and restrain" methods and give birds time to acclimate to their presence and to being in the exam room. They use the time to observe their patients and identify potential problems before putting their hands on them. This makes for happier, more relaxed birds; more thorough veterinary exams; and more accurate lab test results. They may use target training to teach birds to enter or exit a carrier, allow intramuscular injections, or take medication from a syringe. Low-stress handling techniques are taught in veterinary schools, at veterinary conferences, and through organizations such as Fear Free Pets (https://fearfreepets.com), which has an avian veterinary certification program (bird owners can take the course, too, which is heavily focused on behavior).

For information on who's out there to treat your bird and how to find the best veterinary care, turn to Chapter 9. You don't necessarily need a certified specialist — many general-care veterinarians do wonderfully by their avian patients — but you do need a veterinarian who likes to treat pet birds and keeps up on the rapid changes in the field of avian medicine.

**TIP**

Look for a veterinarian whose exam room is set up for your bird's comfort. A good avian exam room is stocked with perches of varying sizes to meet the needs of many different birds, as well as a variety of treats and training supplies (such as target sticks and clickers), towels for wrapping birds if necessary, and scales with perches for easy weighing. Having these items on hand reduces restraint time and stress.

# Having Your Vet Review Your Caging and Husbandry Techniques

With a smaller bird, the initial look-see may reveal problems with the cage and its accessories, because small birds are often brought to the hospital in their everyday environment (not possible with the massive cages designed for their larger relatives).

If you bring the cage, your veterinarian can easily evaluate whether it's appropriate for your bird. Is it the right size? Are the bars spaced correctly? Are the perches, dishes, and toys safe and well positioned? Your veterinarian can offer direction on all these items and more. If you aren't able to bring your bird's cage to your veterinarian's office, ask your vet to review caging basics with you to make sure that your bird has safe housing with enough room to shake some tail feathers.

**TIP**

What makes a great cage? You can find the answers in Chapter 4.

You don't have to bring the cage with your bird. You may find it easier to bring your bird in a carrier (see Chapter 4). With a small bird, even a carrier may not be necessary. Brian sees many small birds arrive safely at the hospital in a brown paper grocery bag — although a carrier is probably a better idea!

After doing a complete review of caging, your veterinarian should ask you about your cleaning routine — how often you change cage liners or litter, how often you clean dishes, how frequently (if ever) you scrub the cage and perches, and so on. When your vet asks about these things, she isn't questioning your housekeeping skills. Instead, the focus is on preventing infectious diseases from gaining a foothold and avoiding cleaning or pest-control products that may be dangerous to your bird. She may have some suggestions for making life easier or may even tell you that you're cleaning too often.

# Feeding Your Bird a Healthy Diet

The revolution in avian nutrition has left behind more than a few breeders and pet stores — and a lot of bird owners, too. Expect a conscientious veterinarian to go over the proper diet for your bird — the main course, limited-quantity treats, and bill-of-fare no-no's.

**TIP**

Whenever you can, use food as a vehicle for delivering medication to your bird. You know what Mary Poppins always said: "Just a spoonful of sugar helps the medicine go down!" With birds, of course, it's not sugar, but something special such as bread, scrambled eggs, oatmeal, peanut butter, or pastries, all of which mix or absorb easily with liquid medication. Choose something that has a high value for your particular bird. You can also ask your veterinarian if medication can be compounded by a specialty pharmacy into a flavorful treat that appeals to your bird. *Remember:* The goal isn't to trick your bird into taking medication but to give it to him in a less stressful way.

If your bird's diet should be improved, your veterinarian should work with you on a plan to gradually convert your bird to better eating habits. (It's not just a matter of changing foods one day.) Expect some follow-up phone calls to make sure things are going well and to better ensure your success. Diet change is a learning process, and it helps if your teacher is truly invested in helping *you* teach your bird how to switch to a new diet safely and effectively.

**TIP**

Although your veterinarian may sell or recommend a line of foods that is perfectly adequate for your bird's nutritional needs, other products on the market may be just as good. Ask not only for a recommendation but also for an evaluation of the handful of products that may suit your bird. If your veterinarian emphasizes the brand she carries in her office, you should be able to ask why without risking offense. It's a fair question, and it should be met with an honest answer — even if the veterinarian admits she just likes the products she recommends better.

## Performing a Behavioral Checkup

Your veterinarian can tell a lot about your bird's adjustment to life in your household — and your patience and consistency — by gauging how comfortable you are with each other. Even the most well-meaning owners fall into some bad habits when it comes to behaviors. The result can be the conversion of a sweet-natured baby into a feathered adversary who is difficult, demanding, and possibly even dangerous.

Brian tends to spend a great deal of time on behavior issues, assessing his patients to see where they draw the line and watching their owners' reactions. When he encounters a bird who won't put up with much handling, he shows clients better ways to interact with their birds without putting pet or person at risk and suggests ways to remedy the situation over the long term.

Even if everything's going well, an attentive veterinarian takes the time to discuss problems that may appear, what to watch for, and how to get through trying situations unscathed. Some birds go through an adolescent period that's not much different from a human one, with hormones raging and fights over control and good manners cropping up on a daily basis. Coping with these difficult stages is key to the survival of your bird–human relationship.

## Introducing a New Bird to Your Household without Endangering the Birds You Already Have

Three words to remember: *closed aviary concept.* You can find much more about this subject in Chapter 13, but it can be summed up this way:

*Don't risk the health of the birds you have by introducing a potentially sick one.*

**TIP**

How can you keep your birds safe? Preventive health screening, common sense, and quarantine. Your veterinarian can explain safe ways to keep a new bird separate and for how long. When you get the okay to bring your birds together, your veterinarian should also have some tips on how to handle the introduction to prevent injuries and promote companionship.

# Ordering Blood Tests

When it comes to avian health, the emphasis is on preventive care. One facet of this care is establishing what's normal for your bird. One of the ways your veterinarian determines your bird's personal health profile is by drawing blood for a *baseline complete blood count* (CBC). This test, one of the more basic in both human and veterinary medicine, is a gauge of good health, as well as a diagnostic tool to help determine the presence and type of illness. In birds, the CBC test measures four or five variables, including red blood cell (RBC) levels and total white blood cell (WBC) count, as well as differential white cell counts. Your veterinarian may also suggest certain blood chemistries. Results of baseline blood testing help to fill in some of the gaps in your veterinarian's understanding of the overall health of your bird and help her to get a feel for what's going on under those beautiful feathers (kind of like checking under the hood of a car).

**TECHNICAL STUFF**

A veterinarian typically obtains blood samples by *venipuncture* (the insertion of a small needle into a vein). Venipuncture is generally the preferred method, using neck, leg, or wing veins for the draw. Although popular in the past, collection of blood samples by toenail clip is much less desirable today. How would *you* like to have your blood tested by clipping your nails back until they bleed? We wouldn't, either!

# Screening for Bacteria, Viruses, and Fungi If Necessary

Some veterinarians may suggest screening for bacteria, taking a swab across the roof of your bird's mouth, her eyes, or her nose (if discharge is obvious), or getting a sample from her feces or a swab of her fanny, more formally known as the *cloaca.* Your veterinarian can then have one or more tests performed to spot any troublemakers among the normal beneficial bacteria, viruses, and fungi that may be present. Although once almost a standard screening test, these types of microbiological sampling tests are less commonly pursued unless there is a specific reason to do so in a particular bird.

Two tests are commonly performed: *Gram stain* and *bacterial culture.* Gram stain is a less specific test to give the veterinarian an idea of what general kinds of bacteria may be present. A bacterial culture, which involves growing and identifying bacteria, provides a precise identification of bacteria present, as well as the ability to test those bacteria for their sensitivity to antibiotics, if treatment is indicated. Choosing the most effective antibiotic helps to prevent development of antibiotic resistance, one of the biggest threats to global health — human and animal alike — in the world today. Because the common sampled sites are not sterile, careful interpretation is required to properly use the results of these tests.

# Testing for the Specific Causes of Some Diseases

*Psittacine beak and feather disease* (PBFD) is a serious and contagious viral disease affecting so-called "old-world birds" — species from Africa, Australia, and Indonesia. If your bird is a representative of one of these species, your veterinarian may suggest a blood test to determine whether PBFD is present. Given good care and a low-stress environment, some birds can live with PBFD for years. Your veterinarian can advise you as to what the test results mean and how your bird should be retested or treated, if necessary.

TIP

Any time you acquire a new bird, both the new bird and your current birds should be tested for PBFD before you introduce them to each other.

Another disease your veterinarian may want to test for is *chlamydiosis,* also known as *psittacosis* — not only for your bird's sake but possibly for your own. The bacterial disease, caused by *Chlamydia psittaci,* can, albeit rarely, cause illness in humans, ranging from mild flulike signs to pneumonia.

For more on PBFD, psittacosis, and other infectious diseases, see Chapter 10.

# Determining Your Bird's Gender

Although birds can definitely tell the difference, we humans (even veterinarians) can't easily tell the boys from the girls in a great many species. This ambiguity may have no bearing on how good a pet your bird becomes, but some people can't stand not knowing the gender of their birds. Their reasons may have nothing to do with an interest in breeding. They may want to know whether to choose a masculine or feminine name, for instance, while others want to be prepared for potential problems down the line, such as reproductive problems in females.

When we can't tell birds apart based on color — as in Eclectus parrots — or other visible characteristics, the answer is testing. A veterinarian can use a surgical procedure to determine gender, but more commonly she uses a blood sample or any newly formed feather (called a *blood feather* or *pin feather*) to check a pet bird's DNA. DNA testing takes a couple of weeks to process.

**TECHNICAL STUFF**

The Eclectus parrot is one bird even we humans can't confuse when it comes to figuring out which are males and which are females. The male is bright green with red patches under his wings, while the female is a shimmery purple with red head and tail. They're among the more handsome birds around. Each member of the pair is so different that the two genders were once believed to be different species. In scientific terms, they are *sexually dimorphic,* meaning males and females have obvious differences in appearance.

**REMEMBER**

After you settle the gender issue, give serious consideration to providing your bird a unique identity with a microchip. Your veterinarian may suggest this safety measure, a device the size of a grain of rice that can be inserted into the bird's breast muscle. A microchip can help you recover your bird if he disappears and prove your ownership if someone steals him. For more on microchips and other forms of bird ID, see Chapter 5.

# Considering Vaccination

Unlike dogs and cats, birds don't get a series of baby shots — not yet, anyway. A couple of vaccinations exist, one for a potentially deadly infectious disease called *polyomavirus* (see Chapter 10), and another for West Nile virus. Their use is a topic of much discussion in the avian community, by breeders, retailers, and veterinarians alike. Some professionals advise vaccinations for all birds, while others recommend shots only for breeding birds or for those going to a place with a potentially high level of exposure, such as a pet store or where mosquitoes are more likely to be present (mosquitoes can carry West Nile virus). Still others don't recommend inoculation at all.

We ride the fence on the issue. Your veterinarian isn't wrong if her opinion differs, but she should let you know about the vaccine and why she is or isn't recommending it. If you choose to vaccinate your bird, she'll need a booster shot 14 days later.

# Chapter **17**

# Ten Questions to Ask When Buying a Bird

ove at first sight? Slow down a little! When it comes to buying a bird, you need to be a savvy consumer, with your head more in control than your heart, and your wallet firmly in your pocket — or better yet, left at home — until you have good answers to some crucial questions.

**REMEMBER**

Restrain your urge to buy until you're sure what kind of bird is the right match for you. If you go to a bird shop or breeder without a solid understanding of the differences between species, you may well end up falling in love with a pretty bird who doesn't really agree with your personality and lifestyle. Check out Chapter 2 for more on how to choose; Chapter 19 lists our picks of good starter birds.

## Where Do You Get Your Birds?

The world is full of people selling pets who are better suited for another line of work. To them, a bird (or a puppy or a kitten) is nothing more than a product to make as cheaply as possible and sell as profitably as possible. Aside from the philosophical question of whether a living creature should be treated like an object — we certainly don't think so — birds who are produced in a strictly bottom-line manner may not make good companions.

REMEMBER

Healthy bird babies come from healthy parents, are raised in healthy environments on healthy foods, and are lovingly socialized by human "godparents." They're not the stressed-out "production units" you may find with a mass producer. For a bird to have a chance as a good companion, he needs to have an idea of what a human being looks, sounds, and smells like, a chance to bond to a species that doesn't look very much like his own.

Because we've seen the sick and unsocialized babies who are the direct result of poor-quality breeding and marketing practices, we think your best bet is dealing with an experienced local breeder or a shop that buys from one. (Brian, for example, sells his macaw babies through reputable bird shops because he doesn't want people dropping in at his home.)

TIP

Ideally, you want to deal directly with a seller who either breeds her own birds or buys from locals she has confidence in. Most shops are happy to share the sources of their birds; an ethical and principled operation is proud of the quality of the birds it has for sale. Other shops prefer not to reveal the names of their breeding sources — sometimes at the request of the breeders — but can assure you that they're local, can provide references from other buyers and from veterinarians (more on that later in this chapter), and stand behind the quality of the birds they sell.

WARNING

An individual or shop that cannot or will not tell you the source of its pets — or that makes some vague reference to a large production facility — is probably not your best bet for a healthy bird with good potential as a companion. "We get our birds from lots of local breeders and from a few large producers" may not be a sign of good quality control; the health of the babies is often only as good as the health of the poorest-quality supplier, because of the highly infectious nature of some types of disease. In general, the fewer the number of breeders supplying a store, the better.

Depending on where you live and the type of bird you're hoping to buy, a reputable aviculturist may not live in the same state as you are. In some areas — California, Florida, and Texas among them — breeding and selling companion birds is a big industry, with lots of participants, both large and small, professional and hobbyist. Trying to find a breeder in the Midwest, though, may be as difficult as finding beach toys during wintertime — they're around, but not that common. A reputable bird store deals only with good breeders, whether they're in the same city or hundreds of miles away.

TIP

How do you know whether you're dealing with a reputable breeder or bird shop? We give you the inside track in Chapter 3.

# How Many Birds Do You Sell per Year?

With this question, the idea is to ensure that a seller is able to pay attention to birds as individuals. Although a reputable shop may sell 200 to 300 birds or sometimes more per year, all healthy and well-socialized, any retail outlet that moves markedly more than that number ought to set off alarms in your head.

Socialization and health are everything in this game, and in our experience, large-scale operations aren't able or willing to pay as much attention to these factors as quality care requires. And how can a breeder, with hundreds or thousands of breeding pairs housed in colonies without any concern about who's mating with whom, possibly be in tune with a bird's predisposition to congenital problems or current state of health? Get 'em hatched, pack 'em up, and ship 'em out by the thousands isn't the way to produce a healthy new family member, in our opinion.

**WARNING**

Even though you're taking a risk with a mass-produced bird — and possibly supporting some questionable businesses — you also have to remember that smaller isn't necessarily better when it comes to bird breeding. A careless, sloppy, or uninformed breeder can mess up one clutch of baby birds just as surely as a mass producer can ruin thousands. Some small-scale hobbyists are excellent; others aren't. Some large breeding operations are excellent; others aren't. Health and socialization are key!

**TECHNICAL STUFF**

A *clutch* is bird-speak for what you find in a nest — eggs laid at the same time from a particular breeding pair, incubated and hatched at one time.

# What Are the Terms of the Sales Contract and Post-Purchase Warranty?

A bird who may appear perfectly healthy at the time of sale may, in fact, be harboring an infectious disease or birth defect that can limit the quality of her life, if not eventually kill her. Such a situation can be heartbreaking, of course, but it can also be financially devastating. Some parrots carry price tags into the thousands — and tens of thousands — of dollars, not to mention the significant expense of cages and other must-have bird equipment for a bird you may not have long and can't afford to replace.

Make sure the sales contract spells out what happens if something goes wrong — if the bird gets sick or dies, for example. Nothing can make up for the sadness of losing a bird, but a contract spelling out terms of replacement or compensation with a good post-purchase warranty can at least offset some of the financial burden and provide a measure of protection to both buyer and seller.

Expect a seller who has the bird's welfare in mind to strongly recommend or require you to have the bird examined by a qualified veterinarian of your choice within a certain time frame — 48 to 72 hours is a common recommendation. The veterinary exam ensures to your own satisfaction that your new bird is healthy. The seller should lay out the ground rules if the bird is not healthy — full refund, store credit, or other alternative that is acceptable to you.

**TIP**

For more information on protecting your rights in the purchase process, see Chapter 3.

# What Are Your References?

Ask the seller for names of recent buyers (within the last year or so). Call a couple of previous buyers and ask what they thought of their dealings with the shop or breeder, as well as what kind of companions their birds have turned out to be. A good sign: Aviculturists or shops that stay in touch with buyers and are always available to help out with behavior or husbandry recommendations. Satisfied customers continue to patronize a bird shop for boarding, grooming, and supplies.

A veterinary reference is important, too. Ask store owners or breeders for the name of the veterinarian who treats their birds. If the business can't provide one, don't buy. A seller who treats her own birds or who doesn't believe in or practice preventive veterinary care isn't the kind of person from whom you can safely buy. Who knows what illnesses are brewing in birds with such precarious beginnings? The seller certainly doesn't, and you're smart to skip the opportunity to find out.

# How Old Is This Bird?

Most novice bird owners are better off with a young bird, one without the "baggage" of past relationships. But because of their real or perceived value, problem parrots are often sold time and time again, with each owner hoping to recoup at least part of the purchase price while dumping an unmanageable bird on someone else. Although finding older birds who make wonderful pets is within the realm of possibility, the only sure way to know a bird's history is to buy a *weaned* baby (one capable of eating without assistance) from a reputable source.

A reliable seller knows the age of the bird; ideally, a hatch date appears on the paperwork that comes with the bird. If a bird was raised by parents, not by human hands — perfectly acceptable if he has been socialized — an exact hatch date may not be known, but the seller should be able to give you an estimate that's pretty close. Good breeding practices include good recordkeeping: When you see evidence that the paperwork has been taken care of properly, most often so has the bird!

**TIP**

In some species, you can determine approximate age by markings or eye color — both of which change as a bird matures. For instance, male African ringneck parakeets develop a black ring around the neck when they're 18 to 36 months old.

Keep in mind that young is good, but unweaned babies often are not. Few new bird owners have the expertise to hand-feed, wean, and socialize an unweaned baby, like the one shown in Figure 17-1. Don't buy into old-fashioned thinking suggesting that your bird is destined to bond better if you buy him unweaned, and don't fall for a lower price for an unweaned baby. Too many novices who buy unweaned babies end up with dead birds. Cockatiels and budgies are weaned by 6 to 8 weeks of age; larger parrots range from 14 weeks up to 6 months.

**FIGURE 17-1:**
Cute as they are, unweaned babies such as this blue-fronted Amazon aren't the best pets, especially for first-time buyers.

*Photograph by Brian L. Speer, DVM*

**TIP**

Some nonprofit organizations work not only to rescue birds with problems but also to educate prospective adopters so they have a better chance of making the newly forming relationship work. By requiring classes for adopters, these organizations help to ensure educated bird owners are prepared to deal with any health or behavior problems in their new pets. We highlight some of these groups in the appendix at the back of this book. They deserve your support.

## Does This Bird Have Any Medical Problems, Past or Current?

This question may require some tact — you don't want to accuse someone of trying to sell you a sick bird. Still, you have a right to know — and a need to know — the bird's medical history. If the bird you fancy is currently being treated for an illness, don't buy her until a veterinarian has certified the bird's return to good health. Not all problems are easily remedied, so don't take a chance. If the bird recovers and you still want her, fine.

**WARNING**

You want to feel confident that the seller has a history of using a veterinarian. Overreliance on home remedies and guesswork is a red flag. A tactful way to find out whether the bird's illness has been properly addressed is to ask for a copy of the medical records so your own veterinarian can review them. If there are no medical records because the seller hasn't used a veterinarian for care, beware!

## Does This Bird Have Any Behavioral Problems?

Many birds end up in new homes because their owners can't deal with behavior problems. In general, a novice bird keeper is better off avoiding birds with behavior problems, but if you feel capable of taking on the challenge, be sure you understand what you're likely to face.

Feather picking is pretty obvious, because the afflicted bird may look more like a plucked chicken than a parrot in full, colorful plumage. Don't fall for that old line, "He's just molting." He may not be. Other potential problems may not be so straightforward. Some birds don't like men; others don't like women. Some are afraid of people with glasses or have no basic training in good behaviors, such as stepping onto a hand or perch. Others scream constantly for attention — usually because that's what their previous owners have inadvertently taught them.

Go into any such a situation with your eyes open and be determined to work on the problem in full knowledge that some sad situations can't be fixed. Others require a great deal of time and patience. Some birds get passed around more than a foot-ball, growing more unhappy and insecure with each change of family (wouldn't you?). If you aren't willing to put some time and effort into a problem bird, don't consider taking one on. Parrots are highly intelligent — it's one of the reasons they're so popular. But it's also one of the reasons "recycled" birds are such an iffy proposition. When a bird has had a rough life, he often bears psychological scars that can make him a challenging companion indeed.

# How Have You Socialized This Bird?

If the answer to this question is "Huh?," consider looking elsewhere when shopping for anything except birds who aren't meant to be handled, such as members of the finch family, canaries included.

**REMEMBER**

Birds don't have to be hand-fed to be socialized — that's a myth we'd like to correct. Parent-raised birds have wonderful pet potential, as long as they're handled, played with, and talked to by humans while they're growing. You don't expect every kitten or puppy to be bottle-fed from birth, do you? Of course not! Mother dogs and cats do a wonderful job of raising their own offspring, and as long as the babies are handled and exposed to humans, they have no problem transferring their affection from their mothers and littermates to members of their new, human family. The same is true of birds: It's perfectly fine to let a bird's parents do the raising, as long as the babies are socialized by humans.

If the bird you're thinking of buying *has* been hand-raised, that's fine, too, provided you realize that the overall handling, not the hand-feeding, makes the difference.

A dependable breeder or bird shop can explain how the birds have been socialized, how they've been handled, and how much time they've spent with people. You *don't* want to hear, "She's a nice bird, and if you can get her out of the cage, she's yours." (You can find out more about socialization in Chapters 3 and 13.)

**WARNING**

Because of the economic realities of hand-feeding less-expensive birds — the profit margin just isn't there — many budgies and some cockatiels aren't socialized at all. From an economic perspective, nurturing an Eclectus parrot or hyacinth macaw (both with price tags in the hundreds to thousands of dollars) makes more sense than to lavish that much attention on a parakeet who may fetch as little as $10. If you find a socialized budgie or cockatiel, you're in luck! But if you end up with a bird who's largely wild, you can work toward building trust and a good relationship (see Chapter 5).

## What Have You Been Feeding This Bird?

If the seller says, "Seed," run! All-seed diets are not healthy for birds and shorten their lives in the long run. You have to wonder what else could be wrong with a bird whose seller doesn't know this basic fact. Some bird folks make their own diets from a nutritious blend of "people food" and seeds. Others feed one of the balanced pelleted diets, supplemented with fresh fruits and vegetables.

TIP

Our recommendation is to support a seller who already has the bird on one of these commercial diets and to stick with it when you take your bird home. Research shows that pelleted diets keep birds healthy. They make caring for a pet bird easier, too, because you won't have to figure out your bird's nutrition needs every day and fix meals from scratch. The makers of commercial pellets have already done that job.

REMEMBER

Pellets aren't the whole story — you need to supplement commercial foods with a healthy dose of fruits, vegetables, and other foods. Don't worry, though: Avian nutrition isn't that complicated. Check out Chapter 6 for diet tips that can put your bird on the right track.

## May I Visit and Get to Know the Bird Before Buying?

We include this question because it's a good idea to spend some quiet time observing any bird you're considering before bringing out your wallet. You need to look at a bird as an individual, not just go by what you think is normal for each species. A *Pionus* parrot may, indeed, have more in common with another *Pionus* parrot than with an African grey, but that doesn't mean personality differences don't exist among individual birds.

One of Brian's favorite stories is from the first clutch of blue-and-gold macaws he raised — Uno, Dos, and Tres. Dos literally hatched with an attitude problem, and she still pretty much has one, 38 years later. Fortunately, she lives with a person who's a good fit for her personality, but getting her through her "childhood" was a challenge from the first crack in her egg! Although they had the same parents, she and her nestmates were very different.

**TIP**

Look beyond the beautiful plumage and try to pick up clues from the bird you plan to share your life with. Observe quietly, and see how the bird responds. Is he interested in your attention? Afraid? Indifferent? If you let him perch on your hand, does he seem to relax? Can you get a sense of the individual bird? Do you like him? Do you think he likes you?

If you've carefully considered all the other questions in this chapter, we give you permission to fall head over heels in love. In fact, we encourage it!

# Chapter **18**

# Ten (Or So) Must-See Avian Websites

L ots of possibilities exist for bird lovers on the Internet. A list of ten sites can't begin to hit all the best bird resources online, which is why we've fudged and offered you more than ten. But even a hundred wouldn't do the job, nor would a thousand. If you type the word *parrot* into Google, you'll find that the subject triggers hundreds of millions of suggested places to look. The word *bird*? Billions!

## Fun for Kids — and Adults, Too

You can't go wrong with *National Geographic* when it comes to finding out information about animals — birds included. From pet birds to penguins, the National Geographic Kids site (https://kids.nationalgeographic.com/animals/birds) offers the following:

» All kinds of neat facts about bird species, including anatomy, locomotion (some birds swim and run instead of fly), and eating habits

» Videos of birds visiting the veterinarian with tips on their care

» Slide shows with amazing photos of weird and wonderful birds from around the world

» Quizzes, games, and NatGeo's well-known colorful maps

# Behavior Help and Then Some

Parrot behavior consultant Barbara Heidenreich dishes on solving behavior problems, parrot species, conservation, and more at Good Bird, Inc. (www.good birdinc.com), and at Barbara's Force Free Animal Training (www.barbarasffat. com). These sites include training terminology and success stories, FAQs about parrot behavior, ways to teach birds to take medication or receive veterinary care, how to reduce screaming, health research information, downloadable lost-bird flyers, and links to rescue organizations and sanctuaries.

At AllPetBirds.com (www.allpetbirds.com), you can find all kinds of information about living with birds, from what to know about popular species to training tips, checklists, and toys. We especially love the video of the Senegal parrot being clicker-trained for such tricks as Fetch and Play Dead. Subscribe to the "Bird is the Word" e-zine or take a quiz to determine the best pet bird for you. The quiz said the top match for Kim was a parakeet and included the medium-size parakeets like her late African ringneck, Larry, who lived to be 29 years old.

Parrot Wizard Michael Sazhin guides parrot peeps on using positive reinforcement to teach and safely interact with their birds. His website, Trained Parrot Blog (www.trainedparrot.com), isn't fancy, but it offers parrot care and training videos, advice on living harmoniously with parrots, tips on reading parrot body language and clicker training, and other useful information. The focus is on positive reinforcement and having an equitable relationship with your bird.

Best in Flock (www.bestinflock.com), described as "musings about life with parrots," covers parrot training, enrichment, nutrition, and more. Recent blog posts address important topics on living with parrots, including helping them stay calm during fireworks, whether parrots are good at delayed gratification, and favorite parrot items.

Finally, if you want to take a deep dive into behavioral science, we highly recommend the courses of Susan Friedman, PhD, available through www. behaviorworks.org. It's perfect for the bird owner who wants a greater understanding of learning and behavior delivered by an internationally renowned expert in parrot care and training.

**REMEMBER**

If your bird is suffering from a behavior problem — or if you are! — check out our tips for preventing and fixing bad bird habits in Chapter 12.

# Enraptured over Raptors

Raptors aren't pets — far from it — but birds of prey are cool. The folks at the Raptor Center at the University of Minnesota's College of Veterinary Medicine understand the essential coolness of these fierce and fascinating birds, and they've got a fabulous website to prove it (www.raptor.umn.edu).

The center is an internationally known medical facility for birds of prey, with an emphasis on "medical care, rehabilitation, and conservation of eagles, hawks, owls, and falcons." The center's website is a great place to find out about these birds, as well as to sponsor the care, feeding, and training of one. The organization relies on donations to keep going. Sponsorships start at $25 per year and include information on the bird of your choice, as well as a newsletter.

**TECHNICAL STUFF**

No one knows exactly when the sport of *falconry* (hunting with a trained raptor) began, but it was well established in Asia and the Middle East more than 4,000 years ago. It gradually spread to Greece, Italy, and the rest of Europe. In Western Europe, hawking, as it was also known, achieved widespread popularity in the Middle Ages.

The Raptor Center's website offers information and education on such topics as what to do with an injured raptor or updates on current cases in the center's veterinary clinic. Look for links to other raptor programs around the world, too.

Other fascinating raptor sites include Audubon (www.audubon.org/features/birds-of-prey), the Birds of Prey Foundation (www.birds-of-prey.org), the Center for Birds of Prey (www.thecenterforbirdsofprey.org), and the Orange County Bird of Prey Center (www.ocbpc.org).

# Help Us Get Home

If nothing else, the Bird HotLine website (www.birdhotline.com), founded in 1998, packs the power to persuade you of the importance of preventing birds from having an escape route out of the house. Although some birds are stolen, many are lost through an open door or window. The website is filled with heartbroken owners who realized in a fraction of a second how easily a flighted bird can, well, fly!

The Bird HotLine is an amazing labor of love, an attempt to use the Internet to link bird lovers worldwide into a bird patrol, looking for lost pets. The site lists not only birds who have been lost or stolen but also birds who have been found. The best part, of course, is the collection of stories with happy endings — those birds who are safely reunited with their owners (far too few, sadly, in comparison to the number of lost birds listed).

Education is another goal of the Bird HotLine. Its creators note that anyone who finds a dog or cat immediately thinks about locating an owner, but too many folks who find a bird assume the rule is "finders, keepers." That notion has a chance of changing as website visitors read and share stories about how much these pets are missed.

The site also offers some basic bird-care guidelines, but really, that's secondary to the outstanding work of these bird lovers. Join the bird patrol today!

Other options for posting lost or found birds can be found at 911 Parrot Alert (www.911parrotalert.com) and ParrotForums.com (www.parrotforums.com/lost-found). The ParrotForums.com community also hosts discussions focusing on such topics as birds and toys, bird allergies, safe household cleaners, appropriate pain relief, types of birds, feather plucking, scientific articles on parrots, and much more.

**WARNING**

Although the cooperative efforts of the bird patrol are commendable, don't rely on the kindness of strangers to ensure your lost bird's return. Birds are valuable, difficult to trace, and easily sold with no questions asked for quick cash, which makes them enticing to burglars. If your bird turns up in someone else's hands, you may have a hard time proving you are your pet's owner. That's why identification such as a microchip is important. For more information on microchips and other forms of identification, turn to Chapter 5.

# Meet Alex, the Star

Alex the African grey (shown in Figure 18-1) may be the best-known parrot in the world, and that's in no small measure due to more than two decades of work by Dr. Irene M. Pepperberg, who has helped to revolutionize people's understanding of the intelligence of birds.

The Alex Foundation (www.alexfoundation.org) showcases Dr. Pepperberg's research and relationship with Alex, and it's a must-see for anyone who wants to know more about parrots. Through their research, Pepperberg and her colleagues have shown that birds such as Alex are not just gifted mimics; they actually understand a great deal of what they say. The foundation's goal is to expand the base of knowledge about the cognitive and communicative abilities of parrots.

**FIGURE 18-1:**
Alex is arguably the world's best-known African grey, even years after his death.

Alex, who sadly died unexpectedly of cardiovascular disease in 2007 at the age of 31, was able to count; identify objects, shapes, colors, and materials; and understand the concepts of same and different. Pepperberg and her associate, Suzanne Gray, currently study avian cognition with two other African greys, Athena and Griffin.

The website of the Alex Foundation contains many of the articles written about Alex and Pepperberg, as well as research published by Pepperberg. Fascinating stuff, with some scientific links you can't find elsewhere (look under the About heading for Research and Links).

# Birds of a Feather, Flocking Together

A visit to the website of the American Federation of Aviculture (AFA; https:// afabirds.org) can enlighten and gratify you. Without the AFA and other activist groups, the companionship of a bird might be out of reach for all of us. The AFA was formed in 1974 in response to legislation that would have greatly restricted the ability to keep birds, in response to concerns over diseases threatening to damage the poultry industry.

Today, the Texas-based organization is a federation of bird clubs and organizations representing thousands of individual aviculturists. Its goals are to advance and improve breeding and husbandry practices and living conditions for exotic birds; raise awareness of bird-related conservation, research, and legislation; and ensure long-term self-sustaining populations of exotic birds both in captivity and in the wild. It also publishes digital and printed editions of *AFA Watchbird* and offers online courses in aviculture. Stop by to keep an eye on what's happening with legislation affecting birds.

TIP

*Aviculture* is a fancy term for the breeding and keeping of birds in captivity; it's also used to represent the entire industry of bird keeping, from breeders and bird stores to magazines and companies that manufacture cages, food, and equipment.

# Sources for Health Information

In the history of veterinary medicine, the Association of Avian Veterinarians (AAV) counts as a fairly recent entry, but its growth is indicative both of the number of birds as pets and in bird owners' interest in keeping them healthy. Founded in 1980, the AAV has more than 1,700 members, including veterinarians, veterinary technicians, veterinary students, and other professionals who work with birds in private practices, colleges and universities, zoos, government, and industry. The international education and scientific organization works to promote the care and welfare of all types of birds in areas including companion bird medicine and surgery, conservation, wildlife, zoological medicine, and more.

The AAV website (www.aav.org) reflects the group's goals, with information both for the public and for member veterinarians, all geared toward improving avian health. Through the website, you can gather basic health information, order pamphlets or articles, or search for an AAV member in your area.

TIP

The easiest way to find an avian veterinarian in your area is to search the AAV's website for all AAV members in your state and then scan the list to see which ones are near you.

Another great resource is the Schubot Center for Avian Health at Texas A&M University (https://vetmed.tamu.edu/schubot). They conduct research into health issues affecting companion, wild, and exotic birds. Recent and long-standing research projects and programs include interactions between stress hormones and blood parasites in birds along elevation gradients, the Ara Genomes Project (`https://vetmed.tamu.edu/schubot/research/the-ara-genomes-project`), and the Tambopata Macaw Project (`https://vetmed.tamu.edu/macawproject`).

**TIP**

One important website to keep in mind is that of the ASPCA National Animal Poison Control Center (`www.aspca.org/pet-care/animal-poison-control`). Keep the toll-free number (888-426-4435) in a prominent spot in your home and make sure everyone knows where it is. If your bird takes a bite out of a toxic plant, food, or other substance, or is showing signs of poisoning such as vomiting, diarrhea, lethargy, tremors, or falling off her perch, to name just a few, call the National Animal Poison Control Center immediately if your veterinarian isn't available. The call is toll-free, but there is a charge for the service. The fee is well worth it if your bird's life is on the line.

# Helping Birds in Need

Birds don't always have it so easy, which is why groups spring up to help pet birds and to assist in preserving wild birds and their habitats. We focus on one of each because we support them and because we think their websites are useful and entertaining.

The Gabriel Foundation (`https://thegabrielfoundation.org`) is a Colorado-based charity that works to rescue, rehabilitate, and rehome unwanted pet birds, as well as educate bird owners about proper care of their pets. Gabriel was the hyacinth macaw of founder Julie Murad, who lost the bird as a result of improper care by the bird's breeder and a veterinarian. The loss propelled Murad into a life dedicated to helping birds, and the foundation now shelters birds waiting for adoption, some with special physical and emotional needs. The birds are listed on the website, along with information on how to adopt and other ways to honor Gabriel's memory by helping out this nonprofit group.

Preserving birds in their ever-more-endangered environment, as well as ensuring that they flourish as companions, is the focus of World Parrot Trust (WPT; `www.parrots.org`). The website includes information on conservation projects, podcasts featuring avian experts from around the world, questions and answers from experts, species profiles, links to parrot bloggers (including WPT's executive director Jamie Gilardi, PhD), social networks, and articles about why wild birds deserve our concern.

Phoenix Landing (www.phoenixlanding.org) is a nonprofit organization dedicated to the well-being of parrots. The facility hosts educational events on avian care and nutrition, helps birds in need find new homes, supports research and conservation of wild parrots, and advocates standards of care for birds. An online newsletter presents information about upcoming classes, highlights adoptable birds, illuminates volunteer opportunities, and shares parrot news from around the world.

# Chapter **19**

# Ten Best Birds for Beginners

When it comes to birds, too many people get in over their heads, choosing a pet who's too large, too loud, too expensive, and ultimately, too much to handle. If your list of must-have birds includes only the largest and most colorful parrots, expand your horizons and consider some other birds with great pet potential before you buy.

The world of birds is large, with more than 300 species of parrots alone — although, of course, not all of them are commonly available as pets. Some of these species are perfect for the first-time owner, in different ways. Some are good because they don't need — or want — to be handled, and some for the opposite reason — because they're feathered love sponges.

In this chapter, we present an admittedly subjective list of birds — some well-known, some not — that are reasonably priced, reasonably sized, and just plain reasonable to live with.

REMEMBER

Deal with a reputable breeder or bird store when shopping for any pet; otherwise, all those wonderful traits we attribute to birds may be nonexistent in the animals you encounter. Some pet retailers see birds as goods to be bred, shipped, and sold as quickly and efficiently as possible. Rapid stock turnover may be a great plan for merchandising widgets, but it's not ideal for pets. Deal with people who sell healthy, well-socialized birds, and you can count on the best start possible.

**TIP**

For more information on choosing a bird and finding a reputable source from which to buy, see Chapters 2 and 3. When you think you have a good seller, Chapter 16 provides the questions you need to ask to help you confirm your instinct.

You may have noticed that we don't include any of the large parrot species such as macaws and cockatoos in our suggestions for beginners. Until you really have a good sense of what it means to share your life with a bird, it may be best to hold off committing to ownership of one of these large, loud, strong, long-lived species.

# Canaries and Finches

Canaries are actually finches, so we've combined them in this section. The canary — among the oldest, most popular, and most varied pet birds in the world — is known for his vocal talents and vibrant color. Canaries hail originally from the Canary Islands, which were not named for their most famous residents but for the dogs the Romans found there. (*Canis* is Latin for "dog.")

Wild canaries are green and yellow, but when folks think of them today, they most often conjure up a brilliantly colored yellow bird, thanks, mostly, to the Sylvester-outsmarting cartoon character, Tweety Bird.

In fact, canaries come in many colors and varieties, thanks to centuries of selective breeding. Canaries can be sleek or plump in body type, smooth or puffy when it comes to feathers, with colors from yellow to bright orange to green and brown. If you want a singer, though, make sure your new bird is a male; female canaries don't sing.

Although still one of the more popular birds in the world, the canary isn't talked about as much for its pet potential as it used to be. And that's a shame, because the bird is perfect for beginners who aren't sure they want as much interaction as some other species require. The canary is happy to hang out in a cage and entertain you with beauty and song. In fact, he'd rather *not* be handled.

Because they don't require or desire handling, the canary can be a good pet for kids, providing song and beauty and allowing youngsters to observe the wonder of birds close-up.

Finches, little charmers who embody the word *vivacious,* are also mostly hands-off birds. Finches are flashy, fast-moving, and fun to watch, with a lively, constant twittering that's considerably below the decibel level parrots are capable of attaining. Several species of finches are available as pets, but for beginners, the most easily available are the zebra finch and the society finch. Gouldian finches (see Figure 19-1), also known as Lady Gouldians or rainbow finches, are greatly admired for their brightly colored plumage.

**FIGURE 19-1:** Finches like this Lutino Gouldian are delightful and beautiful pets for beginning and experienced bird keepers alike.

The zebra (so named for striping, especially on the tail and face) is an Australian native who's available in many distinctive varieties that differ in color — more variety than you can find in any other finch species. And anyone can tell the girls from the boys when it comes to the common gray zebras: Boys have bright orange cheeks and dark orange flanks, and girls don't.

Society finches are a human creation — one of the few species of pet birds that never existed in the wild. Also called the Bengalese finch, the society comes in many colors and patterns and is an easy keeper who's comfortable in human surroundings, as you may expect from a thoroughly domesticated species.

Finches do better in a social situation, so plan on buying two or more and giving them a cage with plenty of space to exercise their wings. These birds get around by flying, and unlike parrots, they don't climb for exercise.

Because they're perfectly content to live without handling, finches make an excellent aviary bird. They're always a delight to observe. For this reason, the finch is also good for a caged bird in an older child's room.

**REMEMBER**

Because finches are small, some people believe they don't need much in terms of cage size — and that's wrong. Finches need room to fly, and when housed with others of their kind, they need enough space to have a bit of territory to call their own. They need enough space and subspaces in their living quarters to be able to choose to be seen or not. When they're too crowded, territorial battles between cage-mates are common. (For more on cages, see Chapter 4.)

# Budgies (Parakeets)

At last, a bird in the hand! Because of their low price and easy availability, budgerigars (commonly known in the United States as parakeets) are often treated as throwaway birds — easily purchased, easily disposed of, easily replaced. This deplorable attitude keeps people from valuing these birds for their affectionate personality. Some budgies even become very good talkers, albeit with tiny little voices.

**TECHNICAL STUFF**

The name *budgerigar* comes from Australia's native humans, the Aborigines. Four syllables is a mouthful, which is probably why some people started calling these brightly colored birds "parakeets." Although the name isn't wrong, it's imprecise. All budgies are parakeets, but not all parakeets are budgies. Many species of parakeets exist, and many of them are available as pets, including the Quaker (see the "Quaker Parakeets" section, later in this chapter), grey-cheeked, ring-necked, and canary-winged, to name a few.

Budgies (like the one shown in Figure 19-2) are commonly found in two major varieties, differentiated by body type: The narrow American and the huskier English. Colors now reach far beyond the green or blue of decades ago. Because these birds are sold so inexpensively (especially the American), hand-raising doesn't pay, so few breeders invest the time or trouble. Budgies can be tamed by gentle, patient handling and can bond closely to their human companions. Others are more suited to life as cage birds and prefer not to be handled.

**TIP**

Hand-raised budgies are worth seeking out for their excellent pet potential. For more on how to find a healthy, happy baby bird, see Chapter 3.

**FIGURE 19-2:**
Tufted budgies
have a crest of
feathers that stick
up and forward.

Photograph by Brian L. Speer, DVM

For a child old enough to understand the need for gentle, respectful handling, budgies are ideal pets. But don't let their reputation as a great child's pet keep you from considering one as a companion for an adult. These active, loving, entertaining birds are easy to keep and relatively quiet.

**WARNING**

Dealing with a good source is important when buying any pet bird, but finding a reliable seller is even more important with budgies. Mass-produced birds are harder to tame because they haven't been socialized, and they may be more prone to life-threatening health problems.

# Chickens

One of the big surprises of the past 20 years has been the rise in popularity of chickens as pets. People no longer keep them simply for their ability to lay eggs; many people have discovered the joys of cuddling a chicken or teaching one tricks. Chickens (shown in Figure 19-3) are full of personality, inexpensive to purchase, and easy to keep in any environment, including small city spaces. Cute chicken diapers allow them to be house pets as well. Outdoors, they eat bugs in your yard and fertilize it with their droppings. Bonus: delicious fresh eggs!

**FIGURE 19-3:**
Chickens are no longer found only in farmyards; they're surprisingly popular as urban and suburban pets.

*Photograph courtesy of Elizabeth Anderson Lopez*

Chickens come in a variety of sizes, colors, and patterns. You can choose chickens based on personality, type of plumage, or the color of the eggs they produce: blue, green, brown, olive, speckled, or classic white. Some that we recommend as great beginner birds include sweet and fluffy Buff Orpingtons, friendly Barred Rocks (once described as the Labradors of chickens), Rhode Island Reds for their hardiness, and Ameraucanas, with their pretty green eggs.

**TECHNICAL STUFF**

The color of the eggs a chicken produces is determined by genetics. Different types of chickens lay eggs of different colors. For instance, Barred Rocks and Rhode Island Reds lay brown eggs; Ameraucanas lay green eggs; Easter Eggers lay blue, green, and pink eggs; and Leghorns lay white eggs. All eggs start out white; pigment, if it's going to be there, is deposited as the egg develops. Chickens with white earlobes usually produce white eggs.

# Cockatiels

Cockatiels (shown in Figure 19-4) are exceptionally popular, and justifiably so. These small parrots are flat-out loving, and they live to snuggle and be petted. If you only recognize the gray bird with orange patches, you may be surprised at how many colors are available these days, thanks to the work of some highly energetic aviculturists.

Photograph by Kim Campbell Thornton

**FIGURE 19-4:** Cockatiels come in a variety of color mutations and can be charming companions.

Some cockatiels learn to talk, but many, particularly the males, are better at whistling. This bird is another who can be a good choice for children, as long as the kids understand the need for careful handling.

Cockatiels can become whatever you make them. When you give one plenty of love and interaction, you can expect to come up with a real winner.

# Quaker Parakeets

The Quaker (shown in Figure 19-5) didn't acquire its name from any religious leanings. The bird is thought to have earned the descriptive title through one of the common noises it makes or the quivering of its youngsters when they beg for food.

Green with a silvery front, Quakers are active and upbeat, and they like to vocalize. Some learn to talk, while others love to whistle. All can be loving if socialized when young and given consistent, respectful handling.

**FIGURE 19-5:** Quakers are named for the quivering motions of their babies.

We have to admit to little hands-on experience with Quaker parakeets, but the lack of acquaintance isn't because we don't like them. They're illegal in California, where we live, because they're considered a threat to native species and agribusiness because of their ability to adapt to a wild lifestyle. Although we can't really say we agree with the policy, we can say the Quaker is well worth considering if you live in places where they're legal.

Other states in the United States that ban them include Connecticut, Georgia, Hawaii, Kentucky, Pennsylvania, Rhode Island, Tennessee, and Wyoming. A few other states regulate them in one way or another. For information on the latest restrictions where you live, check with your state's Department of Agriculture or fish and game authorities.

# Poicephalus Parrots and Parrotlets

The small African parrots known collectively as *Poicephalus* are an easygoing bunch. Of the species available as pets, Senegals (like the one shown in Figure 19-6) are probably the most common; they're handsome little birds with a gray head, green back and wings, and yellow-orange underside. Other species in the group include the Meyer's, Jardine, cape, red-belly, and brown-head — all known for their small size (a little bigger than a cockatiel) and affectionate personalities. They aren't the best talkers, but some manage verbalization quite well. Their noise level isn't too bad.

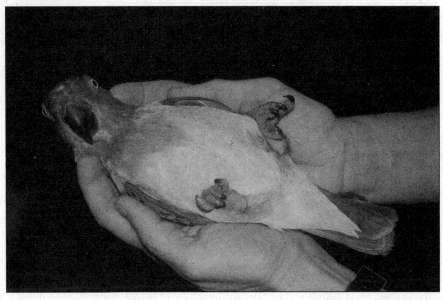

**FIGURE 19-6:** Affectionate and playful Senegal parrots are popular members of the *Poicephalus* family.

*Photograph by Brian L. Speer, DVM*

*Poicephalus* can be devoted to their owners, and after they decide you're trustworthy, they're especially fond of having their heads and necks scratched — in fact, they beg for it, tipping their heads and leaning over to expose their necks for a good scratch.

An even smaller parrot to consider: the parrotlet (shown in Figure 19-7). Don't let their small size fool you; these 5-inch dynamos are all parrot — active, inquisitive, loving, and demanding. Two varieties are commonly available as pets — the Pacific and the green-rumped — but more species are becoming increasingly available. Apple-green or blue in hue, parrotlets are quieter than some of their larger relatives, but some develop the gift of gab.

FIGURE 19-7:
Parrotlets are the
classic "big bird in
a small package."
This is a blue
mutation Pacific
parrotlet.

*Photograph by Brian L. Speer, DVM*

Another one to consider is a newer, less aggressive little bird on the block: the lineolated parakeet. Quiet and calm, they enjoy walking as much as flying and enjoy playing in water. Approximately the same size as a budgie or lovebird, these friendly and funny parakeets can learn to talk and whistle.

TIP

Some species are better talkers than others, picking up words, phrases, and household sounds with little or no effort on the part of their owners. Other species are able to mimic a few sounds if their owners work with them patiently. For information on which species are the best talkers, see Chapter 2. For tips on speech training, see Chapter 7.

# Pionus Parrots

*Pionus* parrots are sometimes overlooked because they're just not as flashy as other parrots — their beauty is more subtle. But what they lack in bright colors they make up for with winning personalities.

Several species of *Pionus* (see Figure 19-8) are available as pets, including Maximilian, blueheads, dusky, bronze-winged, and white-capped. *Pionus* are slightly larger than the *Poicephalus*, but they're still small enough to be easy to keep and handle. Their personalities are considered among the more sedate, and they're not excessively loud. (Nor are they considered fantastic talkers, although they're certainly capable of learning a few phrases.) The word most connected with the *Pionus* is *sweet*, and it fits — socialized, well-handled birds are unparalleled as loving companions.

**FIGURE 19-8:** *Pionus* parrots tend to be easygoing and can be quieter than other parrots. This is a blue-headed *Pionus*.

*Photograph by Brian L. Speer, DVM*

And when you're in love with one, you can appreciate the subtle beauty of these birds — the plumage of a healthy *Pionus* has an almost iridescent quality about it.

# Pyrrhura Conures

The conures (see Figure 19-9) are one of the larger groups of parrots, with more than 100 species and subspecies. As pets, conures are well-represented, too, with about a dozen available, including such well-known birds as the jenday, dusky, and sun. These three belong to the *Aratinga* genus, but our best-for-beginners picks belong to another category, the *Pyrrhura* genus. (Does it seem like we always choose the ones that are hard to spell and pronounce?)

*Photograph by Brian L. Speer, DVM*

If you find it easier, call them either green-cheeked or maroon-bellied, because these are the most commonly available species in the category. Whatever you call them, though, you can look forward to a lovely pet. Both species are much, much quieter than the sun conure (but then, so are some rock bands). Enthusiasts say the *Pyrrhura* is affectionate and playful. Colors aren't as dramatic as the red-and-gold sun, but the greens of the lesser-known conures still make for an attractive companion. Some may even grace you with a few acquired phrases.

Although *Aratinga* conures such as the sun may not be the best choice for beginners, their colorful appearance and clownish personalities have won them plenty of fans — and a starring role in the movie *Paulie*. (Paulie was a blue-crowned conure.) For more on *Aratinga* conures, see Chapter 3.

# Amazon Parrots

Amazons (like the one in Figure 19-10) are a little bigger and more expensive than many of the birds we describe in this chapter, but they're just too darn appealing to leave off the list. Amazons are among the best talkers around, especially the yellow-naped species. Amazons are also beautiful and brilliant, and they love to clown around. When Brian hears a bird entertaining herself and everyone around her in the waiting room of his hospital, he knows without looking that it's an Amazon. They love to be in the limelight, and they seem to feed off the attention they attract.

**FIGURE 19-10:**
A green-cheeked Amazon, also known as a Mexican red-headed parrot. These medium-size birds are funny, playful, and affectionate, with a somewhat milder personality than other Amazons.

*Photograph by Brian L. Speer, DVM*

Amazons are midsize parrots. They're very active birds who truly enjoy spending time with the people they love. An Amazon appreciates his toys, too, and is one of the easier birds to train to perform certain behaviors.

**TIP**

Some Amazon species are easier to live with than others. For beginners, we like to recommend the lilac-crowns, blue-fronted, red-lored, and white-fronted. These smaller species are less likely to push, are generally quieter, and are all around easy to handle.

**WARNING**

A potential problem for beginners: Amazons can be *too* smart. As with any parrot, you need to be sure you're giving your bird lots of structured socialization, a fair share of toys, and plenty of exercise (see Chapters 5 and 12).

# Peach-Faced Lovebirds

Peach-faced lovebirds are beautiful, active, and playful. Talking is possible, but it's not what these small parrots are known for. A well-socialized peach-faced can be your best pal for years, if you don't leave him to waste away alone in a cage. When hand-raised and socialized with humans, these little guys love to be handled, carried around in your shirt pocket or under the hair on your collar. They're very affectionate, not overly loud, and capable of picking up a few phrases.

Lovebird species commonly available as pets include the Fischer's, black-masked, and peach-faced, with the last being the more popular. Peach-faced lovebirds also come in many interesting color mutations, including Lutinos, olives, and pieds.

# Chapter 20

# Ten Common Dangers to Your Bird's Life

Birds are hardy creatures in many ways, survivors both in the evolution game — where they boast residency in nearly every ecological niche — and in the challenging role of sharing their lives with us.

Although life in the rain forest, outback, or wherever their natural habitat may be harbors plenty of risks, so, too, does the modern human dwelling. Some of these hazards are obvious, and others manage to sneak up on bird owners who don't realize what's happening until it's too late. We don't want you to be in that sad latter group.

REMEMBER

Your bird's best protection is a safe but fun cage and an observant human companion. But you need to know what to look out for to keep your bird safe. To help build your awareness, we share a list of the more common dangers in this chapter. Read them all, and give your home the once-over, removing or reducing any risks you find.

# Predators

Predators think birds are fair game, and you really can't blame them. The best you can do to protect your bird is to remember who's sharing your happy home — and who may drop by uninvited.

Some predators are more obvious than others and are especially dangerous to birds living in outdoor aviaries. Rats, mice, raccoons, and opossums all would relish a taste of your bird. Although they may not pose much of a risk to bigger pet birds, they can be a formidable danger to smaller ones.

More common are the predators we live with and call companions: dogs and cats. Aside from the obvious danger from teeth and claws, dogs and cats can transmit infectious elements in their saliva that can do in your bird.

WARNING

Don't take a chance. Although some pets seem to get along wonderfully with birds, don't ever discount the power of instinct — never leave birds unattended with dogs and cats.

TIP

If your bird is attacked by *any* animal, call your veterinarian immediately, even if everything seems fine. You may not be aware of internal damage, and the prompt administration of appropriate antibiotics may be necessary to ward off a potentially life-threatening infection. Even cat saliva on a bird's feathers is enough to introduce an infection that could kill the bird.

For more on keeping birds safe from cats and dogs, see Chapter 5. Emergency-care guidelines — what can wait and what can't — are in Chapter 10.

# Flying Free

Flying is one of those things that adds to the incredible appeal of birds, their mystique, and their wonder. Birds are not the only creatures who fly, of course. A zillion insects manage it, as do mammals such as bats. But birds do it with style, with grace, and, often, with a flash of brilliant color. We admire and envy them, because only recently in human experience have we taken to the sky — and let's be honest, blasting place to place inside a jet-propelled metal tube hardly has the same panache.

But when it comes to most companion birds, flying out into the wide, wild world is too dangerous to risk, although some committed and experienced bird lovers allow their birds to fly free in certain circumstances — when they've built a relationship that will help ensure the bird returns to the hand.

REMEMBER

Inside the home, protect your bird by restricting access to rooms with dangers such as hot stoves, gas burners, overhead fans, fireplaces, and open dog mouths, for instance. Keep toilet lids down so your bird doesn't fly into the toilet.

TIP

Finches and canaries are happier if not handled or allowed out, and their feathers should be left alone so they can fly in their cages for exercise (which means they need a cage large enough to do so!). See Chapter 4 for cage-selection guidelines.

The best way to enjoy flighted birds is in the wild, and a great way to do that is to take up bird watching. Find out all about this fast-growing hobby in *Bird Watching For Dummies,* by Bill Thompson III (Wiley).

# An Open Door or Window

Your bird may love you, but that doesn't mean she won't seize the opportunity provided by an open door or window. And even if she's not inclined to consciously attempt an escape, taking flight is an instinctive move for a bird who's spooked or frightened.

The best way to prevent losing your bird in this way is to put screens on your doors and windows and be careful about opening any route to the great outdoors. If you like to take your bird with you when you go out, use a travel carrier or cage, or consider one of the harness-and-leash getups available online, in bird-supply catalogs, or through the ads in bird magazines.

TECHNICAL STUFF

A lost bird is a double tragedy because colonies of escaped pets can be a threat to native birds by displacing them from their habitats. Former pet birds do very well in warm states such as Arizona, California, and Florida, as well as in a number of countries, but they can also do surprisingly well in colder climates. Monk or Quaker parakeets are such successful colonizers that they've been banned in several states as a danger to native birds and agriculture. Colonies of these birds have been spotted as far north as Chicago.

Look for tips on how to encourage an escaped bird to come home in Chapter 7. You can find a website dedicated to reuniting lost birds with their owners in Chapter 18, as well as in the appendix.

# Inhalants

Remember the historical accounts about canaries being put to service in mine shafts? Coal miners once used the birds as early-warning systems to alert them to the presence of dangerous gases. Because birds are highly sensitive to toxic fumes, a sick (or dead) canary meant gases were building up to toxic levels — a clear signal that miners had to get out to save their own lives.

Although this practice has been replaced by more accurate — and certainly more humane — monitoring equipment, the fact remains that birds have sensitive respiratory systems. In our tightly sealed homes, they can die quickly from use of aerosol products or cookware with nonstick coatings. Remove your bird to a safe place before using insecticides and cleaning products, even those that seem as benign as air freshener. Be especially careful about insecticides: Read the label and look for ingredients such as pyrethrin, fenoxycarb, and Precor, all of which are safe around birds, but only after the application has dried.

WARNING

Perhaps the most insidious danger is from nonstick cookware, such as Teflon or Silverstone. When overheated, these products emit fumes that can kill your bird quickly — without harming humans or other mammals. You can't smell or see the gases, so the only way to protect your bird is to keep your feathered friend out of the kitchen when you're using such cookware or when setting your oven's self-cleaning feature.

Although many folks recommend simply getting rid of nonstick cookware, such a compromise is impractical for many people. The risk of using a suspect product is greatly reduced if you monitor it closely — not allowing pots and pans to overheat — and ensure that your bird is always safe in another room when you're cooking or baking. Also keep an eye out for nonstick surfaces in other household objects, such as irons, toaster ovens, self-cleaning ovens, and heat lamps, as well as for aerosol products that promise protective coatings for your cookware.

REMEMBER

Seemingly every new product sparks a rumor of toxic risk. Although we agree it's good to be cautious, check with an avian veterinarian to set the record straight on any rumor you hear.

A final inhalant caution: Don't smoke around your bird, and don't leave cigarette butts where your pet can get hold of them. Cigarette smoke and tobacco are just as bad for your pets as they are for you.

# Toxic Plants

Birds are great chewers, and sometimes that tendency gets them into trouble. They can ingest metals and other inorganic items that are toxic — more on that later in this chapter — as well as nibble plants that can do them some damage.

Although we encourage giving your pet bird some plant material to destroy (it's good exercise and fights boredom), a few common plants are worthy of off-limits warnings. They include avocado, members of the philodendron (dumb cane) family, lily of the valley, foxglove, and oleander. If you aren't sure about a certain plant in your household, check with your veterinarian or a pet poison control hotline.

Most of these plants "just" make your pet sick, but a few of them can kill. If your bird tangles with any of these, call your veterinarian. And don't forget: Even "good" plants can cause problems if they've been sprayed with insecticide.

**TIP**

If you have any of these plants, move them out of reach. Better yet, don't allow your bird access to any plants at all, except for untreated and nontoxic branches you put in the cage for perches and chewing material.

You can find more information about using tree branches as perches — including which ones are safe — in Chapter 4.

# Certain Foods

**WARNING**

Although we recommend sharing healthy human food with your bird, don't hand over even a *morsel* of avocado, chocolate, or anything with caffeine in it.

Birds can also be sensitive to foods that have spoiled or grown mold. Give your bird fresh food only and remove it from the cage before it has a chance to spoil.

**REMEMBER**

Because you don't know what was sprayed on any fruit or vegetable you buy, be sure to wash any produce before offering it to your bird.

We cover healthy food choices for your bird in Chapter 6, along with everything you need to know about proper nutrition.

# Heavy Metals

Although sometimes the clinical signs may be a bit different, both zinc and lead poisoning are common metal-associated problems. Less commonly, copper and other metals can be problematic. Historically, the most common danger of heavy-metal poisoning is from lead, which can be found in weights for fishing and for curtains, bell clappers, solder, some types of putty or plaster, some linoleum, stained glass, costume jewelry, leaded foils from champagne and wine bottles, batteries, some ceramic glazes, the backs of some mirrors, paints, and galvanized wire.

No pet owner is going to feed a fishing weight to a pet, but as always, the inquisitive nature of birds puts them at risk. The energetic chewing of a parrot can even reveal lead paint many layers down on the walls of an old house. Sources of zinc in the household are also common; they include dried flakes of paint and galvanized bits of metal.

Keep an eye out for dangerous metals in your bird's environment, but some things you may worry about aren't a problem. Pencil leads, for example, aren't made of lead anymore, and, contrary to some long-held beliefs, you have nothing to fear from regular black newspaper ink or "child-safe" paints.

# Over-the-Counter Medications

If you ever consider, even for a second, giving your bird some medication just because you think it may help, we implore you: Stop!

**WARNING**

Over-the-counter human medications, even those as seemingly benign as aspirin, acetaminophen (Tylenol), or vitamins, can poison your bird. Commonly available bird products — such as antibiotics, mite sprays, or feather-picking "remedies" — should likewise be avoided.

**REMEMBER**

Always check with your veterinarian before giving *any* health product to your bird. And don't guess on dosages for medications prescribed for your bird, or overdose with the idea that if a little is good, more must be better. Birds are small compared to humans, so the margin of error when it comes to medications is slimmer. Follow your veterinarian's directions precisely on any medication sent home with your bird.

**REMEMBER**

Birds are clever and exceptionally interested in exploring and tasting. Keep not only medications — those pharmacy containers are appealing to play with — but also any questionable household product out of your bird's reach. Some to watch out for include mothballs, rodent poisons, cleaning fluids, deodorants, matches, carpet fresheners, and flea products meant for dogs and cats. Don't leave your bird free to explore in areas where such products may be stored!

# Your Feet

With the exception of finches and canaries, birds need and appreciate "out time" — periods of freedom beyond the cage for playing and socializing. Besides flying, their means of locomotion includes the same bipedal mode we use — they walk around on their own two feet.

Sometimes that mobility means a lot of exploring on the ground, which can present some hazards. Being on the ground puts your birds within reach of dogs and cats, and it also makes them easy to step on. And a human foot — backed up by human weight — can cause some real damage to delicate avian bones.

**WARNING**

We advise not allowing your bird to wander around on the ground at all, but if you do so, make a habit of looking down before you plant your big feet. Better still: Let your bird hitch a ride on you, preferably on your shoulder or hand.

# Electrical Cords

Birds are lifelong chewers, and one of the things they sometimes investigate is an electrical cord.

**REMEMBER**

Our best advice is to do just as you would with a puppy: Keep all cords out of chewing range. Tuck them away out of your bird's reach or cover them with tough plastic cable covers.

» Keeping your bird safe

» Helping others

# Chapter **21**

# Ten Disaster-Planning Tips for Bird Lovers

Tornado, earthquake, hurricane, fire, flood — if you were faced with any of these and had to leave your home, would you know how to help your bird? Disaster-planning experts advise you to take your pets with you when told to evacuate, but that plan isn't as easy as it sounds.

Sandwiched between the idea of taking your pets with you and the reality of accomplishing a safe evacuation is a lot of thought and planning. To help you prepare for all sorts of unplanned events, in this chapter we walk you through the process of being ready for the worst — and hoping for the best.

The good news: When it comes to disasters and pets, consideration for preparedness has changed a great deal in recent years — all for the better. Once left to their own survival instincts in times of calamity, animals today are the focus of a lot of planning, with organizations in place to complement those caring for human victims.

In fact, a model program started by the California Veterinary Medical Association positions a veterinarian in each county to help coordinate animal relief efforts. Other states are starting to see the light, too, with veterinarians, shelter groups, and specially trained disaster teams from the Sacramento, California–based United Animal Nations Emergency Animal Response Service prepared to do for animals what the Red Cross does for people — on an international basis!

These positive developments are the result of a growing realization that animals need help, too, and that some people choose to put their lives in danger rather than abandon their pets.

Despite all this progress, your bird's chances of surviving any kind of crisis still depend mostly on you. Don't put off preparing for the unexpected. No one likes to think about the possibility of catastrophe, but your pets are counting on you.

## Consider the Possibilities

Disaster preparedness starts with a simple question: What if? Ask yourself that question, and then consider not only the kind of crisis you're most likely to face, but also special challenges such as your being away from home when disaster strikes.

People need to rely on each other during emergencies, and this fact is just as true when it comes to your pets. Get to know your neighbors and talk about how you might help each other out. Find out from local shelters and veterinary organizations what their emergency response plans are.

Veterinary connections can be tricky for bird owners. Because you need someone experienced in avian care, your veterinarian may not be located anywhere near you. Brian's clients, in fact, come to him from all over Northern California, and some drive for hours to bring their birds to him. In a disaster, you may not have the luxury of relying on a veterinarian who's nearby. Make sure you're familiar with nearby veterinary hospitals, especially those offering round-the-clock and emergency care. Keep a current list of local veterinarians willing and able to provide care or board your birds in an emergency situation. Know who's agreeable to consulting with your regular veterinarian by telephone or online, if needed, to coordinate and possibly enhance the level of care your birds receive. Make note, too, of shops with a special interest in or focus on birds, particularly those that board birds.

REMEMBER

A crisis isn't always a community-wide event. When considering your options, think about what would happen if you were suddenly injured or hospitalized from a car accident, say, or a heart attack or stroke.

# Make a Contact List

All you really need is a sheet of paper or two, slipped into a plastic page protector you can pick up at any office-supply store. Handwrite the info or print it out from your home computer. (If you keep the master list on your computer, you can update it easily and print out a current version every so often. Beats cross-outs and erasures!)

**REMEMBER**

Your wisest move is to have a list of emergency contacts to cover everything for you and your family. But for the purpose of this book, we're just concerned with your birds.

List the name, location, and phone number of your regular veterinarian, and then the same information for nearby backup hospitals and emergency clinics. Same goes for local humane societies and animal-control shelters, animal groups, and bird shops. Include friends and neighbors, as well as your local office of emergency services.

The final step: Put the list where you know you can find it (attach it to the refrigerator with a magnet, for instance). Better yet, make a few copies — one for the house, one for the car, one for work, and so on.

**TIP**

You can also keep this information on your phone, but having a hard copy is wise in case your battery dies.

# Make Sure Your Bird Carries ID

Many birds survive disasters, but too many will never see their families again unless there's a way to determine their identity and family connections. Although you may be lucky enough to avoid being separated from your bird, you need to be ready for that possibility. One way to contribute to a continued connection is to ensure your bird has identification. (You also need to make a "Lost Bird" kit, which we cover later in this chapter.)

Your bird may have a leg band already. If so, be sure to note the identifying letters and numbers. Whether your bird is banded or not, we highly recommend you have your bird microchipped. This simple procedure provides permanent identification for your beloved companion.

For more information on leg bands and microchips, see Chapter 5.

# Make and Trade Bird-Care Files

Prepare a couple of files with up-to-date veterinary records, your bird's microchip or leg band numbers, your veterinarian's phone number and address, feeding and medication instructions, recent pictures of your bird, and written descriptions noting any unique markings or other physical details.

Talk to other animal-loving friends, ask them to do the same for their pets, and then trade files. The more people who know about your bird and how to care for him, the better.

# Collect Food and Supplies

At the top of the list of disaster gear is a travel cage or carrier for any bird whose regular lodgings aren't portable — anything bigger than a finch or budgie, in most cases. You probably already make use of a travel cage or carrier for trips to your veterinarian or for any other travel outside the home — we talk about choosing one in Chapter 4. The key, in a time of crisis, is to make sure you know where the cage is and how you can get to it easily — an emergency isn't the time to look for a ladder or dig through junk in the basement or attic. Before an emergency strikes, make sure you can get your bird to enter the cage without a great deal of effort on your part or trauma to your bird.

Also keep a few days' supply of food on hand, along with bottled water. Our recommendation for a pelleted diet (see Chapter 6 for more on nutrition) lends itself well to feeding your bird on the run. Pack some of your bird's favorite dried fruits, nuts, and seeds, too. Don't forget to rotate disaster supplies on a regular basis, so they're always fresh.

Include any medication your bird takes regularly. Get an extra supply of maintenance medication and put it in rotation — use it after your current medication runs out, and put the refill in the disaster kit. That way, your "disaster" medicine is always current. And finally: Toys! Your bird will need to take out her stress on something, and better it be toys than you or her own body.

# Keep a First-Aid Kit Fully Stocked

Every bird-lover needs basic first-aid supplies packed into a neat, portable kit. Make sure the kit includes scissors, cloth towels, and paper towels. Don't forget styptic powder for cauterizing bleeding nails or beak tips, if needed. If your kit doesn't have a first-aid booklet, tuck one inside. Consider keeping two kits — one for home, and one for the car. It's also a good idea to take a pet first-aid course so you'll feel confident in the event of an emergency.

**WARNING**

One of the problems with first-aid kits is that you're always picking at them in everyday life — a little ointment here, some gauze there, and where did the scissors go? Be sure to promptly replace any supplies you use. Otherwise, when you really need your kit, the cupboard may be bare.

For a complete list of basic first aid supplies for birds — along with help in recognizing an emergency — see Chapter 10.

# Plan, Plan, Plan, and Practice

With your research done and your supplies assembled, the next logical step is a real plan for what to do "in case." Design strategies for what to do if you're home, or if you're at work, and make sure everyone in the family knows about them — children included!

Rehearsals are a great idea. If you've been through something once or twice, the act has a better chance of becoming second nature — get the travel cage, get the bird, get the supplies, get everything in the car, and let's go! A dry run can also point out any problems with your plan, which you can then remedy.

# Keep Your Bird Secure — and Separate

Disasters can bring out the best in people and pets — but they can also bring out the worst. Your bird is bound to be scared, stressed, and disoriented, and he's likely to feed off your uncertainty as well. Keep your bird secure in his travel cage, and keep handling to a minimum. Be alert to your bird's body language — even sweet-natured pets may strike out in fear. Try to maintain as regular a schedule as possible, feeding at normal times if you can.

To help your bird maintain his good health, keep him away from other pets if at all possible, especially other birds who may be carrying heaven-knows-what diseases.

## Keep a "Lost Bird" Kit Ready

The onset or aftermath of a disaster isn't the best time to get flyers printed up, so make up some generic ones and keep them with your emergency supplies. In the biggest type size you can manage, center the words *LOST BIRD*, along with a clear picture of your feathered friend. Beneath that, include a description of your bird, including identifying marks or colors, and a space to add the phone number where you can be reached, as well as backup contacts, friends, relatives, neighbors, or your veterinarian. Print up a hundred copies and keep them in a safe, dry, and accessible place.

TIP

A staple gun enables you to post your notices; keep one loaded and tucked in with a supply of thumbtacks and electrical tape.

If your bird becomes lost, post flyers in your neighborhood and beyond, as well as distributing them at veterinary hospitals and shelters. Relying on the kindness of strangers is nice, but offering a reward may inspire some folks to be just a little bit kinder.

## Be Prepared to Help Others

You may survive a disaster nearly untouched, but others in your community may not be so fortunate. Contact your local humane society and veterinary organization now to train as a volunteer so you can help out in an emergency. Disaster-relief workers do everything from distributing food to stranded animals to helping reunite pets with their families — and helping find new homes for those who need them.

Not only is volunteering a good thing to do, but it's also the *right* thing for anyone who cares about animals and people.

# Appendix

# Resources

Throughout this book, we mention products, supplies, groups, and services that can help make things better for you and your bird — or all birds, in the case of some groups. We put a collection of resources together here, so you can find what you need.

## Aviculture and Veterinary Organizations

The following groups are a great resource for bird lovers, whether you're looking for an avian veterinarian, trying to find information on breeding birds, or wanting to make a donation toward avian health research:

>> **American Federation of Aviculture (AFA;** https://afabirds.org**):** Members of the AFA include aviculturists (bird breeders), bird owners, veterinarians, and others with an interest in avian health, bird keeping, and conservation. The AFA provides information about legislation, courses on bird care for children and adults, and aid for bird owners and aviculturists affected by storms, earthquakes, fires, and other disasters.

>> **American Holistic Veterinary Medical Association (AHVMA;** www.ahvma. org**):** Check this site if you're seeking a veterinarian who practices integrative medicine or for information about holistic medicine or therapies.

>> **ASPCA Animal Poison Control Center (**www.aspca.org/pet-care/ animal-poison-control**; 888-426-4435):** Veterinarians or pet owners can call this hotline for advice from veterinary toxicologists on toxic substances that birds may have ingested or come into contact with. A consultation fee of $75 may apply.

>> **Association of Avian Veterinarians (AAV;** www.aav.org**):** Besides being a great resource for finding an avian veterinarian or learning more about birds, the AAV also has a research fund that supports scientific research into such topics as heart disease and feather-damaging behavior.

>> **Pet Poison Helpline (**www.petpoisonhelpline.com**; 855-764-7661):** Veterinarians or pet owners can call this hotline for advice from veterinary toxicologists on toxic substances that birds may have ingested or come into contact with. A fee of $59 per incident applies.

>> **Schubot Center for Avian Health at Texas A&M University** (https://vetmed.tamu.edu/schubot): Pet, wild, and exotic birds all benefit from the Schubot Center's mission of conservation, teaching, and research into avian health, genetics, and population management.

# Behavior and Care

The following websites and blogs contain top-notch information about living with, caring for, and training birds, as well as species descriptions, enrichment tips, and information on body language:

>> **All Pet Birds:** www.allpetbirds.com

>> **Best in Flock:** www.bestinflock.com

>> **Bird HotLine:** www.birdhotline.com

>> **Good Bird, Inc.:** www.goodbirdinc.com

>> **ParrotForums.com:** www.parrotforums.com

>> **Trained Parrot Blog:** www.trainedparrot.com

# Books

Birds are in! An amazing array of newly published and classic books are available on every facet of birds. In the following list, we include a number of general-interest bird books, from avian intelligence to bird watching to the wonders of wild birds, as well as a couple of good bird-care guides that can serve as a supplement to *Birds For Dummies*.

>> *Alex & Me,* **by Irene Pepperberg (HarperCollins):** This is the remarkable story of the relationship between a cognitive researcher and the African grey parrot who together brought the brilliance of parrots to the forefront and broke new ground in our understanding of intelligence.

>> *The Beak of the Finch: A Story of Evolution in Our Time,* **by Jonathan Weiner (Vintage):** In his Pulitzer Prize–winning book, science writer Jonathan Weiner documents Charles Darwin's theory of natural selection in action as he follows the field studies of Rosemary and Peter Grant, who observe rapid adaptation

of finches in the Galapagos Islands over a 25-year period, including why the finches' beaks are crucial to their survival.

>> *The Bird Way: A New Look at How Birds Talk, Work, Play, Parent, and Think,* **by Jennifer Ackerman (Penguin Books):** Acclaimed science writer Jennifer Ackerman delves into the latest understanding of bird life and behavior with engaging writing that brings the science of birds to life.

>> *Birder on Berry Lane,* **by Robert Tougias (Imagine):** Do you bird in your backyard? You can learn a lot that way. In these essays, Robert Tougias shares his own observations of seasonal backyard bird life on his New England acreage.

>> *BirdNote: Chirps, Quirks and Stories of 100 Birds from the Popular Public Radio Show,* **edited by Ellen Blackstone (Sasquatch Books):** Even if you think you know a lot about birds, you're sure to learn more from this not-so-trivial-pursuit of interesting information about 100 species, complete with color illustrations.

>> *Birdology,* **by Sy Montgomery (Atria Books):** From chickens to hummingbirds, naturalist Sy Montgomery celebrates the strangeness and sagacity of seven species of birds, captivating readers with a wealth of knowledge about these "winged aliens."

>> *Birds by the Shore,* **by Jennifer Ackerman (Penguin Books):** Essays on bird life and other natural history of the Delaware shore explore not only "shorescapes" but also the deepest desires and sorrows of the human heart.

>> *Crazy For Birds* **by Misha Maynerick Blaise (Penguin Books):** Fun facts about birds and whimsical illustrations by the author combine to draw readers in to the ways humans and birds have connected over the centuries, as well the many different ways birds live.

>> *Every Penguin in the World: A Quest to See Them All,* **by Charles Bergman (Sasquatch Books):** Who doesn't love penguins? Author Charles Bergman takes his passion for them around the world, introducing readers through words and photos to the 18 species he seeks out in the wild.

>> *The Feather Thief: Beauty, Obsession, and the Natural History Heist of the Century,* **by Kirk Wallace Johnson (Penguin Books):** The theft of rare bird skins and feathers from a natural history museum is the catalyst for a tale of obsession, feathers, and fly-fishing, a true-crime story that's stranger than fiction.

>> *Feathers: The Evolution of a Natural Miracle,* **by Thor Hanson (Basic Books):** Their beautiful feathers are at least one of the things that attract us to birds. For biologist Thor Hanson, an interest in vulture feathers set him on the path to writing about what is arguably the most diverse and functional form of body covering in the world. Kim flew through this book.

» *Feeding Your Pet Bird,* **by Petra M. Burgmann (Barron's Educational Series):** The author builds on what we've shared about bird nutrition, going into detail about the dietary needs of companion birds, how birds eat in the wild, how to tell when your bird's diet is deficient, and much more.

» *The Genius of Birds,* **by Jennifer Ackerman (Penguin Books):** This predecessor to *The Bird Way* looks at the wide spectrum of avian intelligence, including their ability to craft tools, their amazing navigation skills, and their complex vocalizations.

» *H Is for Hawk,* **by Helen Macdonald (Grove Press):** Grieving for her father, falconer Helen Macdonald acquires a 10-week-old goshawk she names Mabel and sets out to train this most challenging of raptors. Her story brings together memoir, falconry, raptor biology, Arthurian legend, the architecture of a human–bird bond, and the transformation of a life after death.

» *The Hidden Lives of Owls,* **by Leigh Calvez (Sasquatch Books):** Naturalist Leigh Calvez brings readers along on her journey to learn more about the owls who have always fascinated her.

» *How Birds Work,* **by Marianne Taylor (The Experiment):** We address the basics of bird bodies in Chapter 7, but if you want to take a deeper dive into avian anatomy, Marianne Taylor reveals the secrets beneath the feathers, as well as their dinosaur beginnings and modern bird biodiversity.

» *Imperial Dreams: Tracking the Imperial Woodpecker through the Wild Sierra Madre,* **by Tim Gallagher (Atria Books):** Adventure writer and bird expert Tim Gallagher travels the world in search of rare and interesting birds. This book takes him to the wilds of northern Mexico where he risks encounters with drug lords and bandits in a quest for a glimpse of the imperial woodpecker.

» *The Life of Birds,* **by David Attenborough (Princeton University Press):** With nearly 200 color photos and vivid writing, famed naturalist David Attenborough takes newbie bird watchers on a tour of avian evolution, feathers, flight, song, courtship, and other elements of bird life.

» *Mastering Bird Photography: The Art, Craft, and Technique of Photographing Birds and Their Behavior,* **by Marie Read (Rocky Nook):** Want to take better bird photos? Award-winning wildlife photographer Marie Read sets you on the path, with 16 illustrated chapters that start with the basics and move on to equipment, technique, creative vision, field craft, and more.

» *Parrots of the Wild: A Natural History of the World's Most Captivating Birds,* **by Catherine A. Toft and Timothy F. Wright (University of California Press):** Parrots have been described as "the most human of birds." This book is a scholarly but reader-friendly look at these fascinating birds, ranging from evolution to conservation.

>> *That Quail, Robert,* **by Margaret Stanger (William Morrow):** An abandoned quail chick raised in a home falls in love with people and they with . . . her. Yes, Robert turned out to be Roberta, and the classic love story between bird and humans has won hearts for decades.

>> *The Thing with Feathers,* **by Noah Strycker (Riverhead Books):** Noah Strycker wonders what birds would learn if they studied us. They might, in fact, discover that we have a lot in common with them. In his book, he looks at the amazing intersections between bird and human behavior and reflects on what we can learn from each other.

>> *Wesley the Owl,* **by Stacy O'Brien (Atria Books):** In this girl-meets-owl love story, biologist Stacy O'Brien brings up and spends the next 20 years with Wesley the barn owl, in the process gaining remarkable insights into the behavior, intelligence, and communication abilities of the wild and solitary but passionate, playful, and emotionally fragile birds.

>> *What It's Like to Be a Bird,* **by David Allen Sibley (Knopf):** Artist and birder David Allen Sibley answers a wide range of questions about bird behavior, coloration, senses, and more. As a bonus, he illustrates the book with his own gorgeous artwork. This book is the kind you can skip around to what interests you most or open to any page and learn something new.

# Conservation Groups, Research, Reference Resources, and Raptors

Many bird species are endangered in the wild — often for such reasons as development-related habitat loss, competition for nest sites from other species, and predation. A number of organizations support avian conservation or conduct research about birds that increases our knowledge of them. We encourage you to support such groups, including the following, in order to preserve birds in the wild:

>> **The Alex Foundation (**www.alexfoundation.org**):** In memory of the world-famous grey parrot who was known for breaking the "bird brain" belief and demonstrating the real intelligence of nonhuman animals, the Alex Foundation supports research into the cognitive and communicative abilities of parrots.

>> **American Bird Conservancy (**https://abcbirds.org**):** Here you can find a bird of the week, bird facts, watch lists (birds that need conservation action), searches for lost species, tips on living a bird-friendly life, and more.

>> **Audubon** (www.audubon.org): Audubon's website has a North American bird guide, information on native plants to draw birds to your home, bird calls, and articles on everything you could possibly think of regarding birds — including one on how they smell!

>> **Birds of the World** (https://birdsoftheworld.org): This website from the Cornell Lab of Ornithology at Cornell University offers identification information, news, citizen science, avian studies, and other scholarly content. You can subscribe for $7.99 per month or $49 per year.

>> **Center for Birds of Prey (CBP;** www.thecenterforbirdsofprey.org): In Awendaw, South Carolina, the CBP offers group education programs on natural history and conservation for all ages, as well as free-flight demonstrations of falcons, owls, and other raptors.

>> **Orange County Bird of Prey Center** (www.ocbpc.org): Sick and injured birds receive treatment and rehabilitation at this Southern California facility and are then released back into the wild whenever possible. The birds who stay become ambassadors for their species, helping to educate visitors and raise funds for the center's operation.

>> **Parrots International** (https://parrotsinternational.org): This organization focuses on conservation of wild parrots and improving the welfare of companion parrots. Its website has information about global parrot conservation projects.

>> **Raptor Center, University of Minnesota** (https://raptor.umn.edu): At the University of Minnesota's Raptor Center, virtual programs introduce viewers to raptors in flight, eating, and being cared for. It also addresses what to do if you find an injured raptor and how to observe and photograph raptors without disturbing them. The center is also known for expertise in raptor medicine and surgery.

>> **World Parrot Trust (WPT;** www.parrots.org): With the dual mission of saving wild parrots and improving parrot care, the WPT offers an online parrot encyclopedia, photos, and videos; presents podcasts featuring avian experts from around the world; and has an "Ask the Expert" feature, to name just a few of its benefits.

# Periodicals, Podcasts, Websites, and Apps

Reading about and listening to information on birds brings enjoyment as well as new knowledge. The following are print, audio, and online resources for bird lovers:

>> *Australian BirdKeeper* (`https://birdkeeper.com.au`): Even if you don't live in Australia, this magazine offers articles on keeping and breeding all kinds of species, from African parrots to zebra finches. One year of six issues is $140 with international delivery. It also publishes and sells book about parrots, reptiles, and amphibians.

>> *Birding* (`www.aba.org/magazine`):This magazine, published bimonthly by the American Birding Association (ABA), is available both in print and online. An annual membership to the ABA costs $49, and a subscription to the magazine is included in the membership.

>> **BirdNote** (`www.birdnote.org`): This podcast includes sounds and stories about birds. You can find the podcasts wherever you like to listen to podcasts, including Apple Podcasts, Spotify, and Stitcher.

>> *BirdWatching* (`www.birdwatchingdaily.com`): Colorful and informative, this website addresses bird identification, what to put in bird feeders for different species, photography tips, and science news about birds. A bimonthly print magazine is $26.95 annually. A digital subscription, available on Kindle, is available for the same price.

>> **Lafeber** (`https://lafeber.com/pet-birds/avian-expert-articles`): Lafeber makes bird food, but its blog is an excellent resource on birds, with posts on training, behavior, health, nutrition, and fun stuff like the types of music birds like.

>> *Living Bird Magazine* (`https://join.birds.cornell.edu/page/14522/donate/1`):This quarterly magazine, published by the Cornell Lab of Ornithology, covers such topics as salt marsh conservation and its effects on humans and birds; bird-collision studies and ways to protect birds from building strikes; and on a lighter but equally informative note, the ways birds display affection. The magazine is included with a membership to the Cornell Lab of Ornithology; it costs $44 per year.

>> **Merlin** (`https://merlin.allaboutbirds.org`): This free app from the Cornell Lab of Ornithology, helps you identify the birds you see. You can find the app in the Apple App Store or at Google Play.

>> *PsittaScene* (`www.parrots.org/psittascene`): This quarterly magazine, published by the World Parrot Trust, covers bird behaviors, updates about WPT field studies, interviews with avian experts, parrot-related tourism, and profiles of parrot species, to name just a few of its topics. A subscription costs $40 per year.

# Rescue and Adoption Organizations

Regular animal shelters are usually not equipped to handle birds. Many groups have been organized in response to the need, offering education, rescue, and adoption services, some for specific species and others for multiple types of birds. Check out the following:

>> **A-Parrot to A-Flamingo Inc., Parrot Rescue:** http://aparrottoa flamingoinc.zoomshare.com

>> **Beauty of Birds:** www.beautyofbirds.com/rescue.html

>> **Companion Parrots Re-homed:** www.companionparrots.org

>> **Exotic Avian Sanctuary of Tennessee:** https://tnavianrescue.org

>> **Feathered Friends Sanctuary & Rescue:** www.feathered-friends.com

>> **Foster Parrots:** www.fosterparrots.com

>> **The Gabriel Foundation:** https://thegabrielfoundation.org

>> **Greyhaven Exotic Bird Sanctuary:** https://greyhavenbirds.com

>> **Mickaboo Companion Bird Rescue:** www.mickaboo.org

>> **New Life Parrot Rescue:** www.nlpr.org.uk

>> **The Oasis Sanctuary:** www.the-oasis.org

>> **Palomacy Pigeon & Dove Adoptions:** www.pigeonrescue.org

>> **Parrot Education & Adoption Center:** www.peac.org

>> **Phoenix Landing:** www.phoenixlanding.org

>> **The Tropics Exotic Bird Refuge:** www.parrotrefuge.com

>> **Tucson Parrot Rescue:** www.tucsonparrotrescue.com

# Toys and Supplies

If you find a great bird shop in your area (Chapter 3 tells you how to know whether you're really in the right place), you can look forward to reliable advice and proper supplies. The following are catalog/online merchants we know and recommend:

>> **All Parrot Products:** www.allparrotproducts.com

>> **Birdie Buddy:** www.mybirdiebuddy.com

- **Bonka Bird Toys:** https://bonkabirdtoys.com
- **Caitec:** www.caitec.com/bird-products
- **Chewy:** www.chewy.com/b/bird-941
- **The Leather Elves:** https://theleatherelves.ecwid.com
- **Noah's Ark and Novelty:** www.noahsarkandnovelty.com/premabito.html
- **Planet Pleasures:** https://planetpleasures.com
- **Squawk Box:** www.squawkboxes.com
- **Super Bird Creations:** www.superbirdtoys.com
- **Tidy Seed:** www.tidyseed.com

# Index

# About the Authors

**Brian L. Speer DVM, DABVP (Avian Practice), DECZM (Avian):** Brian is one of only a handful of veterinarians recognized as an avian specialist in both the United States and Europe. His specialty practice, the Medical Center for Birds (www.medicalcenterforbirds.com), draws the bulk of its clientele from all over California and adjacent western states, and he regularly consults on cases from around the globe.

A graduate of the University of California, Davis, School of Veterinary Medicine, Dr. Speer has limited his practice to provide exclusive care to birds since 1989. Patients include everything from finches, budgies, and cockatiels to larger parrots, chickens, waterfowl, falcons, eagles, flamingos, and more. Active in teaching and "paying it forward," he is dedicated to training students, interns, and residents to excel at the delivery of excellent health care. He has lectured throughout the United States and in numerous other countries for veterinary and avicultural audiences. Brian has authored a number of peer-reviewed publications on avian medicine and surgery, helping to contribute to the advancement of the specialty. He has served the Association of Avian Veterinarians as chair of the Aviculture Committee, as a member of the board of directors, and as president. He has also served the North American Veterinary Conference as the chair of the avian program, as well as coordinator for the exotics programs. A recipient of the Lafeber Award, the Western Veterinary Conference Educator of the Year award, and the North American Veterinary Conference Speaker of the Year award, he is thankful for these honors, and remains focused on finding ways to teach, help, and collaborate even better with others in the future.

Brian lives on the fringes of the San Francisco Bay Area, with his family, two dogs, one cat, and menagerie of bird residents of a number of different species (including 12 macaws; Big Bird and Ernie, the two emus; pigeons; geese; chickens; and ducks), and three tortoises who are just outright cool in their own way.

**Kim Campbell Thornton:** Kim is an award-winning writer with hundreds of articles and more than 25 books to her credit. With her veterinary partner, Dr. Marty Becker, and dog trainer, Mikkel Becker, she writes the weekly feature *Pet Connection,* which is offered through Andrews McMeel Syndication and appears in newspapers across the country, as well as online. Kim is also content manager for Fear Free Happy Homes, which promotes education on pet behavior and care; relief of fear, anxiety, and stress in pets; and building a great relationship with animals. She's an Elite Fear Free Certified Professional who has taken continuing education in avian behavior and care.

Among the more than 50 awards given to Kim's work are a win in the American Society of Journalists and Authors "How-To" category for a piece on teaching dogs to avoid snakes; a two-time win of the Dr. Jim Richards Cornell Feline Health Center Veterinary Issues Award for pieces on the feline skin microbiome and on oral contraceptives for feral cats, presented by the Cat Writers Association; and a Maxwell Medallion from the Dog Writers Association of America for her essay on the journey to life-saving heart surgery for her dog.

Kim lives in Lake Forest, California, with her husband and two Cavalier King Charles Spaniels, Harper and Keeper. She is an avid traveler and has become an avid bird watcher in the process.

**Gina Spadafori:** Gina is the author or coauthor of more than a dozen books on pets and their care. A former syndicated pet-care columnist, she now works as a writer covering the business and future of veterinary medicine for a Fortune 100 company. She and her animals — dogs, cats, goats, chickens, and the occasional visiting horse — live on a small acreage near Sacramento, California.

# Dedication

To the anchors in my life: my wife, Denise, our children Robin and Cody, and all of my family, immediate and extended. And to the birds, with gratitude for opening up the opportunity for such a wonderful ride into the almost magical feathered world they can share with us all.

—Brian L. Speer

To Larry (the) Bird and Spike, who introduced me to the joys of living with birds. And to my husband, Jerry, for being my in-house tech consultant on so many occasions.

—Kim Campbell Thornton

To Patrick, the Senegal parrot who was my adored little muse.

—Gina Spadafori

# Authors' Acknowledgments

We could not have written this book without the contributions of many other people who shared information, experiences, and photographs. They include Rachel Baden, DVM; Amy Baggs; John and Diane Claridge; Daleen Comer; Deb Eldredge, DVM; Deborah Davidson Harpur; Liz Harward; Melody Hennigh of Busy Beaks Academy; Heather Houlahan; Claudia Hunka of Your Basic Bird; Emily Hurt; Melissa Kauffman; Kristi Krause, DVM; Elizabeth Anderson Lopez; Shelmarie Main; Liz Moe; Arden Moore of Pet First Aid 4U; Julie Murad of The Gabriel Foundation; Lisa D. Myers of Feathered Follies; Omar's Exotic Birds, for allowing Kim to photograph birds there; Irene Pepperberg of The Alex Foundation; Jenn Prendergast; Chan Quach; Julie Rach; Cait Reyes-Macanliss; Vicki Aquino Ronchette; Sarah Rehkopf Schoefernacker; Wailani Sung, DVM, DACVB; Scott Weldy, DVM; Sara Whitehurst; and Elizabeth Young of Palomacy Pigeon and Dove Adoptions.

A very heartfelt thank you to Brian's staff at the Medical Center for Birds, all of whom worked so hard to maintain the busy practice and help keep everyone healthy through the COVID-19 pandemic, and made it possible for him to have time to write this book and edit the second volume of a professional text at the same time.

The folks at Wiley deserve to take a bow as well. Many thanks to Kelsey Baird, Vicki Adang, Michelle Hacker, and Elizabeth Kuball.

## Publisher's Acknowledgments

**Acquisitions Editor:** Kelsey Baird

**Managing Editor:** Vicki Adang, Michelle Hacker

**Project Editor:** Elizabeth Kuball

**Copy Editor:** Elizabeth Kuball

**Production Editor:** Mohammed Zafar Ali

**Cover Image:** © Feng Wei Photography/ Getty Images